MW01119692

DETENTION OF TERRORISM SUSPECTS

Controversial erosions of individual liberties in the name of anti-terrorism are ongoing in liberal democracies. The focus of this book is on the manner in which strategic discourse has been used to create accepted political narratives. It specifically links aspects of that discourse to problematic and evolving terrorism detention practices that happen outside of traditional criminal and wartime paradigms, with examples including the detentions at Guantanamo Bay and security certificates in Canada.

This book suggests that biased political discourse has, in some respects, continued to fuel public misconceptions about terrorism, which have then led to problematic legal enactments, supported by those misconceptions. It introduces this idea by presenting current examples, such as some of the language used by US President Donald Trump regarding terrorism, and it argues that such language has supported questionable legal responses to terrorism. It then critiques political arguments that began after 9/11, many of which are still foundational as terrorism detention practices evolve. The focus is on language emanating from the US, and the book links this language to specific examples of changed detention practices from the US, Canada, and the UK.

Terrorism is undoubtedly a real threat, but that does not mean that all perceptions of how to respond to terrorism are valid. As international terrorism continues to grow and to change, this book offers valuable insights into problems that have arisen from specific responses, with the objective of avoiding those problems going forward.

Detention of Terrorism Suspects

Political Discourse and Fragmented Practices

Maureen Duffy

·HART·
PUBLISHING
OXFORD AND PORTLAND, OREGON
2018

Hart Publishing

An imprint of Bloomsbury Publishing Plc

Hart Publishing Ltd	Bloomsbury Publishing Plc
Kemp House	50 Bedford Square
Chawley Park	London
Cumnor Hill	WC1B 3DP
Oxford OX2 9PH	UK
UK	

www.hartpub.co.uk
www.bloomsbury.com

Published in North America (US and Canada) by
Hart Publishing
c/o International Specialized Book Services
920 NE 58th Avenue, Suite 300
Portland, OR 97213-3786
USA

www.isbs.com

HART PUBLISHING, the Hart/Stag logo, BLOOMSBURY and the
Diana logo are trademarks of Bloomsbury Publishing Plc

First published 2018

© Maureen Duffy 2018

Maureen Duffy has asserted her right under the Copyright, Designs and Patents Act 1988 to be
identified as Author of this work.

British Library Cataloguing-in-Publication Data

A catalogue record for this book is available from the British Library.

ISBN:	HB:	978-1-84946-864-0
	ePDF:	978-1-50990-401-3
	ePub:	978-1-50990-400-6

Library of Congress Cataloging-in-Publication Data

Names: Duffy, Maureen, author.

Title: Detention of terrorism suspects : political discourse and fragmented practices / Maureen Duffy.

Description: Oxford [UK] ; Portland, Oregon : Hart Publishing, 2018. |
Includes bibliographical references and index.

Identifiers: LCCN 2017050988 (print) | LCCN 2017050501 (ebook) |
ISBN 9781509904006 (Epub) | ISBN 9781849468640 (hardback : alk. paper)

Subjects: LCSH: Detention of persons. | Imprisonment. | Terrorists—Legal status, laws, etc. |
Terrorism—Prevention—Law and legislation. | War on Terrorism, 2001–2009.

Classification: LCC K5437 (print) | LCC K5437 .D84 2018 (ebook) | DDC 344.05/325—dc23

LC record available at https://lccn.loc.gov/2017050988

Typeset by Compuscript Ltd, Shannon
Printed and bound in Great Britain by TJ International Ltd, Padstow, Cornwall

To find out more about our authors and books visit www.hartpublishing.co.uk. Here you will find extracts,
author information, details of forthcoming events and the option to sign up for our newsletters.

'It's so much darker when a light goes out than it would have been if it had never shone.'[1]

You left us suddenly and far too soon, and our lives are forever diminished. You will always live on in our hearts. This book is dedicated to you.

---

[1] John Steinbeck, *The Winter of Our Discontent* (New York, Penguin Classics, 2008) 678.

PREFACE

I was driving to work near Chicago as the shocking news of the terrorist attacks of 11 September 2001 ('9/11') unfolded on the radio. I was stopped in unusually heavy traffic, as Chicago traffic was somehow affected by the horrible developments out East. I listened to escalating and incomprehensible news reports, trying, without success, to get a phone signal to check on family and friends. The radio reported an evacuation at the Sears Tower, directly in front of us, and I tried not to look at it, afraid that I would see a plane fly into it. People were crying in the cars around me.

This research journey began later that month, again as I was driving to work. I heard a short radio report, which said that there had been concerns about people 'disappearing' at the US border. The people, the report said, were largely originally from Muslim countries, raising fears that the US government was secretly arresting certain people.

This report was different from those preceding it, which focused entirely on the horror of the attacks that had personally affected me and people I loved. In the days after hearing this report about disappearances, I tried to find more information on it, but there was little to be found for quite some time. That radio report sparked an alarm that has never stopped since, and I pursued it through two graduate programmes at McGill University, in Montreal, which began two years later.

This book is based on my doctoral dissertation, which I wrote and defended at McGill University. It is impossible for me to find adequate words to thank my doctoral supervisor, Professor René Provost, for his advice, amazing patience, diligence, and encouragement throughout my doctoral programme.

Much has changed in my life since this journey began, including moves to two cities in a new country; a new career; the addition of beloved members to our family; and the sudden, shattering deaths of two cherished family members. That day in 2001 feels distant in many ways, but developments since then have continued to engage my interest and concerns in this area.

This book is the next step in that research journey. I cannot possibly name all of the people who have helped me along the way, but they know who they are, family and friends both, and that I am deeply grateful. A special thank you to Bill Asquith and Francesca Sancarlo of Hart Publishing for their diligence, patience and understanding. Finally, thank you to the three anonymous peer reviewers for their encouraging and helpful suggestions.

All errors are my own.

TABLE OF CONTENTS

Part II: Fragmented Practices

INTRODUCTION

I am, by calling, a dealer in words; and words are, of course, the most powerful drug used by mankind. Not only do words infect, egotise, narcotise, and paralyse, but they enter into and colour the minutest cells of the brain, very much as madder mixed with a stag's food at the Zoo colours the growth of the animal's antlers.[1]

I. Introductory Comments: Words and Fear

As of 2017, both domestic and international terrorist attacks are distressingly regular occurrences. The list of places where sudden terrorist attacks have recently struck seems to expand daily: Paris, Brussels, Nice, Berlin, London, Quebec City, New York, Istanbul, Jakarta, Baghdad, Ankara, Berlin, Orlando, Aleppo, Jerusalem, Kandahar, Mogadishu, Stockholm, Garissa, Manchester, Barcelona—and so many others. Many of these attacks, rightly or wrongly, have been attributed to groups like Daesh, suggesting an international component to terrorism that has significantly expanded since the 9/11 attacks in New York.[2]

No rational person can fail to be outraged by such violent attacks on civilians. Following the attack in Manchester in May 2017, in which children were killed and were likely targeted, Prime Minister Theresa May described the attack as one of the worst terrorist attacks in the UK, adding that it 'stands out for its appalling, sickening cowardice—deliberately targeting innocent, defenceless children and young people who should have been enjoying one of the most memorable nights of their lives'.[3] Among recent horrors, this one seemed to reach an enhanced level of cruelty. It is clearly necessary to respond to such horrors, but the parameters of that response are not always so straightforward.

As of mid-2017, several national jurisdictions had declared a state of emergency after terrorist attacks. By definition, a state of emergency suggests that another

---

[1] Rudyard Kipling, 'Speech, Annual Dinner, Royal College of Surgeons' (1923) *Telelib*, www.telelib. com/authors/K/KiplingRudyard/prose/BookOfWords/surgeonssoul.html.

[2] Daesh is also known by other names, including ISIS, ISIL or IS. The decision to refer to the group as Daesh in this book was intentional and is explained more in ch 1.

[3] Gordon Rayner et al, 'Soldiers Deployed on Streets in Race to Foil Second Terror Attack after Threat Level Raised to "Critical"' *Telegraph Online* (23 May 2017) www.telegraph.co.uk/news/2017/05/23/ theresa-may-increases-uk-terrorist-alert-critical-manchester. This discussion of these events is current as of 7 June 2017.

attack is imminent and it, justifiably, can enhance a feeling of fear, while allowing a government what it needs to respond to the perceived emergency. The mechanism can occur in different forms. The UK, for instance, raised its terror threat level to the highest level of 'critical' after the Manchester attack.[4] Sometimes, such a state is necessary, but sometimes the argument can be made that it is a pretext for enhancing Executive governmental powers. While states of emergency are designed to be temporary, the timing of these declarations has varied. France has been renewing a state of emergency since 2015, after a series of high-profile attacks there.[5]

Turkey has repeatedly extended a state of emergency, after several events that included a coup attempt, a gunman killing 39 people in an Istanbul nightclub and a series of other high-profile attacks attributed to Daesh.[6] This state of emergency was extended in April 2017, after a referendum to amend the constitution, giving more centralised power to the President.[7] Under the state of emergency, citizens check a gazette every day to see what new decrees are published. Extraordinary procedures are required for Parliament to overturn these decrees, and the constitutional court has not accepted any challenges.[8]

The controversial Philippines President Rodrigo Duterte declared martial law in May 2017 on the Island of Mindanao, after conflict between the military and a group allegedly connected to Daesh, and he publicly said that he might extend it across the Philippines.[9] Duterte is infamous for encouraging murders of suspected drug dealers or users, promising pardons and immunity for their killers, resulting in the deaths of more than 7,000 people. He has invoked Hitler as a role model for these mass killings and has allegedly used this campaign as a pretext for killing his political opponents.[10] In discussing permissible conduct by the military, he told listeners at a military camp that, under his martial law declaration, they were allowed to rape up to three women, with later claims that the remark was intended as a joke.[11]

States of emergency, whether formal or simply a creation of political commentary, give rise to a notion that standard constitutional protections must and can be

---

[4] ibid.

[5] See Jean-Claude Paye, 'Sovereignty and the State of Emergency: France and the United States' (2017) *Monthly Review: An Independent Socialist Magazine* 1; 'Éditorial, Vers un état d'urgence permanent?' (2017) *Esprit* 3–10; Nadim Houry, 'Breaking France's Addiction to its State of Emergency' (2017) *Open Democracy*, www.opendemocracy.net/can-europe-make-it/nadim-houry/breaking-france-s-addiction-to-its-state-of-emergency.

[6] 'Turkey to Extend State of Emergency by Three Months' (2017) *Al Jazeera*, www.aljazeera.com/news/2017/04/turkey-extend-state-emergency-months-170418034656371.html.

[7] ibid.

[8] ibid.

[9] 'Philippines President Duterte Declares Martial Law on Mindanao Island' *BBC News* (23 May 2017) www.bbc.com/news/world-asia-40022529.

[10] Jeremy Scahill, 'Trump Called Rodrigo Duterte to Congratulate Him on His Murderous Drug War: "You are Doing an Amazing Job"' *The Intercept* (23 May 2017) theintercept.com/2017/05/23/trump-called-rodrigo-duterte-to-congratulate-him-on-his-murderous-drug-war-you-are-doing-an-amazing-job.

[11] 'Philippines' Duterte under Fire for Second Rape Joke' *BBC News* (27 May 2017) www.bbc.com/news/world-asia-40072315.

set aside. How such states of emergency play out varies and, because such emergency declarations give extraordinary powers to the government, abuse can sometimes be the result. For instance, one report notes that Turkey's two emergency decrees took away detainee protections against ill-treatment. The report quoted police officers in Turkey as asserting impunity for killing and for torture during the state of emergency.[12] After the failed coup attempt in 2016, Turkey detained approximately 40,000 people and there have been allegations of mistreatment of the prisoners during their detention.[13] Almost 90,000 civil servants, including 'teachers, police and military officials, doctors, judges and prosecutors', were fired, based on allegations that they were linked to a terrorist organisation that posed a risk to national security.[14]

When a state of emergency is extended repeatedly, the obvious concern is that the urgent will become the new normal. In late May 2017, Amnesty International accused France of using its increased powers, under the state of emergency, to clamp down on peaceful protest.[15] A representative called on President Emmanuel Macron to 'stop the misuse of anti-terrorism powers and end France's dangerous and dizzying spiral towards a permanent state of emergency'.[16]

As terrorist attacks, and governmental responses to such attacks, continue unabated around the world, it is important to look to the nature of these responses, especially as certain responses have become increasingly normalised. While terrorist attacks present an obvious threat, poor responses to attacks can create risks of their own. This book does not address all responses to terrorism, but, instead, focuses primarily on practices relating to the detention and interrogation of terrorism suspects.

In theory, most people would agree that fear-based decision-making does not lead to good outcomes, but fear continues to drive many national responses to terrorism. This fear ebbs and flows, generally driven to heights when a new attack occurs, and then sometimes calming a bit before the next attack. Whose fear is at issue can be a factor in disassembling some of the governmental responses. Is it the government itself that is acting out of fear, or is the government undertaking actions in a climate of fear, knowing that a frightened population will be more likely to agree to its agenda?

---

[12] 'A Blank Check: Turkey's Post-coup Suspension of Safeguards against Torture' *Human Rights Watch* (24 October 2016) www.hrw.org/report/2016/10/24/blank-check/turkeys-post-coup-suspension-safeguards-against-torture.

[13] ibid; Amnesty International, 'Turkey' in *Amnesty International Report 2016/17: The State of the World's Human Rights*, 2017, www.amnesty.org/en/documents/pol10/4800/2017/en, 367 (hereinafter *Amnesty International: Turkey*).

[14] *Amnesty International: Turkey*.

[15] Amnesty International, 'France: Unchecked Clampdown on Protests under Guise of Fighting Terrorism' (31 May 2017) www.amnesty.org/en/latest/news/2017/05/france-unchecked-clampdown-on-protests-under-guise-of-fighting-terrorism.

[16] ibid.

Piotr Cap, who has written extensively about the use of particular tools in political discourse, notes that 'manufacturing fear and social anxiety is a central feature of modern public discourse, serving to justify policies which include the policy-makers and their audiences in a joint course of action aimed to prevent or neutralize the threat'.[17] With fear as an underpinning thread, some governmental leaders use discourse tools that are designed to persuade. Such tools have been used successfully in the face of certain high-profile events, such as after the 9/11 terrorist attacks in the US.

Political discourse is rarely simply descriptive or objective. Those in the political world generally seek to achieve a particular objective by using the mechanisms of public conversation that they employ. This may or may not be appropriate, of course, depending on the circumstances. Either way, the power of rhetoric styles in public conversations cannot be overlooked. As Cap points out:

> Public discourse is essentially strategic: there exist observable and systematic ways in which interests of the top actors—politicians, institutional leaders, lawmakers, media management—are performed linguistically. Public leaders use a plethora of rhetorical means to manage their power, status and credibility in the service of a social consensus. The aim is to receive people's approval of policies involving both sides, the leader and her audience, in a joint course of action.[18]

Cap draws from the work of Habermas to continue:

> [P]ublic communication—including state political discourse as well as voices of various non-governmental bodies and 'grass-roots' initiatives—has the continued goal of maximizing the number of 'shared visions', that is, common conceptions of current reality as well as its desired developments.[19]

As a result of these characteristics, public discourse has been called 'coercive' in nature.[20] This coercion can be exercised in different ways, including:

> [S]etting agendas, selecting topics in conversation, positioning the self and others in specific relationships, making assumptions about realities that their hearers are obliged to at least temporarily accept in order to process the text or talk. Power can also be exercised through the control of others' use of language—that is, through various kinds and degrees of censorship and access control.[21]

Beyond these overarching approaches to political persuasion, certain rhetoric techniques can have the effect of increasing the likelihood that a particular viewpoint will be accepted by a given audience. These techniques are discussed in greater detail in chapter two.

---

[17] Piotr Cap, *The Language of Fear* (London, Palgrave Macmillan, 2016) xi.
[18] ibid 2.
[19] ibid xi (citations omitted).
[20] See ibid.
[21] ibid.

This book provides a way of looking at fast-moving legal developments, not just in the area of terrorism detentions, but with an approach that could be used to critique many other areas of the law that have developed, or will develop, in times of crisis. This approach draws from various disciplines, particularly that of legal philosophy and discourse analysis, but is one that is not as commonly applied in the field of law.[22] This work draws heavily on specific threads from the theory laid out by Chaim Perelman and Lucie Olbrechts-Tyteca in their famous work *The New Rhetoric*, with variations to that work as expounded on by other scholars over the years.[23] This is not intended to be a comprehensive assessment of the field of argumentation theory, but rather to take one aspect of that field, and primarily one thread from the work of Perelman and Olbrechts-Tyteca, and to use that thread as a foundation in an argument critiquing a particular post-9/11 detention narrative. The idea is to demonstrate that if that thread can reveal new understandings of that narrative, a more comprehensive use of understandings from this field might reveal even more.

This book does this through a critique of political conversations surrounding terrorism, with an in-depth look at US-generated language after the 9/11 attacks, and how various structural aspects of that language led directly to changed, problematic legal norms regarding the detention and interrogation of terrorism suspects in several countries. Rather than looking to traditional notions of what is 'legal', it seeks to critique the legitimacy of the changes by pointing out argumentation flaws in the political commentary that led directly to legal changes. Many of these flaws continue to dominate public discourse today. Examples of such political commentary are given throughout this book. Some examples, particularly in the Introduction and the Conclusion, relate to different scenarios, outside of the terrorism context, to illustrate the larger point about the power of reconsidering how discourse is built.

Addressing terrorism, of course, is not a simple matter, and terrorism is designed to provoke fear. So fear is a reasonable reaction. But for those in positions of power, whether in terms of influencing public opinion or in enacting laws, fear cannot be the driving force behind determining proper responses, either in terms of their own fears or in terms of exploiting the fears of others. While the forms of terrorism are constantly evolving, terrorism itself has been a dominant global issue long enough so that some baseline capacity for calm reflection, and for learning from past mistakes in promoting future responses, should exist by now. However, this does not always seem to be the case. Fear has a direct correlation with the

---

[22] Some discussion of argumentation theory as applied in law can be found in recent works in the field of philosophy of law. See, eg, Mirjami Paso, 'Rhetoric Meets Rational Argumentation Theory' (2014), 27(2) *Ratio Juris* 236; Francis J Mootz III , 'Perelman's Theory of Argumentation and Natural Law' (2010) 43(4) *Philosophy and Rhetoric* 382.

[23] See Chaim Perelman and Lucie Olbrechts-Tyteca, *The New Rhetoric: A Treatise on Argumentation*, translated by John Wilkinson and Purcell Weaver (Notre Dame, IN, University of Notre Dame Press, 1969).

effectiveness of political commentary, when those in power seek agreement from a population to measures that may otherwise be seen to infringe human rights. Frightened people can be persuaded of the truth of illogical premises when they might not be so easily convinced when in a less fearful state of mind. Thus, the underpinning of fear is a critical thread running through any review of political conversations around terrorism responses and how they arise, and it provides a background theme to the specific issues raised in this book.

One major argument in this book is that faulty, fear-based or fear-supported assumptions dominated public discourse after 9/11 and led directly to faulty legal responses in some places. Terrorism detention and interrogation practices, in particular, reflected these false popular assumptions, and this book focuses especially on the development of those practices after 9/11. If many of the false assumptions that created bad practices after 9/11 still dominate public discourse, this does not bode well for future responses to an expanding and mutating international threat.

Terrorism discourse and terrorism responses have developed differently in different places, for obvious reasons. The post-9/11 narrative, however, clearly emanated out of the US, as the target of the attacks, and had differing impacts on other jurisdictions.[24] It is thus the American discourse that will be the starting point in assessing changes that appear to have emanated from there.

II. Narratives Create Perceptions of Truth

In law, political narrative controls responses more than is often recognised. This can happen on different levels. The largest level, of course, in the fight against terrorism is the simple good-versus-evil narrative, which, for example, is laced throughout post-9/11 American discourse.[25] Richard Jackson, who has written about the use of political discourse to persuade the public about agreeing to the so-called 'War on Terror', argues, in the post-9/11 US context, that:

> [T]he public language of the American administration has been used to construct a whole new world for its citizens. Through a carefully constructed public discourse, officials have created a new social reality where terrorism threatens to destroy everything that ordinary people hold dear—their lives, their democracy, their freedom, their way of life, their civilisation. In this new reality, diabolical and insane terrorists plot to rain down weapons of mass destruction across western cities, while heroic warriors of freedom risk their lives in foreign lands to save innocent and decent folk back home; good battles evil and civilisation itself stands against the dark forces of barbarism.

...

[24] See generally Kent Roach, *The 9/11 Effect: Comparative Counter-terrorism* (New York, Cambridge University Press, 2011) (comparing different national responses to the 9/11 attacks).

[25] See generally Adam Hodges, *The 'War on Terror' Narrative* (Oxford, Oxford University Press, 2015) (assessing numerous speeches made by George W Bush in the construction of this narrative).

In this way, the *language* of the 'war on terrorism' normalises and reifies the *practice* of the 'war on terrorism'; it comes to be accepted as part of the way things naturally are and should be. Language and practice, in other words, reinforce each other—they constitute the reality of counter-terrorism.[26]

A narrative, of course, has no impact on legal standards without effective buy-in from the public, legislative bodies and courts. Therefore, broad narratives, such as the good-versus-evil paradigm, are not enough, on their own, to elicit support and legal changes. The presentation of the narrative is everything. An effective narrative must have layers of elements in order to persuade people. Thus, for example, the 9/11 attacks were described not as a criminal act, but as an act of war. Immigrants were treated as presumptive terrorists. Dissent was equated with support for terrorism. Vivid images, such as Condoleezza Rice's notorious 'mushroom cloud' over Manhattan, were used to scare and thus persuade people.[27] Layering points and techniques can create a complete narrative picture. Among those who accept the narrative as indisputable truth, these beliefs can then become difficult to refute. Deconstructing this successfully created narrative is not easy, especially when many layers and differing techniques were created to build the narrative in the first place.

Beyond content, though, is the method of argument chosen. This can perhaps be thought of as the procedural aspect of the argument. The right methodology, used with the right audience, can be more influential than the actual substance of the points made. It is not just the words used, or a recourse to fear, that can be significant, but the actual techniques the speaker uses to create and promote an argument. In determining, after the fact, the appropriateness of the result, it can therefore be useful to break down the procedural pieces that went into building the argument to see if any flaws in the technique can be identified.

Relevant issues, drawn from the work of legal philosophers, include how well the original argument was tailored to a particular audience, especially considering the particular values that audience might hold, and how the argument is tailored to those values.[28] One might consider whether logical arguments had to be sacrificed to appeal to high emotions or to the emotions expressed by a specific audience. Another obvious consideration is the motivation of those who originally advanced the arguments and whether that motivation corresponded with the motivation that was presented as the rationale. Consistent with that inquiry, an issue arises as to whether the original proponent of the argument was concerned

---

[26] Richard Jackson, *Writing the War on Terrorism* (Manchester, Manchester University Press 2005) 1–2.

[27] See 'Sen. Byrd: Rice Responsible for "Most Overblown Rhetoric Administration Used to Scare the American People"' *Democracy Now!* (26 January 2005) www.democracynow.org/2005/1/26/sen_byrd_rice_responsible_for_most (discussing controversy over Condoleezza Rice's statements before the invasion of Iraq, which were renewed as she faced confirmation hearings for the position of Secretary of State).

[28] See Perelman and Olbrechts-Tyteca, above, n 23.

with a particular end and whether that concern overrode the means used. Is the method of argument used one that would appeal to a universal audience, and thus 'valid', or one that is more likely to appeal to a more finite, specific audience, and thus just 'effective?'[29]

A. The Power of Language: Using a New Narrative to Dispel a Long-Standing False Narrative

A vivid picture, painted through language, can significantly change the way in which a factual scenario is viewed and can make an audience perceive its pre-conceived truths in different lights. A compelling example of this phenomenon arose in a speech given by Mitch Landrieu, the Mayor of New Orleans, in May 2017, accompanying his decision to remove four Confederate monuments. When explaining his decision, Landrieu invoked the language of terrorism, and of the reliance on a false narrative, to critique the continued existence of the monuments whose removal he was ordering. Under his direction, four major monuments to the Confederacy were taken down in the spring of 2017 as part of a wider move-ment to remove such monuments in the US South, the former home of the Con-federacy. The decision to do so was part of an initiative to recognise the horrors of slavery and to avoid painting an unrealistic, glorified view of what happened before and during the US Civil War.[30]

Tension had surrounded the removal of the monuments. A group of White Supremacists had previously held a candlelight march protesting against the deci-sion, chanting phrases from the Nazi era and evoking memories of nighttime ral-lies by the Ku Klux Klan.[31] A New Orleans state representative, Karl Oliver, posted a comment on Facebook that, among other things, suggested that those responsible for removing the statues 'erected in loving memory of our family and fellow South Americans … [those who] destroy historical monuments of OUR HISTORY, they should be LYNCHED'.[32] Although Oliver later apologised for this, the statement gave an indication of the types of tensions surrounding the issue.[33] Lynching of African Americans is a well-known, notorious part of the history of the US South.

Mayor Landrieu made a moving and important speech, which was clearly designed to reconfigure the narrative around the monuments. This language

---

[29] See ibid 27.

[30] See Tegan Wendland, 'With Lee Statue's Removal, Another Battle of New Orleans Comes to a Close' *NPR* (20 May 2017) www.npr.org/2017/05/20/529232823/with-lee-statues-removal-another-battle-of-new-orleans-comes-to-a-close.

[31] See Jonah Engel Bromwich, 'White Nationalists Wield Torches at Confederate Statue Rally' *New York Times* (14 May 2017) www.nytimes.com/2017/05/14/us/confederate-statue-protests-virginia.html?_r=0.

[32] Kate Royals, 'Rep. Karl Oliver: Those Removing Confederate Monuments "Should Be Lynched"' *Mississippi Today* (21 May 2017) mississippitoday.org/2017/05/21/rep-karl-oliver-those-removing-confederate-monuments-should-be-lynched (emphasis in original).

[33] See ibid.

quickly became widely reproduced. He reminded listeners of the rich and diverse culture of New Orleans, but added:

> But there are also other truths about our city that we must confront. New Orleans was America's largest slave market: a port where hundreds of thousands of souls were brought, sold and shipped up the Mississippi River to lives of forced labor[,] of misery[,] of rape, of torture.

> America was the place where nearly 4,000 of our fellow citizens were lynched, 540 alone in Louisiana; where the courts enshrined 'separate but equal'; where Freedom riders coming to New Orleans were beaten to a bloody pulp.

> So when people say to me that the monuments in question are history, well what I just described is real history as well, and it is the searing truth.

> …

> And it immediately begs the questions: why there are no slave ship monuments, no prominent markers on public land to remember the lynchings or the slave blocks; nothing to remember this long chapter of our lives; the pain, the sacrifice, the shame … all of it happening on the soil of New Orleans.

> So for those self-appointed defenders of history and the monuments, they are eerily silent on what amounts to this historical malfeasance, a lie by omission.

> There is a difference between remembrance of history and reverence of it. For America and New Orleans, it has been a long, winding road, marked by great tragedy and great triumph. But we cannot be afraid of our truth.[34]

Mayor Landrieu specifically sought to deconstruct the false narrative that had given rise to the monuments in the first place. They were, he said, part of a 'movement which became known as "The Cult of the Lost Cause", whose members sought to rewrite history to hide the truth, which is that the Confederacy was on the wrong side of humanity'.[35] He restated what the monuments symbolised— not noble reminders of a glorious history, but as actual elements of 'terrorism', explaining:

> These statues are not just stone and metal. They are not just innocent remembrances of a benign history. These monuments purposefully celebrate a fictional, sanitized Confederacy; ignoring the death, ignoring the enslavement, and the terror that it actually stood for.

> After the Civil War, these statues were a part of that terrorism as much as a burning cross on someone's lawn; they were erected purposefully to send a strong message to all who walked in their shadows about who was still in charge in this city.[36]

---

[34] Derek Cosson, 'Transcript of New Orleans Mayor Landrieu's Address on Confederate Monuments' *The Pulse* (19 May 2017) pulsegulfcoast.com/2017/05/transcript-of-new-orleans-mayor-landrieus-address-on-confederate-monuments. The speech is reproduced in its entirety in the Appendix.

[35] ibid.

[36] ibid.

After using historical quotes to argue that the main objective of the Confederacy was to promote white supremacy and to continue the practice of slavery, he continued reframing the narrative:

> Now, with these shocking words still ringing in your ears, I want to try to gently peel from your hands the grip on a false narrative of our history that I think weakens us and make straight a wrong turn we made many years ago so we can more closely connect with integrity to the founding principles of our nation and forge a clearer and straighter path toward a better city and more perfect union.[37]

A powerful aspect of this language is that it seeks to refute a long-standing, often-cherished, but false narrative. Under this narrative, the Confederacy arose in a noble battle to preserve States' rights. Instead, Mayor Landrieu presented factual underpinnings to his listeners that should have been the foundation of the true narrative all along. He urged listeners, people who have grown up with this idealistic narrative, to go back in time to approximately 1865, when this false narrative was created. He told them to replace the flawed parts of the narrative with actual truth and he suggested that this was critical to moving forward in the present day. His proposed deconstruction of the narrative is similar to the goal of this book in relation to parts of the post-9/11 narrative, going back to the beginnings of the narrative in order to find a better way forward.

Another of Mayor Landrieu's narrative points was that the same symbol, or the same words, or the same stories can actually mean different things to different people.[38] Describing a stone on which slaves were forced to stand as they were sold, Mayor Landrieu reminded his audience that the plaque at this site only mentions that President Andrew Jackson and Henry Clay once spoke there. 'A piece of stone—one stone. Both stories were history. One story told. One story forgotten or maybe even purposefully ignored', he said.[39]

Mayor Landrieu was not suggesting that going back in time to correct the original narrative would fix all that was wrong. But it was a necessary first step to moving forward in a more positive direction:

> This is … about showing the whole world that we as a city and as a people are able to acknowledge, understand, reconcile and, most importantly, choose a better future for ourselves, making straight what has been crooked and making right what was wrong.
>
> Otherwise, we will continue to pay a price with discord, with division, and yes, with violence.[40]

He explained the dangers of trying to move forward with this significant false narrative looming: 'To literally put the [C]onfederacy on a pedestal in our most

---

[37] ibid.
[38] See ch 2 below and the discussion of Kafka's Parable, and how the short Parable can mean so many different things to different people.
[39] Cosson, above, n 34.
[40] ibid.

prominent places of honor is an inaccurate recitation of our full past, it is an affront to our present, and it is a bad prescription for our future … Centuries-old wounds are still raw because they never healed right in the first place.'[41]

Answering critiques that the removal of the monuments erased history, he argued: 'We have not erased history; we are becoming part of the city's history by righting the wrong image these monuments represent and crafting a better, more complete future for all our children and for future generations.'[42] He also downplayed the heavy prominence the Confederacy tended to be given among people in the region, saying: 'Instead of revering a 4-year brief historical aberration that was called the Confederacy we can [by retroactively correcting this false narrative] celebrate all 300 years of our rich, diverse history as a place named New Orleans and set the tone for the next 300 years.'[43]

His general characterisation of the true role of the Confederacy was dramatically different from the dominant narrative in the area:

> The Confederacy was on the wrong side of history and humanity. It sought to tear apart our nation and subjugate our fellow Americans to slavery. This is the history we should never forget and one that we should never again put on a pedestal to be revered.[44]

Mayor Landrieu then drove his point home by concluding with a famous passage from the Second Inaugural Address of President Abraham Lincoln, delivered just as the Civil War was ending and calling for national unity, for reconciliation, for help to 'bind up the nation's wounds, to do all which may achieve and cherish … a just and lasting peace among ourselves and with all nations'.[45]

This ending had a narrative significance, not just for the words, but also because Mayor Landrieu was advocating ending an era of reverence for the Confederacy by quoting the US President who led the North in defeating the Confederacy in the Civil War. This suggests a dramatic shift in the suggested narrative. Although he did not say so explicitly, the implication was that, in going back in time, one proper starting point in reconfiguring the narrative about this part of New Orleans history would be to begin with Lincoln's speech, which, in itself, symbolically began the conclusion of the war, and to rebuild the narrative from that very different foundation. This remarkable series of events demonstrates the power of narratives, and the value not just in moving forward from a narrative that is problematic, but in going back in time to try to fix the underlying flaws in the initial narrative.

Thus, Mayor Landrieu invoked the modern language of terrorism to present a competing narrative about what these monuments mean to New Orleans residents whose families are descended from slavery. He also recognised that the

---

[41] ibid.

[42] Cosson, above, n 34.

[43] ibid.

[44] ibid.

[45] ibid (quoting the Second Inaugural Address of Abraham Lincoln, *The Avalon Project* (4 March 1985), avalon.law.yale.edu/19th_century/lincoln2.asp)).

construction of a narrative does not have to be merely forward looking, but can involve going back in time to fix the rotten structural components of the end product.

III. Assessing an Argument after the Fact

This example demonstrates that it is not just valid to critique an argument as it is happening, or going forward. If, after the fact, a reassessment of legal changes is undertaken, one potentially strong approach is to actually start with the end product and break down the argumentation methods used to reach that end point. If there are concerns about those argumentation elements not based on opinion about the substance, but based on the strength of the methods used to build the argument, this might suggest that something was structurally wrong with the argument to begin with.

It is not that there is never calm critique, after the fact, of actions taken in times of crisis. The Commission on Wartime Relocation and Internment of Civilians in the US, for instance, acknowledged that the interment of citizens of Japanese-American ancestry was the result of 'racial prejudice, wartime hysteria, and a failure of political leadership'.[46]

However, it is less common for a more nuanced assessment of past arguments themselves, as described above, to take place. That is why Mayor Landrieu's speech and accompanying actions were so remarkable. The idea is simple. If a legal change is based on a false premise, or the structure of the underlying argument used to bring about the change is faulty, then this might provide an additional basis for questioning the change. In other words, an argument should make sense. If the building blocks used to create that argument are flawed, then the argument and the resulting conclusion are likely also to be flawed. This type of critique provides a logic-based method of challenging arguments in general, and it is used here to provide a line of critique in challenging the argumentation so often applied in the area of terrorism detentions. In so doing, it questions the effectiveness of the argumentation components that led to legal changes, rather than offering technical arguments about the legal changes.

This style of critique is familiar in the area of philosophy, and specifically even in the area of legal philosophy, where the field of so-called 'argumentation theory' is well established.[47] However, this type of critique is rarely undertaken in the study of law, which is surprising, considering that so much of law is based on the

---

[46] United States Congress, 151(6) *Congressional Record* (21 April–5 May 2005) 7954.
[47] See, eg, Perelman and Olbrechts-Tyteca, above, n 23. This theory is explained in much more detail in ch 2.

effectiveness of argumentation. This suggests a possible gap in the way in which legal enactments are critiqued. More importantly, it suggests an avenue for those who seek to critique certain legal changes to present obvious problems with how the changes came to be.

Law, particularly in common law jurisdictions, such as those discussed herein, is evolution. By its very nature, it involves a series of changes over time, usually starting from some baseline point. Rules about the proper basis for that evolution exist in such common-law notions as *stare decisis*, where the decisions of certain courts are binding on others, and such notions are designed to ensure a certain consistency for those who are subject to the law. Moreover, while laws may evolve, there is often an underpinning idea against which changes must be measured in order for the law to have legitimacy. Constitutional law provides probably the most pointed example of this, as those countries having a written constitution will often make arguments as to whether, for instance, a new piece of legislation is constitutional. Much of the jurisprudence relating to anti-terrorism detentions has been promulgated under this dynamic, such as the *Charkaoui I* case in Canada, measured under Canada's Charter of Rights and Freedoms, or the *Boumediene* decision in the US, based on the Supreme Court of the United States' reading of the US Constitution's habeas corpus provision.[48] In the UK, a similar process is undertaken when alleged human rights violations are measured for validity against the European Convention on Human Rights (ECHR), a scenario expected to continue, in spite of threats by the current government to withdraw from the Convention.[49] These different instruments have generally served as baseline measures when courts have assessed the validity of post-9/11 anti-terrorism detention practices.

While this is the formal structural basis under which the validity of many laws and undertakings can be measured, does this mean that this is the only form of evolutionary process that can shed light on the viability of legal norms?[50] In various disciplines, argumentation theory can be used as a lens through which to assess cultural and legal phenomena.[51] Argumentation theory, borrowed primarily

---

[48] See *Charkaoui v Canada (Citizenship and Immigration)* [2007] 1 SCR 350, 2007 SCC 9 (hereinafter *Charkaoui I*); *Boumediene v Bush*, 553 US 723 (2008).

[49] See, eg, *A (FC) and Others (FC) (Appellants) v Secretary of State for the Home Department (Respondent)* [2004] UKHL 56 (hereinafter *Belmarsh Detainees Case*) (discussing detentions for non-citizens in relation to the ECHR); see also Christopher Hope, 'Britain to Be Bound by European Convention on Human Rights until 2022' *The Telegraph* (26 April 2017) www.telegraph.co.uk/news/2017/04/26/britain-likely-bound-european-convention-human-rights-2022 (indicating that earlier statements about the UK withdrawing from the ECHR have largely been repudiated or just not repeated, suggesting that compliance will continue at least for the immediate future).

[50] See generally Jürgen Habermas, *Between Facts and Norms: Contributions to a Discourse Theory of Law and Democracy* (Cambridge, Polity Press, 1996) (suggesting that discourse theory provides a means of determining the legitimacy of laws promulgated through the democratic process because the process can provide one potential indicator of validity); Jürgen Habermas, *Theory of Communicative Action, Vol I: Reason and the Rationalization of Society* (Boston, Beacon Press, 1981).

[51] See, eg, Trudie Govier, *A Delicate Balance: What Philosophy Can Tell Us about Terrorism* (Cambridge, MA, Westview Press, 2002).

from the field of philosophy, can be explicitly used by those in law to consider the structural soundness of particular normative innovations.[52] A question arises as to whether the legitimacy of laws can be assessed through this use of argumentation theory, not to undertake a positivist measure of the laws against a baseline within the existing legal system, but to look in a broader sense at the structural soundness of the argumentation that always underscores the development of new legal regimes, particularly those subject to the type of controversy associated with post-9/11 terrorism detention practices. This book seeks to make a small contribution to one potential application of this argumentation theory to a particular range of normative legal changes, viewed through the lens of the public discourse that surrounded those changes. As described in more detail in chapter two below, the analysis draws from a number of other theoretical foundations as well.[53]

Similar to the suggestion by Jürgen Habermas when laying out his ideas of discourse theory, this approach provides a practical way to look at argumentation as a social practice.[54] The objective is to reconstruct the normative underpinnings that make up the discourse used for effective arguments. On the other hand, if these underpinnings have flaws, this could be a possible indicator that any normative changes resulting from that particular argument should be more closely examined. However, according to Habermas, these presuppositions cannot be definitively assessed solely through the logical properties of argument, nor does this book suggest that they are. Rather, Habermas suggests that there are different aspects of argumentation, of which the process of argumentation is only one. The process of argumentation is most similar to what is considered to be traditional logical argumentation.[55]

As noted in the translator's introduction to Habermas' work *Between Facts and Norms*:

> When a claim is contested, actually bringing about such rational acceptance requires actors to shift into a *discourse*, in which, the pressures of action having been more or less neutralized, they can isolate and test the disputed claim solely on the basis of arguments.[56]

In the crisis atmosphere that immediately followed the 9/11 attacks, a number of baseline presumptions quickly emerged and appear to have been accepted as foundational truths for various forms of extraordinary detention practices. This phenomenon played out differently in various places, but many of these practices had commonalities in terms of the discourse foundations on which they were established.

---

[52] See, eg, Perelman and Olbrechts-Tyteca, above, n 23.

[53] See ch 2 below for a more detailed exposition of the theoretical approaches applied throughout this book.

[54] Habermas, *Theory of Communicative Action*, above, n 50, 26.

[55] ibid.

[56] Habermas, *Between Facts and Norms*, above, n 50, at xv; see also generally Thomas McCarthy, *The Critical Theory of Jürgen Habermas* (Cambridge, MA, MIT Press, 1978); Michael Salter, 'Habermas's New Contribution to Legal Scholarship' (1997) 24 *Journal of Law & Society* 285 (reviewing Habermas' book *Between Facts and Norms*).

Much of this discourse emanated out of the US, the target of the attacks, and initially was reasonably tinged with a sense of urgency and an initial notion that an unprecedented attack required an unprecedented response. This sense of urgency was echoed across a number of national jurisdictions, which began to look to their own responses in light of the attacks and the resulting discourse of crisis. The quickly emerging premises were not necessarily tested outside of this atmosphere of crisis, especially as they were initially seen as temporary. These premises about what causes terrorism, or what is needed to stop it, quickly became embedded in the political and popular lexicon. This discourse led to a number of controversial and sometimes unprecedented infringements on long-standing constitutional protections, particularly for those suspected of involvement in terrorism.

Over time, many of these presumptions solidified, and they have now gained acceptance as familiar. As the practices are increasingly normalised, critique of them becomes problematic and difficulties arise in determining the proper future steps to take. For various reasons, including the crisis atmosphere under which the practices arose, differences in values across national jurisdictions and differences in judicial treatment of government initiatives, the narrative surrounding how suspected terrorists should be detained has ultimately become somewhat fractured. Frequently, inconsistent standards are now applied to different terrorism suspects, with some being detained entirely outside of the criminal justice system, and the bases for these discrepancies are often difficult to explain.

Many factors were assembled to paint the picture that emerged immediately after the 9/11 attacks. When one looks back to where the justification for certain changes began, one can shift the proverbial kaleidoscope, reassembling these pieces to create a new, perhaps equally viable, picture from the same constituent parts. This can provide insights into new ways to view these practices. By looking back, it may be possible to construct a new way of looking forward.

IV. US-Generated Anti-terrorism Discourse in 2001 versus 2017

In 2017, much of the terrorism-related public conversation bears a striking similarity to conversations that happened in 2001 after the 9/11 attacks. The mechanisms of distributing information, and of refuting it, may differ dramatically between the two points in time, but the underlying governmental messages are still very much the same. What is especially clear is that much of the discourse described here, from 2017, has drawn from the narrative that was deemed acceptable after 9/11. Had the post-9/11 discourse been more carefully broken down and critiqued, specifically in terms of how it was connected to legal changes, there is a possibility that the 2017 discourse might be different and that the mistakes of the past would not be recurring in the present day. It is therefore important to look at language that emanated from the US after the 9/11 attacks, particularly where it was directly related to the construction of structurally unsound legal changes. The events of 9/11 are chosen as a starting point because the attacks provide a sequence of events, over a compact period of time, that helps to advance this assessment, and because there are some aspects of terrorism-detention practices that became fragmented in specific ways because of 9/11. Part of the reason for this is because the post-9/11 period was so widely publicised and there was a particular discourse that grew out of the attacks.

What is too often missing from the current political discussion regarding terrorism detentions is a review of past political conversations, including what has been discussed in the past, what has been learned, what was a mistake and what can be done differently. Instead, many of the responses to international threats, such as that posed by Daesh, often give rise to knee-jerk reactions that resemble some of those that arose after 9/11. It is unclear what lessons have been learned in a post-9/11 world, and that may be because many of the problematic practices that arose out of 9/11, and the assumptions on which they were based, have become deeply entrenched in the public consciousness and are now seen as normal.

V. Overview of the Book

There are many aspects of the fight against terrorism that have engaged academic attention before 9/11 and certainly since then. This book focuses on one issue—that of extraordinary Executive detention practices undertaken after the attacks, many of which continue in different forms to this day. Practices in the US especially are emphasised, with examples also drawn from Canada and the UK, and occasionally another jurisdiction, where a commonality was apparent across post-9/11 responses.

A. Some Parameters

A work such as this can likely not set enough parameters. Some are set here and others appear throughout the book. This book is ambitious in its scope, and this ambition could only be pursued with certain clear limitations. First, this work does not intend to provide a comprehensive assessment of post-9/11 terrorism detention practices in the named jurisdictions. That has already been done, in a much better way than this book could ever possibly contemplate.[57] Instead, where different detention scenarios are discussed, they are intended as specific examples

---

[57] See, eg, Kent Roach, *The 9/11 Effect: Comparative Counter-Terrorism* (New York, Cambridge University Press, 2011) (comparing different national responses to the 9/11 attacks).

of situations in which a dominant political discourse, or conversation, appears to have resulted in particular legal changes regarding terrorism detentions. No claim is made that practices were uniform across, or always within, jurisdictions before 9/11. However, the examples chosen for this book are used to show that common points of argumentation led to different, and often irreconcilable, practices being pursued in comparable cases, specifically in response to 9/11.

This book also recognises the inherent risks in any comparative undertaking, as different jurisdictions have different histories, cultures, constitutional norms and traditions. The UK, for instance, has considerably more experience with the use of Executive detentions in terrorism matters than the US or Canada, and that experience obviously pre-dates 9/11.[58] As such, Executive detentions may seem less shocking to somebody coming from the legal tradition of the UK than they are for somebody from the US or Canada.[59] This difference is acknowledged. However, this very difference supports the argumentation theories set forth in this book, as they reflect the impact of different values and experiences on a dominant political and legal narrative.

Much has been written in valid criticism of national criminal justice systems in relation to terrorism detentions.[60] Much has also been written to critique international humanitarian law in this context.[61] These critiques are complex and important, and their validity is noted. This work, however, does not generally engage with these critiques or with problems within these systems of detention. Instead, it focuses on the post-9/11 development or use of terrorism detention regimes outside of either of these traditional, more established paradigms. That is, in itself, a large area of study.

This book demonstrates a marked preference for the use of the criminal justice system in cases involving detained terrorism suspects.[62] This preference specifically

---

[58] For a thorough discussion of Executive detentions in the anti-terrorism context, see David Bonner, *Executive Measures, Terrorism and National Security: Have the Rules of the Game Changed?* (Burlington, VT, Ashgate Publishing, 2007) (discussing Executive detentions, particularly focusing on their use and history in the UK); pre-9/11 Executive detention measures in a number of jurisdictions, including the UK, are discussed in ch 6 below.

[59] I am originally from the US, where I practised law, and I now hold dual citizenship with the US and Canada. Much of my own background, by definition, informs my perspectives on these matters.

[60] Too many such sources exist to cite them all here. For context, see, eg, Steven Dewulf, 'Human Rights in the Criminal Code? A Critique of the Curious Implementation of the EU and Council of Europe Instruments in Combating and Preventing Terrorism in Belgian Criminal Legislation' (2014) 22(1) *European Journal of Crime, Criminal Law and Criminal Justice* 33; Simon Hallsworth and John Lea, 'Reconstructing Leviathan: Emerging Contours of the Security State' (2011) 15(2) *Theoretical Criminology* 141; see generally Aniceto Masferrer and Clive Walker, *Counter-terrorism, Human Rights and the Rule of Law: Crossing Legal Boundaries in Defence of the State* (Cheltenham, Edward Elgar, 2013); see also generally Wadie E Said, *Crimes of Terror: The Legal and Political Implications of Federal Terrorism Prosecutions* (New York, Oxford University Press, 2015).

[61] See generally Helen Duffy, *The 'War on Terror' and the Framework of International Law* (Cambridge, Cambridge University Press, 2005).

[62] See Gabor Rona and Raha Wala, 'In Defense of Federal Criminal Courts for Terrorism Cases in the United States' in Fionnuala Ni Aolain and Oren Gross (eds), *Guantanamo and Beyond: Exceptional Courts and Military Commissions in Comparative Perspective* (New York, Cambridge University Press, 2013) 137.

relates to the notion of fair procedure or due process.[63] There is some controversy surrounding this view, and this controversy is noted. As will be explained throughout this book, national criminal justice systems continue to be the mechanism used most commonly to process terrorism cases. That is not surprising, given the constitutional traditions of the US, Canada and the UK regarding fair trial on detention.

The objection is not necessarily to the handling of any cases outside of the criminal justice system. It is to a shift in presumptions, which once favoured criminal justice paradigms for terrorism detention. With this presumption, those seeking to deviate from the criminal justice system would need to justify, in a particular case, and with the burden of proof, this deviation. However, as will be described throughout this book, after 9/11, this presumption changed in some cases. Those who used extraordinary detention measures—whether it was the detentions at Guantanamo Bay, immigration detentions or other mechanisms such as control orders—made generalised assertions (often supported by legislative authorisation) that these mechanisms must be available, at the discretion of the Executive. In some respects, it appeared as if those seeking to reinforce the dominance of the criminal justice paradigm were the ones who had to explain why this was necessary, instead of the other way around.[64] Beyond that, ongoing critiques of these various extraordinary detention measures have caused them to be plagued by significant questions as to their legitimacy, which is less often a critique used for criminal prosecutions.

Thus, although extraordinary detention scenarios involved far fewer detainees than criminal proceedings did in the years after 9/11, they represent an important crack in the pre-existing paradigms. Executive detentions may not have been new, but they were often pursued in new, or problematic, ways in response to 9/11. Moreover, in many of these cases, outside of the pre-existing paradigms, people have sometimes been held for years, with no criminal conviction. At some point, even if a detention is initially justified as a short-term, emergency or administrative measure—a point not necessarily conceded here—it becomes unhinged from this short-term mechanism and it becomes problematic. Where people are held for years with no criminal charge, on an accusation of terrorism involvement, with no end in sight, this problem is most significant.[65] Where this happened or, in the

[63] See Larry May, *Global Justice and Due Process* (Cambridge, Cambridge University Press, 2011) (arguing that due process should be a *jus cogens* standard under international law, discussing wide-ranging detentions, such as those at Guantanamo Bay and those in refugee camps).

[64] See, eg, the discussion of the Abdulmutallab case in ch 3 below.

[65] See Joseph Chedrawe, 'Blurring the Civil-Criminal Divide for Process Rights: Closed Material Procedures and the Curious Character of Preventive Security Measures' (2015) 24(1) *King's Law Journal* 1 (talking about some of the controversies in preventive detention measures in security cases); Claire Macken, *Terrorists: Preventive Detention and International Human Rights Law* (Oxford, Routledge, 2011); Fiona de Londras, *Detention in the 'War on Terror': Can Human Rights Fight Back?* (New York, Cambridge University Press, 2011).

case of the US, where torture and targeted killing became normalised, questions arose as to the very nature of national identity and whether this had undergone an unacceptable shift because of this break in paradigms. Thus, even regimes that may no longer be used are important to demonstrate the manner in which this break occurred.[66]

Finally, this book considers how political discourse, or narratives, emanated from the US and led to decisions to institute extraordinary detention practices in a number of cases. Based on this starting premise, the emphasis is necessarily heaviest on the US, as the target of the 9/11 attacks, the source of much of the relevant post-9/11 political language and the jurisdiction that arguably most systematically employed regimes outside of the pre-existing criminal justice paradigms. The US 'War on Terror' approach was not expressly adopted in other jurisdictions, but, as explained throughout this book, other threads of the US argumentation had an impact on some of the detention decisions made in countries like Canada and the UK. Thus, examples from Canada and the UK, and sometimes another jurisdiction, are interlaced in this work where relevant to the particular point being addressed.

B. 'Extraordinary Detention'

As a preliminary definition, 'extraordinary detention', or some similar term, is used to loosely describe terrorism-related detentions, or limitations on freedom, or limitations on judicial process that take place outside of the criminal justice system. For the US, it also includes detentions that the government claims result from war, but which do not fit into the international humanitarian law framework. Because this book addresses a number of practices, some more closely resembling traditional detention than others, it was necessary to identify a single phrase that would collectively describe all of these practices.

These practices are grouped together because they are argued, in this book, to have emerged from the same threads of political discourse. They involve changes from detention standards that existed before 9/11 and that arose because of the 9/11 attacks. Different terms, such as 'extraordinary practices', were considered for this purpose, but the reality is that even where the practices may not technically be considered detentions by some, they are all sufficiently analogous to detentions for the purposes of this discussion. The term 'extraordinary detention' is a play on words, drawing from some of the terms the US used to describe its questionable, altered practices, such as 'extraordinary renditions', which was a US practice of secretly transporting a terrorism suspect to a third country for questioning,

---

[66] See generally Fiona de Londras, 'Can Counter-terrorist Internment Ever Be Legitimate?' (2011) 33(3) *Human Rights Quarterly* 593 (noting that the practice of counter-terrorism detentions tend to be argued as illegitimate, but that there could potentially be factors that could narrow the scope of such detentions and could address some of the legitimacy problems).

generally including torture.[67] 'Extraordinary' in this context does not have a positive connotation.

Since 9/11, in situations involving an 'extraordinary detention', the person held typically does not face a trial before a traditional criminal court. This person might, or might not, have a hearing elsewhere, but the body holding the hearing might have questionable legitimacy, or the procedural protections might be quite abridged from those in a criminal proceeding. If there is a hearing, this hearing does not necessarily involve a conviction, with a full defence and a set sentence, but, more often, involves periodic review to continue detention, with no clear end in sight. The detention, or other deprivation of liberty, is considered extraordinary for the purposes of this work if it takes place as a result of a proceeding that is not included within the criminal justice system, either because the proceeding itself is entirely separate or because traditional procedural protections, such as the right to counsel, the right to specific forms of judicial review or the right to know the nature of the charges or evidence, are abridged on an assertion of national security, in a manner that would not be permitted in a criminal proceeding.

The following definition, employed by the Office of the High Commissioner for Human Rights, in describing the treatment of irregular migrants is comparable to what is meant by 'detention' here: 'administrative deprivation of liberty. Detention is to be considered as confinement within a narrowly bounded or restricted location which the detainee cannot leave'.[68] Thus, somebody might be held under conditions pursuant to a Canadian security certificate. This person might not be allowed to be home alone, or to leave the home, or to use the Internet, or to otherwise engage in activities that people normally can pursue. The person might be required to wear an ankle monitoring bracelet or to provide frequent status updates on his or her whereabouts and activities. The list goes on. This scenario is considered to be 'detention' for this purpose, even if this person is not sitting in an actual cell.

It is recognised that some individual protections might be abridged in the context of a criminal matter, such as where the government asserts a national security justification for keeping evidence secret under section 38 of the Canada Evidence Act.[69] Such a procedure is built into Canada's evidence rules for criminal matters and involves an adjudication as to whether the evidence can be admitted. The Act calls for a separate application before the federal court, and not the trial judge, when the government seeks to withhold evidence based on national security concerns.[70] However, this would not be considered an extraordinary detention

---

[67] See Mark J Murray, 'Extraordinary Rendition and US Counterterrorism Policy' (2011) 4(3) *Journal of Strategic Security* 15; see also Fiona de Londras, 'Prevention, Detention, and Extraordinariness' in Ni Aolain and Gross, above, n 62, 118, 119.

[68] Office of the High Commissioner for Human Rights, Migration Task Force, 'Administrative Detention of Migrants' n 3, *Office of the High Commissioner for Human Rights*, www2.ohchr.org/english/issues/migration/taskforce/docs/administrativedetentionrev5.pdf.

[69] See Canada Evidence Act, RSC, 1985, c C-5, s 38.

[70] ibid.

scenario because it is still within the parameters of a traditional criminal proceeding, and the Supreme Court of Canada has ruled that while section 38 is constitutional, if it would result in an unfair trial, the detainee must be released.[71] This is the inverse from the general situation in the case of many extraordinary detentions, where a detainee can continue to be held even if the procedure followed causes the proceeding to be unfair to the detainee.[72]

Moreover, these 'extraordinary detentions' are specifically used in terrorism-related cases, where the government asserts a security justification for the extraordinary measures. This work therefore does not seek to critique criminal prosecutions for terrorism undertaken under a national constitutional system, again, while recognising that valid critiques of those systems exist. The focus is on situations in which a national government has entirely avoided its criminal justice system, or the traditional rules of war, to detain, or limit freedom somehow, of an individual under some parallel form of justice. It does not suggest that constitutional criminal courts are ideal, but instead suggests that avoiding those systems entirely is a distinct problem to be expanded upon here.

C. Roadmap of the Argument

This book breaks down—or deconstructs—some of the idiosyncratic political discourse surrounding certain extraordinary detention practices, specifically those implemented in a number of liberal democracies after the 9/11 terrorist attacks. In the crisis atmosphere that arose after the attacks, distinctive political language emerged that became familiar and foundational, as several national jurisdictions struggled to decide how best to respond to what seemed to be a new and imminent terrorist threat. This language gave rise to certain ideas about how terrorism should be fought and, in turn, gave rise to specific legal enactments. In subsequent years, it has often been overlooked that this foundational language emerged during a crisis and was not necessarily challenged, even though it continues to undergird certain detention practices. This book focuses on one particular aspect of the response to terrorism—that of detention and, more specifically, what is described above as 'extraordinary detention'.

As a preliminary roadmap to this book, it is divided into two major parts, each containing three chapters. Each of the two parts is named after a portion of the

---

[71] *R v Ahmad*, 2011 SCC 6, [2011] 1 SCR 110 at para 78 (pointing out that 'if the end result of non-disclosure by the Crown is that a fair trial cannot be had, then Parliament has determined that in the circumstances a stay of proceedings is the lesser evil compared with the disclosure of sensitive or potentially injurious information').

[72] For a Canadian example, see the procedure for special advocates in Canada. Immigration and Refugee Protection Act, SC 2001, c 27, ss 85–85.1 (providing greater procedural protection than the prior process, in which the detainee was simply barred from secret evidence, but still not allowing the special advocate to communicate the evidence to the detainee without permission).

subtitle of this book. Part I, 'Political Discourse', makes various arguments relating to the deconstructing and reconstructing of anti-terrorism detention discourse. Chapter one uses specific examples to argue that language can manufacture truth. Chapter two argues that breaking down particular rhetoric, and reassembling it through the vehicles of argumentation theory, can reveal new realities. Chapter three argues that layering different argumentation and language tools in inconsistent ways after 9/11 led to a 'fracturing' of the narrative, and thus of practices, around these detentions.

Part II, 'Fragmented Practices', draws on a specific thread of Perelman and Olbrechts-Tyteca's theory relating to argumentation points of departure and argues that three examples of problematic points of departure in post-9/11 political conversation underscored faulty changes in particular legal standards. This Part draws from the argument in Part I, in which the point is made that there were many layers of problems in terms of what rhetoric was advanced and how it affected legal actions. By expanding on one of these layers of problems, Part II seeks to give some insight into how deeply problematic each individual layer potentially was, with the idea that compiling these layers shows significant flaws in the pathway to these particular legal changes. Chapter four addresses the problematic argument that so much had changed after 9/11 that new detention paradigms were required. Chapter five addresses the common point of departure of the terrorist as the non-citizen Other. Finally, chapter six argues that the often simplistic, binary language used after the 9/11 attacks prevented a more nuanced assessment, in some cases, of proper legal responses in specific situations that were actually much more complex than a binary configuration could demonstrate. Finally, the book draws these points together in concluding that argumentation theory provides a lens for identifying problems with post-9/11 discourse surrounding terrorism detentions, and thus in identifying problematic legal changes that resulted from this rhetoric. With Daesh viewed as a growing threat and increasing calls for multi-layered responses to it, these detention practices, and the foundations on which they were built after 9/11, continue to be important.

D. The Beginning of a Conversation

Lest expectations of this book now be too high, a final introductory parameter is needed. This book does not claim to resolve all, or even most, of the issues it raises. Rather, it suggests something more akin to the beginning of a conversation, a suggestion that the assessments of certain legal changes might begin to take a different direction, and that the pursuit of this different direction may one day provide important insights into these practices. The hope is that this different manner of constructing these conversations will raise issues not just relating to the legitimacy of these particular detention practices, but also regarding the manner in which we move forward on evolving legal norms, especially those that change quickly in times of crisis. The realisation that this can only be the beginning of this conversation came about as this work progressed, and it draws inspiration from Clifford Geertz, in his work *Local Knowledge*, who said, of his own work:

> When, a decade ago, I collected a number of my essays and rereleased them under the title, half genuflection, half talisman, *The Interpretation of Cultures*, I thought I was summing things up; saying, as I said there, what it was I had been saying. But, as a matter of fact, I was imposing on myself a charge. In anthropology too, it so turns out, he who says A must also say B, and I have spent much of my time since trying to say it. The essays below are the result; but I am now altogether aware how much closer they stand to the origins of a thought-line than to the outcomes of it.[73]

This does not suggest that there are not conclusions to be drawn from this work. However, it means that much more can always be said and likely will be said in future works. The groundwork in this book is to argue for a methodology for critiquing specific legal enactments using argumentation theory. Once this groundwork is laid, much more can develop from there.

For now, the conversation begins.

[73] Clifford Geertz, *Local Knowledge* (New York, Basic Books, 1983) 3.

Part I

Political Discourse

When the Supreme Court of the United States refused to hear the appeal from the denial of habeas corpus in *Rumsfeld v Padilla* on the merits, now-retired Justice Stevens chastised the Court for failing to understand the importance of the issue before it, cutting through the then-dominant discourse of necessity and Executive deference, and drawing the issue back to fundamental ideals:

> Whether respondent is entitled to immediate release is a question that reasonable jurists may answer in different ways. There is, however, only one possible answer to the question whether he is entitled to a hearing on the justification for his detention.

> At stake in this case is nothing less than the essence of a free society. Even more important than the method of selecting the people's rulers and their successors is the character of the constraints imposed on the Executive by the rule of law. Unconstrained Executive detention for the purpose of investigating and preventing subversive activity is the hallmark of the Star Chamber. Access to counsel for the purpose of protecting the citizen from official mistakes and mistreatment is the hallmark of due process.

> Executive detention of subversive citizens, like detention of enemy soldiers to keep them off the battlefield, may sometimes be justified to prevent persons from launching or becoming missiles of destruction. It may not, however, be justified by the naked interest in using unlawful procedures to extract information. Incommunicado detention for months on end is such a procedure. Whether the information so procured is more or less reliable than that acquired by more extreme forms of torture is of no consequence. For if this Nation is to remain true to the ideals symbolized by its flag, it must not wield the tools of tyrants even to resist an assault by the forces of tyranny.[1]

The Star Chamber was a court in England, which operated from approximately 1487 until 1641. It evolved over time, growing in use as a political weapon against those who opposed the Crown's policies. Its judges had the power to order imprisonment and torture. Proceedings were, especially later, held in secret, with no right of appeal, and punishment could be severe and quickly enforced. Although the Star Chamber was abolished in 1641, it is still referred to as an expression for a

---

[1] *Rumsfeld v Padilla*, 542 US 426 (2004) (Stevens J, dissenting) (internal citations omitted).

judicial proceeding that is arbitrary, abusive and secret, and as the antithesis of one respecting individual freedoms.[2]

Justice Stevens wrote his opinion in 2004, at a time when public criticism of the actions of then-President George W Bush, in responding to the 9/11 attacks, was more muted than it became later. This quote played prominently in American media at the time, since it showed a striking contrast to the dominant narrative of necessity, safety and unquestioning support for the President. Justice Stevens' comments would have seemed more normal before 9/11, but the public conversation had changed so much by 2004 that they caused a considerable stir.

The quote demonstrates the power of reconfiguring the narrative in a legal context. This first part of the book addresses the different tools through which political discourse can be used to alter perceptions of what is true and what is real. It does so by addressing some of the many layers of tools that can be assembled in different ways to persuade a particular audience of a particular truth, including the use of examples. Thus, each of the three chapters in this part presents a different angle on ways in which the narrative can be deconstructed and then reconstructed to paint a new picture.

---

[2] See Max Radin, 'The Right to a Public Trial' (1931–32) 6 *Temple Law Quarterly* 381, 381–82 (explaining the role of the Star Chamber in the concept of a right to have a trial that is public); Thomas G Barnes, 'Star Chamber Mythology' (1961) 5(1) *American Journal of Legal History* 1 (explaining the background and connotations of references to the Star Chamber, although disagreeing in some of the specifics as to the reputation of the Star Chamber).

1

Language Manufactures Truth:
The Power of Labels

I. The Beginning of the Conversation:
Narratives Wield Great Power

Language matters.

How an argument is constructed and presented has everything to do with the ultimate appeal and success of that argument. In law, the underlying arguments, and how they are put forth, can be a foundational factor in the ultimate development of legal norms. Success can have more to do with how an argument is constructed than with the actual substantive merits of the argument. Missing or flawed elements can undermine an argument. George Orwell talked about the potential practical harm that imprecise language can have:

> Now, it is clear that the decline of a language must ultimately have political and economic causes: it is not due simply to the bad influence of this or that individual writer. But an effect can become a cause, reinforcing the original cause and producing the same effect in an intensified form, and so on indefinitely. A man may take to drink because he feels himself to be a failure, and then fail all the more completely because he drinks. It is rather the same thing that is happening to the English language. It becomes ugly and inaccurate because our thoughts are foolish, but the slovenliness of our language makes it easier for us to have foolish thoughts. The point is that the process is reversible. Modern English, especially written English, is full of bad habits which spread by imitation and which can be avoided if one is willing to take the necessary trouble. If one gets rid of these habits one can think more clearly, and to think clearly is a necessary first step toward political regeneration: so that the fight against bad English is not frivolous and is not the exclusive concern of professional writers.[1]

The old children's rhyme 'sticks and stones may break my bones, but names will never hurt me' sounds good in theory. In some cases, though, a name used can actually create a false sense of reality. The label of 'suspected terrorist' can have profound legal implications, even if the person is never charged with any

---

[1] George Orwell, 'Politics and the English Language' (first published London, Horizon, 1946), reprinted numerous times, www.orwell.ru/library/essays/politics/english/e_polit.

terrorism offence. Public narratives often lead to specific legal outcomes, so precision in public language is required. Unfortunately, such precision is often absent in the public discourse, and certainly in that surrounding terrorism, and this has led to inconsistency in certain terrorism detention practices, which are discussed more in Part II. In some cases, this lack of precision is arguably intentional, where a speaker uses a particular technique to persuade a specific audience.[2]

As one example, Perelman and Olbrechts-Tyteca speak of epithets. They argue that certain ways of describing things can be subject to an underlying agreement between the audience and the speaker. 'The epithet', they note 'is used without justification because it is supposed to set forth unquestionable facts ... It is permissible to call the French Revolution "that bloody revolution", but this is not the only way of qualifying it and other epithets could equally well be chosen.'[3] A particular phrasing, they suggest, can be chosen to express or promote a particular point of view to a particular audience. This kind of argumentation tool is most obvious when two 'symmetrical qualifications with opposite values appear equally possible'. This is especially clear when the viewpoint is potentially controversial.[4]

When focusing specifically on political language, Orwell described it as 'designed to make lies sound truthful and murder respectable, and to give an appearance of solidity to pure wind'.[5] While this work does not go so far as to suggest that all political language is so dishonest, Orwell persuasively suggests that political language is frequently presented in a way that is mainly designed to achieve a certain view of an issue and a desired outcome, often through the use of poor language. This chapter focuses extensively on one small piece of the larger language tools that can be used, arguing that particular 'epithets' or labels or characterisations can have a profound impact on public perception in different terrorism-related situations. It does so through the use of three examples in which an obvious fracturing of the political narrative, or intentional advancement of a particular narrative, has taken place, producing inconsistent, competing and often inaccurate descriptions of the same high-profile events and/or people or entities.

A label is, of course, only one of the many layers of discourse tools that can be used in persuasion. This chapter demonstrates, through example, how just that one layer can, on its own, significantly impact public perceptions. Imagine, then, the potential impact of layering all of the other possible argumentative techniques, many of which are discussed in the following chapters. Much of this book deals with the way in which narratives developed after 9/11, and this chapter sets the stage for that. Problems with post-9/11 narratives (and certainly narratives

---

[2] See Chaim Perelman and Lucie Olbrechts-Tyteca, *The New Rhetoric: A Treatise on Argumentation*, translated by John Wilkinson and Purcell Weaver (Notre Dame, IN, University of Notre Dame Press, 1969) 126 (discussing the importance of the audience in persuasion, which is discussed more fully in ch 2).

[3] ibid.

[4] ibid.

[5] Orwell, above, n 1.

developed before then) continue to provide problematic foundations for some of the narrative that is dominating legal developments today. These problems are demonstrated in the more current examples used in this chapter.

II. Whoever Prevails with Duelling Labels Wins the Day: 'Muslim Ban' or 'Extreme Vetting'?

Duelling narratives were obvious in the 2017 battle between the US Administration and various US courts over two Executive Orders barring, to different degrees, the rights of certain people from certain countries to travel to the US.[6] The nature of the narratives bears a striking resemblance to the types of conversations that occurred after 9/11, showing that little has changed in some respects.[7]

In the terrorism context, a question sometimes arises as to whether governments are themselves acting out of fear or whether they have exploited the fears of their populations in the wake of high-profile attacks. For the so-called 'War on Terror', for example, the novel idea of declaring war on an ideology, or on a type of conduct, required public acceptance that it was 'necessary, desirable and achievable' to follow this path in order to prevent events like those on 9/11 from recurring.[8] It may be true in some cases that the narrative is not just a natural response to the fear of attacks, but that it is carefully designed to garner a certain response and to exploit fears, or even that it is a dishonest exploitation of such fears in some cases.[9] Orwell said: 'The great enemy of clear language is insincerity. When there is a gap between one's real and one's declared aims, one turns as it were instinctively to long words and exhausted idioms, like a cuttlefish spurting out ink.'[10]

This section is not about critiquing the policies behind the Executive Orders, although much could be said there. Rather, it focuses on the presentation of duelling narratives that have arisen around them. It focuses on why such duelling

---

[6] This discussion is current as of late June 2017. See *Executive Order 13769, Protecting the Nation from Foreign Terrorist Entry into the United States* (27 January 2017) 82 Federal Register 8977 (hereinafter *Trump Executive Order I*); Executive *Order 13780, Protecting the Nation from Foreign Terrorist Entry into the United States* (16 March 2017) 82 Federal Register 13209 (superseding *Trump Executive Order I*) (hereinafter *Trump Executive Order II*); see also, eg, *State of Washington; State of Minnesota v Trump et al*, No 17-35105 (9th Cir 2017) (hereinafter *Washington v Trump*); *State of Hawaii et al v Trump*, No 17-15589) (9th Cir 2017) (hereinafter *Hawaii v Trump*); *International Refugee Assistance Project v Trump*, No 17-1351 (4th Cir 2014) (hereinafter *IRAP v Trump*) (each upholding a lower court's injunction on one of the Executive Order travel bans).

[7] See the discussion of the terrorist as the non-citizen Other, below in ch 5.

[8] Richard Jackson, *Writing the War on Terrorism* (Manchester, Manchester University Press, 2005) 1.

[9] See generally Robert Diab, *The Harbinger Theory: How the Post-9/11 Emergency Became Permanent and the Case for Reform* (Oxford, Oxford University Press, 2015) ch 3 (for an extensive discussion of fear-based rhetoric in response to the 9/11 attacks).

[10] Orwell, above, n 1.

political narratives are common and why the victory of one narrative is necessary in order to advance a particular argument. For the purposes of this section, the focus is on the dispute over the proper words to describe the Orders.

To pursue this point means to use sources that are unconventional for a work such as this. Many events are quite recent, as of the writing of this book, and news sources give a sense of how the political discourse has been presented to the public. Trump's use of the social media site Twitter is also unprecedented for a sitting American President. Other national leaders use Twitter, but in a more formal capacity, while Trump regularly uses his own personal page, in addition to the official '@POTUS' page, to vent personal opinions or to talk about policy. Trump's Twitter thus provides a somewhat linear example of the narrative formation that he presents about the Executive Orders, and examples from his Twitter are included here, unusual as such a source might otherwise seem. It is for this reason that his personal Twitter account is frequently cited, and why official statements of other government officials on the same events are not always included. Sean Spicer, Trump's former press secretary, said that Trump's Twitter posts can be taken as official White House statements, although confusion remains as to whether he was including Trump's personal Twitter.[11] Other sources supplement this.

The first of the two Executive Orders, among other things, suspended 'immigrant and non-immigrant entry' into the US for nationals of seven predominantly Muslim countries—Iraq, Iran, Libya, Sudan, Somalia, Syria and Yemen.[12] It also suspended the Refugee Admissions Program for 120 days and indefinitely barred entry to refugees from Syria.[13] In addition, it provided for changing the refugee screening process to give priority to those fleeing religious persecution, but only where the person's religion was a minority religion in the place of origin.[14] The Order captured some people who otherwise had a legal right to enter the US, and it immediately led to confusion and to large protests at many American airports.[15] It also quickly led to high-profile legal rulings staying the Order.[16]

As court proceedings progressed, Trump replaced the first Executive Order with another one, by the same name, which limited entry from six, rather than seven,

---

[11] See, eg, Elizabeth Landers, 'White House: Trump's Tweets are "Official Statements"' *CNN* (6 June 2017) www.cnn.com/2017/06/06/politics/trump-tweets-official-statements/index.html (one of several stories reporting the statements of Press Secretary Sean Spicer that Trump's tweets should be taken as 'official statements', but not indicating whether this included Trump's personal Twitter).

[12] *Trump Executive Order I*, above, n 6.

[13] ibid.

[14] ibid.

[15] See 'Thousands Protest against Trump Travel Ban in Cities and Airports Nationwide' *The Guardian* (30 January 2017) www.theguardian.com/us-news/2017/jan/29/protest-trump-travel-ban-muslims-airports; 'ACLU and Other Groups Challenge Trump Immigration Ban after Refugees Detained at Airports Following Executive Order' *ACLU* (28 January 2017) www.aclu.org/blog/speak-freely/aclu-and-other-groups-challenge-trump-immigration-ban-after-refugees-detained; see also, eg, the cases listed above in n 6.

[16] See, eg, the cases listed above in n 6 (all appellate rulings upholding stays laid down in lower courts).

predominantly Muslim countries, among other differences.[17] At the same time, the government sought to voluntarily dismiss the actions pending over the first Order.[18] Iraq was not included in this second Executive Order, because the Order said it was a country that had a positive relationship with the US, while the other six countries were identified as state sponsors of terrorism.[19]

The legal significance of these Orders continues to be a subject of contention in the US as of the writing of this book.[20] For the purpose of the duelling narratives, there are two points that are important in terms of argument and narrative. The first relates to a dominant political narrative that acts of terror are committed by Muslims and the second regards whether the Executive Orders constituted a 'ban' on travel to the US. Duelling narratives arose on both issues, and arguments over which narrative should win were expressly directed to the language to be used. Thus, this example provides a case study as to how language, even something as simple as one or two words, can completely change a picture.

A. Terrorism or 'Radical Islamic Terrorism'?

An underpinning to the discussion about the so-called 'Muslim ban' is the issue of language used associating Islam with terrorism. Terminology is important, and the underpinnings of language explain a great deal about what the Executive Orders actually were. Trump had campaigned heavily on a plan to rid the world of 'radical Islamic terrorism'.[21] It was not just the objective that has been important to him, but the actual use of that term, which was a significant, specific issue during his presidential campaign. He heavily criticised former President Barack Obama for not using that term.[22] Both Obama and former President George W Bush had intentionally used labels that did not connect terrorism with the Muslim faith.[23]

---

[17] *Trump Executive Order II*, above, n 6.

[18] *Hawaii v Trump*, above, n 6, 6.

[19] *Trump Executive Order II*, above, n 6, section g.

[20] As of the writing of this book, in June 2017, the Supreme Court of the United States granted the government's Petition for Writ of Certiorari regarding two appellate court rulings (with a third issued as the matter was before the Supreme Court). The Court lifted part of a stay on the travel ban, left part in place and set the matter for oral argument in its fall term. *Trump et al v International Refugee Assistance et al*, 582 US ___ (2017) (*per curiam*).

[21] See Samuel Osborne, 'After Criticising Opponents for Not Saying "Radical Islamic Terrorism" Donald Trump Rules it out of Saudi Arabia Speech: President Will Instead Use "Islamist Extremism"' *The Independent* (21 May 2017) www.independent.co.uk/news/world/americas/us-politics/donald-trump-muslim-radical-islamic-terrorism-speech-saudi-arabia-riyadh-a7747651.html (including a video of part of his statement).

[22] Mattathias Schwartz, 'White House Blames Exhaustion for Donald Trump's "Islamic Terrorism" Dog Whistle in Saudi Arabia' *The Intercept* (22 May 2017) theintercept.com/2017/05/22/white-house-blames-exhaustion-for-donald-trumps-islamic-terrorism-dog-whistle-in-saudi-arabia.

[23] Nahal Toosi, 'Breaking with Bush and Obama, Trump Talks about "Radical Islamic Terrorism"' *Politico* (28 February 2017) www.politico.com/story/2017/02/donald-trump-congress-speech-radical-islamic-terrorism-235531.

Trump went a different way, beginning during his campaign. In fact, he made so many statements on this issue that many of them were compiled in the ruling by the Fourth Circuit Court of Appeal, upholding a stay on a portion of one of the Executive Orders.[24] Throughout the campaign, Trump spoke repeatedly of the need to keep Muslims from entering the country. In December 2015, for example, he called for a 'total and complete shutdown' of the entry of Muslims to the US, 'until our country's representatives can figure out what the hell is going on'.[25] Trump once said 'I think Islam hates us'[26] and, during the same interview, '[w]e can't allow people coming into the country who have this hatred'.[27] A Trump spokesperson said '[we]'ve allowed this propaganda to spread all through the country that [Islam] is a religion of peace'.[28] Michael Flynn, Trump's national security advisor for less than a month, made statements such as the following, shortly after the election, calling 'Islamism' a 'vicious cancer inside the body of 1.7 billion people' that must be 'excised'.[29] Trump later said, with regard to his proposal for a ban, 'we're having problems with the Muslims, and we're having problems with Muslims coming into the country'.[30] The former Mayor of New York, Rudy Giuliani, said publicly that Trump had announced a 'Muslim ban' and then asked him how to institute it legally.[31]

Trump's language has varied depending on the audience involved. At times, this type of rhetoric has been more muted, as in early 2017, in a speech he gave before a joint session of Congress, where he said:

> I directed the Department of Defense to develop a plan to demolish and destroy ISIS—a network of lawless savages that have slaughtered Muslims and Christians, and men, women, and children of all faiths and beliefs … [w]e will work with our allies, including our friends and allies in the Muslim world, to extinguish this vile enemy from our planet.[32]

While his language was muted in that respect, Trump still pointedly referred to 'radical Islamic terrorism' in the speech.[33]

Similarly, in May 2017, Trump intended to avoid using the term 'Radical Islamic Terrorism' during his visit to Saudi Arabia, instead reportedly intending to use

---

[24] See *IRAP v Trump*, above, n 6, 18–23 (quoting Trump's interview).

[25] Jenna Johnson, 'Trump Calls for "Total and Complete Shutdown of Muslims Entering the United States"' *Washington Post* (7 December 2015) www.washingtonpost.com/news/post-politics/wp/2015/12/07/donald-trump-calls-for-total-and-complete-shutdown-of-muslims-entering-the-united-states/?utm_term=.96b861dfbc14 (accompanying video).

[26] Schwartz, above, n 22.

[27] *IRAP v Trump*, above, n 6, 20 (quoting Trump's interview).

[28] ibid.

[29] Andrew Kaczynski, 'Michael Flynn in August: Islamism a "Vicious Cancer" in Body of All Muslims That "Has to Be Excised"' *CNN* (22 November 2016) www.cnn.com/2016/11/22/politics/kfile-michael-flynn-august-speech/index.html (including a video of the statement).

[30] *IRAP v Trump*, above, n 6, 20.

[31] ibid.

[32] Toosi, above, n 23.

[33] ibid.

the term 'Islamist extremism and the Islamist terror groups it inspires', which is deemed to be less of an indictment of Islam or an association of the faith with terrorism.[34] Trump's aides attributed his ultimate shift in this plan to an error, induced by exhaustion, when he deviated from the script and called on leaders gathered in Saudi Arabia to join the US in 'honestly confronting the crisis of Islamic extremism, and the Islamists, and Islamic terror of all kinds'.[35]

These examples are different, though, from the intentional use of stronger language on this issue, where the Muslim faith and terrorism are conflated, and it is clear that this juxtaposition is not inadvertent. During the campaign, Trump caused controversy when he suggested a plan for the 'registration' of Muslim immigrants, something his staff subsequently denied that he said.[36] Members of his transition team later said that the plan under contemplation was actually a database of immigrants and visitors from Muslim countries, similar to the *National Security Entry-Exit Registration* (NSEERS) programme instituted by Bush after the 9/11 attacks and later abolished by Obama.[37]

Trump even formalised this position on his campaign website. During subsequent debates over whether his Executive Orders were 'Muslim bans', the statement disappeared from the website, but the Fourth Circuit Court of Appeal had a copy, which it quoted in its decision to uphold an injunction against a specific section of one of the Executive Orders.[38] Called the 'Statement on Preventing Muslim Immigration', the campaign statement begins by stating:

> Donald J. Trump is calling for a total and complete shutdown of Muslims entering the United States until our country's representatives can figure out what is going on. According to Pew Research, among others, there is great hatred towards Americans by large segments of the Muslim population. Most recently, a poll from the Center for Security Policy released data showing '25% of those polled agreed that violence against Americans here in the United States is justified as a part of the global jihad' and 51% of those polled 'agreed that Muslims in America should have the choice of being governed according to Shariah'. Shariah authorizes such atrocities as murder against nonbelievers who won't convert, beheadings and more unthinkable acts that pose great harm to Americans, especially women.

---

[34] Schwartz, above, n 22.

[35] ibid.

[36] See, eg, Harriet Agerholm, 'Donald Trump Seen Calling for Muslim Registry in New Video Despite Denials' *The Independent* (18 November 2016) www.independent.co.uk/news/world/americas/us-elections/donald-trump-muslim-registry-video-president-islam-policies-immigration-a7424511.html (accompanying video).

[37] Abigail Hauslohner, 'Is the Trump Administration Really Going to Launch a Registry for Muslims?' *Washington Post* (16 November 2016) www.washingtonpost.com/news/post-nation/wp/2016/11/16/is-the-trump-administration-really-going-to-launch-a-registry-for-muslims/?utm_term=.de3c35177c2d (including statements by Kris Kobach, who played a role in creating the now-defunct *NSEERS* program, after 9/11).

[38] *IRAP v Trump*, above, n 6, 19–20. This decision contains the full text of Trump's statement from the campaign on Muslim immigration and it also notes that the statement was removed while the case was pending. The statement will thus be quoted as reproduced in this decision.

... Without looking at the various polling data, it is obvious to anybody the hatred is beyond comprehension. Where this hatred comes from and why we will have to determine. Until we are able to determine and understand this problem and the dangerous threat it poses, our country cannot be the victims of the horrendous attacks by people that believe only in Jihad, and have no sense of reason or respect of human life. If I win the election for President, we are going to Make America Great Again.—Donald J. Trump.[39]

When Trump issued his Executive Orders regarding travel, it was widely understood to be pursuant to this and other statements made during the campaign.[40] The countries from which people were banned were all predominantly Muslim countries.[41] The Executive Orders quickly came to be called a 'Muslim ban' in popular discourse, in spite of the government's attempts to quash use of this term.[42] The importance of the narrative is shown by the White House's attempt to offer a different narrative, to stop people from calling the Orders a 'Muslim ban' or, sometimes, a 'ban' at all.[43] The term 'extreme vetting' began to be offered as an alternative description.[44] However, in publicity surrounding the first Executive Order, Trump announced that it was intended to keep out 'radical Islamic terrorists'.[45]

Amidst all of this activity in the US, Canadian Prime Minister Justin Trudeau posted on Twitter, in obvious opposition to the travel ban. He wrote: 'To those fleeing persecution, terror & war, Canadians will welcome you, regardless of your faith. Diversity is our strength #WelcomeToCanada.'[46]

On 29 January 2017, two days after Trump issued his first Executive Order regarding travel, he was still tweeting about terrorism, largely in response to

---

[39] ibid (reproducing the statement from Trump's website, which, the Court noted, had been removed from the campaign website shortly before the oral arguments before it, in May 2017). The statement also disappeared from other sites, such as Trump's Facebook page. As of 23 June 2017, the post was still there, with a blank box under the heading 'Statement on Preventing Muslim Immigration': Donald J Trump, *Facebook* (7 December 2015) www.facebook.com/DonaldTrump/posts/10156386906600725.

[40] See *IRAP v Trump*, above, n 6, 18–23 (laying out a number of relevant statements that Trump and his staff made regarding the Executive Orders).

[41] See *Trump Executive Order I*, above, n 6.

[42] See, eg, Alan Yuhas and Mazin Sidahmed, 'Is This a Muslim Ban? Trump's Executive Order Explained' *The Guardian* (31 January 2017) www.theguardian.com/us-news/2017/jan/28/trump-immigration-ban-syria-muslims-reaction-lawsuits; Daphne Eviatar, 'The New Travel Ban is Still a Muslim Ban' *The Atlantic* (7 March 2017) www.theatlantic.com/international/archive/2017/03/trump-muslim-executive-order-syria-yemen-refugee-bannon-breitbart/518808.

[43] Aaron Rupar, 'After Days of Calling Trump's Muslim Ban a "Ban", the White House is Trying to Walk it Back' *Think Progress* (31 January 2017), thinkprogress.org/spicer-muslim-ban-not-a-ban-trump-5a2ff81bdfa3#.elxh7q43f.

[44] ibid; see also '"Extreme Vetting" Would Require Visitors to US to Share Contacts and Passwords' *The Guardian* (4 April 2017), www.theguardian.com/us-news/2017/apr/04/trump-extreme-vetting-visitors-to-us-share-contacts-passwords.

[45] See, eg, Dan Merica, 'Trump Signs Executive Order to Keep Out "Radical Islamic Terrorists"' *CNN Politics* (30 January 2017) www.cnn.com/2017/01/27/politics/trump-plans-to-sign-executive-action-on-refugees-extreme-vetting.

[46] Justin Trudeau, @JustinTrudeau, *Twitter* (28 January 2017) twitter.com/JustinTrudeau/status/825438460265762816.

adverse court orders obtained over the weekend and in response to the large protests that took place that same weekend. For example, he tweeted: 'Our country needs strong borders and extreme vetting, NOW. Look what is happening all over Europe and, indeed, the world—a horrible mess!'[47] He also tweeted: 'Christians in the Middle-East have been executed in large numbers. We cannot allow this horror to continue.'[48] He posted a statement on Facebook entitled 'Statement Regarding Recent Executive Order Concerning Extreme Vetting'.[49] Among other things, he wrote: 'To be clear, this is not a Muslim ban, as the media is falsely reporting.'[50] Instead, he wrote:

> This is not about religion—this is about terror and keeping our country safe. There are over 40 different countries worldwide that are majority Muslim that are not affected by this order. We will again be issuing visas to all countries once we are sure we have reviewed and implemented the most secure policies over the next 90 days.[51]

That same day, Alexandre Bissonnette, a Canadian citizen, walked into a mosque in Quebec City, Canada, and shot a number of people as they were participating in evening prayers. In the end, six people died and 19 others were injured, five of them seriously. All of the victims were Muslim. Trudeau immediately condemned the shootings as an act of terrorism.[52] Reports after the Quebec City shootings suggested that Bissonnette was known for online trolling against refugees and women and in favour of Trump, but not as somebody who ever espoused violence.[53]

In a statement shortly after the attack, Trudeau said: 'We condemn this terrorist attack on Muslims in a centre of worship and refuge … Muslim-Canadians are an important part of our national fabric, and these senseless acts have no place in our communities, cities and country.'[54] The investigation in Canada was treated as a terrorist attack.[55] Bissonnette was ultimately charged with six counts of first-degree murder and five counts of attempted murder using a restricted firearm, but was not charged with terrorism offences. Such offences require proof regarding

---

[47] Donald J Trump, @realDonaldTrump, *Twitter* (29 January 2017) twitter.com/realDonaldTrump/status/825692045532618753 (each of these Tweets is a separate post, so no 'ibid' designation is used).

[48] Donald J Trump, @realDonaldTrump, *Twitter* (29 January 2017) twitter.com/realDonaldTrump/status/825721153142521858.

[49] Donald J Trump, 'Statement Regarding Recent Executive Order Concerning Extreme Vetting', *Facebook* (29 January 2017) www.facebook.com/DonaldTrump/posts/10158567643610725.

[50] ibid.

[51] ibid.

[52] See Nicolas van Praet et al, 'Suspect in Quebec City Mosque Attack Charged with Six Counts of Murder' *Globe and Mail* (30 January 2017) www.theglobeandmail.com/news/national/quebec-city-mosque-shooting/article33822092.

[53] ibid. The same mosque had been subjected to hate before the attack, including somebody leaving the severed head of a pig, wrapped with bows and ribbons, and a card saying 'bonne appétit' a few months before the attack. Andy Riga, 'Quebec Mosque Shooting Suspect Alexandre Bissonnette Changes Lawyer' *Montreal Gazette* (30 March 2017) montrealgazette.com/news/local-news/quebec-mosque-shooting-suspect-alexandre-bissonnette-back-in-court.

[54] Van Praet et al, above, n 52.

[55] ibid.

intent and, as of late May 2017, government officials were saying that the investigation on that issue was continuing.[56]

After the Quebec City attack, Trump continued to tweet about the first Executive Order on travel, but he never mentioned the Quebec City attack on his Twitter.[57] Kellyanne Conway, a Trump aide, was asked why Trump had been silent on Twitter about the attack, and she said '[h]e doesn't tweet about everything, he doesn't make a comment about everything' and noted that Trump was 'sympathetic to any loss of life'.[58]

The day after the Quebec City attack, Trump was still posting about protests to his Executive Order, saying, in two tweets:

> Only 109 people out of 325,000 were detained and held for questioning. Big problems at airports were caused by Delta computer outage … protesters and tears of Senator Schumer. Secretary Kelly said that all is going well with very few problems. MAKE AMERICA SAFE AGAIN![59]

A little later, Trump tweeted: 'There is nothing nice about searching for terrorists before they can enter our country. This was a big part of my campaign. Study the world!'[60] And later still: 'If the ban were announced with a one week notice, the "bad" would rush into our country during that week. A lot of bad "dudes" out there!'[61]

Although he did not comment on the Quebec City attack on Twitter, Trump did call Trudeau to offer condolences and US support.[62] While Trudeau had publicly

---

[56] Riga, above, n 53; see also 'Police Failed to Warn Quebec Muslims before Mosque Shooting, Survivor Says' *CTV News* (18 May 2017) www.ctvnews.ca/canada/police-failed-to-warn-quebec-muslims-before-mosque-shooting-survivor-says-1.3420371; Jacques Boissinot, 'Why No Terrorism Charges in Quebec Mosque Shooting? It Would Place Extra Burden on Prosecutors: Experts' *National Post* (31 January 2017) news.nationalpost.com/news/canada/quebec-mosque-shooting-terrorism-offences-are-complex-experts-say) (quoting the Crown prosecutor, when asked why terrorism charges were not laid, as saying the events were recent and that the investigation is ongoing); see also Criminal Code, RSC 1985, c C-46, s. 83.01 (Canada) (discussing intent provisions relating to terrorism offences in Canada).

[57] Meagan Fitzpatrick, 'Trump "Sympathetic" But Publicly Silent on Quebec City Mosque Attack' *CBC News* (9 February 2017) www.cbc.ca/news/world/trump-quebec-mosque-tweet-fitzpatrick-1.3973893.

[58] ibid.

[59] Donald J Trump, @realDonaldTrump, *Twitter* (30 January 2017) twitter.com/realDonaldTrump/status/826041397232943104; Donald J Trump, @realDonaldTrump, *Twitter* (30 January 2017), twitter.com/realDonaldTrump/status/826042483155013632 (two tweets combined for this purpose).

[60] Donald J Trump, @realDonaldTrump, *Twitter* (30 January 2017) twitter.com/realDonaldTrump/status/826044059647107073.

[61] Donald J Trump, @realDonaldTrump, *Twitter* (30 January 2017) twitter.com/realDonaldTrump/status/826060143825666051.

[62] Jake Edmiston, 'White House Suggests Quebec Mosque Attack is "Terrible Reminder" of Why Trump is Focusing on National Security' *National Post* (30 January 2017) nationalpost.com/news/canada/pope-francis-hugs-archbishop-of-quebec-at-vatican-meeting-calls-for-mutual-respect-after-quebec-city-mosque-shooting/wcm/4df61bbc-03f2-4726-8382-2ee248514106; Adam Taylor, 'Donald Trump Often Tweets about Terror and Violence, But Said Nothing about an Attack on Muslims in Quebec City' *Washington Post* (2 February 2017) www.washingtonpost.com/news/worldviews/wp/2017/02/02/donald-trump-often-tweets-about-terror-and-violence-but-he-ignored-an-attack-on-muslims-in-quebec-city/?utm_term=.8973d5aada9e.

called the massacre a terrorist attack very shortly after the attack, Spicer said that Trudeau had been 'cautious to draw conclusions on the motives at this stage of the investigation'. He then indicated that Trump agreed.[63]

Spicer actually cited this terrorist attack on a Muslim mosque, by a non-Muslim, as a justification to support Trump's Muslim ban, saying: 'We condemn this attack in the strongest possible terms. It's a terrible reminder of why we must remain vigilant, and why the president is taking steps to be proactive, rather than reactive, when it comes to our nation's safety and security.'[64] Like Trump, Spicer never mentioned that the victims were Muslim or that the shooter was a Caucasian Christian, much less that the shooter had indicated strong support for Trump on social media, apparently energised by a visit to Quebec City by conservative French politician Marine Le Pen the year before.[65]

By 1 February 2017, Trump still hadn't mentioned Quebec City on Twitter. He did mention terrorism again though. For instance, he said: 'Everybody is arguing whether or not it is a BAN. Call it what you want, it is about keeping bad people (with bad intentions) out of country!'[66]

On 2 February, Kellyanne Conway, a chief advisor to Trump, said in an interview that the first Executive Order was justified because of two Iraqi refugees, who she said were the masterminds behind 'the Bowling Green massacre'.[67] She complained about the lack of coverage of this massacre. There was no Bowling Green massacre.[68] Conway later corrected her statement, saying that she meant to say 'Bowling Green terrorists', referring to the fact that the two Iraqis she was describing had lived in Bowling Green. They were sentenced to federal prison after trying to send weapons and money to al-Qaeda in Iraq. No attack actually arose from their activities.[69] While attempting to justify the Muslim ban in this conversation, Conway also did not mention the Quebec City attack.[70]

On 3 February, an Egyptian man, wielding two machetes and two bags of spray paint, and yelling 'Allahu Akbar', injured a soldier who was guarding the museum

---

[63] Daniel Dale, 'The White House Cited the Quebec Mosque Attack to Justify Trump's Policies' *The Star* (30 January 2017) www.thestar.com/news/world/2017/01/30/the-white-house-just-cited-the-quebec-mosque-attack-to-justify-trumps-policies.html.

[64] ibid.

[65] See, eg, Les Perreaux and Eric Andrew-Gee, 'Quebec City Mosque Attack Suspect Known as Online Troll Inspired by French Far-Right' *Globe and Mail* (30 January 2017) www.theglobeandmail.com/news/national/quebec-city-mosque-attack-suspect-known-for-right-wing-online-posts/article33833044.

[66] Donald J Trump, @realDonaldTrump, *Twitter* (1 February 2017) twitter.com/realDonaldTrump/status/826774668245946368.

[67] Samantha Schmidt and Lindsey Bever, 'Kellyanne Conway Cites "Bowling Green Massacre" That Never Happened to Defend Travel Ban' *Washington Post* (3 February 2017) www.washingtonpost.com/news/morning-mix/wp/2017/02/03/kellyanne-conway-cites-bowling-green-massacre-that-never-happened-to-defend-travel-ban/?utm_term=.1b214baeffd7.

[68] ibid.

[69] ibid.

[70] See ibid.

at the Louvre.[71] Nobody was seriously injured in the attack, except for the attacker as soldiers shot him.[72] Soon after the attempt, Trump tweeted: '[A] new radical Islamic terrorist has just attacked in Louvre Museum in Paris. Tourists were locked down. France on edge again. GET SMART U.S.'[73] He did not mention that his Muslim ban did not include Egypt, the Louvre attacker's home country, or Dubai, where the attacker obtained a tourist visa for France, among the seven countries from which people were banned from travel to the US.[74]

While this discussion has focused on the thread of narrative that Trump and his aides laid out, it is notable that refutations to the different components of this narrative abounded. For instance, Chelsea Clinton responded to Trump's tweet about the Louvre attack, writing: 'Very grateful no one seriously hurt in the Louvre attack ... or the (completely fake) Bowling Green Massacre. Please don't make up attacks.'[75] Later that night, Trump tweeted: 'We must keep "evil" out of our country.'[76]

Trump continued to tweet about terrorism over the course of that weekend, mostly to express his outrage at a federal court judge in Seattle who issued a nationwide ban on the first Executive Order regarding travel on Friday, 3 February 2017.[77] For example, on 4 February, Trump tweeted: 'When a country is no longer able to say who can, and who cannot, come in & out, especially for reasons of safety &.security—big trouble!'[78] And: 'Interesting that certain Middle-Eastern countries agree with the ban. They know if certain people are allowed in it's death & destruction!'[79] A short time later: 'The opinion of this so-called judge, which essentially takes law-enforcement away from our country, is ridiculous and will be overturned!'[80] And: 'What is our country coming to when a judge can halt a Homeland Security travel ban and anyone, even with bad intentions, can come

---

[71] 'Louvre Attack: Egyptian Man, 29, Believed to Be Assailant' *BBC News* (3 February 2017) www.bbc.com/news/world-europe-38863431.

[72] ibid.

[73] Donald J Trump, @realDonaldTrump, *Twitter* (3 February 2017) twitter.com/realDonaldTrump/status/827499871011819520.

[74] See Caroline Mortimer, 'Le Louvre Terror Attack: Suspect Identified as Egyptian Abdullah Reda al-Hamany' *The Independent* (3 February 2017), www.independent.co.uk/news/world/europe/louvre-terror-attack-paris-abdullah-reda-al-hamamy-egyptian-tourist-visa-dubai-donald-trump-muslim-a7562361.html; see also *Trump Executive Order I*, above, n 6.

[75] Chelsea Clinton, @ChelseaClinton, *Twitter* (3 February 2017) twitter.com/ChelseaClinton/status/827518183934394370.

[76] Donald J Trump, @realDonaldTrump, *Twitter* (3 February 2017) twitter.com/realDonaldTrump/status/827655062835052544.

[77] See *State of Washington, et al v Donald J Trump*, No C17-0141JLR (WD Wash 2017).

[78] Donald J Trump, @realDonaldTrump, *Twitter* (4 February 2017) twitter.com/realDonaldTrump/status/827864176043376640 (errors in original).

[79] Donald J Trump, @realDonaldTrump, *Twitter* (4 February 2017) twitter.com/realDonaldTrump/status/827865957750161408 (errors in original).

[80] Donald J Trump, @realDonaldTrump, *Twitter* (4 February 2017) twitter.com/realDonaldTrump/status/827867311054974976.

into U.S.?'[81] Later that day, he tweeted: 'Because the ban was lifted by a judge, many very bad and dangerous people may be pouring into our country. A terrible decision[.]'[82] And: 'Why aren't the lawyers looking at and using the Federal Court decision in Boston, which is at conflict with ridiculous lift ban decision?'[83] Later: 'The judge opens up our country to potential terrorists and others that do not have our best interests at heart. Bad people are very happy!'[84]

The next day: 'Just cannot believe a judge would put our country in such peril. If something happens blame him and court system. People pouring in. Bad!'[85] Later: 'I have instructed Homeland Security to check people coming into our country VERY CAREFULLY. The courts are making the job very difficult!'[86]

After moving on to other subjects, Trump came back to it on Twitter on Monday, 6 February 2017: 'Any negative polls are fake news, just like the CNN, ABC, NBC polls in the election. Sorry, people want border security and extreme vetting.'[87] Later that day, he tweeted: 'The threat from radical Islamic terrorism is very real, just look what is happening in Europe and the Middle-East. Courts must act fast!'[88] On 8 February, he wrote: 'If the U.S. does not win this case as it so obviously should, we can never have the security and safety to which we are entitled. Politics!'[89]

This snapshot of a larger narrative makes it quite obvious that terrorism was at the forefront of Trump's personal messaging in the days following the Quebec City attack. Trump and his staff clearly sought to advance a narrative in which terrorists are 'Muslim' or 'radical Islamic terrorists'. It is obvious that they sought to downplay and, to the greatest extent possible, ignore the attack in Quebec City, never referring to the fact that the shooter was a Caucasian, non-Muslim (and apparent Trump supporter) or that the victims were innocent Muslims gathered in prayer. Trump's Twitter silence on the attacks, given his prolific and notorious tweeting, including many tweets about terrorism during that time, speaks volumes. Quebec City is, geographically, much closer to Washington DC than the sites of

[81] Donald J Trump, @realDonaldTrump, *Twitter* (4 February 2017) twitter.com/realDonaldTrump/status/827981079042805761.

[82] Donald J Trump, @realDonaldTrump, *Twitter* (4 February 2017) twitter.com/realDonaldTrump/status/827996357252243456.

[83] Donald J Trump, @realDonaldTrump, *Twitter* (4 February 2017) twitter.com/realDonaldTrump/status/828024835670413312.

[84] Donald J Trump, @realDonaldTrump, *Twitter* (4 February 2017) twitter.com/realDonaldTrump/status/828042506851934209.

[85] Donald J Trump, @realDonaldTrump, *Twitter* (5 February, 2017) twitter.com/realDonaldTrump/status/828342202174668800.

[86] Donald J Trump, @realDonaldTrump, *Twitter* (5 February, 2017) twitter.com/realDonaldTrump/status/828343072840900610.

[87] Donald J Trump, @realDonaldTrump, *Twitter* (6 February 2017) twitter.com/realDonaldTrump/status/828574430800539648.

[88] Donald J Trump, @realDonaldTrump, *Twitter* (6 February 2017) twitter.com/realDonaldTrump/status/828797801630937089.

[89] Donald J Trump, @realDonaldTrump, *Twitter* (8 February 2017) https://twitter.com/realDonaldTrump/status/829299566344359936.

other attacks that Trump had previously posted about, and certainly closer than Paris. People died in Quebec City, but did not die in the Louvre attack in Paris. That in no way lessens the significance of the Paris attack, but suggests that Trump's motivation in his comments was related to the creation of a particular narrative, which supported his preferred policy.

The Quebec City attack simply does not fit the narrative being advanced by the US government. After the Quebec City attack, the US government did not move to bar Caucasian Canadian Christians from entering the US. Instead, its representatives ignored the attacks or largely ignored the identity of the perpetrator, and even, in the case of Spicer, used an anti-Muslim attack on innocent people praying at a mosque by a Caucasian Christian to justify a travel ban on Muslims. This is an extraordinary contortion in favour of a particular narrative. This narrative is being carefully and systematically constructed, not based on facts as they occurred, but based on a wish to advance a particular narrative to support a particular set of legal changes, and no doubt to present an additional narrative to a particular audience that the Trump Administration is tough on terror. Fear, always present in the face of public discussions of terrorism, is thus a tool to advance a questionable end rather than an underlying motivation for the narrative.

On 26 May 2017, three people were stabbed, and two of them killed, in Portland, Oregon, after they came to the defence of two young women, who were being harassed by a man, allegedly Jeremy Joseph Christian, who was shouting anti-Muslim slurs. Christian is reported to have told them to 'go back to Saudi Arabia', told them to get out of 'his country' and said 'that Muslims should die'.[90]

Trump did not mention the attacks on his personal Twitter. The official President of the United States' (known as 'POTUS') Twitter, retweeted by the White House Twitter account, contained a condemnation of the attacks, with Trump saying: 'The violent attacks in Portland on Friday are unacceptable. The victims were standing up to hate and intolerance. Our prayers are w/ them.'[91] However, this post and its retweet did not appear until three days after the attacks.[92] They also appeared after pressure to address the attacks from people like Dan Rather.[93] In calling on Trump to condemn the attacks, Rather accused Trump of a selective narrative, writing in a Facebook post:

> This story may not neatly fit into a narrative you pushed on the campaign trail and that has followed you into the White House. They were not killed by an undocumented

---

[90] Eder Campuzano, 'Man Saw Teenagers, One with Hijab, and Launched into Racial Tirade' *Oregon Live* (27 May 2017) www.oregonlive.com/portland/index.ssf/2017/05/man_saw_teenagers_one_with_hij.html.

[91] President Trump, @POTUS, *Twitter* (29 May 2017) twitter.com/POTUS/status/869204433418280961 (retweeted by the White House page) (hereinafter '@POTUS: Portland Statement').

[92] See ibid.

[93] See Elliot Hannon, 'President of United States Waits Nearly Three Days to Condemn Racist Portland Murders' *The Slate* (29 May 2017) www.slate.com/blogs/the_slatest/2017/05/29/donald_trump_tweeted_21_times_while_not_condemning_white_supremacist_portland.html (the article contains hyperlinks and screenshots to the original tweets).

immigrant or a 'radical Islamic terrorist.' They were killed in an act of civic love, facing down a man allegedly spewing hate speech directed at two teenage girls, one of whom was wearing a hijab. That man seems to have a public record of 'extremist ideology'—a term issued by the Portland Police Bureau.

This 'extremism' may be of a different type than gets most of your attention, or even the attention in the press. But that doesn't make it any less serious, or deadly. And this kind of 'extremism' is on the rise, especially in the wake of your political ascendency. Most people who study these sorts of things do not think that is a coincidence. I do not blame you directly for this incident. Nor do I think other people should. But what a President says, who he has around him, and the tone he sets can set the tone for the nation at large.

…

I hope you can find it worthy of your time to take notice.[94]

When Trump ultimately did condemn the Portland attack in official statements, the language he used was considerably more muted than that used in other instances. He did not post about it on his personal Twitter.[95]

Whether the Portland attack is formally characterised as 'terrorism', or as a hate crime, the trend with such crimes suggests a growing, comparable safety concern, and security is supposed to be at the heart of counter-terrorism efforts. In the spring of 2017, David Anderson QC, the UK Independent Reviewer of Terrorism Legislation, said that a quarter of 'extremists' who are referred to a deradicalisation programme are sympathisers of the far right, saying that far-right extremism is now 'as murderous as its Islamic equivalent'.[96] In the US, attacks by people with far-right sentiments have increased.[97] The Southern Poverty Law Center is currently monitoring more than 1,600 right-wing extremist groups in the US, as well as a rise in so-called 'lone wolf' attacks by those who are not directly affiliated with a group.[98] However, the narrative on such attacks from the US government continues to be muted or non-existent as compared to statements regarding 'radical Islamic extremism'.

While Trump did not mention the Portland attacks on his own Twitter, he did post about terrorism that day. The post was in response to another attack, this time in Egypt, in which gunmen had attacked a bus full of Christian pilgrims, ordering the men to recite an Islamic declaration of faith and beginning to shoot people

---

[94] Dan Rather, 'Open Letter to President Trump' *Facebook* (28 May 2017) www.facebook.com/theDanRather/posts/10158743532925716.

[95] See @POTUS: Portland Statement, above, n 91.

[96] David Anderson QC, 'Prevent Strategy Can Work against Radicalisation … if it is Trusted' *Evening Standard* (15 February 2017) www.standard.co.uk/news/uk/david-anderson-qc-prevent-strategy-can-work-against-radicalisation-if-it-is-trusted-a3467901.html.

[97] See William Parkin et al, 'Analysis: Deadly Threat from Far-Right Extremists is Overshadowed by Fear of Islamic Terrorism' *PBS Newshour* (24 February 2017) www.pbs.org/newshour/updates/analysis-deadly-threat-far-right-extremists-overshadowed-fear-islamic-terrorism.

[98] See Southern Poverty Law Center, 'Hate and Extremism', *Southern Poverty Law Center*, www.splcenter.org/issues/hate-and-extremism; see also Parkin et al, above, n 97.

when they refused. At least 28 people, including children, were killed.[99] Trump's tweet read: 'Terrorists are engaged in a war against civilization—it is up to all who value life to confront & defeat this evil.'[100] The tweet then linked to Trump's longer official statement on the attack, saying, among other things:

> America also makes clear to its friends, allies, and partners that the treasured and historic Christian Communities of the Middle East must be defended and protected. The blood-letting of Christians must end, and all who aid their killers must be punished.
>
> …
>
> Civilization is at a precipice—and whether we climb or fall will be decided by our ability to join together to protect all faiths, all religions, and all innocent life. No matter what, America will do what it must to protect its people.[101]

The Trump narrative has been clear, both from what is said and what is not said. This narrative suggests that Muslims are terrorists and that Christians are victims. Trump uses his Twitter to advance this narrative, and circumstances that conflict with it are either downplayed or simply ignored.

The reality, however, does not correspond so neatly to this narrative. Daesh is seen as probably the most significant current international terrorist threat, although the organisation has characteristics that are different in many ways from other prominent terrorist organisations, and there is some controversy over that designation.[102] The reality is that most of Daesh's victims are not Christian, as the US narrative suggests, but are Muslim. Even before Daesh rose to prominence, reports suggested that, while Sunni extremists were responsible for most terrorist attacks around the world, Muslims were also the largest demographic among the victims. In 2012, the National Counterterrorism Center reported that Muslims comprised between 82 and 97 per cent of the victims of terrorism in the preceding five years.[103]

The rise of Daesh has continued, and increased, this trend. Daesh is normally characterised as a terrorist organisation, and certainly many of the attacks around

---

[99] Declan Walsh & Nour Youssef, 'Gunmen in Egypt Force Coptic Christian Pilgrims from Buses and Kill 28' *The New York Times* (26 May 2017) www.nytimes.com/2017/05/26/world/middleeast/egypt-coptic-christian-attack.html?_r=0.

[100] Donald J Trump, @realDonaldTrump, *Twitter* (26 May 2017) twitter.com/realDonaldTrump/status/868201805934678017.

[101] The White House, Office of the Press Secretary, 'Statement by President Donald J Trump on the Attack in Egypt' (26 May 2017) www.whitehouse.gov/the-press-office/2017/05/26/state-ment-president-donald-j-trump-attack-egypt?utm_source=twitter&utm_medium=social&utm_content=wh_20170526_na.

[102] See, eg, Audrey Kurth Cronin, Council on Foreign Relations, 'ISIS is Not a Terrorist Group' *Foreign Affairs* (March/April 2015) www.foreignaffairs.com/articles/middle-east/isis-not-terrorist-group (quoting then-US President Barack Obama as saying ISIS is 'a terrorist organization, pure and simple' and arguing that this is wrong and that counter-terrorism efforts are unlikely to be effective against the group).

[103] United States Military Academy, West Point, National Counterterrorism Center, *Report on Terrorism* (2011) (indicating that the information is current up to 12 March 2012), 14.

the world, for which it has claimed responsibility, are terrorist in nature. However, it also has indicia of a military group, taking over large areas in Syria and Iraq. Estimates suggest that eight million people live in the territories that have been controlled by Daesh, which themselves are largely Muslim areas.[104]

Reports abound of significant brutality committed against those civilians. Many are killed, refused medical treatment, deprived of already-scarce food or kept from leaving conflict areas so that they can be used as human shields. One witness in Mosul described seeing bodies of those caught while trying to escape hanging from electricity poles.[105] When Daesh took over Mosul, it began using airwaves to announce repressive rules, such as not allowing women to be out of their homes alone, on threat of a public lashing.[106] Men were required to wear beards of a certain length, and smoking or communicating with the outside world was forbidden. Those caught with mobile phones were killed.[107] Homes were robbed, and people were tortured and killed during these robberies.[108] Schools were closed and, when open, girls were not allowed to attend.[109] One article quoted a maths problem from the enforced Daesh curriculum: 'There are 42 bullets and seven unbelievers in front of you. How many shots in your sniper rifle do you have for each?'[110]

Daesh does claim to be fighting and killing those who do not share its claimed beliefs, but this does not mean that its targets are solely Christian. Although Daesh claims to adhere to a form of Sunni Islam, the areas it has overrun are home to many Sunni Muslims, who have suffered terribly under Daesh rule. Approximately 4.2 million Iraqis, who were displaced from their homes, are Sunni Muslims.[111] One Sunni leader said: 'ISIS was a tsunami that swept away the Sunnis.'[112]

In addition, Daesh has also targeted Christians, members of different Shiite groups, Kurds and the Yazidi population.[113] The UN Human Rights Council has

---

[104] Riaz Hassan, 'ISIS and the Caliphate' (2016) 51(4) *Australian Journal of Political Science* 759 (review of the following book: Jessica Stern and JM Berger, *ISIS: The State of Terror* (London, William Collins, 2015)).

[105] Jane Arraf, 'As Iraqi Forces Encircle Mosul, ISIS Unleashes New Level of Brutality on Civilians' *NPR* (18 April 2017) www.npr.org/sections/parallels/2017/04/18/524466679/as-iraqi-forces-encircle-mosul-isis-unleashes-new-level-of-brutality-on-civilian; see also Derek Stoffel, 'Life under ISIS: Mosul Residents Reflect on a Brutal Occupation' *CBC News* (23 March 2017) www.cbc.ca/news/world/life-under-isis-mosul-residents-reflect-on-a-brutal-occupation-1.4034574.

[106] Stoffel, above, n 107.

[107] ibid.

[108] ibid.

[109] ibid.

[110] ibid.

[111] Mustafa Salim and Zakaria Zakaria, 'ISIS: A Catastrophe for Sunnis' *Washington Post* (23 November 2016) www.washingtonpost.com/sf/world/2016/11/23/isis-a-catastrophe-for-sunnis/?utm_term=.938ba647f52a.

[112] ibid (quoting Sheik Ghazi Mohammed Hamoud, a Sunni tribal leader in Iraq).

[113] See United Nations, Office of the High Commissioner for Human Rights and United Nations Assistance Mission for Iraq Human Rights Office, 'Report on the Protection of Civilians in the Armed Conflict in Iraq: 6 July to 10 September 2014', 11–17.

accused Daesh of genocide against the Yazidi people.[114] The Council concluded that:

> ISIS has sought to erase the Yazidis through killings; sexual slavery, enslavement, torture and inhuman and degrading treatment and forcible transfer causing serious bodily and mental harm; the infliction of conditions of life that bring about a slow death; the imposition of measures to prevent Yazidi children from being born, including forced conversion of adults, the separation of Yazidi men and women, and mental trauma; and the transfer of Yazidi children from their own families and placing them with ISIS fighters, thereby cutting them off from beliefs and practices of their own religious community …[115]

Much more can obviously be said about Daesh, but this short explanation makes it clear that Trump's advanced narrative of Muslim-terrorist-versus-Christian victim is simply not accurate, especially when presented as the entire picture. This problematic pattern of Trump's narrative continued (as described above) as a series of attacks struck in different parts of the world in 2017. The indicator of what would generate condemnation, and mention on Twitter, continued to seem to be linked to who was the perpetrator and who was the victim in any given attack.

After the attacks in Manchester on 22 May 2017, for which Daesh claimed responsibility, Trump tweeted a message of sympathy, saying '[w]e stand in absolute solidarity with the people of the United Kingdom', along with a graphic of the American and British flags intertwined.[116]

Trump did not tweet about terrorist attacks in Baghdad on 30 May 2017. The terrorists targeted civilians and 31 people were killed, with many more wounded, in twin attacks. Victims included families at an ice cream shop who were breaking their Ramadan fast, and people near a government office where pensions are collected. Daesh claimed responsibility for these attacks as well, saying that it was targeting Shia Muslims.[117]

Trump was also mostly silent after a terrorist attack in Kabul on 31 May 2017, also during Ramadan, killed 90 people and wounded 400 on a busy shopping street in the diplomatic quarter.[118] His Twitter silence about Kabul is especially notable because the explosion happened not far from the US Embassy, and the US government announced that 11 American contractors working for the Embassy were

---

[114] United Nations, 'UN Human Rights Panel Concludes ISIL is Committing Genocide against Yazidis' (16 June 2016) www.un.org/apps/news/story.asp?NewsID=54247#.WVGV-uvyvRY.

[115] ibid.

[116] Donald J Trump, @realDonaldTrump, *Twitter* (23 May 2017) twitter.com/realDonaldTrump/status/866988278184116224; see also Katrin Bennhold et al, 'Terror Alert in Britain is Raised to Maximum as ISIS Claims Manchester Attack' *New York Times* (23 May 2017) www.nytimes.com/2017/05/23/world/europe/manchester-arena-attack-ariana-grande.html.

[117] Reports have varied as to how many people were killed in two attacks that day. See 'Dozens of Iraqis Killed as Isis Targets Baghdad during Ramadan' *The Guardian* (30 May 2017) www.theguardian.com/world/2017/may/30/baghdad-ice-cream-shop-isis-car-bomb-attack.

[118] See Thaslima Begum, '90 People were Murdered by Terrorists in Kabul This Week. Where is the Minute's Silence for Them?' *The Independent* (1 June 2017) www.independent.co.uk/voices/kabul-isis-explosion-attack-no-one-minutes-scilence-a7767341.html.

injured.[119] Trump did place a condolence call to Afghan President Ashraf Ghani. A summary of the call was placed on The White House Twitter, but the attack was not mentioned on Trump's Twitter or the official Twitter for the President.[120] The disparity in public commentary among these attacks is not solely attributed to Trump, as, at least in North America, the media, while covering the attacks, did not do so with the prominent headlines or minute-by-minute coverage that occurred after attacks in places like Paris, Manchester and London.

On 1 June 2017, Trump did comment, before announcing his decision to withdraw the US from the Paris Agreement, on the attack on a casino in Manila, which left at least 36 people dead, calling it a terrorist attack and saying 'but it is really very sad as to what's going on throughout the world with terror'.[121] He did not post anything about the attack on Twitter. Instead, his tweets that day primarily related to his decision to withdraw from the Paris Agreement.[122] In fact, the Manila attack turned out to have been perpetrated by an indebted gambling addict.[123] The shooter owed more than US$80,000, and the local police ultimately confirmed that the incident was not a terrorist attack and was unrelated to Daesh, as initially thought, but was part of a botched robbery.[124]

Trump also never said anything on his personal Twitter about the attacks in Kabul on 3 June 2017, in which seven people were killed and 119 were wounded, while they were attending a funeral for a protestor killed previously while demanding that the government resign after the 31 May attack. This was the third attack in four days in Kabul.[125]

Daesh claimed responsibility for attacks on and near London Bridge that same day, in which eight people were killed and 48 were injured.[126] Trump did tweet about the attacks, but his tweets had a very different tone from his tweet after the Manchester attack, with a clearly self-serving political agenda regarding gun control, his travel ban and his ongoing feud with London's Mayor. His first tweet was: 'We need to be smart, vigilant and tough. We need the courts to give us back

[119] See, eg, 'Official: 9 Local Guards at U.S. Embassy in Kabul Killed, 11 Americans Injured in Bombing' *CBS News* (31 May 2017) www.cbsnews.com/news/kabul-afghanistan-suicide-truck-bomb-attack-americans-wounded.

[120] Catherine Putz, 'Kabul and London Attacks: What's Wrong with US President Trump's Reaction?' *The Debate* (6 June 2017) thediplomat.com/2017/06/kabul-and-london-attacks-whats-wrong-with-us-president-trumps-reaction; The White House, @WhiteHouse, *Twitter* (31 May 2017) twitter.com/WhiteHouse/status/870040046467923969.

[121] Putz, above, n 120. Reports varied as to whether 36 or 37 people died.

[122] See, eg, Donald J Trump, @realDonald Trump, *Twitter* (1 June 2017) twitter.com/realDonaldTrump/status/870412262900740096.

[123] 'Manila Casino Attack: Philippine Police Say Gunman was Indebted Gambler' *ABC News* (4 June 2017) www.abc.net.au/news/2017-06-04/philippine-police-say-manila-casino-attacker-indebted-gambler/8588102.

[124] ibid.

[125] Sune Engel Rasmussen, 'At Least Seven Killed in Suicide Bombing at High-Profile Funeral in Kabul' *The Guardian* (3 June 2017), www.theguardian.com/world/2017/jun/03/kabul-explosions-afghanistan-people-killed-funeral-salim-ezadyar; see also Putz, above, n 120.

[126] Caroline Davies et al, 'Death Toll from London Bridge Attack Rises after Body Found in Thames' *The Guardian* (7 June 2017), www.theguardian.com/uk-news/2017/jun/04/foreign-nationals-victims-of-london-terror-attacks.

our rights. We need the Travel Ban as an extra level of safety!'[127] Only after citing the attacks to advance his agenda did he express support. He then tweeted: 'Whatever the United States can do to help out in London and the U.K., we will be there—WE ARE WITH YOU. GOD BLESS!'[128]

This message of support was followed with less supportive tweets. The next day: 'We must stop being politically correct and get down to the business of security for our people. If we don't get smart it will only get worse[.]'[129] Then: 'At least 7 dead and 48 wounded in terror attack and Mayor of London says there is "no reason to be alarmed!"'[130] Then: 'Do you notice we are not having a gun debate now? That's because they used knives and a truck!'[131]

Even after it became clear that Trump was quoting London's Mayor, Sadiq Khan, who happens to be a Muslim, out of context, Trump continued his criticism, tweeting: 'Pathetic excuse by London Mayor Sadiq Khan who had to think fast on his "no reason to be alarmed" statement. MSM is working hard to sell it!'[132] Initially, Khan's office responded that it was busy addressing the attacks and had no time to respond to Trump's remarks.[133] Later, as Trump continued his attack even after it was clear that he took Khan's comments out of context, Khan called on the British government to cancel Trump's planned state visit.[134] A different narrative emerged when the US Embassy in London tweeted messages of condolence and support, including: 'I commend the strong leadership of the @MayorofLondon as he leads the city forward after this heinous attack.' The tweet was signed by the Acting Ambassador at the US Embassy in London, Lewis Lukens.[135]

On 7 June 2017, Daesh claimed responsibility for two terrorist attacks in Tehran, Iran, killing 13 and injuring over 45.[136] The US State Department issued a statement condemning the attacks and offering condolences.[137] Trump did

---

[127] Donald J Trump, @realDonaldTrump, *Twitter* (3 June 2017) twitter.com/realDonaldTrump/status/871143765473406976.

[128] Donald J Trump, @realDonaldTrump, *Twitter* (3 June 2017) twitter.com/realDonaldTrump/status/871145660036378624.

[129] Donald J Trump, @realDonaldTrump, *Twitter* (4 June 2017) twitter.com/realDonaldTrump/status/871325606901895168.

[130] Donald J Trump, @realDonaldTrump, *Twitter* (4 June 2017) twitter.com/realDonaldTrump/status/871328428963901440.

[131] Donald J Trump, @realDonaldTrump, *Twitter* (4 June 2017) twitter.com/realDonaldTrump/status/871331574649901056.

[132] Donald J Trump, @realDonaldTrump, *Twitter* (4 June 2017) twitter.com/realDonaldTrump/status/871725780535062528 ('MSM' refers to mainstream media); see also Julian Borger, 'Cancel Donald Trump State Visit, Says Sadiq Khan, after London Attack Tweets' *The Guardian* (6 June 2017) www.theguardian.com/us-news/2017/jun/05/donald-trump-attack-courts-travel-ban-london.

[133] Chris Iorifida, 'The Ongoing History of the Trumps and London Mayor Sadiq Khan' *CBC News* (6 June 2017) www.cbc.ca/news/world/trump-family-london-mayor-feud-1.4147806.

[134] Borger, above, n 132.

[135] US Embassy London, @USAinUK, *Twitter* (4 June 2017), twitter.com/USAinUK/status/871435629569212416.

[136] Thomas Erdbrink and Mujib Mashal, 'At Least 12 Killed in Pair of Terrorist Attacks in Iran' *New York Times* (7 June 2017) www.nytimes.com/2017/06/07/world/middleeast/iran-parliament-attack-khomeini-mausoleum.html?_r=0.

[137] Heather Nauert, Department Spokesperson, 'Terrorist Attacks in Tehran' *US Department of State* (7 June 2017) https://www.state.gov/r/pa/prs/ps/2017/06/271625.htm.

not post about the attacks on Twitter, but he responded in a statement, saying: 'We grieve and pray for the innocent victims of the terrorist attacks in Iran, and for the Iranian people, who are going through such challenging times ... We underscore that states that sponsor terrorism risk falling victim to the evil they promote.'[138] Iran's Foreign Minister Javad Zarif responded the next day, calling Trump's statement, as well as sanctions approved that day by the US Senate, '[r]epugnant', accusing the US of backing the terrorists and saying the 'Iranian people reject such claims of U.S. friendship'.[139]

On 19 June 2017, in London, a British citizen drove a van into a group of Muslims who were leaving a service at a nearby mosque, killing one person and injuring 11. The suspect has been charged with terrorism-related offences and the Crown is arguing that he was 'motivated by extreme political views and a personal hatred of Muslims'.[140] An imam from the mosque shielded the suspect because he was afraid of a mob attack.[141] The US State Department officially condemned the attack and offered help, and, in so doing, the spokesperson called it a 'terrorist attack'.[142] Trump did not tweet anything about the attack.[143] In an article in *The Guardian* condemning Trump's silence, the author wrote: 'So, rather than condemn Trump's Twitter feed, let us embrace it for the ethical, intellectual and political barometer that it is. Let us welcome his Twitter rants and silences for making us confront what he could have said, and what we should say.'[144]

Trump was by no means alone in emphasising attacks by Muslim perpetrators on non-Muslim, generally Christian, victims. Some studies suggest, for instance, that the media disproportionately covers attacks along the same lines.[145] Conflicting narratives also arose during this time, but it was clear that Trump was attempting to advance this specific narrative. Not everybody was convinced. In describing the travel ban, the Fourth Circuit Court of Appeal spoke of 'an Executive Order that in text speaks with vague words of national security, but in context drips with religious intolerance, animus, and discrimination'.[146]

---

[138] The White House, 'Statement by the President on the Terrorist Attacks in Iran' (7 June 2017) www.whitehouse.gov/the-press-office/2017/06/07/statement-president-terrorist-attacks-iran.

[139] Javad Zarif, @JZarif, *Twitter* (7 June 2017), twitter.com/JZarif/status/872649473352232960.

[140] 'London Mosque Attack Driver on Trial for "Terrorism"' *Al Jazeera* (23 June 2017) www.aljazeera.com/news/2017/06/london-mosque-attack-driver-charged-terrorism-1706231123 56082.html.

[141] ibid.

[142] Heather Nauert, Department Spokesperson, 'United States Condemns Attack outside of London Mosque' *US Department of State* (19 June 2017), www.state.gov/r/pa/prs/ps/2017/06/272021.htm.

[143] Christian Christensen, 'Trump's Silence after the London Mosque Attack Speaks Volumes' *The Guardian* (20 June 2017) www.theguardian.com/commentisfree/2017/jun/20/donald-trump-silence-london-mosque-attack-speaks-volumes.

[144] ibid.

[145] See, eg, Erin M Kearns et al, 'Why Do Some Terrorist Attacks Receive More Media Attention than Others?' (March 2017) https://papers.ssrn.com/sol3/papers.cfm?abstract_id=2928138 (finding that, between 2011 and 2015, attacks in the US by Muslim perpetrators received 449 per cent more coverage than other attacks).

[146] *IRPA v Trump*, above, n 6.

B. A Ban or Not a Ban?

Both the description that the Executive Orders applied to 'Muslims' and that it was, in fact, a 'ban' were disputed. In some ways, the two ideas fit together and are seen as one issue, but the public disputes over the terminology sometimes split them into two ideas. The preceding section addresses some of the rhetoric specifically around whether Muslims were targeted. There were similarly duelling narratives regarding whether the orders were a 'ban', although to a much lesser extent, since much of the legal controversy was about whether the orders targeted people based on religion.[147] Still, a review of public statements shows that there was a bit of a battle over whether to use this term too, which sometimes went beyond the argument of whether the notion was being wrongly applied to Muslims. It adds to the picture over the contentious nature of which term was correct.

On 31 January 2017, Spicer spoke to the media, actually insisting that the first Executive Order did not constitute a 'ban', but, instead, was 'extreme vetting'. Referring to the fact that it was only people from the seven identified countries who were not allowed to enter the US, he said: 'It can't be a ban if you're letting a million people in ... If 325,000 people from another country can come in, that is by nature not a ban.'[148] Spicer had, in fact, called the order a '90-day ban' two days before in a White House press release.[149] The day before this press conference, Trump had also tweeted: 'If the ban were announced with a one week notice, the "bad" would rush into our country that week. A lot of bad "dudes" out there.'[150]

However, at the 31 January press conference, Spicer blamed the media for this confusion, saying, in relation to Trump: 'He's using the words the media is [*sic*] using ... I think the words that are being used to describe it derive from what the media is calling this. [Trump] has been very clear that it is extreme vetting.'[151]

Trump continued to refer to the Executive Order as a ban even after Spicer tried to direct the media to call it 'extreme vetting'. On 1 February 2017, Trump tweeted: 'Everybody is arguing whether or not it is a BAN. Call it what you want, it is about keeping bad people (with bad intentions) out of [the] country!'[152] On 4 February, he tweeted: 'Interesting that certain Middle-Eastern countries agree with the ban. They know if certain people are allowed in it's [*sic*] death & destruction!'[153] Later

---

[147] See, eg, the cases cited above, n 6.

[148] Christina Wilkie, 'Sean Spicer Insists Muslim Ban is Not a "Ban", But He and Trump Both Called it One' *Huffington Post* (31 January 2017) www.huffingtonpost.ca/entry/sean-spicer-muslim-ban_us_5890ed19e4b0522c7d3da0bd.

[149] ibid.

[150] Donald J Trump, @realDonaldTrump, *Twitter* (30 January 2017) https://twitter.com/realDonaldTrump/status/826060143825666051.

[151] Wilkie, above, n 148.

[152] Donald J Trump, @realDonaldTrump, *Twitter* (1 February 2017) twitter.com/realdonaldtrump/status/826774668245946368?lang=en.

[153] Donald J Trump, @realDonaldTrump, *Twitter* (4 February 2017) https://twitter.com/realDonaldTrump/status/827865957750161408.

that day, he tweeted: 'What is our country coming to when a judge can halt a Homeland Security travel ban and anyone, even with bad intentions, can come into U.S.?'[154] And next: 'Because the ban was lifted by a judge, many very bad and dangerous people may be pouring into our country. A terrible decision.'[155] On 5 February, he tweeted: 'Why aren't the lawyers looking at and using the Federal Court decision in Boston, which is at conflict with ridiculous lift ban decision?'[156]

By early June 2017, Trump made it clear that he was conceding that the orders were a 'ban'. In a series of tweets on 5 June, he wrote: 'People, the lawyers and the courts can call it whatever they want, but I am calling it what we need and what it is, a TRAVEL BAN!'[157] Then: 'The Justice Dept should have stayed with the original Travel Ban, not the watered down, politically correct version they submitted to S.C.'[158] Later still: 'In any event we are EXTREME VETTING people coming into the U.S. in order to help keep our country safe. The courts are slow and political!'[159] Finally: 'That's right, we need a TRAVEL BAN for certain DANGEROUS countries, not some politically correct term that won't help us protect our people!'[160]

Those involved in this wavering discussion did not explain why they deemed the use of the word 'ban' to have varying degrees of controversy attached to it. The most likely explanation—and this is speculation—is that there was concern that a complete ban on entry would be more likely to be struck down in court as too broad. Those involved were clearly aware of pending litigation.

III. Motive and Omar Mateen: Immutable Characteristics Can Lead to a Label that Could Obscure True Motive and Undermine Systemic Responses

On 12 June 2016, Omar Mateen entered the Pulse nightclub in Orlando, Florida, and started shooting. He ultimately killed 49 people, and wounded 58 others, in what was, as of that date, the worst mass shooting in the US by a single shooter,

---

[154] Donald J Trump, @realDonaldTrump, *Twitter* (4 February 2017) https://twitter.com/RealRealDonaldT/status/827981080422645760.

[155] Donald J Trump, @realDonaldTrump, *Twitter* (4 February 2017) twitter.com/realDonaldTrump/status/827996357252243456.

[156] Donald J Trump, @realDonaldTrump, *Twitter* (4 February 2017) https://twitter.com/realDonaldTrump/status/828024835670413312.

[157] Donald J Trump, @realDonaldTrump, *Twitter* (5 June 2017) twitter.com/realDonaldTrump/status/871674214356484096 (capital letters in original).

[158] Donald J Trump, @realDonaldTrump, *Twitter* (5 June 2017) twitter.com/realDonaldTrump/status/871675245043888128 ('S.C.' is a reference to the Supreme Court of the United States).

[159] Donald J Trump, @realDonaldTrump, *Twitter* (5 June 2017) twitter.com/realDonaldTrump/status/871679061847879682.

[160] Donald J Trump, @realDonaldTrump, *Twitter* (5 June 2017) twitter.com/realDonaldTrump/status/871899511525961728.

and the worst attack on the LGBT community in the US.[161] While the actual facts of the shooting, in terms of the name of the perpetrator and what happened, were not heavily disputed, the proper label to attach to Mateen was the subject of considerable public dispute in the early days after the attacks. This dispute was important as an illustration that the rush to a label can be based on immutable characteristics and that this can override other factors in the public perception. Because there were so many potential narratives about Mateen, different groups seized upon the shooting to advance different political agendas.[162] The way that information was used showed some of the assumptions regarding labels that have become embedded in public discourse regarding terrorism, among other things. Mateen himself made statements that were clearly designed to attribute a particular motive to his actions, but, as discussed below, there was considerable reason, from the beginning, to question what he said.

The previous section of this chapter underscored its larger point with the significant difference that social networking sites like Twitter can make in terms of a public narrative about certain events. Less emphasised, but still important, is the way in which media have dramatically expanded in recent decades. Organisations like CNN, which was founded in 1980, provide news coverage around the clock.[163] The rise of the Internet has obviously amplified this immediacy. It is through these vehicles that the Mateen story quickly spread and competing narratives about his motive arose. It is possible that the truth lies somewhere at the intersection of some of these motives and that it does not necessarily fit neatly into one compartment.

Different stages are characteristic of the way that the mass media report on a mass-casualty attack. One of these stages involves trying to identify characteristics of the attacker that would somehow explain motive.[164] This stage of reporting about Mateen developed in different, often inconsistent, directions shortly after the Pulse shooting. One developing critique relates to differences in public assumptions depending on who the perpetrators and victims are. Muslim perpetrators are likely to be associated more quickly with terrorism, while those attacks perpetrated by Caucasian, non-Muslim perpetrators are more likely to be perceived as

---

[161] Associated Press, '49 Victims of Pulse Massacre Remembered in Daylong Services' *CBC News* (12 June 2017) www.cbc.ca/news/world/49-victims-of-pulse-massacre-remembered-in-daylong-services-1.4156176.

[162] See, eg, RR Reno, 'In the Aftermath of the Orlando Killings by Omar Mateen, LGBT Activists Saw an Opportunity to Redouble Pressure on Religious Groups' (2016) 265 *First Things: A Monthly Journal of Religion and Public Life* 69.

[163] See Jennifer L Murray, 'Mass Media Reporting and Enabling of Mass Shootings' (January 2017) 17(2) *Cultural Studies—Critical Methodologies* 114 (assessing the different stages of reporting of mass shootings and how this has changed).

[164] See ibid (identifying seven distinct stages to media coverage of such events, with the fourth being to compare the attack to others deemed similar to try to attribute characteristics to the killer).

another issue, often relating to serious mental illness.[165] One study of media coverage in the US between 2011 and 2015 suggested that domestic terrorism tends to be portrayed as the result of mental illness by the perpetrator, and thus more of an isolated event, while terrorist attacks driven by extremist interpretations of Islam are more likely to be viewed as significant and more of a threat overall, as well as a threat from the outside.[166]

The label used to describe Mateen could change the perception of the entire incident, even when the underlying facts of what happened remain the same. In some ways, the labels gave rise to the perceptions of his motive rather than the other way around. This is not to say that Mateen's motivation was not relevant, because, in criminal law, of course the motivation matters. Motive is important, both in terms of determining charges in individual cases and in terms of prevention of future violence. A problem arises, though, when the search for the motivation starts not necessarily with conduct or evidence, but with quick assumptions based on immutable characteristics of the perpetrator, such as citizenship or national origin. These factors appear to have been prominent in the early search for Mateen's motivation.[167]

One thing about labels is that they are short, easily communicated and easily understood. A label can contribute to a strong headline and it can be attention-grabbing in a speech. Whether a particular label enters the public consciousness often depends on the role of the media and how careful they are about using, or repeating, labels that accurately describe rather than oversimplifying or sensationalising.[168] The scenarios discussed in the following sections should thus all be considered through the lens of how the media covered these events.

A. Mateen's Citizenship Status and Allegations of Islamic Terrorism Ties

Mateen was killed at the scene of the attacks. While early assumptions arose as to who he was and why he did it, it emerged over time that he did not neatly fit into the categories used to describe him. This is important, because, even though he

---

[165] See Kearns, above, n 145 (finding that, between 2011 and 2015, attacks in the US by Muslim perpetrators received 449 per cent more coverage than other attacks); Shankar Vedantam, 'When is it "Terrorism"? How the Media Cover Attacks by Muslim Perpetrators' *NPR* (19 June 2017) http://www.npr.org/2017/06/19/532963059/when-is-it-terrorism-how-the-media-covers-attacks-by-muslim-perpetrators.

[166] See Kearns, above, n 145.

[167] See ch 5, below, for a more detailed discussion of citizenship and national origin as creating presumptions regarding who is a terrorist.

[168] For a critique relating to the different labels the media have used to describe Omar Khadr, a high-profile Canadian citizen and long-time Guantanamo Bay detainee, see Maureen T Duffy, 'A 'Convicted Terrorist' by Any Other Name' *ABlawg* (13 May 2015) ablawg.ca/2015/05/13/a-convicted-terrorist-by-any-other-name (critiquing the media for often unquestioningly accepting the terminology used to describe Khadr, which is generally inaccurate, oversimplified and prejudicial).

was killed at the scene, the category into which he was placed would have been significant in the disposition of his case if he had survived. It could still have a significant impact on larger governmental responses. Beyond that, the Mateen narrative shows that differing labels can sometimes be used for the same underlying conduct, suggesting some fracturing in terms of the effectiveness of responses.

One of the first facts to emerge about Mateen was that he was a US citizen, of Afghan descent. This narrative was fuelled by reports that he was a person of interest in an FBI investigation that was closed a couple of years earlier.[169] Much was immediately made of his citizenship, with one article describing him as 'a New York-born son of an Afghan immigrant'.[170] Another article said: 'He's an American citizen and he has family that are not—his parents are Afghan.'[171]

To be clear, again, Mateen himself created some of the narrative through statements he made during the attacks.[172] Although Daesh later also claimed responsibility, even from the beginning, investigators were not convinced that Mateen's statements reflected his true motive, and it is known that Daesh has claimed responsibility for attacks in which it played no part, other than perhaps 'inspiring' the perpetrator through its publicity.[173]

Tying Mateen's motivation to Daesh was not unreasonable, given Mateen's own efforts to make this connection and Daesh's claim of responsibility. For example, Mateen told a negotiator that he was an 'Islamic soldier' and pledged allegiance to Daesh.[174] He also pledged allegiance to the Daesh leader, as well as mentioning, with admiration, the Tsarnaev brothers, who carried out the Boston Marathon bombing.[175] He blamed US airstrikes that happened the previous month, which killed Abu Wahib, Daesh's alleged leader, for his shooting spree.[176] At one point, he

---

[169] See, eg, 'Omar Mateen: 5 Fast Facts You Need to Know' *Heavy* (12 June 2016) heavy.com/news/2016/06/omar-mateen-pulse-orlando-florida-shooting-gunman-attack-name-photos-facebook-motive-terrorism.

[170] Hannah Parry, 'Omar Mateen Blamed Pentagon Air Strike Which Killed Iraqi ISIS Leader for "Triggering" His Orlando Terror Attack during Calls with Police Negotiator' *Mail Online* (28 September 2016) www.dailymail.co.uk/news/article-3811839/Omar-Mateen-blamed-Pentagon-air-strike-killed-Iraqi-ISIS-leader-triggering-Orlando-terror-attack-calls-police-negotiator.html (reproducing the transcripts that had just been made publicly available).

[171] 'Omar Mateen: Terrorist was 29-Year-Old Islamic Radical' *TMZ* (12 June 2016) www.tmz.com/2016/06/12/terrorist-omar-mateen-gay-nightclub-murder.

[172] See, eg, Spencer Ackerman, 'Omar Mateen Described Himself as "Islamic Soldier" in 911 Calls to Police' *The Guardian* (20 June 2016) www.theguardian.com/us-news/2016/jun/20/omar-mateen-911-calls-orlando-shooting-fbi-release-isis (including transcripts of the calls between Mateen and the police during the attacks).

[173] ibid; Greg Myre, 'What Does it Mean When ISIS Claims Responsibility for an Attack?' *NPR* (24 May 2017) http://www.npr.org/sections/thetwo-way/2017/05/24/529685951/what-does-it-mean-when-isis-claims-responsibility-for-an-attack.

[174] Ackerman, above, n 172.

[175] Parry, above, n 170.

[176] ibid; see also Steve Visser and John Couwels, 'Orlando Killer Repeatedly Referenced ISIS Transcripts Show' *CNN* (24 September 2016), www.cnn.com/2016/09/23/us/orlando-shooter-hostage-negotiator-call/index.html (both pages reproducing the actual transcript).

said that his name was 'Islamic soldier' and told a dispatcher 'call me Mujahideen, call me the soldier of God'.[177] He also said he had fasted and prayed for Ramadan on the day of the shooting.[178]

Others were quick to pick up on this possible motive. The day of the attacks, then-presidential candidate Trump used the shooting to advance his campaign agenda regarding 'radical Islamic terrorism', tweeting: 'Appreciate the congrats for being right on radical Islamic terrorism, I don't want congrats, I want toughness & vigilance. We must be smart!'[179] He also tweeted: 'What has happened in Orlando is just the beginning. Our leadership is weak and ineffective. I called it and asked for the ban. Must be tough.'[180]

Trump issued a longer statement about the attack, framing it in terms of the campaign. He said: 'Last night, our nation was attacked by a radical Islamic terrorist.' He criticised Obama and Clinton for refusing to use the words 'Radical Islam' and he described Mateen as: 'The terrorist … the son of an immigrant from Afghanistan who openly published his support for the Afghanistan Taliban and even tried to run for President of Afghanistan. According to Pew, 99% of people in Afghanistan support oppressive Sharia Law.'[181] Contemporaneous reports did indicate that Mateen's father had run for President of Afghanistan and had supported the Taliban in the past.[182] The Congressman whose district covered the area of the Pulse shooting made similar remarks, saying the attacks were motivated by ideology and noting: 'Let me put it this way … the nationality of family members is indicative.'[183]

Some responses in this area had more nuance. US Congressman Adam Schiff issued a press release shortly after the attacks, calling it an 'ISIS-inspired act of terrorism', arguing for a distinction between 'ISIS-inspired' attacks and 'ISIS-directed' attacks:[184]

> This attack is so painfully reminiscent of the terrible attack at the Batlaclan [*sic*] Theatre in Paris, and other ISIS-inspired attacks in recent years … The fact that this shooting took place during Ramadan and that ISIS leadership in Raqqa has been urging attacks during this time, that the target was an LGBT night club during Pride … Whether this attack was also ISIS-directed, remains to be determined.[185]

---

[177] Parry, above, n 170.

[178] ibid.

[179] Donald J Trump, @realDonaldTrump, *Twitter* (12 June 2016) twitter.com/realDonaldTrump/status/742034549232766976.

[180] Donald J Trump, @realDonaldTrump, *Twitter* (12 June 2016) twitter.com/realDonaldTrump/status/742096033207844864. This tweet is also another example of the use of the word 'ban', as discussed above.

[181] Krishnadev Calamur et al, 'Orlando Nightclub Attack: What We Know' *The Atlantic* (15 June 2016) www.theatlantic.com/news/archive/2016/06/orlando-nightclub-shooting/486713.

[182] 'Omar Mateen: 5 Fast Facts', above, n 169.

[183] ibid.

[184] ibid.

[185] ibid.

When asked, soon after the attack, about whether Mateen had a connection to radical Islamic terrorism, an FBI agent said there were 'suggestions' that he 'may have leanings' that way.[186] On 12 June, *TMZ* ran a headline saying: 'Omar Mateen: Terrorist was 29-year-old Islamic Radical.'[187] Then-President Obama said, shortly after the attacks, that the attack seemed to be 'an example of the kind of home-grown extremism that all of us have been concerned about.'[188] Saudi Arabia revealed, at around the same time, that Mateen had visited the country twice for a religious pilgrimage.[189]

After headlines ran describing Mateen's pledge to Daesh, a Daesh representative issued a statement saying 'a soldier of the Islamic State has carried out the attack.'[190] Shortly after the attacks, by contrast, then-FBI Director James Comey said '[s]o far, we see no indication that this was a plot directed from outside the United States, and we see no indication that he was part of any kind of network', although he suggested that Mateen might have been radicalised over the Internet.[191]

The day after the shootings, the *New York Times* described it as 'the worst act of terrorism on American soil since Sept. 11, 2001, and the deadliest attack on a gay target in the nation's history'.[192] Florida's Governor, Rick Scott, said: 'Yesterday's terror attack was an attack on our state and entire nation.'[193] The following days contained public discussions of whether Mateen was on the terrorism watchlist and thus should have been prevented from getting guns.[194]

Some, however, began to suggest that this association of Mateen with Islamic extremism was a false narrative. One author wrote:

> Since his attack on the Pulse gay nightclub in Orlando, the developing narrative surrounding Mateen's life is that of a troubled human being who had a history of domestic violence, a struggle with his sexual orientation, as well as an inclination toward a radical version of Islam. However, in addition to recently pledging allegiance to the Islamic State group, Mateen had previously shown support for both al-Qaida and Hezbollah, who have radically different interpretations of Islam and are in fact bitter enemies.

---

[186] ibid.

[187] 'Omar Mateen: Terrorist was 29-Year-Old Islamic Radical' *TMZ* (12 June 2017) www.tmz.com/2016/06/12/terrorist-omar-mateen-gay-nightclub-murder.

[188] Lizette Alvarez et al, 'Orlando Gunman was "Cool and Calm" after Massacre, Police Say' *New York Times* (13 June 2016) www.nytimes.com/2016/06/14/us/orlando-shooting.html.

[189] ibid.

[190] Pamela Engel, 'There's a Key Difference between the Orlando Attack and Past ISIS-Claimed Massacres' *Business Insider* (12 June 2016) www.businessinsider.com/isis-statement-orlando-shooting-attack-2016-6.

[191] Jason Dearen and Terrance Harris, 'Orlando Mourns its Dead; Gunman May Have Been "Homegrown"' *CTV News* (13 June 2016) www.ctvnews.ca/world/orlando-mourns-its-dead-gunman-may-have-been-homegrown-1.2942974?autoPlay=true.

[192] Alvarez et al, above, n 188.

[193] ibid.

[194] See, eg, Russell Berman, 'Could Congress Have Stopped Omar Mateen from Getting His Guns?' *The Atlantic* (14 June 2016) www.theatlantic.com/politics/archive/2016/06/closing-the-terror-gun-loophole-might-not-have-stopped-the-orlando-massacre/486863.

This suggests Mateen had an extremely shallow and confused understanding of Islam as he failed to comprehend the social and political differences between the diferent [*sic*] groups. Hezbollah are currently fighting against the Islamic State and other radical Sunni groups in Syria.[195]

This comment itself suggests a questionable narrative, since if Mateen was actually confused about the groups, this did not mean he was showing a misunderstanding over Islam, but over the groups who wrongly claim to act on behalf of Islam in carrying out objectives often characterised as terrorism. These are two very different things.

Two days after the shootings, *Time* magazine ran an article that said, among other things: 'Omar Mateen was one of the least interesting people you never met. Rage isn't interesting; hatred isn't interesting; intolerance and misogyny and homophobia aren't interesting. If you ever had happened to meet him you'd probably have tried to forget him.'[196] It continued:

That same dark bargain—personal enlargement through mass violence—is what all terrorist organizations, but particularly ISIS, offer their murderous foot soldiers. If the U.S. and other countries are going to confront the growing threat that such groups present, the first step is to understand better what's in the mind of those front line killers.

…

Even people like Mateen, who apparently did self-radicalize, are part of the group-think if not the actual group. 'Whether [radicalization] involves direct personal contact with others or the person is just developing these ideas in his or her own mind, it's obviously not done in a social vacuum … [quoting Harvard psychologist and philosopher Joshua Green].'[197]

The article then summarised a supposed explanation of Mateen's actions, saying:

All the same, the Orlando shooter, like so many terrorists, was nothing more than an ideological opportunist—a lonely, angry, violent man who likely would have found his way to murder one way or another. ISIS and other groups help people like him weaponize their hate, and in the bargain, provide them a flash of dark fame. But their ugly moment passes. No less a monster than Osama bin Laden wound up a shrunken old man, rocking in front of his television while he watched videotapes of his greatest atrocities. Then a Navy SEAL shot him in the head. Thus all terrorists.[198]

These statements generally demonstrate that much of the public narrative pointed to Islamic extremism as the motive behind Mateen's actions.

---

[195] 'Orlando Shooter's Wife: The FBI Told Me Not to Tell the Media He was Gay' *AlterNet* (16 June 2016) http://www.alternet.org/sex-amp-relationships/fbi-told-orlando-shooters-wife-not-tell-us-media-he-was-gay.
[196] Jeffrey Kluger, 'This is What Drove the Orlando Killer' *Time* (14 June 2016) time.com/4368275/mateen-orlando-why-he-killed.
[197] ibid (internal citations omitted).
[198] ibid.

How the narrative developed is important, especially during a time in which there has been so much larger discussion about extremism and terrorism and how best to address these risks. Mateen's own statements, and those of Daesh, provided significant support for this narrative, although, as discussed below, not necessarily unequivocal support. What is notable in the narrative is the speed with which Mateen's citizenship and national origin emerged as major factors in determining his motive. The Quebec City shooter, a Canadian citizen and a Caucasian, committed an act quite similar to what Mateen did, and his citizenship and national origin were not similarly used as starting points to find his motive, although they are arguably as relevant in that case as in Mateen's. If, in fact, Mateen's motive was something other than what he claimed it to be, then these attacks do not necessarily add to the narrative of how governments should be responding to Islamic extremism. A misleading narrative could lead to the wrong legal responses. As time passed, information emerged that suggested that the initial narrative about Mateen's motivation was not so clear at all.

B. Allegations that the Shootings were an Act of Homophobic Rage

Another narrative that quickly emerged was that Mateen had rage towards people in the LGBT community. Mateen's father went to lengths to advance this narrative and to dispel that of an association with Islamic extremism. He was quoted as saying that Mateen attacked the nightclub, which was popular in the LGBT community, after extreme anger when he saw two men kissing in Miami several months earlier.[199] He said:

> We were in downtown Miami, Bayside, people were playing music. And he saw two men kissing each other in front of his wife and kid, and he got very angry ... They were kissing each other and touching each other, and he said: 'Look at that. In front of my son, they are doing that.' And then we were in the men's bathroom, and men were kissing each other.
>
> ...
>
> This had nothing to do with religion.[200]

Thus, Mateen's father insisted that his son's actions constituted a hate crime rather than an act of terrorism. There has been a tendency to silo these crimes into different legal responses in some cases, so this distinction is important. These two possible motivations were sometimes combined in the public narrative.

---

[199] 'Omar Mateen: 5 Fast Facts', above, n 169; Pete Williams et al, 'Gunman Omar Mateen Described as Belligerent, Racist and "Toxic"' *NBC News* (13 June 2016) www.nbcnews.com/storyline/orlando-nightclub-massacre/terror-hate-what-motivated-orlando-nightclub-shooter-n590496.
[200] Williams, above, n 199.

One reporter wrote, the day after the attacks, 'investigators probing gunman Omar Mateen's massacre [of] at least 49 people at a popular gay nightclub in Florida are trying to determine whether terrorism, homophobia or both pushed him over the edge'.[201] Attorney General Loretta Lynch said: 'People often act out of more than one motivation … This was clearly an act of terror and an act of hate.'[202]

If one assumes that these two motivations were both present, then this presents a different scenario from the one motivated solely by religious extremism or by hate of a particular group.

C. Allegations that Mateen was Angry Over Being Gay

Yet another narrative about Mateen's motives emerged with reports that Mateen himself had been a familiar patron at the Pulse nightclub and may himself have been gay.[203] Mateen's father vehemently denied that Mateen was gay.[204] He allegedly told one reporter: 'If he was gay, why would he do something like this?'[205]

Several people came forward after the attacks to allege that they had met Mateen at gay clubs, had encountered him online or had had romantic encounters with him.[206] This, it was reported, prompted an investigation into whether Mateen might have been motivated by self-loathing and revenge.[207] Mateen's ex-wife speculated that this was true. As of late June 2016, the FBI had reported that it had not found any independent corroboration of this.[208]

Even the narratives describing Mateen as gay were divided as to how that fit into his motive. Some suggested that he had self-loathing over his being gay, possibly because of his father's views of gay people or because of the conflict between this and his religious beliefs.[209]

---

[201] ibid.

[202] Frances Robles and Julie Turkewitz, 'Was the Orlando Gunman Gay? The Answer Continues to Elude the F.B.I.' *New York Times* (25 June 2016) www.nytimes.com/2016/06/26/us/was-the-orlando-gunman-gay-the-answer-continues-to-elude-the-fbi.html.

[203] ibid.

[204] ibid.

[205] Chris Spargo et al, '"Omar Mateen was Gay": Orlando Terrorist Pursued a Relationship with Male Classmate, was a Regular at Gay Bars Including Pulse for the Past Decade, and Used Hookup Apps like Grindr to Meet Men' *Daily Mail* (14 June 2016) www.dailymail.co.uk/news/article-3639961/Orlando-terrorist-went-gay-club-Pulse-dozen-times-got-drunk-belligerent-talked-wife-kid-massacring-49-people-there.html (this article is not cited for the truth of its assertions, but to demonstrate the narrative that was presented).

[206] Robles and Turkewitz, above, n 202.

[207] ibid.

[208] ibid.

[209] ibid.

D. Allegations that Mateen was an Unstable, Violent Substance Abuser

Possibly related and possibly separate was the narrative that Mateen was generally a violent person, as evidenced by allegations from his first wife, who said she actually had to be rescued by relatives from his abuse.[210] She said he was unstable and violent, and would attack her because of trivial reasons, such as the laundry not being done.[211] She also expressed scepticism about the theory that Mateen was driven by Islamic extremism, saying she saw no sign of this during their time together.[212] She said he had a history of taking steroids and expressed a belief that his instability was behind the attacks.[213] Mateen's autopsy confirmed physical changes suggesting heavy use of steroids.[214]

E. Allegations that Mateen was Bullied

Still others argued that the media were too quick to put easy labels on Mateen. One writer accused the FBI of ignoring any evidence that did not fit its Islamic terrorist narrative, saying:

> The personal details about Mateen, from his vicious abuse of his first wife to credible accounts of a secret gay life to the reports of his mental instability and the autopsy results confirming him as a heavy abuser of steroids, have been forgotten or apparently suppressed by the FBI. Taken together, these elements of Mateen's person [*sic*] profile directly contradicted the popular portrayal of the mass killer as an Islamic extremist acting in the name of ISIS. Unsurprisingly, they have fallen down the Orwellian memory hole.[215]

Documents released by the government approximately a month after the shootings reveal yet another potential narrative. They suggested that Mateen had made repeated allegations of racial and religious harassment at work. Among the

---

[210] Suzanne Moore, 'Omar Mateen's Domestic Violence was a Clue to His Murderous Future' *The Guardian* (13 June 2016) www.theguardian.com/commentisfree/2016/jun/13/omar-mateen-domestic-violence-clue-murderous-future.

[211] 'Ex-wife of Suspected Orlando Shooter Omar Mateen Says He was Unstable and Violent: "He Beat Me"' *National Post* (12 June 2016) nationalpost.com/news/world/ex-wife-of-suspected-orlando-shooter-omar-mateen-says-he-was-unstable-and-violent-he-beat-me/wcm/106fe9af-997b-4158-9e0e-9bc84136e319.

[212] ibid.

[213] Moore, above, n 210.

[214] Del Quentin Wilber, 'Orlando Gunman was HIV-Negative, and Probably a Long-Term Steroid User, Autopsy Shows' *LA Times* (15 July 2016) www.latimes.com/nation/la-na-mateen-steroid-hiv-20160715-snap-story.html.

[215] Max Blumenthal, 'Disturbing New Documents Reveal Orlando Shooter Omar Mateen's Allegations of Racial Harrassment [*sic*] by Police Co-workers' *AlterNet* (1 August 2016) www.alternet.org/grayzone-project/new-documents-shocking-accounts-orlando-shooter-omar-mateen-alleging-racial (including a link to the actual documents).

extensive allegations, for example, Mateen claimed that a sheriff at the court-house where he worked said: 'Don't you Arabs sleep with goats?'[216] He alleged that another person, a deputy, said 'we need to kill all the fucking Muslims' and would stand behind him, flipping the clip on his gun holster to intimidate him.[217] Mateen said another employee repeatedly called him 'Aladdin' and that others suggested he was primitive, spoke of killing Muslims, offered him bacon and mocked him about praying.[218] He claimed that after every high-profile terrorist attack, deputies would confront him, implying that he knew more about it.[219]

Mateen was later investigated for statements he made about loyalty to Islamic extremist groups, but said he made these statements to get co-workers to stop harassing him. After the Boston attack, for instance, he said that he was harassed, so he told co-workers that the attackers were his cousins, among other comments, claiming a connection to known terrorists. He said he made such statements to get them to 'leave me alone'.[220] Bullying had been cited as a motivation behind other mass shootings in the US, such as the Columbine High School shooting in 1999, although such narratives also tend to be more complex than is generally perceived.[221]

In describing how little attention was paid to the conflicting evidence about Mateen's motives, especially evidence that conflicted with the dominant narrative of Islamic extremism, one author commented on how that false, or at least incomplete, narrative was being used to advance legal and political changes:

> As the facts that could have interrupted the official narrative fell by the wayside, Congress and state legislatures exploited the tragedy to push for an expansion of undemocratic databases of 'terror' suspects and the discriminatory no-fly list. As Sarah Lazare reported for AlterNet, police departments across the country have been leveraging the attack to lobby for expanded arsenals of military gear. At both Republican and Democratic conventions, Orlando has been invoked to summon fears of Islamic extremism at home and to gin up support for military action abroad. Meanwhile, new information continued to surface that complicated the simplistic war on terror narrative even further.[222]

Shortly after the attack, the FBI had also confirmed prior reports that Mateen told them he made statements of support for terrorism to stop co-workers from harassing him. They had closed that earlier investigation.[223]

---

[216] ibid.
[217] ibid.
[218] ibid.
[219] Blumenthal, above, n 215.
[220] ibid.
[221] Peter Lagman, 'Columbine, Bullying, and the Mind of Eric Harris' *Psychology Today* (20 May 2009) www.psychologytoday.com/blog/keeping-kids-safe/200905/columbine-bullying-and-the-mind-eric-harris (arguing that the dominant narrative that Harris was bullied does not necessarily account for his actions).
[222] Blumenthal, above, n 215.
[223] Alvarez et al, above, n 188.

F. The Narrative Matters

Legally, the issue of Mateen's motivation is important, certainly for governments seeking to prevent similar acts of violence in the future. As noted above, some narratives suggested that Mateen had more than one motivation, and potential motivations may overlap. It may be true that it was both an act of terrorism and a hate crime, but several other motivations could have been factors as well, and the extent of particular motivations, among several possibilities, has not clearly emerged.

If the narrative of a motive of Islamic extremism is false, if it was just a smokescreen that Mateen created to hide his true motives, aided by Daesh for its own self-serving motives, this raises the risk of undermining any response based on this belief. This would not only raise questions about the public narrative surrounding Mateen, but also surrounding Daesh, and the legitimacy of responses based on an assumption that Mateen had a particular motivation. Similarly, if this was only part of a configuration of motives attributable solely to Mateen, this could have different implications for proper responses.

Because this attack so quickly gained traction in the popular conversation as an act of international terrorism, the narrative was different from that after other high-profile mass shootings in the US, which are distressingly common. After incidents like the shooting of 26 people, of whom 20 were first-graders, at Sandy Hook Elementary School, or that in the movie theatre in Aurora, Colorado, in which 12 people were killed and approximately 70 were injured, widespread cries for gun control were prominent.[224]

With Mateen, the commentary on gun control appeared more muted. It often focused on rules allowing those on a terrorism watchlist—and he was apparently not on such a list, except during the brief prior period when he was investigated—to have access to guns.[225] Obama did make a statement regarding gun control, connecting some of these shootings, but he distinguished this case when he said: 'The motives of this killer may have been different than mass shooters in Aurora or Newtown, but the instruments of death were so similar.'[226] Even when credible evidence emerged that Mateen's claims to be connected to Daesh—in part fuelled by Daesh—may have been a smokescreen, the tone of this public narrative did not significantly shift. This is in spite of the fact that, ultimately, Mateen's actions could

---

[224] See, eg, Polly Mosendz, 'Read: Transcript of President Barack Obama's Speech on Gun Control' *Newsweek* (5 January 2016) www.newsweek.com/obama-transcript-gun-control-president-speech-411953 (reproducing transcript of Obama's speech, in which he cited high-profile incidents of gun-related deaths in the US, including Sandy Hook and Aurora, and called for reasonable gun control); see also 'Colorado Theater Shooting Fast Facts' *CNN* (2 July 2017) www.cnn.com/2013/07/19/us/colorado-theater-shooting-fast-facts/index.html (listing the victims and total numbers).

[225] See Del Quentin Wilber, 'Omar Mateen was Taken off a Terrorist Watch List, But Keeping Him on it Wouldn't Have Stopped Him from Buying Guns' *LA Times* (16 June 2016) www.latimes.com/nation/la-na-orlando-nightclub-shooting-live-omar-mateen-was-taken-off-a-terrorist-1465772737-html-story.html.

[226] ibid.

turn out to have more in common with the attacks at Sandy Hook and at Aurora, among many others, as a random outburst of violent rage than with advancing the objectives of Daesh. The narrative heavily controls the direction of the response.

IV. 'A Rose by Any Other Name …': Strategically Naming an International 'Terrorist' Group is Key to the Narrative[227]

Having referred to this group as 'Daesh' throughout this work, this last section will argue that the very label used to name the group, which has emerged as arguably the most significant international terrorist group as of 2017, has been fraught with confusion. The larger label of 'terrorism' is itself somewhat controversial when applied to this group, which has different dimensions to its devastating activities. Beyond that, even the general meaning of the word 'terrorism' is controversial. This book does not need to enter that particular fray, as the subject of the varied definitions of terrorism has been well addressed in other works.[228] However, controversies over the word's meaning are briefly acknowledged in order to demonstrate some of the layered confusion that arises in this area from the use of imprecise or political language. Mark Burgess describes this obstacle in the discourse:

> Defining terrorism has become so polemical and subjective an undertaking as to resemble an art rather than a science. Texts on the subject proliferate and no standard work on terrorism can be considered complete without at least an introductory chapter being devoted to this issue.[229]

This book will deviate from this pattern by not attempting to establish a settled definition of the term, as it is not necessary for the points made here. Rather, it is noted that the meaning of 'terrorism' is, indeed, so amorphous and controversial as to make it difficult to establish a definitive and all-encompassing explanation of what it means, leading to difficulties in determining systematic responses.[230]

---

[227] The full quote is: 'A rose by any other name would smell as sweet.' Juliet says the line in *Romeo and Juliet*, suggesting that it does not matter that Romeo has the name of her father's enemy. This quote has been altered by certain editors from its original form, and the most well-known current version is the one used here. See William Shakespeare, *Romeo and Juliet*, Act II, Scene II.

[228] See, eg, Sudha Setty, 'What's in a Name? How Nations Define Terrorism Ten Years after 9/11' (2011) 33 *University of Pennsylvania Journal of International Law* 1 (using examples from the US, the UK and India to suggest that the definitions relating to terrorism have changed in the years since 9/11, purportedly in favour of heightened security, with the result being an adverse impact on certain minority groups and questions arising as to whether these jurisdictions have departed from certain values relating to the Rule of Law); Anthony Richards, *Conceptualizing Terrorism* (Oxford, Oxford University Press, 2015).

[229] Mark Burgess, 'Terrorism: The Problems of Definition' *Center for Defense Information* (1 August 2003) www.cdi.org/friendlyversion/printversion.cfm?documentID=1564.

[230] See Setty, above, n 228.

Much of the post-9/11 discourse, such as the declaration of a 'War on Terror', tends to suggest that this is a phenomenon that lends itself to an easy characterisation, which is not at all always the case. This section will, however, address some of the unique complications that arise when this particular label is applied to this particular group, as well as those surrounding the actual name of the group.

Words and names can be chosen strategically to drive a particular narrative, and such choices can be made by actors on all sides of an issue. The name for this group is an example of conflicting and deliberate decisions, by political actors and even by the group itself, to give the group one of several different names, depending on what narrative is intentionally being advanced. This is a discourse tool that has not necessarily been used with other groups and it illustrates the importance of names.

A. ISIS or ISIL or IS or Islamic State or Daesh or …?

An obvious example of the importance of the narrative is found in the very name of the group, beyond its general characterisation. The group is known alternatively by various names, including the Islamic State of Iraq and the Levant ('ISIL'), the Islamic State of Iraq and Syria ('ISIS'), Islamic State ('IS') and Daesh (derived from the Arabic).[231] The group itself has changed its own designation, recently expressing a wish to be called 'Islamic State', indicating recognition of a Caliphate and obviously trying to present itself as the representative of Islam.[232] This is one of several areas in which the group has intentionally used language to advance its objectives.[233]

Many news organisations call the group 'ISIS', while Obama referred to it as 'ISIL', and some speculate that is because he preferred to ignore the inclusion of Syria in the 'ISIS' designation.[234] Trump regularly refers to the group as 'ISIS', unlike his predecessor, and has criticised Obama for calling the group 'ISIL'.[235] The US State Department, however, refers to the group as 'Daesh'.[236] The British and

---

[231] See Philip Ross, 'ISIL, ISIS, Islamic State, Daesh: What's the Difference?' *International Business Times* (23 September 2014) www.ibtimes.com/isil-isis-islamic-state-daesh-whats-difference-1693495.

[232] ibid.

[233] Major Theresa Ford, US Army, 'How Daesh Uses Language in the Domain of Religion' (March–April 2016) *Military Review* 16.

[234] See Jaime Fuller, '"ISIS" vs "ISIL" vs. "Islamic State": The Political Importance of a Much-Debated Acronym' *Washington Post* (20 January 2015) www.washingtonpost.com/blogs/the-fix/wp/2015/01/20/isis-vs-isil-vs-islamic-state-the-political-importance-of-a-much-debated-acronym-2; see also Matt Wilstein, 'Chuck Todd Knows Why Obama Prefers "ISIL" to "ISIS"' *Mediaite* (8 September 2014), www.mediaite.com/tv/chuck-todd-knows-why-obama-prefers-isil-to-isis.

[235] David Pugliese, 'ISIL, ISIS or DAESH? Ottawa's Past Efforts to Change its Term for Terrorist Group Plagued by Confusion' *The National* (2016) www.nationalpost.com/m/wp/news/blog.html?b=news.nationalpost.com/news/canada/canadian-politics/isil-isis-or-daesh-ottawas-past-efforts-to-change-its-term-for-terrorist-group-plagued-by-confusion.

[236] ibid.

French governments call the group 'Daesh', sometimes spelled 'Daech' in French, as a shorthand for the translation of the group's full Arabic name, 'al-Dawla al-Islamiya fi Iraq wa ash-Sham'.[237] In Canada, the government also decided to start calling the group 'Daesh'.[238] It had previously called the group 'ISIL', and the Privy Council Office caused confusion by ordering that it be changed from 'ISIL' to 'ISIS'.[239]

Some news organisations use 'Islamic State', which has also been controversial. This name, preferred by the group itself, implies a system of organised government rather than a terrorist or militant group and, some say, gives the group unwarranted legitimacy.[240]

Even in this book, a conscious decision on the importance of labels is apparent in the choice to call the group 'Daesh', because this translation of its name has a pejorative connotation.[241] Daesh leaders have expressed anger over the name, threatening to punish anybody inside the territory it controls if they use 'Daesh', and the decision to use this designation in this book was intentional as a response.[242] Specifically, Daesh 'threatened to cut the tongue of anyone who publicly used the acronym Daesh, instead of referring to the group by its full name, saying it shows defiance and disrespect'.[243]

This book is not the first work to make this choice for this reason. One military author in the US notes the importance of the group's proper name thus:

> What we call the enemy is important. The fact that we and our friends and allies have yet to definitively agree on a name for this enemy speaks volumes about our lack of understanding. We use acronyms interchangeably, such as ISIS for Islamic State of Iraq and Syria, or ISIL for Islamic State of Iraq and the Levant. Using those names and their acronyms, however, gives these terrorists the religious and political veneer they seek. Those names acknowledge that the group is Islamic, and that it is a state. Neither premise, however, is legitimate. Therefore, this article uses the name Daesh, which is based on the Arabic acronym for the Islamic State in Iraq and Syria. Daesh sounds similar to an Arabic word that means to bruise or crush; the group's leaders consider the word insulting. This article uses it with the intent to strip away any religious or political legitimacy that other acronyms suggest.[244]

The author points out how several other countries have thus adopted the use of 'Daesh' for the group and speculates that countries like the US continue to use the other names because they do not understand the significance of language to the group's success.[245] Language is so important to Daesh, she argues, that language is

---

[237] See Ross, above, n 231; Pugliese, above, n 235.
[238] Pugliese, above, n 235.
[239] ibid.
[240] See Ross, above, n 231.
[241] See ibid; Pugliese, above, n 235.
[242] See Pugliese, above, n 235.
[243] Ford, above, n 233 (citing the Associated Press).
[244] ibid.
[245] ibid.

the weapon that should be used to fight back, such as by using terminology that delegitimises Daesh in its quest to be viewed as the heir to Islam, accomplished in part by refusing to adopt Daesh's preferred terminology.[246]

This view, while certainly well supported, may be overly generous to the US government, suggesting a mere misunderstanding, when circumstances have suggested that the power of language is actually well understood and used in a strategic way. As discussed at length in chapters four to six of this book, language was the building block on which the US-declared 'War on Terror' was created. As two authors note: 'Words shape and affect policy. The issue is not simply nomenclature; it is the policies that derive from the assumptions and concepts embedded in the term.'[247] The fractured way in which the group is even named in political discourse, they suggest, undermines the actual fight against Daesh.[248]

Although this book focuses on the one example of the importance of the group's name, other aspects of Daesh's linguistic choices are also intentionally designated to give the impression of a close association with the Prophet Muhammad, and of Daesh being the regime that has inherited religious authority from the Prophet.[249] Language is critical to all levels of their functioning, beginning even with the most basic issue of the group's name.

In an odd twist, problems arose when the acronym 'ISIS' gained wide use so quickly, because there were companies bearing that name, which then ran into a concern over being confused with the militant group. Some changed their names as a result.[250] Obviously, the battle over the public narrative is problematic, as unrelated organisations rushed to distance themselves from this new, dominant narrative.

B. Terrorism or Militants or Religion or Government or ...?

Although, as explained above, this book will not attempt to resolve the ongoing conflict about what 'terrorism' means, the word 'terrorism' is used to describe Daesh, and this may be overly simplistic and misleading in some ways.[251] Indeed, this designation is commonly used to describe this group by major political

---

[246] ibid.

[247] Asaf Siniver and Scott Lucas, 'The Islamic State Lexical Battleground: US Foreign Policy and the Abstraction of Threat' (2016) 92(1) *Journal of International Affairs* 63 (quoting Robert S Litwak, 'What's in a Name? The Changing Foreign Policy Lexicon' (2001) 54(2) *Journal of International Affairs* 376).

[248] ibid.

[249] ibid.

[250] See, eg, John Adams, 'Isis Wallet Picks a New Name' *American Banker* (3 September 2014) www.americanbanker.com/news/isis-wallet-picks-a-new-name?feed=00000158-bab1-dda9-adfa-fef7649f0000 (describing the decision to change the name after a survey of users showed a strong association of the group with the militant group).

[251] Siniver and Lucas, above, n 247.

figures.[252] However, one author notes that Daesh has more military equipment than the French Army, and has invaded and assumed power at different times in large geographical territories, with the indicia of a military force. This is not the norm for groups that are called terrorist groups.[253] Another author describes Daesh as 'a hybrid organisation that combined terrorist tactics, military precision, religious ideology, and technological and bureaucratic innovation'.[254] Another wrote that Daesh is 'unquestionably that of a mercenary army. [Daesh] is neither a rebellion, nor a guerrilla movement, and even less a terrorist entity'.[255]

In Syria, for instance, Daesh has caused widespread devastation. Mass graves were found in Palmyra, and Daesh destroyed priceless antiquities there and in other places.[256] It captured Palmyra for the second time in December 2016, several months after the city had been reclaimed by Syrian and Russian forces. It did so while government forces were focused on the battle then taking place over Aleppo. Syrian forces took the city back in March 2017.[257] Daesh is accused of widespread atrocities during its time of occupation.[258]

These military actions are not typical of a terrorist organisation, but other actions attributed to Daesh are. Daesh has claimed responsibility for numerous recent attacks in places like Paris, Brussels, Manchester and London. These attacks, sudden and vicious and directed at civilians, do bear more resemblance to what has traditionally been considered terrorism.

Some evidence suggests that Daesh is splintered and is not one cohesive group, and that these splinter groups may be behind some of these attacks, and may be sufficiently distinct to be deemed separate from the main Daesh organisation.[259] Other evidence suggests that Daesh has been so successful in its propaganda campaigns that it has 'inspired' people in different parts of the world to launch terrorist attacks, not as actual affiliates of Daesh, but simply by people who decided on their own to act and to associate their actions with Daesh. When such people have acted, Daesh has falsely given the impression of involvement by claiming responsibility. As discussed above, there is evidence that this might have been the case with Omar Mateen, but that is not the only instance.

The person who shot and killed a Canadian soldier at the National War Memorial in Ottawa, for instance, had claimed allegiance to Daesh, and a spokesperson

---

[252] See, eg, 'President Obama's Speech on ISIS' *CNN* (10 September 2014) politicslive.cnn.com/Event/President_Obamas_speech_on_ISIS (describing US plans to destroy the 'terrorist group known as ISIL').

[253] Siniver and Lucas, above, n 247.

[254] Ben Fishman, 'Defining ISIS' (2016) 58(1) *Survival* 17.

[255] Xavier Raufer, 'The "Islamic State", an Unidentified Terrorist Object' (2016) 25(2) *Polish Quarterly of International Affairs* 45.

[256] Martin Chulov, 'Syrian Regime Recaptures Palmyra from Islamic State' *The Guardian* (2 March 2017), www.theguardian.com/world/2017/mar/02/syrian-regime-recaptures-palmyra-from-islamic-state.

[257] ibid.

[258] ibid.

[259] See Lori Hinnant, 'That's Not a Cell, That's a Terrorist Group: ISIL Network that Attacked Brussels Continues to Grow' *National Post* (11 April 2016) news.nationalpost.com/news/world/thats-not-a-cell-thats-a-terrorist-group-isil-network-that-attacked-brussels-continues-to-grow.

for Daesh later praised his actions. However, an investigation suggested that this gunman was not directly associated with Daesh, but just admired them based on what he had seen of them in the news.[260]

Thus, a wide range of atrocities have been attributed to Daesh, or a group connected to Daesh. In some instances, the acts have been acts of terrorism; in others, they have had more of a military aspect, and beyond that of a typical internal insurgency. Each scenario is different and it is reasonable that the responses to the risks presented by each must also be different. Public discourse that ignores these distinctions can lead to problematic responses that might persuade the public that action is being taken, but may do little to really address the threat.

This discussion just scratches the surface of the proper designation to place on Daesh's activities and it is not intended to do more than that. Rather, it provides a summary view of some of the problems that can arise by grouping widely disparate activities under one label, such as that of terrorism or a military group, which theoretically can lead to problems in the responses, since different activities can require different responses. The label, in terms of the name to be used for the organisation, is also much more complex than can, perhaps, be captured in one word. For this group in particular, the reality may be much more complex than much of the dominant political discourse would suggest.

V. Conclusion

As stated at the outset of this chapter, language matters.

This chapter focused primarily on one aspect of persuasive language, regarding labels. The examples presented in this chapter demonstrate how even that one element can have a significant impact on how a particular event, entity or person is viewed and treated.

Labels can be used strategically in political discourse. The examples herein show how labels can, even on their own, significantly alter how something is perceived. Labels that are applied in popular political commentary tend, whether they are accurate or not, to become embedded in people's understanding of the underlying thing that is being described.[261] By creating an association of something or somebody with a name that is clearly negative, one can cause others to have a preconceived response, which evades the normal level of nuance that one might otherwise apply in assessing the issue.[262] A label can be a "'cognitive shortcut", which

---

[260] See 'ISIS Praises October Slaying of Soldier in Ottawa; Calls for Attack in West' *Global News* (26 January 2015) globalnews.ca/news/1793629/isis-praises-october-slaying-of-soldier-in-ottawa.

[261] Katarzyna Molek-Kozakowska, 'Labeling and Mislabeling in American Political Discourse,' in Urszula Okulska and Piotr Cap (eds), *Perspectives in Politics and Discourse* (Amsterdam, John Benjamins Publishing Company, 2010) 83.

[262] ibid 85.

saves "cognitive misers" the effort of processing the incoming information, examining its logic and remembering details'.[263] As one author explains: 'As a result of labeling, complex categories are simplified, sometimes through straightforward associations to what the majority finds loathsome or scary.'[264]

As explained more fully in the next chapter, labels are only a very small part of the arsenal of argumentation tools that can be layered to carry a given point and to persuade a particular audience. The examples in this chapter show the importance and persuasive strength of just that one discourse tool. A carefully layered political discourse, then, which combines this with other argumentation strategies, can be a powerful vehicle for persuasion and, as argued in the second part of this book, can significantly change legal structures as a result.

---

[263] ibid 85–86.
[264] ibid 86–87.

2

Breaking Down and Reconstructing Discourse Can Reveal New Realities

I. Introduction: Fractured Narratives and Manufactured Confusion

The preceding chapter gives examples of types of rhetorical tools that can affect perceptions of truth. It suggests that 'truth' is not always something that is objectively seen. The way in which an argument is constructed has everything to do with its success. The starting point of a debate, understandings of what can be assumed to be true and what must be proven to be true, the burden of proof on such questions, and the overarching imposition of values are among the critical points to be assessed in considering the efficacy and outcome of an argument.[1] This is hardly a new concept, as politicians, theorists and lawyers have known this for a long time. While these structural building blocks are often recognised as a strategic component, looking forward, to developing a successful argument, they are not as often considered after the fact, when one is looking at a policy that was built on the back of a particular argument and directed at the public, legislative bodies and judicial bodies. These components, however, can be as useful in assessing the structural soundness of past changes as they are in laying out a future argumentation strategy, as demonstrated in the Introduction to this book, through Mayor Landrieu's speech.

The study of law and language is not new and, indeed, it has become well established as its own discipline. Possibly because of the way this field has developed, it 'remains fragmented', with a large number of different modes of scholarship.[2] This work may add to that fragmentation, in the use of particular threads of language analysis to undertake its argument. Argumentation theory is the study of elements of effective argument or rhetoric. This theory provides the theoretical lens

---

[1] Chaim Perelman and Lucie Olbrechts-Tyteca, *The New Rhetoric: A Treatise on Argumentation*, translated by John Wilkinson and Purcell Weaver (Notre Dame, IN, University of Notre Dame Press, 1969).

[2] Elizabeth Mertz and Jothie Rajah, 'Language-and-Law Scholarship: An Interdisciplinary Conversation and a Post-9/11 Example' (2014) 10 *Annual Review of Law and Social Science* 169.

through which this book views particular changes to anti-terrorism detention practices in places like the US, Canada and the UK in direct response to the 9/11 attacks. This is just one of the many potential threads that could be pursued.[3]

This work breaks post-9/11 discourse into pieces, seeking to reassemble them to suggest new perspectives. A metaphor is helpful to explain this methodology. Although that of a puzzle comes to mind, this metaphor does not work, because the pieces of a puzzle can only be reassembled into a single, one-dimensional picture, and there are no alternatives. Instead, a metaphor of a kaleidoscope better explains this process of disassembling and then reassembling the same components into possibly equally valid, but entirely different, pictures. It is not intended to suggest illusion, although the working of a kaleidoscope does involve a certain form of illusion between the mirrors and the use of light. Rather, the idea here is to use the metaphor to explain the methodology applied and the idea of the intended outcome—that a reconfiguration of a picture can come about through such a reconfiguration of the component parts. It is also implied that the elements that are changed into the new picture tend to be those that are of questionable validity, but sometimes a change in emphasis is possible, without necessarily undermining the validity of the prior iteration. The concept of a kaleidoscope as metaphor has been used in other contexts, notably by novelist Marcel Proust and anthropologist Claude Lévi-Strauss.[4]

The objective is to consider whether the picture changes when the component parts are disassembled and then thus reassembled, much like the process that takes place when one turns a kaleidoscope. When a kaleidoscope is turned, two complete, but different, pictures emerge, even though all of the same component parts are used, with the change being the result of an alteration in position and emphasis for those parts. Each picture may be potentially legitimate, or at least have indicia of legitimacy, as it is rare that only one definitive truth can emerge from any given situation, but more than one picture can certainly be constructed from the same component parts. Indeed, some elements of post-9/11 discourse and detention practices may well be sound and may remain static, but altering other elements, which are not necessarily so, still presents a different overall picture. Similarly, if some of the elements in the kaleidoscope picture are structurally unsound, collapsing them repositions the other elements to change the overall outlook as well. Thus, this metaphor explains the methodology used in this book to assess threads of argumentation.

By breaking down the discourse and foundational components of an implemented policy, one can expose new views on those changes that are not available simply from looking at the final product and, in relation to legal changes, may

---

[3] See ibid.

[4] See, eg, Marcel Proust, 'Remembrance of Things Past, Part II' in *Within a Budding Grove*, translated by CK Scott Moncrieff and Terence Kilmartin (Paris, Pleiade, 1919); Claude Lévi-Strauss, *The Savage Mind* (Chicago, University of Chicago Press, 1968) 36–37; Joseph Campbell, *Masks of God: Primitive Mythology* (New York, Penguin, 1987) 61.

not be available by applying validity arguments within the existing framework of legal analysis. This assessment of the steps leading to a particular policy is one important tool in determining whether the policy is sound and whether it should be pursued going forward. It can also provide insight into responses in other situations that may not be factually identical. In relation to terrorism detentions, constitutional presumptions favoured the use of the criminal justice system, for the most part, before 9/11 in liberal democracies. After the attacks occurred, political argumentation tools were successful in changing this presumption in some cases and, in some instances, the presumption shifted to favour a system outside of the criminal justice system for these detainees. In the US, where much of this rhetoric originated, a corresponding shift occurred in terms of the audience for the political rhetoric. An overwhelming wave of support for the President initially manifested in the early days after the attacks and a corresponding wave of support for the idea of a strong response to those responsible for the attacks rose with it. This meant that there was not the typical plurality of voices debating some of these issues, which might have otherwise tempered the significant impact of the argumentation tools that were employed.

An effective argument, of course, is one that works, or one that will:

> [C]reate or increase the adherence of minds to the theses presented for their assent. An efficacious argument is one which succeeds in increasing this intensity of adherence among those who hear it in such a way as to set in motion the intended action (a positive action or an abstention from action).[5]

Perelman and Olbrechts-Tyteca speak of the difficulty of disengaging a belief once it has taken root. They note that 'a belief, once established, can always be intensified, and, on the other hand ... argumentation is a function of the audience being addressed'.[6] When the post-9/11 political commentary arose in such a charged atmosphere of fear, with other views muted or outright silenced, it was much easier for those advancing the political speech to connect with, and persuade, their audiences that these changes in detention and interrogation strategies were absolutely necessary and right. Once people have internalised certain beliefs, they tend to view arguments in favour of the belief as correct and to resist arguments suggesting that their belief is wrong.[7] A belief thus created is very hard to refute.

The particular audience in the US, and the values that dominated at that time, had a great deal to do with what kind of argumentation approach would work. The idea of values, which underscores much of Perelman and Olbrechts-Tyteca's work, has some controversy, as it suggests a certain subjectivity to the traditional idea of objectivity in arguments. However, the manner in which persuasion was successfully used after 9/11, even when arguments were presented with significant structural flaws, suggests that they are right, and that perceptions of truth, even on

---

[5] Perelman and Olbrechts-Tyteca, above, n 1, 45.
[6] ibid.
[7] ibid.

something with the appearance of objectivity, can vary depending on the particular audience and the values the audience holds.

Because there seems no longer to have been a solid presumption in favour of criminal justice in all cases, competing detention narratives sprang up and were treated as if they were parallel and equal possibilities. This led to a fracturing—or inconsistency—of the narrative within particular countries, but also across jurisdictions that originally set about to have a unified response to the attacks. Different standards arose in order to deal with comparable situations, with no obvious basis for the differences.

A starting presumption, however, in favour of criminal justice detention standards that have been long-standing, and generally successful, in addressing the threat of terrorism might have led to a more unified conversation in terms of how to address detentions of terrorists. To be clear, most cases of terrorism suspects continued to be handled under the criminal justice systems in the countries reacting to 9/11.[8] Nevertheless, an option arose for some governments, under which they could opt out of using that system in specific cases, without being required to do much to rebut the presumption in favour of the criminal justice system, and this fracturing in particular cases arose in response to 9/11.

To operate under such a presumption does not necessarily mean that the criminal justice system is adequate in all cases. It would mean, however, that those arguing that it is not adequate would bear the burden of proof on that issue, on a case-by-case basis, instead of the burden falling on those arguing in favour of using the pre-existing criminal justice system, as actually seems to have played out.[9]

Post-9/11 American rhetoric was distinctive and persuasive in many ways and for many reasons. Some of this rhetoric may have simply been the natural response to a horrific attack. Some may have been created with the hope of persuading a particular audience to approve a particular type of action. Some may have been used not to clarify, but to obfuscate reality. And some of the rhetoric may have simply been confusing, perhaps unintentionally, or perhaps actually intended to confuse people so they more easily deferred the decisions to those in positions of power. Finally, some of the rhetoric may actually have been seemingly clear and consistent, but perceived differently by different audiences. Whatever the motivation, it was assembled in such a way, at such a time and to such an audience to cause a structural crack in the legal narrative surrounding detention and interrogation practices for those accused of terrorism.

---

[8] See, eg, Steve Swann, 'UK Terror Convictions Rising, BBC Jihadist Database Shows' *BBC* (6 July 2017) www.bbc.com/news/uk-40483171?ocid=socialflow_facebook&ns_mchannel=social&ns_campaign=bbcnews&ns_source=facebook; 'Who Are Britain's Jihadists?' *BBC* (5 July 2017) www.bbc.com/news/uk-32026985 (a searchable database of particular UK terrorism convictions).

[9] chs 3–6, below will address this issue in much more detail.

II. The Same Scenario, or the Same Words, with Different Meanings for Different People

An example of some of the confusing nature of post-9/11 American discourse emerged in a much-parodied statement made by then-US Secretary of Defense Donald Rumsfeld. In explaining the challenges facing the US in its attempts to address the post-9/11 risk of terrorism, and specifically responding to allegations that evidence of weapons of mass destruction in Iraq was lacking, Rumsfeld commented:

> [A]s we know, there are known knowns; there are things we know we know. We also know there are known unknowns; that is to say we know there are some things we do not know. But there are also unknown unknowns—the ones we don't know we don't know. And if one looks throughout the history of our country and other free countries, it is the latter category that tend to be the difficult ones.[10]

This statement was intended to create acceptance of the US's plan to invade Iraq, which, unlike other, preceding post-9/11 US governmental actions, was facing pushback, both within the US and internationally.[11]

Rumsfeld's words demonstrate an undercurrent sense that there was an unknown danger lurking, implying that this preventive action was necessary to prevent this unknown danger from striking. The unknown nature of this threat served to excuse national governments from making a specific showing that their initiatives had a direct link to addressing the threat, thus allowing for sometimes broad measures with questionable connections to the prevention of terrorism. Such language may have had particular resonance at that time because of the manner in which the 9/11 attacks occurred, striking suddenly, and with great initial confusion over who the attackers were, in a busy metropolitan city, with the use of ordinary passenger planes, against iconic towers, on what was otherwise a typical, sunny Tuesday in September.

In the aftermath of these particular attacks, it is reasonable that the public and law-makers, especially in the US, would prove to be receptive audiences for an argument that unprecedented changes were needed to prevent an unknown and only vaguely identified threat. Thus, the boundaries were more easily blurred. Favourable political discourse may have had a greater impact in that environment than it might when not coming on the heels of a horrific attack that so many people watched taking place on live television. Thus, the atmosphere in which the discourse is delivered was a critical component of its success.

---

[10] Donald Rumsfeld, 'DoD News Briefing—Secretary Rumsfeld and Gen Myers' *US Department of Defense* (12 February 2002) www.defense.gov/transcripts/transcript.aspx?transcriptid=2636.

[11] See ibid.

III. An Example: Kafka and Shifting the Kaleidoscope

Untangling the detention narrative that has emerged since 9/11 is an extraordinarily complex task. One method for attempting to do so is to break down the component parts that led to these varying scenarios in order to question whether matters that were treated as foundational premises were, in fact, valid or, if valid, if they were the only possible presumptions. However, even when broken down, the constituent parts may mean different things to different people. The most seemingly straightforward situation can be subject to differing interpretations if one changes starting points and argumentation elements, much, again, as one does in turning a kaleidoscope. It can even change based on subjective experiences of those listening to the arguments or on different interpretations of the same words.

Kafka's Parable from *The Trial* presents a compact example of this idea. Kafka's name is often invoked in discourse surrounding claims that a system of justice has elements of the arbitrary or the chaotic. Post-9/11 detention regimes in particular have been described as 'Kafkaesque' because of sometimes seemingly arbitrary detention, secret evidence, secret allegations and brutal interrogation methods.[12] This comparison likely draws from Kafka's short story about torture, *In the Penal Colony*, or from *The Trial*.[13]

In *The Trial*, Joseph K ('K') is arrested and imprisoned for an unknown crime, and is ultimately executed after a judicial proceeding in which he is unable to ascertain the rules, to understand the evidence or even to understand that with which he has been charged.[14] In the post-9/11 era, often characterised by secrecy

---

[12]   See, eg, Steven T Wax, *Kafka Comes to America: Fighting for Justice in the War on Terror—A Public Defender's Inside Account* (New York, Other Press, 2008); Maureen Webb, *Illusions of Security: Global Surveillance and Democracy in the Post-9/11 World* (New York, City Lights Books, 2007); Geoff Brumfiel, 'Physicians Protest Colleague's Terrorism Detention' *Nature News* (November 2010) www.nature.com. ezproxy.lib.ucalgary.ca/news/2010/101108/full/news.2010.592.htm (noting 'his colleagues are publicly protesting what they describe as his Kafkaesque detention'); Kevin Johnson, 'Rights Groups Detail 'Kafkaesque' U.S. Detentions' *USA Today* (27 June 2005) www.usatoday.com/news/washington/2005-06-26-detentions_x.htm; Andrew Grice and Nigel Morris, 'Britain War Crimes: UK terror Suspects Being Held in "Kafkaesque World"' *The Independent* (23 February 2006) groups.yahoo.com/group/IslamicNewsUpdates/message/6333 (original no longer available, reproduced at Yahoo Groups); Murray Dobbin, 'Harper's Hitlist: A Kafkaesque Nightmare for Abandoned Canadians' *Rabble.ca* (7 April 2010) rabble.ca/news/2010/04/harpers-hitlist-kafkaesque-nightmare-abandoned-canadians; Michael Kinsley, 'The Name is Kafka … Franz Kafka' *Washington Post* (16 June 2006) www.washingtonpost.com/wp-dyn/content/article/2006/06/15/AR2006061501795.html; Deborah Sontag, 'Who is This Kafka That People Keep Mentioning?' *New York Times Magazine* (21 October 2001) www.nytimes.com/2001/10/21/magazine/who-is-this-kafka-that-people-keep-mentioning.html?pagewanted=all; Frédéric Mégret, 'Justice in Times of Violence' (2003) 14(2) *European Journal of International Law* 327, 340 (citing Franz Kafka, *In the Penal Colony* (1914) as an example of Kafka as 'the *visionnaire* of our society's propensity for the absurd' in critiquing the argument that terrorists should be 'judged expeditiously').

[13]   See Franz Kafka, 'In the Penal Colony' in Franz Kafka, *The Metamorphosis and Other Stories*, translated by Donna Freed (New York, Barnes & Noble, 1996); Franz Kafka, *The Trial* (New York, Schocken Books, Inc, 1935).

[14]   Kafka, *The Trial*, above, n 13.

in detentions, proceedings, charges and evidence, and in a world in which 'special' tribunals, such as the US Military Commissions, have been created, or advocated, solely to address the allegedly pervasive threat of terrorism, the comparison to Kafka's world has a certain intuitive appeal. It is, however, quite a surface comparison, and neither Kafka's world nor the post-9/11 world is so easily and obviously explained.

The Parable is a smaller part of this work, which is a story told to K in *The Trial* and may be more useful to demonstrate how a meaning may seem straightforward in the first instance, but may actually be amenable to a wide range of different interpretations. On some level, it raises insights as to the meaning of law, which can be extrapolated to the more practical realm that is the focus of this book.[15] Indeed, it seems that post-9/11 detention discourse was often Kafkaesque, not just in presenting elements of the arbitrary and even sometimes of the absurd, but also in the way it was structured to suggest that more established scenarios were sometimes not an option.

The Parable is short and, as such, will be reproduced in its entirety here, as the following discussion refers to the text:

> **BEFORE THE LAW** stands a doorkeeper. To this doorkeeper there comes a man from the country and prays for admittance to the Law. But the doorkeeper says that he cannot grant admittance at the moment. The man thinks it over and then asks if he will be allowed in later. 'It is possible', says the doorkeeper, 'but not at the moment.' Since the gate stands open, as usual, and the doorkeeper steps to one side, the man stoops to peer through the gateway into the interior. Observing that, the doorkeeper laughs and says: 'If you are so drawn to it, just try to go in despite my veto. But take note: I am powerful. And I am only the least of the doorkeepers. From hall to hall there is one doorkeeper after another, each more powerful than the last. The third doorkeeper is already so terrible that even I cannot bear to look at him.' These are difficulties the man from the country has not expected; the Law, he thinks, should surely be accessible at all times and to everyone, but as he now takes a closer look at the doorkeeper in his fur coat, with his big sharp nose and long, thin, black Tartar beard, he decides that it is better to wait until he gets permission to enter. The doorkeeper gives him a stool and lets him sit down at one side of the door. There he sits for days and years. He makes many attempts to be admitted, and wearies the doorkeeper by his importunity. The doorkeeper frequently has little interviews with him, asking him questions about his home and many other things, but the questions are put indifferently, as great lords put them, and always finish with the statement that he cannot be let in yet. The man, who has furnished himself with many things for his journey, sacrifices all he has, however valuable, to bribe the doorkeeper. The doorkeeper accepts everything, but always with the remark: 'I am only taking it to keep you from thinking you have omitted anything.' During these many years the man fixes his attention almost continuously on the doorkeeper. He forgets the other doorkeepers, and this first one seems to him the sole obstacle preventing access to the Law. He curses his

---

[15] See Robin West, *Narrative, Authority and Law* (Michigan, University of Michigan Press, 1993) 84 (advocating reading various of Kafka's works for their 'tremendous and multiple insights into the nature of law').

bad luck, in his early years boldly and loudly; later, as he grows old, he only grumbles to himself. He becomes childish, and since in his yearlong contemplation of the doorkeeper he has come to know even the fleas in his fur collar, he begs the fleas as well to help him and to change the doorkeeper's mind. At length his eyesight begins to fail, and he does not know whether the world is really darker or whether his eyes are only deceiving him. Yet in his darkness he is now aware of a radiance that streams inextinguishably from the gateway of the Law. Now he has not very long to live. Before he dies, all his experiences in these long years gather themselves in his head to one point, a question he has not yet asked the doorkeeper. He waves him nearer, since he can no longer raise his stiffening body. The doorkeeper has to bend low toward him, for the difference in height between them has altered much to the man's disadvantage. 'What do you want to know now?' asks the doorkeeper; 'you are insatiable.' 'Everyone strives to reach the Law', says the man, 'so how does it happen that for all these many years no one but myself has ever begged for admittance?' The doorkeeper recognizes that the man has reached his end, and, to let his failing senses catch the words, roars in his ear: 'No one else could ever be admitted here, since this gate was made only for you. I am now going to shut it.'[16]

A. Kafka's Parable and 'The Law'

On a first reading, Kafka's Parable suggests, by its own words, that a man has faced some puzzling obstacles in attempting to access the law. However, this seemingly straightforward story has been the subject of considerable debate over what it really means. Kafka himself added to this lack of precision in the way in which his character, the Priest, explains the story in *The Trial*.[17] The Priest recounts, and then explains, the Parable to K. His interpretation suggests that the man must accept what he is told about the law, because it is the law, and it exists as a framework to permissible conduct.[18] The legality, or even fundamental justice, of the situation is found solely in the fact that the legal structures and procedures have been followed to the letter, even if these structures and procedures are completely incomprehensible.

However, one might spin the kaleidoscope to present an entirely different view of this same story. A less narrow view might be, for instance, inspired by Kahn's *The Cultural Study of Law*.[19] Kahn critiques the tendency of legal scholarship to view the law within the narrow and internal ambit of law reform, an approach that suggests that there are certain fundamental structural elements within which any conception, or study, of the law must operate.[20] In critiquing this approach, Kahn

---

[16] Kafka, *The Trial*, above, n 13, 213–15. This Parable is sometimes published as a separate entity called 'Before the Law'. See Jacques Derrida, 'Before the Law' in Jacques Derrida, *Acts of Literature* (New York, Routledge, 1992) 181 (the wording varies somewhat in different translations).

[17] Kafka, *The Trial*, above, n 13.

[18] For an exposition of positivist and other views of the law, see Ronald Dworkin, *Law's Empire* (London, Collins, 1986).

[19] Paul W Kahn, *The Cultural Study of Law: Reconstructing Legal Scholarship* (Chicago, University of Chicago Press, 1999).

[20] ibid.

talks about some of the flaws in the perceived structure, as well as in the nature of the discourse that gives rise to this form of scholarship:

> By taking up the project of legal reform, however, the scholar becomes a participant in legal practice and, therefore, a part of the very object that he or she set out to investigate. This collapse of the distinction between the subject studying the law and the legal practice that is the object of study is the central weakness of contemporary legal scholarship ... the legal scholar comes to the study of law already understanding herself as a citizen in law's republic. She is committed to 'making law work', to improving the legal system of which she is a part. Collapse refers to the failure of an analytic possibility, not some sort of transitional experience.[21]

Kahn's approach suggests that, by stepping outside of the law as constructed by normative standards and not perceiving it from the view of an inside participant, one can truly assess its nature. What, then, would happen if one were to view Kafka's Parable outside of the dominant public and political discourse of legal instruments? Spinning the kaleidoscope, and allowing for different perspectives outside of the normative framework, reveals more than one viable scenario as to what the Parable means. One possibility is that Kafka is presenting the story of an arbitrary denial of access to justice, presented as denial of access to 'the Law'. Viewed through this lens, the ending is significant, when the man asks the Doorkeeper why nobody else has sought access while he waited, and the Doorkeeper explains that this door exists only for him, that this denial of access applies only to him and thus suggests, perhaps, that the road to the law is different for him than it is for everybody else. Viewing this story through a cultural lens rather than through a strict structural lens, one might argue that it is not dispositive to look to what the existing legal structures require, because the structures themselves are flawed in their foundation and must be set aside for a higher conception of law, or at least for a different understanding of the nature of the law. If the Parable is perceived as relating to access to justice, one might thus argue that the arbitrary denial of access for this man is an obvious violation of the Rule of Law.[22]

Lord Thomas Bingham wrote, in his formulation of the elements of the Rule of Law, that: 'The law must be accessible and so far as possible intelligible, clear and predictable.'[23] Denying the man from the country access to the law for unexplained reasons, with no recourse and through a set of standards to be applied only to him raises questions in relation to legitimacy under a conception of the Rule of Law, regardless of whether the process of doing so conforms to technical normative standards. On the other hand, there is the possibility that everybody has an individual door leading to the Law and that the scenario of the man from the country is thus not arbitrary, but shares commonalities to what others

---

[21] ibid 7.

[22] For one articulation of the parameters of the Rule of Law, see Tom Bingham, *The Rule of Law* (London, Penguin Group, 2010) 37 (among other things, Lord Bingham writes, the Rule of Law demands equal access to justice).

[23] ibid.

seeking the law face. There is not enough information in the Parable to know, but the possibility seems open.

Others may, however, spin the kaleidoscope yet again, to formulate an entirely different picture based on these same facts. An equally possible interpretation to the one above is that the man is somewhat of a fool, passively believing what he is told about this being the only path to the law, and sitting there, without protest, without researching his options and without challenging what he is told until he dies. Rather than being unjustly barred from access to the law, the man has essentially imprisoned himself and is thus to blame for his own predicament. This view of the story presents an entirely different picture in terms of Kafka's representation of the meaning of the law and suggests, not that the government has done something wrong in arbitrarily denying him access to justice, but that, instead, the man has foolishly wasted his life and has failed to avail himself of alternative, and potentially available, means of access simply because he has failed to consider possibilities outside of the four corners of the normative standards with which he has been presented. This interpretation is supported by the description of the man, over the years, focusing his full attention on this Doorkeeper and this door, and forgetting about all the other Doorkeepers and all the other doors. Then again, this fact could symbolise the way that assumptions lead to the view that only one narrative is possible and equally viable, while competing narratives become marginalised and ultimately forgotten. Recalibrating the lens and applying a cultural study of law would raise some concerns about the legitimacy of the framework itself and would not provide passive compliance as the only viable option, or even as an acceptable option.

The nature of the characters in the Parable can change, under this cultural view, and depending on the factual perspective from which the assessment starts. Even reading the exact same words set forth in this short Parable, readers' different values and subjective views can cause the meaning to shift. If, for instance, one assumes that the man is powerless before the stronger law and that he is an innocent seeking redress, then the facts to follow are viewed through this lens and the picture presented is that of a tragic, unjust, unacceptable outcome. If, however, one were to reverse the roles, to blame the man for his misfortune and to present the Doorkeeper as the long-suffering, patient character, as Kafka himself does, through the priest telling the Parable, the scene shifts and empathy with the characters shifts as well.

Kafka includes, in his unfinished novel, a conversation that discusses what the story might mean, and which undertakes this shift in the characters, to paint the Doorkeeper as the one deserving of sympathy.[24] The priest who tells the story defends the Doorkeeper by explaining that he is only following his duty and that it is not up to the Doorkeeper to question the process. The priest explains:

> The patience with which [the Doorkeeper] endures the man's appeals during so many years, the brief conversations, the acceptance of the gifts, the politeness with which

---

[24] See Kafka, *The Trial*, above, n 13.

he allows the man to curse loudly in his presence the fate for which he himself is responsible—all this lets us deduce certain feelings of pity.[25]

Thus, the priest assumes that the man from the country is himself responsible for his own situation. Is that responsibility a function of the man's insistence on believing he must wait outside the door or is it something larger, such as a presumption that the man is guilty of something that means he deserves to sit indefinitely outside the door, with no right of access? Indeed, if it is vindication in a criminal proceeding that the man from the country seeks, the presumption should, under traditional principles, be one of innocence, not of guilt, as the priest's comments seem to imply.

K laments that under the priest's perspective of the story, all that the Doorkeeper says must simply be accepted—a rather positivistic view—but the priest disagrees, saying 'it is not necessary to accept everything as true, one must only accept it as necessary'.[26] Thus, the image shifts and the man becomes the antagonistic character, with the Doorkeeper as the noble guardian of the law, willing to adhere to this important task through years of tribulation and harassment from this problematic man. This latter interpretation can be further bolstered by another shift in the perception of the man as an outside, even aggressive intruder, seeking to break down the very structures protecting the proverbial 'Law' and stopped only by the great dedication of the Doorkeeper. The same facts can be seen quite differently, not just based on the lens through which they are viewed, but also based on the starting presumptions of the person looking through the lens.

There are other potential interpretations as well, such as the larger possibility that there is, in fact, no law at all. Rather, it might just be that one person, the Doorkeeper, is simply stronger than the other and able to impose his will accordingly.[27] Or, alternatively, the man is wrong in assuming there is law and that he has some entitlement to it, continuing to annoy the patient Doorkeeper for years based on this assumption. Much of the ambiguity about the nature of law may well reflect Kafka's larger sense that the law is not as clear as one might believe:

> Our laws are not generally known; they are kept secret by the small group of nobles who rule us. We are convinced that these ancient laws are scrupulously administered; nevertheless it is an extremely painful thing to be ruled by laws that one does not know ... The very existence of these laws, however, is at most a matter of presumption ... There is a small party who are actually of this opinion and who try to show that, if any law exists, it can only be this: The Law is whatever the nobles do.[28]

The Parable arguably shares many factual characteristics with the post-9/11 detention story, with arguments on one side of arbitrary denial of access to justice, and

---

[25] ibid 217.
[26] ibid 219–20.
[27] Compare Franz Kafka, 'The Problem of Our Laws' in Nahun N Glatzer (ed), *Franz Kafka: The Complete Stories and Parables* (Berlin, Schocken Verlag 1971) 437–38.
[28] ibid.

arguments on another side of necessity and of a proverbial Doorkeeper standing as the sole guardian of law and order, of 'freedom' and even of fundamental safety against an outside intruder.[29] If adjusting the lens to view the same component parts can so significantly change the view of a story as seemingly simple as Kafka's Parable, it seems inescapable that the much larger and more complex story of post-9/11 rhetoric and legal changes can also be deconstructed, viewed through a new lens and thus seen in many different lights.

Jacques Derrida was one of many scholars to discuss the possible meaning of Kafka's Parable. Derrida suggests a range of lenses through which the parable might be viewed, such as the idea that the word 'Before' in the title of 'Before the Law' may mean more than one thing. It may have a procedural aspect, as in being brought before a judge or other judicial body. Alternatively, it could be temporal rather than spatial and refer to a circumstance that occurred before the law came into being, an assumption, if accepted, that would add an additional dimension to the various potential interpretations provided above.[30] Derrida gives the passage an existential spin, suggesting that the door is only there for the man, because each must reach an end via an individual path.[31] He notes that the man from the country believes 'the law ... should be accessible at all times and to everyone. It should be universal'.[32] Derrida speculates about the factors that might make the law inaccessible, such as illiteracy, thus adding additional potential nuance to the story's meaning.[33] He also speculates about the type of 'law' intended in Kafka's parable, such as whether it is moral law, natural law or some other type.[34]

B. Kafka, the Law and Anti-terrorism

Given the way that anti-terrorism detention measures developed in several liberal democracies after 9/11, this sort of reconfiguring of the kaleidoscope lens can also significantly change the overall picture presented. If one starts with the 'us against them' notion and with the clear and unequivocal 'good versus evil' rhetoric quickly espoused in particular by the US government after the attacks, the picture takes on an absolute and irrefutable perspective, in which nothing must be held back to fight a great evil and in which asserted necessity becomes paramount, with all opposition to these initiatives deemed to be obstacles to this necessity. Safety becomes supreme, and stark images, such as that publicly espoused by then-US

---

[29] See, eg, President George W Bush, 'Address to a Joint Session of Congress and the American People' *The White House* (20 September 2001) georgewbush-whitehouse.archives.gov/news/releases/2001/09/20010920-8.html.

[30] Jacques Derrida, 'Before the Law' in Jacques Derrida, *Acts of Literature* (New York, Routledge, 1992).

[31] ibid.

[32] ibid 196–97.

[33] Derrida, above, n 30, 197.

[34] ibid 192.

Secretary of State Condoleezza Rice, of a mushroom cloud, presumably over an American city, are enough in their own right to justify any action, often on the barest assertions of necessity. Disagreement with the measures taken are seen through an equally stark lens, either as misguided or even as an assertion in favour of the terrorists themselves.[35] Much of this discourse, which began in the political arena, worked its way into normative legal developments.

Many of these discourse strategies could arguably be encompassed under the relatively newly articulated concept of 'lawfare', which is a term gaining increasing use to describe 'using—or misusing—law as a substitute for traditional military means to achieve an operational objective'.[36] It is increasingly obvious that the legalities of various measures are argued in the public forum and that persuasive techniques through political discourse are used to bolster assertions relating to various legalities. Presented with this starting point as a foundation for building detention and interrogation structures, it is not surprising that many of these structures arguably represented a significant shift from pre-existing norms.

If, however, one begins with a more nuanced perspective, not just relating to the nature of the cast of characters, but also to the necessity and cost of various responses, the focus can be adjusted and the picture may change. If the actual threat is more closely examined to define its parameters, if the nature of the 'enemy' is identified with more precision, and if the actual links between proposed responses and the threat are more clearly articulated, it is entirely possible that a new, viable picture of appropriate parameters for terrorism detentions could emerge. This is not to say that turning the kaleidoscope will reveal an absolute truth, or a truth at all, but it may reveal that the current picture is, itself, not an absolute and unequivocal truth. Turning the kaleidoscope should, at the very least, present another viable perspective from a reconstruction of the same parts and, at the very least, serve to help provide a more complete picture than that which currently exists. Therefore, in order to assess the measures implemented particularly since 9/11, it appears that a useful undertaking would be to deconstruct the rhetoric and legal structures that were so quickly espoused after the attacks, to apply a more broad, cultural perspective to the threat and to the responses implemented, and to then turn the kaleidoscope to see what emerges.[37] An underlying premise herein is that before national jurisdictions can move forward in addressing the threat of terrorism, they must go back to examine the structures that were often so

---

[35] CNN Transcripts, 'Interview with Condoleezza Rice; Pataki Talks about 9-11; Graham, Shelby Discuss War on Terrorism' *CNN* (8 September 2002) transcripts.cnn.com/TRANSCRIPTS/0209/08/le.00.html (quoting Condoleezza Rice as saying: 'The problem here is that there will always be some uncertainty about how quickly he can acquire nuclear weapons. But we don't what [*sic*] the smoking gun to be a mushroom cloud'); see also Piotr Cap, *Legitimisation in Political Discourse: A Cross-disciplinary Perspective on the Modern US War Rhetoric* (Newcastle, Cambridge Scholars Press, 2006).

[36] Michael P Scharf and Shannon Pagano, 'Foreword: Lawfare!' (2010) 43 *Case Western Reserve Journal of International Law* 1 (quoting Charles J Dunlap, Jr , 'Lawfare Today: A Perspective' (2008) 3 *Yale Journal of International Affairs* 146).

[37] Drawing again on the approach of the cultural study of law as laid out in Kahn, above, n 19.

hastily assembled after 9/11 in order to attempt to ensure that future initiatives are built on a solid foundation. Going back is thus critical to moving forward.

Kafka's simple Parable thus serves as a sort of capsule example for this book, with some dominant themes. The first is the notion that the man, presented as an everyman, is steadfast in his belief that the law is universal and available to all, but that he learns, too late, through the final statement of the Doorkeeper that this may not be true and that the law can, in fact, be arbitrary and unpredictable, and really only accessible to some. This discovery calls into question the meaning of law itself. The second theme is the idea of unquestioning acceptance of normative standards of the law or, alternatively, quick acceptance of the justifications underlying these normative standards, even where the standards appear inconsistent with other ideals that themselves are generally included within the meaning of the 'law'. If law is a dynamic, interactive entity rather than simply a set of written, normative instructions, one must deconstruct paradigms that have been implemented to consider alternative narratives. This is especially so in the case of post-9/11 detention practices, in which there have been questions raised as to how these changes may have infringed on constitutional protections. If reconfiguring the kaleidoscope presents a viable image that does not carry such a contention of constitutional violation, identifying that alternative scenario is certainly worthwhile. Breaking down the elements that were built into these detention paradigms is thus a first step towards determining whether the kaleidoscope can be turned at all.

What if, as presented in the Parable and in Kafka's larger story, *The Trial*, the uniformity of judicial process were to vanish, and consistency in procedure and rules were replaced by arbitrary, incomprehensible rules that ultimately deny a party access to a judicial body to ever present a case or defend against an allegation? Moreover, what if, in denying that access, no viable alternative is presented? Finally, what if this shift towards the arbitrary is accompanied by the suggestion that the changes must be accepted without question or if the only justification is a generalised, unsubstantiated statement of necessity? Does such a shift change the underlying structure of what is understood to be the law?

Access to the law, if the law is seen as some form of justice, is expected to be non-discriminatory, predictable and a means to an end.[38] When this process is subverted, made available only to some or infused with arbitrary rules that destroy a sense of predictability, the implications can be significant, and not simply confined to the particular cases directly affected by this shift. In Kafka's Parable, the man seeks access to the law through what he believes to be the only possible route, but through a route he cannot understand, which is arbitrary, seems to him to single him out for disparate treatment and serves as a roadblock rather than a means of achieving justice. What Kafka's story lacks under this interpretation is a

---

[38] See Bingham, above, n 22; AV Dicey, *An Introduction to the Study of the Law of the Constitution*, 5th edn (London, Macmillan, 1897).

sense of reasoning as to why such a subversion might be permissible. Absent the priest's bare assertion of 'necessity', as he tells the story to K, no further reason is presented, and one must speculate as to whether an appropriate reason would lend a different perspective to the plight of the man from the country. The outcome of the story, if it does represent a denial of access to justice, is not limited to the man himself, but has an impact on everybody who expects to be protected under the larger umbrella of the Rule of Law, as what happened to him, if permissible, could arguably happen to anybody. Indeed, although the reader knows this door is just for this man, it is entirely possible that similarly inaccessible doors already exist for everybody else as well.

Thus, *The Trial*, in relation to the novel itself, can serve as a metaphor for post-9/11 detention practices, as a simple, stark story that serves as a cautionary tale for the way that some argue liberal democracies are heading with their anti-terrorism detention measures. Rather than focusing on the larger story, this book uses the Parable in its metaphorical sense to demonstrate that there are differing, and often marginalised, views that might better characterise possible post-9/11 approaches to detention practices. However, in order to truly make the comparison between the Parable and post-9/11 detention practices, one must question the meaning of the Parable in order to deconstruct its elements and to see how viewing it from different angles changes its meaning. The same methodology could be followed to assess post-9/11 changes, so it appears that Kafka's tale might demonstrate a comparative element that goes beyond the elements of the story itself.

IV. 'Deconstructing' Anti-terrorism Detention Discourse

As a preliminary matter, the terms 'anti-terrorism' and 'counter-terrorism' are often used interchangeably, and they are used differently in different countries. In the US, the Department of Defense has adopted definitions in which 'anti-terrorism' refers to defensive measures, while 'counter-terrorism' refers to assertive, proactive steps to prevent terrorism.[39] For the purpose of this work, for the sake of consistency, those definitions will be adopted, and most of the measures described here would be deemed anti-terrorism measures.

As discussed earlier, the detention regimes that national jurisdictions used after 9/11 were largely initially structured in an environment of crisis, with a perception of an imminent and horrific threat. These initial steps, while often altered, in many ways served as building blocks for future developments in terrorism detention practices. However, it does not appear that a departure of the sense of

---

[39] US Department of Defense, *DOD Dictionary of Military and Associated Terms*, *Department of Defense*, www.dtic.mil/doctrine/new_pubs/dictionary.pdf (using a different spelling norm, of 'antiterrorism' and 'counterterrorism'.),17, 57.

imminent crisis led to a full deconstruction, or adequate challenging, of the initial presumptions on which the detention structures were established. An overwhelming amount of scholarship has been produced since 9/11, with debates over the appropriate paradigm to follow in enunciating proper detention standards. Yet, a question arises as to whether the issue is best addressed by selecting from among those existing paradigms or whether the premises on which the paradigms themselves were built should be challenged in order to suggest an approach to fighting terrorism.

Deconstruction is a term of art, often attributed to Jacques Derrida, and the term is used in this book in a similar, but not identical, sense, as Derrida himself has indicated that there is much misunderstanding about his notion of deconstruction and that it is a technique that does not necessarily apply universally.[40] The intention herein is not to break down existing terrorism detention structures in a pejorative or partisan manner, but to examine the process by which the current structures were built and to address many of the tensions in the discourse surrounding them, such as the constant tension that seems to exist between those advocating for such regimes and those arguing that they represent an impermissible incursion into traditional and fundamental constitutional norms relating to individual rights. Although Derrida himself suggests that deconstruction does not necessarily have universal application, his deconstruction approach has been posited as an important methodology for approaching the analysis of legal norms for several reasons:

> First, deconstruction provides a method for critiquing existing legal doctrines; in particular a deconstructive reading can show how arguments offered to support a particular rule undermine themselves, and instead, support an opposite rule. Second, deconstructive techniques can show how doctrinal arguments are informed by and disguise ideological thinking. This can be of value not only to the lawyer who seeks to reform existing institutions, but also to the legal philosopher and the legal historian. Third, deconstructive techniques offer both a new kind of interpretive strategy and a critique of conventional interpretations of legal texts.[41]

Derrida and other philosophers have used a form of deconstruction to address the phenomenon of terrorism itself.[42] However, such deconstruction has not been specifically applied to post-9/11 detention practices and, as it is a useful practice for understanding terrorism, it is also a methodology that leads to a better understanding of the nature of post-9/11 detention practices. Similarly, the notion of

---

[40] See generally Peter Goodrich et al (eds), *Derrida and Legal Philosophy* (Basingstoke, Palgrave Macmillan, 2008); Jacques Derrida, *Of Grammatology*, translated by Gayatri Chakravorty Spivak (Baltimore, Johns Hopkins University Press, 1998); compare Perelman and Olbrechts-Tyteca, above, n 1.

[41] JM Balkin, 'Deconstructive Practice and Legal Theory' (1987) 96 *Yale Law Journal* 743, 744.

[42] See Eveline T Feteris, *Fundamentals of Legal Argumentation: A Survey of Theories on the Justification of Judicial Decisions* (Dordrecht, Kluwer Academic Publishers, 1999) 22–24 (explaining the various authors for and approaches to deconstructing and reconstructing argumentation through different lenses).

reconstruction has also been applied to the phenomenon of terrorism, but not specifically to the shifts in detention paradigms since 9/11. The methodology of first deconstructing and then reconstructing the steps followed in building post-9/11 detention practices is similar to that applied within this book, drawing in part on the approaches taken on similar issues by scholars like Derrida and Jürgen.[43]

As new approaches to terrorism detention and process were carved out in the days after 9/11, much of the early, crisis-laden discourse served as building blocks to anti-terrorism initiatives. As time passed, these structures gained an aura of familiarity, and debates over the threshold presumptions faded within much of the academic literature, as well as on the political front. The deconstruction espoused herein aims to return to that starting point to consider some of the underlying premises—both implicit and explicit—that led the argument and the legal normative changes to its present form.

This analysis is also aided, again, by aspects of Kahn's cultural study of law, in which norms are not examined within the framework they create, but rather are viewed through a new lens outside of those frameworks in order to yield new perceptions. Kahn describes the relationship between genealogy and architecture in assessing law. He notes: 'Architecture is bound by genealogy—we cannot make something out of nothing.'[44] As Kahn suggested in his approach:

> I have described the current state of legal studies and proposed a new object for a discipline of law: not legal rules, but the imagination as it constructs a world of legal meaning. I have argued that this discipline must combine a genealogical and an architectural approach. Genealogy traces the history of the central concepts of a legal order; architecture looks at the structure of those concepts and their relationships to each other. Together they take up the problem of the 'historical a priori', in its double aspect of contingency and necessity—i.e., the historically contingent, conceptual conditions of our experience of law's rule.[45]

In order to effectively assess the legitimacy of current anti-terrorism standards and certainly in order to speculate as to viable future developments, it is necessary to break down the existing structures into some of their constituent elements, to look at the architectural process that was used to build them, and to assess the validity and soundness of those structures through this methodology. The present and the future cannot be effectively assessed without a breakdown of what has happened in the past.

These initial post-9/11 debates remain relevant for various reasons. First, the detention-related responses since 9/11 have not had the characteristics of temporary, emergency measures, but rather have, in certain cases, gained indicia of

---

[43] See, eg, Giovanna Borradori, *Philosophy in a Time of Terror: Dialogues with Jürgen Habermas and Jacques Derrida* (Chicago, University of Chicago Press, 2003); see also WJT Mitchell, 'Picturing Terror: Derrida's Autoimmunity' (1987) 33(2) *Critical Inquiry* 277.

[44] Kahn, above, n 19, 43; see also Michel Foucault, *Archaeology of Knowledge*, translated by AMS Smith (London, Tavistock Publications Ltd, 1972).

[45] Kahn, above, n 19, 91.

permanence, thus making the underlying points of departure on which they were built of continuing relevance. Second, terrorism is very much an ongoing threat, as so many recent attacks around the world have painfully reiterated. Third, this area remains one involving considerable controversy, and national jurisdictions continue to espouse new and controversial approaches to terrorism detentions, often based on past practice and past presumptions. Deconstructing the post-9/11 discourse and the presumptions on which many of the present and ongoing structures have been, at least in part, built could provide a more effective framework for any future practices.

The impact of the 9/11 attacks was arguably, and understandably, the most profound in the US. Discourse emanating from that time suggested a sense of reinforcement of US identity as being associated with 'freedom', but the actions undertaken in its War on Terror suggested a certain fracturing of that narrative, even in relation to American identity.[46] The 9/11 attacks were, on some level, a defining moment for the US, but it appears that they left a conflict between the self-perception of those in the US and the actuality that arose from post-9/11 terrorism detentions, as asserted support for defending freedom accompanied an increased willingness to deprive certain people of individual liberty without the protection of constitutional safeguards afforded to others.[47]

V. Deconstructing and Reconstructing the Post-9/11 Discourse Using Argumentation Theory

While this book focuses on the past status of terrorism discourse, it does so because the presumptions of the past continue into the future. Discourse analysis relating to terrorism can 'demonstrate the linguistic and discursive means through which the future is claimed and appropriated by dominant groups and institutions'.[48]

Once it has been determined that post-9/11 discourse can be deconstructed, the question remains as to how best to do it. What elements of that narrative should be assessed, broken down and re-examined? Argumentation theory, a field loosely described as an interdisciplinary approach in which elements of logic can be studied to determine the validity of conclusions, among other things, provides a useful

---

[46] See generally Joseph Margulies, *What Changed When Everything Changed? 9/11 and the Making of National Identity* (New Haven, Yale University Press, 2013) 5–6 (disputing the assumed nature of such changes).

[47] Examples abound and many are discussed throughout this book. For a Canadian example, see Maureen T Duffy and René Provost, 'Constitutional Canaries: The Elusive Quest to Legitimize Security Certificates in Canada' (2009) 40 *Case Western Journal of International Law* 531 (critiquing the Canadian approach to security certificates, which use the immigration system to detain some non-citizens suspected of terrorism involvement).

[48] Patricia L Dunmire, '"Emerging Threats" and "Coming Dangers"' in Adam Hodges and Chad Nilep, *Discourse, War and Terrorism* (Amsterdam, Hodges, 2007) 19.

lens through which to view deconstructed elements of the post-9/11 narrative.[49] This large, and ambitious, way of approaching this issue is, with some exceptions, narrowed in this work to an examination of particular post-9/11 American rhetoric, examining the factors that went into attempted and successful persuasion in political speech.

While terrorism is not a new phenomenon, and it was certainly not new on 9/11, it appears that a distinctive form of argument structure and a somewhat novel form of discourse developed after the 9/11 attacks to persuade members of the public, and of the national legislative branches and the judiciary, that a new type of danger was looming, which justified unprecedented governmental action.[50] This scenario is useful to study because it happened in a relatively compact period of time, driven by some unusual circumstances, and it resulted in swift changes in certain terrorism detention practices, again in a relatively compact amount of time.

After the attacks, Derrida argued in favour of the deconstruction of the concept of terrorism, with one author characterising his argument as the

> only politically responsible course of action because the public use of it, as if it were a self-evident notion, perversely helps the terrorist cause. Such deconstruction consists, as if it were a self-evident notion, in showing that the sets of distinctions within which we understand the meaning of the term *terrorism* are problem-ridden. In [Derrida's] mind not only does war entail the intimidation of civilians, and thus elements of terrorism, but no rigorous separation can be drawn between different kinds of terrorism, such as national and international, local and global.[51]

The post-9/11 terrorism rhetoric, which was arguably fuelled by a political discourse disseminated by a cooperative media, was used to advance a number of presumptions, on which new detention and interrogation standards were built, and the specific language often implied that the underlying presumptions were truths that had already been established rather than simply assumed.[52] Derrida expressed surprise at what he perceived to be a certain naïve willingness on the part of the media to exploit the trauma of 9/11 to feed the notions of what may occur in the future.[53]

Where that much controversy swirled around the very meaning of even basic concepts on which detention structures were built, it is reasonable to assume that such questions remain, unless they were definitively resolved before the measures based on them were implemented. The anti-terrorism detention initiatives undertaken in a number of countries, and particularly, for the purpose of this work, since 9/11, drew on the way in which discourse was presented and perceived, especially

---

[49] See, eg, Perelman and Lucie Olbrechts-Tyteca, above, n 1.

[50] A more detailed discussion of this phenomenon is presented in ch 4; see also Cap, above, n 35 (describing the threat-based discourse used after 9/11 and its use in seeking support for various governmental actions); Borradori, above, n 43.

[51] Borradori, above, n 43, xiii.

[52] ibid.

[53] ibid.

in the early days after the attacks.[54] Public discourse often contained stark binaries, with either/or presentations of the issues—examples include the idea that those opposing anti-terrorism measures must support terrorists, that liberty must give way to security in all instances and that terrorism was either a crime or a war.[55] If nuances to these extreme positions arose, they often still retained the either/or characterisation, with, for example, the idea of finding a proper 'balance' between freedom and security fitting within the limiting parameters of this box.[56] While this position has some degree of nuance and is one that is challenged later in this book, it still has a certain starkness to it in the assumption that civil liberties must give way to security in order to achieve balance.

It is self-evident that states have some degree of responsibility in trying to prevent terrorist attacks, and it is this general notion of state responsibility that has often been invoked to argue that certain approaches must be taken to combat terrorism.[57] At the same time, various legal theories, international instruments and national constitutions establish a degree of state responsibility towards individuals in terms of fundamental notions of fair judicial process. It is the perceived conflict between these two general principles that has given rise to much of the distinctive discourse in the anti-terrorism detention context, certainly since 9/11 and, on some levels and in some places, before 9/11. The narrative is often presented in unequivocal terms, with little room for nuance, or is often based on certain premises that have never really been seriously questioned.[58] For instance, Robert Jackson notes:

> As a term of elite and popular discourse, terrorism has come to possess clearly observable ideographic qualities. That is, like 'freedom', 'democracy' and 'justice', 'terrorism' now

---

[54] See, eg, Michael E Tigar, *Thinking about Terrorism: The Threat to Civil Liberties in Times of National Emergency* (Chicago, American Bar Association, 2007).

[55] A detailed discussion of the use of binaries in anti-terrorism discourse is presented in ch 6 below.

[56] See ch 6 below; see also Robert Chesney and Jack Goldsmith, 'Terrorism and the Convergence of Criminal and Military Detention Models' (2008) 60 *Stanford Law Review* 1079; Richard B Zabel and James J Benjamin, Jr , *In Pursuit of Justice: Prosecuting Terrorism Cases in the Federal Courts* (2008), *Human Rights First*,www.humanrightsfirst.org/wp-content/uploads/pdf/080521-USLS-pursuit-justice. pdf; Richard B Zabel and James J Benjamin, Jr, *In Pursuit of Justice: Prosecuting Terrorism Cases in the Federal Courts: 2009 Update and Recent Developments* (2009), *Human Rights First*, www.humanrightsfirst. org/wp-content/uploads/pdf/090723-LS-in-pursuit-justice-09-update.pdf (accepting to some extent the delineation of the crime-versus-war binary as a starting point, regardless of whether advocating for or against the dominance of the criminal-justice system); Government of the United Kingdom, *Counter-terrorism Strategy (CONTEST)* (12 July 2011) www.gov.uk/government/publications/counter-terrorism-strategy-contest, 50 (stating '[o]ur priority is always to prosecute people suspected of terrorist-related activity in this country').

[57] For a comprehensive discussion of the parameters of state responsibility in fighting terrorism, see Vincent-Joël Proulx, *Transnational Terrorism and State Accountability* (Oxford, Hart Publishing, 2012).

[58] As discussed in ch 4 below. See, eg, Sudha Setty, 'What's in a Name? How Nations Define Terrorism Ten Years after 9/11' (2011) 33 *University of Pennsylvania Journal of International Law* 1 (making it clear that even fundamental concepts like the meaning of terrorism are not well settled); see also Richard Jackson, 'Constructing Enemies: "Islamic Terrorism" in Political and Academic Discourse' (2007) 42(3) *Government and Opposition*, 394, 395.

functions as a primary term for the central narratives of the culture, employed in political debate and daily conversations, but largely unquestioned in its meaning and usage.[59]

The process by which changes were undertaken had, at its heart, not just the perceived facts of what happened and what constituted the threat, but also the values and political views of those presenting and receiving the narratives about it.

In approaching the post-9/11 terrorism detention structures through the lens of a cultural study of law, it helps to review, in some depth, the particular architecture of the arguments that underscored these structural changes. Altering long-standing fair-trial protections is a substantial undertaking and any justification offered for doing so should be carefully scrutinised. Breaking down the post-9/11 detention alterations into their component parts, and examining the discourse used and the methodology by which arguments to justify the changes were structured can provide a meaningful view into the viability of those changes.[60]

Looking at the validity of argumentation, of course, has a long history in the field of philosophy certainly, but also in the legal theory realm. The methodology employed in this book is influenced by some of Robert Alexy's *Theory of Legal Argumentation,* which, in turn, draws on the preceding, famous work of legal philosophers Chaim Perelman and Lucie Olbrechts-Tyteca, as originally established in their work *The New Rhetoric* and refined throughout the years.[61] Perelman and Olbrechts-Tyteca's work dates back many years, but has been used in building ideas in philosophy since they published *The New Rhetoric* and was important to the development of Alexy's work. One part of Alexy's work, in turn, has been described as: 'One of the most important books in the philosophy of law in the post-war period, essential reading for legal theorists.'[62] This chapter requires an explanation of these theories, or at least of the aspects of the theories that are utilised in this book. To lay out this theoretical approach is to demonstrate the many possible argumentation strategies that can be layered in painting a specific narrative. Each one of these strategies, as demonstrated in chapter one, can have a substantial impact on the public narrative. Combined, these tools wield great power.

Perelman and Olbrechts-Tyteca's work is distinguished from prior prominent works because they place a heavy significance on subjective values and particular audiences as tools in effective argumentation. Their experiences in Belgium under

---

[59] Jackson, above, n 58.

[60] See generally Robert Alexy, 'Discourse Theory and Fundamental Rights' in Augustín José Menéndez and Erik Oddvar Eriksen, *Arguing Fundamental Rights* (Dordrecht, Springer, 2006) 15 (noting that '[t]he relation between discourse theory and fundamental rights is close, deep, and complex').

[61] See generally George Pavlakos (ed), *Law, Rights and Discourse* (Oxford, Hart Publishing, 2007) (containing various essays exploring the theoretical works of Robert Alexy, including a chapter in which Alexy himself responds to each of the authors); Robert Alexy, *A Theory of Legal Argumentation: The Theory of Rational Discourse as Theory of Legal Justification* (Oxford, Oxford University Press, 1989); Perelman and Olbrechts-Tyteca, above, n 1.

[62] Lawrence B Solum, 'Legal Theory Bookworm *Legal Theory* (20 February 2010) lsolum.typepad. com/legaltheory/2010/02/legal-theory-bookworm-2.html; see also Matthias Klatt, 'Robert Alexy's Philosophy of Law as System' (14 June 2017) papers.ssrn.com/sol3/papers.cfm?abstract_id=2984327.

Nazi occupation proved formative in their later views.[63] Perelman, who was Jewish himself, founded an organisation that has been credited with saving thousands of Jewish people from murder by the Nazis.[64] Olbrechts-Tyteca was not Jewish, but has been honoured by Yad Vashem as one of 'The Righteous Among the Nations' for her work on behalf of Jewish people in danger, and she worked with an organisation founded by Perelman's wife, Fela.[65] In assessing rhetoric after his own personal experiences as a Jewish survivor of the Nazi occupation of Belgium, some have suggested that Perelman's infusion of notions of justice and values into the study of rhetoric was driven by the traumatic experience he suffered during the Holocaust.[66] In that sense, it seems appropriate to assess these ideas through the response to a later, quite different, traumatic event in the 9/11 attacks.

Before the publication of *The New Rhetoric*, approaches to the analysis of rhetoric and argumentation often focused on the elements of rhetoric to arrive at an objective truth. Perelman and Olbrechts-Tyteca's work, by contrast, melds many of these objective ideas with a strong thread of subjectivity, suggesting that there are subjective features to the use of argumentation, not to communicate truth, but to seek adherence to a particular point or belief.[67] The question, then, is not how people seek the truth, but how people convince others of a particular truth, regardless of whether it is actually an objective truth. In a work completed shortly before his death, Perelman explained that developments 'oblige … me to state precisely, in order to avoid all misunderstanding, that I understand by rhetoric—the theory and practice of persuasive communication'.[68]

Alexy's work looks to discourse as a descriptive notion of the nature of law. Law is, he has noted, properly viewed through the lens of argumentation or discourse, and it exists as 'predominantly a social practice, albeit one that has the structure of rational argumentation'. He connects law to other areas involving reasoning, such as morality and ethics, and posits that law shares a 'discursive structure' with those fields.[69] Thus, his theory negates a central point in the theoretical works on legal positivism, under which law is distinct from morality and ethics, and he characterises his work as a response to positivism.[70] His approach provides some support for the notion that the structural soundness of normative measures can,

---

[63] Alan G Gross and Ray D Dearin, *Chaim Perelman* (Carbondale, Southern Illinois University Press, 2002) 5–7.

[64] ibid 3.

[65] See Yad Vashem, 'The Righteous among Nations: Olbrechts FAMILY', *Yad Vashem*, db.yadvashem.org/righteous/family.html?language=en&itemId=4017965.

[66] See David A Frank, 'A Traumatic Reading of Twentieth-Century Rhetorical Theory: The Belgian Holocaust, Malines, Perelman, and de Man' (2007) 93(3) *Quarterly Journal of Speech* 308.

[67] Feteris, above, n 42 (compiling Perelman's ultimate theory from various works to draw conclusions as to his concluding approach).

[68] Chaim Perelman et al, 'Rhetoric and Politics' (1984) 17(3) *Philosophy & Rhetoric* 129.

[69] Pavlakos, above, n 61, 1.

[70] See Robert Alexy, *The Argument from Injustice: A Reply to Legal Positivism* (Oxford, Clarendon Press, 2002) 3–10; see also Robert Alexy, 'On Necessary Relations between Law and Morality' (1989) 2(2) *Ratio Juris* 167.

at least in part, be assessed by looking at the underlying argumentation structure that built it.

Alexy draws from various German and Anglo-Saxon legal theorists in building his idea of rational discourse in legal philosophy.[71] As a starting point, he describes a ruling of the first panel of the German Federal Constitutional Court from 1973, in which the Court wrote that all judicial rulings must be based on 'rational argumentation'. He posits, early in his work, that rationality can be 'extended to any situation in which lawyers engage in debate'. Beyond its interest to legal theorists, he suggests, rational argumentation is a practical requirement, for lawyers certainly, as well as for 'every citizen active in the public arena'.[72]

Alexy goes on to explain, then, that the validity of legal judgments cannot be fully determined by an assessment of logical factors alone. For example, one might have a case in which both parties have presented normative components and accepted factual premises needed to prevail, but discretion lies with the decision-maker, and this discretion cannot so easily be described through objective criteria.[73] However, even in the case of such value judgments, questions can be assessed as to the extent to which they can be explained through rational criteria, a process he refers to as the 'objectivization of value-judgments'.[74] He explains:

> Finding answers to these questions is of great theoretical and practical significance. At the very least, the scientific status of jurisprudence is dependent on the answers we give. In addition, our answers will have considerable bearing on the problem of the legitimacy of regulating social conflicts by judicial decisions.[75]

At the same time, Alexy acknowledges that consensus about major social issues, or at least a consensus sufficient to deal with the practical implications of those issues, is quite rare.[76] Still, a certain form of discourse can be identified that relates to the validity of legal outcomes. Empirical discourse relates to things like the frequency of certain forms of argument. Analytical discourse relates to the 'logical structure of actual or possible arguments'. Normative discourse relates to the validity of criteria for justifying legal determinations.[77] In assessing the rationality of legal discourse, Alexy looks to a number of scholars, including the argumentation theory of Perelman and Olbrechts-Tyteca, which will be expounded upon in the following sections.[78] Alexy considers portions of their rhetorical theory, which he describes as going back to the ideas of traditional argumentation expounded by people like Aristotle. He incorporates their work with approval of their ideas.[79]

---

[71] See generally ibid Alexy, *The Argument from Injustice*, above, n 70.
[72] ibid vii (quoting BVferGE (Decisions of the Federal Constitutional Court) 34,269 (287)).
[73] ibid 7.
[74] Alexy, *The Argument from Injustice*, above, n 70, 7–13.
[75] ibid 7.
[76] ibid 13.
[77] Alexy, *The Argument from Injustice*, above, n 70, 15.
[78] ibid 16.
[79] ibid 155–56.

A. Speaker as Audience: The Post-9/11 Audience was Especially Receptive to the Persuasion Used

Thus, a prominent factor in the theories of both Alexy and Perelman and Olbrechts-Tyteca has to do with a subjective element in argumentation—the receptiveness of the intended audience to the message given. For an argument to succeed, the audience must assent to the premises presented and it must also assent to each step of the proof presented to support the argument.[80] Perelman and Olbrechts-Tyteca's idea of the audience includes a notion under which discourse is used to 'condition' the audience.[81]

As noted earlier, the post-9/11 period, especially in the US, was unusual in that there was overwhelming popular and legislative support for extraordinary actions by the President to address those deemed responsible for the attacks. This is demonstrated in many ways, but one example is the *Authorization for Use of Military Force*, passed by the US Congress on 14 September 2001 and giving broad discretion to the President to take action against those who might have been involved in the attacks. The specific authorisation says:

> That the President is authorized to use all necessary and appropriate force against those nations, organizations, or persons he determines planned, authorized, committed, or aided the terrorist attacks that occurred on September 11, 2001, or harbored such organizations or persons, in order to prevent any future acts of international terrorism against the United States by such nations, organizations or persons.[82]

The unusually wide range of authority given, with extreme deference to the President, is unusual in an authorisation of such a magnitude, and this Authorization was used for years to justify a broad range of actions.[83] Perelman describes the type of situation in which persuasive techniques work especially well when in an atmosphere of no or muted opposition, citing to the example of a funeral eulogy, in which clearly nobody is going to contest the thesis set forth by the speaker.[84] This background atmosphere, tempered by pervasive fear and an unusual deficiency in countervailing arguments, set the stage for

---

[80] ibid 158.

[81] Perelman and Olbrechts-Tyteca, above, n 1, 160.

[82] *Authorization for Use of Military Force* (AUMF), Pub L 107–40, 115 Stat 224. In late June 2017, a House committee voted to approve the repeal of the AUMF. As of the writing of this book, the repeal is not law. See Jeremy Herb and Deirdre Walsh, 'House Panel Votes to Repeal War Authorization for Fight against ISIS and al Qaeda' *CNN* (29 June 2017) www.cnn.com/2017/06/29/politics/house-panel-repeal-war-authorization-isis-al-qaeda/index.html.

[83] See, eg, Matthew C Weed, *2001 Authorization for Use of Military Force: Issues Concerning its Continued Application* (14 April 2015) *Congressional Research Service*, fas.org/sgp/crs/natsec/R43983. pdf (explaining that the AUMF is not the sole authority for ongoing military action, but that the US government was continuing to rely on it for actions against Daesh, while simultaneously asking Congress for an updated authorisation).

[84] Perelman et al, above, n 68, 130.

arguments to succeed in the early days after 9/11 that might have failed in a different atmosphere.

A capsule example of the mood of the audience among the US population after 9/11 arose in the Dixie Chicks controversy about a year and a half later. Just before the US invaded Iraq, Natalie Maines, the lead singer of the Dixie Chicks, made the following comment during a concert: 'Just so you know, we're on the good side with y'all. We do not want this war, this violence, and we're ashamed that the President of the United States is from Texas.'[85] While there was no formal backlash from the government, a popular backlash was immediate and devastating, with radio stations refusing to play their songs and even leading to death threats and other harassment.[86] The passage of time lessened the controversy, and the Dixie Chicks later addressed the controversy in their music, especially in the song, 'Not Ready to Make Nice', released in 2006. Written by Maines, she said of the backlash:

> I made my bed, and I sleep like a baby
> With no regrets, and I don't mind saying
> It's a sad, sad story
> When a mother will teach her daughter
> That she ought to hate a perfect stranger
> And how in the world
> Can the words that I said
> Send somebody so over the edge
> That they'd write me a letter
> Saying that I better
> Shut up and sing
> Or my life will be over?[87]

There were, of course, protests against the 2003 invasion of Iraq, in the US and elsewhere, and that invasion ultimately altered the post-9/11 mood of the US. However, at the time of Maines' comments, before the invasion and to an audience of country music fans, such dissent caused an extreme backlash. The possible truth of what Maines said, even as just an expression of her opinion, was lost in what appeared to be a significant disconnect with the audience to whom the comments were delivered. It therefore had the opposite effect of persuasion, even if it was a message that would likely have been welcome to a different audience.

---

[85] 'Is Country Music Read to Forgive the Dixie Chicks?' *The Guardian* (19 November 2015) www.theguardian.com/music/2015/nov/19/the-dixie-chicks-tour-is-country-music-ready-to-forgive.

[86] Jeremy V Adolphson, '"Mad as Hell": Democratic Dissent and the Unpatriotic Backlash on the Dixie Chicks' (27 March 2014) 26(1) *Journal of Popular Music Studies* 47.

[87] The lyrics are reproduced in several places, including *Metrolyrics*: www.metrolyrics.com/not-ready-to-make-nice-lyrics-dixie-chicks.html.

In order to persuade, Perelman and Olbrechts-Tyteca suggest, the speaker must connect with the values of the particular audience to which the persuasion is directed. In a sense, the persuasive speaker becomes the audience, adapting the argument and values to those that will most likely persuade that specific audience.[88] There is a distinction between a 'universal audience', which adheres to logical conviction, and a 'particular audience', to whom the speaker directs the discourse and which is subject to the arts of persuasion.[89] In addressing a so-called 'universal audience', if such a thing truly exists, there is less need for persuasion or tailoring, and the argument is theoretically built solely on principles deemed to form the most logical progression of steps. For a 'particular audience', however, the adaptation of the argument, and of the speaker, must occur.[90] The idea of the 'universal audience' has been debated at length since the publication of *The New Rhetoric*, and especially the misconception that the 'universal audience' is the only one qualified to hear a truthful argument.[91] For this purpose, it is unnecessary to delve too deeply into that debate, since the relevant point here is the existence of the particular audience and its specific role in persuasion regarding terrorism detention after 9/11, and that part of Perelman and Olbrechts-Tyteca's work is less disputed. It is noted, though, that Perelman and Olbrechts-Tyteca did view the particular audience as one assembled by the speaker and, after 9/11, this was not necessarily so, since people were predisposed to hear particular messages by the events of the attacks.[92] For this purpose, the idea of the particular audience will still be used.

In the case of post-9/11 practices, as with perhaps many other modern incidents, those in the position of making and advancing decisions faced a difficult question in terms of audience. The attacks had a public element to them not only because of the terrible loss of life, but also because a significant portion of the attacks, including the horror of people jumping from the Twin Towers and the second plane strike, took place on live television.

Three years after the attacks, one author described it thus:

> Then came September 11, 2001, the millennial catastrophe—just a little late. Airplanes fell from the sky, thousands died and an entirely new kind of horror gripped the human imagination. Time, too, played its role, but time as warped by television, which created

---

[88] Perelman and Olbrechts-Tyteca, above, n 1, 19–26 (noting that this form of rhetoric depends on the particular nature of the audience for whom the argument is intended); see also Richard Long, 'The Role of Audience in Chaim Perelman's New Rhetoric' (1983) 4 *Journal of Advanced Composition* 107 (saying 'in a phenomenological sense, argumentation achieves meaning only when the audience registers in the speaker's consciousness and vice versa. Rather than merely analyze the audience, the rhetor becomes the audience. The two merge, become one, and the union results in action. In this respect, Perelman's new rhetoric transcends audience analysis').

[89] Long, above, n 88, 108–09.

[90] Perelman and Olbrechts-Tyteca, above, n 1, 160.

[91] See, eg, JE Sigler, 'The New Rhetoric's Concept of Universal Audience, Misconceived' (2015) 29(3) *Argumentation* 325.

[92] See ibid 329; see also Scott F Aikin, 'Perelmanian Universal Audience and the Epistemic Aspirations of Argument' (2008) 41(3) *Philosophy and Rhetoric* 238.

a global simultaneity, turning the whole human race into a witness, as the awful events were endlessly replayed, as if those bodies leaping from the Twin Towers would never hit the ground. Nightmare in broad daylight. New York's World Trade Center collapsed not just onto the surrounding streets but into the hearts of every person with access to CNN. Hundreds of millions of people instinctively reached out to those they loved, grateful to be alive. Death had shown itself in a new way. But if a vast throng experienced the terrible events of 9/11 as one, only one man, the President of the United States, bore a unique responsibility for finding a way to respond to them.[93]

Those watching became first-hand witnesses to the events of that day. Even if people did not see the attacks on live television or on countless replays, the unusual presence of two film-makers, Jules and Gédéon Naudet, created another level of witnesses. The Naudet brothers were making a documentary on a fire-fighter recruit and happened to be in the area when the attacks happened. They captured the events of the New York attacks, from beginning to end, including rare footage of the first plane hitting the North Tower and scenes from inside the World Trade Center as rescue personnel tried to contain their shock and work to save people. This documentary became the film *9/11* and provided a rare minute-by-minute view of events that otherwise would only be heard about after the fact on news reports.[94]

Particularly within the US, the days after 9/11 were therefore characterised by considerable grief, anger and fear of another attack. Rumours abounded as to other terrorist plots, people were given instructions for setting up contact networks in the event of another attack, and collective nerves were rattled by reports of ongoing anthrax attacks.[95]

Presenting a case to the public under these circumstances would present challenges in relation to the different educational levels and levels of understanding of the attacks and the responses thereto. At the same time, national leaders had to explain the attacks and appropriate responses to the other branches of government, and explanations given to elected legislative bodies might vary from those given to judicial bodies, something that was complicated by an atmosphere in which large percentages of the public continued to closely listen to those arguments. The post-9/11 discourse may have had some unique characteristics in terms of the high interest level of all layers of the audience, but it shares some characteristics of problems common for those in political life.[96] Such a dynamic might arguably always be an issue in a democracy, but the sense of personal affront, personal risk

---

[93] James Carroll, 'The Bush Crusade' *The Nation* (September 2004), www.thenation.com/article/bush-crusade.

[94] The documentary is available on YouTube. Jules and Gédéon Naudet, *9/11*, www.youtube.com/watch?v=6bDN5iVXD7E.

[95] This is based on my personal recollections living in the US at the time.

[96] See Perelman and Olbrechts-Tyteca, above, n 1, 19 (describing the nature of the audience for one speaking before Parliament as including not just those before him or her, but the wider public who will be reached by the discourse as well).

and personal involvement in the 9/11 attacks could be argued to be higher for the average citizen than in relation to many other public matters.

A question arises, then, as to whether argumentation strategies designed to appease a distraught populace or to persuade that audience of a certain course of action were then transferred to arguments presented before legislative bodies and courts. This question could be raised in any scenario in which a highly public event is the subject of a reassessment of existing legal norms. The blending of audiences that may have occurred after 9/11 is not completely distinct in that respect, although it may have had specific distinct elements. This, in itself, makes the sort of analysis applied to the scenario surrounding 9/11 relevant to other situations as well, so reviewing it in the 9/11 context has broad appeal.

Ultimately, the intent in addressing all of these audiences was to persuade. Perelman and Olbrechts-Tyteca note that any argument is built upon the audience, reminding readers that 'the end sought by eloquence always depends on the speaker's audience, and he must govern his speech in accordance with their opinions'.[97] The important issue, they note, is not what the speaker knows or believes to be true, but that the speaker is familiar with the knowledge or beliefs of those being addressed.[98] Structural logic might be a good indicator of an effective argument, but it means nothing if that logic is not accepted by a particular audience, as, they say, 'passions and reasons are not commensurable'.[99] A persuasive speaker must therefore take into account emotional factors dominant in the intended audience, and the early days especially after the 9/11 attacks had a high level of emotional charge to them. Therefore, the same argument might not be effective with members of the public as with courts and legislative bodies, and yet it was impossible for these arguments not to overlap. Perelman and Olbrechts-Tyteca point out the problem with different layers of audience:

> Argumentation aimed exclusively at a particular audience has the drawback that the speaker, by the very fact of adapting to the views of his listeners, might rely on arguments that are foreign or even directly opposed to what is acceptable to persons other than those he is presently addressing.[100]

In describing this phenomenon as 'the contact of minds', Perelman and Olbrechts-Tyteca explain that a common language that can be understood by the audience is necessary. It is not, however, all that is needed, and they use the example of *Alice in Wonderland*, involving a world in which the parties all speak the same fundamental language, but in which the inhabitants feel no motivation to actually communicate with each other.[101] They quote Aristotle in describing the need for the speaker to connect with an audience and in suggesting that the logical quality of an argument could, indeed, be tainted because of the need to alter it to so connect,

---

[97] ibid 23 (citations omitted).
[98] ibid 24.
[99] Perelman and Olbrechts-Tyteca, above, n 1, 24 (citations omitted).
[100] ibid 31.
[101] ibid 14–15.

depending on the nature of the audience. Aristotle went so far as to suggest that discussions not take place with certain audiences, as it would too extensively taint the logic of the underlying argument:

> A man should not enter into discussion with everybody or practice dialectics with the first comer as reasoning always becomes embittered where some people are concerned. Indeed, when an adversary tries by every possible means to wriggle out of a corner, it is legitimate to strive, by every possible means, to reach the conclusion; but the procedure lacks elegance.[102]

Thus, the idea is that argumentation is a dynamic, interactive process, which by definition morphs based on characteristics not only of the speaker, but of the intended audience as well. These parties must be considered when the elements of any argument are being considered. In any politically charged situation in which emotions run high, problems are likely to emerge in this subjective factor in terms of presenting a persuasive argument, and, in the course of persuading the public of something, a risk always arises that this same type of discourse, slanted towards emotion and sometimes away from logic in order to tailor itself to the audience, will make its way into normative legal developments.

B. Post-9/11 Political Speech was Focused More on 'Persuading' Rather than on 'Convincing' in Seeking Buy-in after the Attacks

Beyond the nature of the audience, the rationality of an argument can also be assessed in terms of the objective sought. Perelman and Olbrechts-Tyteca posit that a person concerned with achieving a specified action through the presentation of an argument to an audience is more concerned with persuading than with convincing, as they define conviction as 'the first stage in progression toward action'.[103] For somebody concerned more with the rational nature of an argument rather than with effecting a particular end, convincing is more important than persuading.[104] They define 'persuading' as 'argumentation that only claims validity for a particular audience'. 'Convincing', by contrast, they apply to argumentation that presumes to gain the adherence of every rational being'.[105] Put another way, they equate persuasion with action and conviction with intelligence.[106] Those arguments that gain the acceptance of the universal audience are deemed

---

[102] ibid 16–17 (quoting Aristotle, *Topics*, VIII, 14, 164b).
[103] Perelman and Olbrechts-Tyteca, above, n 1, 27. At this stage they appear to be using 'convincing' and 'conviction' as interchangeable terms.
[104] ibid.
[105] ibid 28 (specifically differing from Kant, who put forward a more distinct differentiation between conviction and persuasion as two 'different types of belief').
[106] Perelman and Olbrechts-Tyteca, above, n 1, 29 (drawing in part from Kant's ideas in Immanuel Kant, *Critique of Poor Reason*, preface to the first edition (1781)).

'valid', while those that only gain acceptance by a particular audience are merely 'effective'.[107]

Political rhetoric, by definition, must be 'effective', as it is addressed to the public and is designed to gain the adherence of those who vote. Therefore, in an atmosphere charged with anger and public fear, politicians may feel compelled to cater to public opinion and to present arguments that appease those public sentiments. This does not, however, mean that the arguments presented are necessarily those that make the most logical sense, and that the arguments may have proven persuasive does not necessarily support validity in relation to those arguments. A question arises as to whether, in persuading much of the public as well as lawmakers and some judicial bodies, of the need for altered detention and interrogation standards after 9/11, national governments presented arguments that had the ability to 'convince' rather than to merely 'persuade' in the sense described by Perelman and Olbrechts-Tyteca.

Perelman and Olbrechts-Tyteca also point to one of the elements of Aristotle's notion of rhetoric—that of 'epidictic' rhetoric, sometimes referred to just as 'praise-and-blame' rhetoric, a technique that can have a strong persuasive effect, particularly when directed to a large audience composed of members of the public. According to Perelman and Olbrechts-Tyteca, the importance of the use of this form of rhetoric had previously been wrongfully dismissed by numerous scholars and, in fact, it tends to play an integral role in the art of persuasion to a given audience.[108] They explain:

> Unlike the demonstration of a geometrical theorem, which establishes once and for all a logical connection between speculative truths, the argumentation in epidictic discourse sets out to increase the intensity of adherence to certain values, which might not be contested when considered on their own but may nevertheless not prevail against other values that might come into conflict with them. The speaker tries to establish a sense of communion centered around particular values recognized by the audience, and to this end he uses the whole range of means available to the rhetorician for purposes of amplification and enhancement.[109]

Particularly in the US after 9/11, as explained at various points throughout this book, audiences were especially receptive to this type of epidictic discourse. As explained in much more detail in various parts of chapters four to six, and particularly in chapter five, a sense of nationalism arose in the US after the attacks, which is hardly surprising, and which quickly developed into an 'us-against-them' type of rhetoric. In some other countries that responded to the attacks, a similar discourse arose, either in the sense of identifying quite heavily with the US, especially in the early days after the attacks, or in a larger notion that it was all Western democracies, or democracies in general, that were under attack, still resulting in

---

[107] ibid; see also Alexy, above, n 61, 164.
[108] Perelman and Olbrechts-Tyteca, above, n 1, 49.
[109] ibid 51.

a form of resurgence of certain nationalistic ideas and a closing of ranks against a perceived danger from outside.[110] These ideals were certainly used as the basis for appeals from particular governmental officials for particular changes.[111] Subjective beliefs can heavily impact understanding, even of seemingly objective events.

Subjectivity is an unavoidable element in the understanding of seemingly objective events. People impose their own experiences, beliefs, and values to create individual views of factual scenarios. The differences that can arise were demonstrated by an example earlier in this chapter, in regard to Kafka's Parable. Clifford Geertz recognised this in relation to law when he said:

> Law, as I have been saying, somewhat against the pretensions encoded in woolsack rhetoric, is local knowledge; local not just as to place, time, class, and variety of issue, but as to accent—vernacular characterizations of what happens connected to vernacular imaginings of what can. It is this complex of characterizations and imaginings, stories about events cast in imagery about principles, that I have been calling a legal sensibility. This is doubtless more than a little vague, but as Wittgenstein, the patron saint of what is going on here, remarked, a veridical picture of an indistinct object is not after all a clear one but an indistinct one. Better to paint the sea like Turner than to attempt to make of it a Constable cow.[112]

Geertz similarly suggests that even facts are filtered through a subjective lens and that while they are widely believed to be objective in nature, this is not actually so:

> The realization that legal facts are made not born, are socially constructed, as an anthropologist would put it, by everything from evidence rules, courtroom etiquette, and law reporting traditions, to advocacy techniques, the rhetoric of judges, and the scholasticisms of law school education raises serious questions for a theory of administration of justice that views it as consisting, to quote a representative example, 'of a series of matchings of fact-configurations and norms' in which either a 'fact-situation can be matched with one of several norms' or 'a particular norm can be … invoked by a choice of competing versions of what happened'. If the 'fact-configurations' are not merely things found lying about in the world and carried bodily into court show-and-tell style, but close-edited diagrams of reality the matching process itself produces, the whole thing looks a bit like sleight-of-hand.
>
> It is, of course, not sleight-of-hand, or anyway not usually, but a rather more fundamental phenomenon, the one upon which all culture rests: namely, that of representation … the point here is that the 'law' side of things is not a bounded set of norms, rules, principles, values, or whatever from which jural responses to distilled events can be drawn, but part of a distinctive manner of imagining the real … The problem it raises is how that representation is itself to be represented.[113]

---

[110] For example, see the discussion of the headline in France's *Le Monde* published shortly after the attacks, noting 'Nous sommes tous Américains', in ch 5 below.

[111] See ch 4 below for a description of some of these changes and ch 5 below for a discussion of this appeal to nationalism.

[112] Clifford Geertz, *Local Knowledge* (New York, Basic Books, 1983) 215.

[113] ibid 173.

The intention here is not to suggest that only one or two narratives are legitimate, or to definitively suggest that all aspects of the present narrative lack legitimacy. Some aspects of the post-9/11 narrative were arguably legitimate, while others continue to be subject to much more debate. Beyond these debates, though, it is possible that there might be equally viable and competing narratives for any given situation and that, in relation to post-9/11 narratives, there might, arguably, be at least one narrative that is more sound than the one currently continuing to develop in this area. Just as the kaleidoscope must be turned to reconstitute the parts into a new picture, only one picture may be viewed at any given time, even though additional pictures may later be revealed by turning the kaleidoscope again.

This methodology does provide a useful manner through which to examine the processes of argumentation since 9/11, as it can give insights into ongoing debates over detention paradigms, as well as potentially giving insights into the larger issue of how we construct laws rather than just within the anti-terrorism realm. Argumentation theory is already used, at least implicitly, in the daily practice of law, as arguments are built with an eye to structuring existing law and facts to build a persuasive case. It is arguably also useful to assess the discourse that leads to normative legal changes, as this shines a light on the process, potentially exposing structural flaws that may undermine the stability of the final product.

Remember, for each of these argumentation tools, it is just one of many that can be configured at different levels to paint a narrative picture. Subjectivity may serve as differing filters through which argumentation can be made, but the tools used even for a subjectively favourable audience are important. For instance, as will be discussed in considerable detail in chapter six, a particular type of binary discourse developed, which tended to state the danger and the necessary response in simplistic, either/or types of language, and which left little room for nuance and, almost of necessity, put audiences in a position of being told they had to choose one option or the other.[114] This type of language is obviously not confined only to post-9/11 discourse, but it was an important aspect of the specific public narratives that arose after the attacks. Combined with the sort of nationalistic language and emphasis on group identity expounded upon in chapter five especially, the discourse that dominated early after the attacks appears to fit well into Perelman and Olbrechts-Tyteca's idea of 'epidictic' discourse defined above.

C. 'Inertia' or 'Normalisation' or 'Path Dependency' Set in Once Enough People were Persuaded to Bring about Legal Changes in Detention Standards, Especially in the US

Once persuasion works, and an audience has accepted a dominant narrative, it is very difficult to undo this accepted new narrative in people's minds. Perelman

---

[114] See ch 6 below.

and Olbrechts-Tyteca call this 'inertia'.[115] Foucault refers to it as 'normalisation'.[116] Other scholars, in a range of disciplines, describe a notion of 'path dependency', in which a phenomenon continues along a certain path based on past decisions.[117] Dennis Grube has described this in terms of 'sticky' political rhetoric, in which public speakers become bound by their past words in making future policy statements, which could be an obstacle to going back to deconstruct discourse.[118] Although somewhat different, these ideas all have a relationship to each other.

Alexy advocates for Perelman and Olbrechts-Tyteca's notion of 'inertia', as the idea that 'an opinion that has been accepted in the past may not be abandoned again without sufficient reason'.[119] The term 'inertia' is based on the scientific notion of inertia, which derives from the study of physics. Inertia, in the study of physics, refers to the resistance of an object to a change either in its stationary state or in its state of motion—an object at rest tends to stay at rest and an object in motion tends to stay in motion.[120] The idea, when applied to argumentation theory, then, would be that there may be resistance to accepting a particular idea, or to implementing a change, at the outset. However, once this resistance is overcome, and the idea or change is accepted, the idea of inertia begins to favour the change rather than the pre-existing idea. It is now difficult to move against the new idea. Thus, while inertia itself refers to resistance to movement, or stopping movement, it can undergo an overarching shift in which a change is ultimately accepted, and thus the changed idea is then supported by the inertia in its favour, or resistance to change.[121] A similar concept, put in different terms, can be found in Foucault's idea of normalisation in which an idea, previously not accepted, gains initial acceptance and, as time passes, gains indicia of familiarity, or normalises.[122] When this happens, there is a resistance to changing it back and a tendency to put the burden on anybody seeking this reversion to the prior iteration rather than on those supporting the changed version.

---

[115] Perelman and Olbrechts-Tyteca, above, n 1, 105–07.

[116] Michel Foucault, *The History of Sexuality*, vol 1, translated by Robert Hurley (New York, Random House, 1978) 89, 144 (discussing normalisation, rather than law, as a basis for power); see also Andrew W Neal, 'Normalization and Legislative Exceptionalism: Counterterrorist Lawmaking and the Changing Times of Security Emergencies' (2012) 6(3) *International Political Sociology* 260 (undertaking a review of UK counter-terrorism legislation at different times, during perceived crisis and times not perceived as crisis, and concluding that measures beginning as emergency measures normalise over time).

[117] See generally Dennis C Grube, 'Sticky Words: Towards a Theory of Rhetorical Path Dependency' (2016) 51(3) *Australian Journal of Political Science* 530.

[118] ibid.

[119] Alexy, above, n 61 (citing Perelman and Olbrechts-Tyteca, above, n 1, 106).

[120] See Isaac Newton, *Newton's Principia: The Mathematical Principles of Natural Philosophy*, translated by Andrew Motte (New York, Daniel Adee, 1846) (American edition, in the public domain), online: *US National Archives*, ia600300.us.archive.org/8/items/ncwtonspmathema00newtrich/newton-spmathema00newtrich.pdf, 73–74.

[121] See Alexy, above, n 61, 171 (citing Perelman and Olbrechts-Tyteca, above n 1, 106).

[122] See, eg, Foucault, above, n 116.

Turning again to post-9/11 discourse, especially that undertaken shortly after the attacks, one might argue that politicians and law-makers employed a form of discourse designed to appease public fears, and that the discourse may have had this as an objective more than a logical acceptability in terms of the proper approach to terrorism detentions. Once this discourse was put out for public consumption, incorporating—as will be discussed later in this book—a peculiar form of terminology that evolved specifically in relation to the attacks, the passage of time lent the new language and these initial persuasion-oriented responses a certain air of familiarity. Many of the changes undertaken shortly after the attacks, in a climate of crisis and aimed at appeasing a frightened and angry populace, may well have been reasonable (or not) when designed to address an unknown and apparently imminent threat, and an assertion of necessity might support such short-term measures in a way they would not support them if they became normalised and permanent. Once they were implemented and normalised to become familiar and accepted, the inertia may have then favoured the changes, putting the burden on those seeking to continue to dispute these changes rather than on those supporting the changes. A form of inertia had set in, where the changes gained some indicia of familiarity without ever having been supported through the formalistic requirements of logical argumentation, and with the inertia now supporting the changes thus normalised.

An example of this phenomenon flows from the US in the continued use of the Guantanamo Bay detention camp in Cuba. When the camp and the 'Military Commissions' first began to be used in 2001–02 to house and 'try' terrorism suspects, they were subject to great controversy, sometimes called a 'legal black hole' and generally denounced as failing to meet US and international standards for detention and fair trial.[123] Obama campaigned on a promise to close the Guantanamo Bay prison. Of course, while he did not bring new detainees there and he did decrease the number of prisoners held there, he did not close the prison.[124] Trump promised to begin using the camp again. In mid-2017, it was reported that the US government was preparing to bring new prisoners there.[125] US Attorney General Jeff Sessions, who visited the camp in the summer of 2017, called it 'very fine place' and said there was no 'legal reason' to stop the US from sending detainees there.[126]

While the governmental language in 2017 may mirror the type of language used by the US government under George W Bush in 2001, the public response is quite different. Many people are simply used to the idea of Guantanamo Bay being used

---

[123] See, eg, Johan Steyn, 'Guantanamo Bay: The Legal Black Hole' (2004) 53(1) *International and Comparative Law Quarterly* 1; Peter Jan Honigsberg and Erwin Chemerinsky, *Our Nation Unhinged: The Human Consequences of the War on Terror* (Berkeley, University of California Press, 2009).

[124] See Rebecca Kheel, 'Trump Officials Signal Intent to Begin Refilling Guantanamo' *TheHill* (8 July 2017) thehill.com/policy/defense/341051-trump-officials-signal-intent-to-begin-refilling-guantanamo.

[125] ibid.

[126] ibid. See chs 4–6 for further discussions of the arguments supporting and opposing the present use of the Guantanamo Bay detention centre and the military commissions.

this way and it does not have the shock effect that it did in the beginning. In other words, it has normalised, and the inertia supports its continued use. This is in spite of the fact that there remain very serious concerns with its use and in spite of the fact that the underlying arguments used to support its creation, presented in the wake of the 9/11 attacks, have never really been revisited. Normalisation suggests that these problematic foundations will not be revisited.

The process under which changes came about and became accepted is critical. This is especially so if this process raises questions about whether validity was adequately assessed as the beginning, and whether this failure continues to the present-day practices. Moreover, if, indeed, some of the starting premises for these changes are themselves seriously flawed, this means that argumentation techniques may have been superimposed on an existing fact pattern to bring about a fundamental change in conceptions of the Rule of Law, without the components of the Rule of Law necessarily being fully considered. A complicated situation such as the disposition of cases involving terrorism suspects would call for careful analysis of the argumentation techniques applied to justify often significant changes in constitutional standards and that does not always appear to have occurred.[127] Before moving forward on this foundation, it is important to look back.

VI. Against this Backdrop, Post-9/11 Terrorism Detention Discourse Successfully Involved the Use of Effective Argumentation Tools

The elements described in the preceding sections—a favourable environment in which rhetoric can be presented unopposed, a favourable particular audience, values of the listeners, and the idea of inertia, normalisation and/or path dependency—all serve as background factors that make important contributions to the study of post-9/11 discourse in this work. It is against this background that this book explores the particular argumentation tools that were used in structuring the arguments themselves. Theoretical discussions of argument structures outline the role of particular elements—building blocks of arguments—and how the assembly of those elements can impact the outcome.[128] On its face, it appears obvious that such principles would be validly applied to legal argumentation, a discipline in which practice is built upon the success or failure of argument strategy. Premises and presumptions, of course, form a fundamental component of traditional

---

[127] See Perelman and Olbrechts-Tyteca, above, n 1, 187 (noting that '[p]ersuasive discourse is effective because of its insertion as a whole into a situation which is itself usually rather complicated').

[128] See Frans H van Eemeren et al, *Fundamentals of Argumentation Theory: A Handbook of Historical Backgrounds and Contemporary Developments* (Mahwah, NJ, Lawrence Erlbaum Associates, 1996) 103 (explaining various theories of argument structure and how they interact).

legal arguments. Concepts such as the presumption of innocence or the burden of proof permeate modern notions of legal proceedings. However, these concepts have a wider application to non-traditional components of legal structures, such as the role they play in the formation of policies, which, ultimately, may lead to the development of legal norms.[129]

In developing their analysis, Perelman and Olbrechts-Tyteca began not with the presumptions that fuelled the arguments, but with the end arguments that were deemed successful, from a range of sources, looking back from that starting point at the various steps undertaken to build the arguments.[130] In so doing, they concluded that there were certain characteristics of successful arguments, and of the premises/points of departure on which they were based, that were designed to appeal, on various levels, to specific audiences.[131] This approach of looking back is similar to Derrida's notion of deconstruction, but somewhat different from the approach taken in this book.[132] In this work, the idea is not to start with a successful argument necessarily, but to start with arguably problematic legal outcomes and to deconstruct the arguments that led to them to determine their soundness. Still, this approach of looking back that Perelman and Olbrechts-Tyteca and Derrida have employed is instructive.

Some terminology should be explained. Some terms, already introduced in this book, have common usage, but may be used in a particular way as the book proceeds. Other terminology is specific to the elements of rhetoric applied in this book. Argumentation theorists, from Perelman and Olbrechts-Tyteca to others, such as Frans van Eemeren et al, refer to 'points of departure' as the pivotal starting point for any successful argument.[133] A 'premise' is something that may be created to specifically appeal to a given audience and thus used as the point of departure for the argument being presented to that audience. Perelman and Olbrechts-Tyteca refer to two classes of premises—the 'real' and the 'preferable'—and van Eemeren et al later explained this distinction as follows:

> In premises relating to reality, a claim is laid to recognition by the universal audience. This class of premises comprises facts, truths and presumptions. Premises relating to what is preferable have to do with the preferences of a particular audience. This class comprises values, value hierarchies, and *loci*.[134]

---

[129] See generally James B Freeman, *Acceptable Premises: An Epistemic Approach to an Informal Logic Problem* (Cambridge, Cambridge University Press, 2005) ix–xi (describing when a premise can be accepted as valid and when it is subject to questioning, thus subjecting the one putting it forth to a burden of proof of its validity).

[130] See Perelman and Olbrechts-Tyteca, above, n 1, 10.

[131] See generally ibid.

[132] See, eg, Goodrich et al (n 40); Jacques Derrida, *Of Grammatology*, translated by Gayatri Chakravorty Spivak (Baltimore, Johns Hopkins University Press, 1998); Borradori, above, n 43.

[133] Van Eemeren et al, above, n 128, 102 (explaining points of departures as starting points for an argument).

[134] ibid.

Van Eemeren et al explain that 'facts and truths' are premises that are not subject to discussion or debate—for example, 'Madrid is the capital of Spain'.[135] Presumptions are defined as:

> [P]remises that imply that something is real or actual. They too are regarded as enjoying the agreement of the universal audience. In contrast to facts and truths, however, it is expected, perhaps even assumed, that the supposition involved will at some stage be confirmed. An example of a presumption is the supposition that a person's actions will say something about that person's character. When such a presumption is used as a premise, everyone is taken to agree with it and it is expected that cases will occur which confirm the presumption.[136]

Similarly, the definition of values is presented as:

> [P]remises that are related to the preference of a particular audience for one thing as opposed to another. They serve as guidelines in making choices: 'As personal liberty is very important, I shall vote for the party that will provide more police.' Values are also a basis for the forming of opinions: 'I prefer grape juice to coke, because I like natural products.'[137]

Van Eemeron et al note that: 'Agreement over values makes a common course of action possible.'[138] In addition to values themselves, they expand upon Perelman and Olbrechts-Tyteca's notion of 'value hierarchies', in which the person presenting an argument must be aware of the subjective perspective placed on different values by a specific audience—an example, perhaps, in terrorism discourse being whether a particular audience is more likely to value notions of individual liberty or those of personal safety.[139]

All of these things, among others, can be points of departure for an argument. While it is important to distinguish the different meanings of these ideas, for the sake of consistency and to avoid confusion, the beginning points of arguments discussed later in this book will be grouped together under the concept of 'points of departure'.

Even the notion of where to start an argument and how to construct that start can be subject to considerable controversy. In so doing, and in deconstructing the elements of arguments and turning the kaleidoscope to view them through the lens of argumentation theory, one might completely change the path down which an argument might travel or one might simply see an established argument in a new light.

---

[135] ibid.
[136] ibid 103.
[137] Van Eemeren et al, above, n 128, 103 (internal citations omitted).
[138] ibid.
[139] See ibid 102–03.

VII. Conclusion

This chapter has set the stage for some of the many layers of argumentation techniques that might be used to put together a particular narrative. This is not to suggest that there is not a concept of 'truth', but rather that perceptions of what is true can sometimes vary greatly depending on these argumentation methods. It can, in some cases, be possible to have different, plausible views of the same scenario.

The example of Kafka's Parable shows how even a short narrative can be seen in varying lights, with the same words meaning different things to different people. Perceptions can change because of things like starting perceptions and values. On some level, Kafka may have intended his short Parable to have significant nuance and varying potential interpretations, as even the conversation between K and the Priest demonstrates. However, by shifting the points of departure, the emphasis to be placed on certain factors and the values superimposed on the Parable, it is surprising how many viable interpretations emerge as to what it means. The same narrative may mean different things to different people.

A significant criticism of the post-9/11 discourse is that it was sometimes built on argumentation factors quite similar to some of those described by scholars like Alexy and Perelman and Olbrechts-Tyteca, undertaken in an atmosphere of a perceived crisis and designed to persuade a particular audience of the need for a particular response.[140] This sometimes happened with the speaker drawing heavily on techniques designed to persuade rather than to convince via logic. Like Kafka's Parable, the presentation of necessary detention shifts was often couched in language that suggested that the situation was much more straightforward than it perhaps was.

Deconstructing the discourse to view it through the lens of somewhat formalised argumentation theory can allow for a particular turning of the kaleidoscope and for a presentation of the issues from a new perspective. This chapter has used some aspects of argumentation theory to suggest a framework for reconsidering particular aspects of the post-9/11 American narrative and, beyond that, for reassessing particular legal changes that were enacted in a number of national jurisdictions. The next chapter redirects the conversation to some of the public narratives that emerged in the years after 9/11, which, in turn, will set the stage for the discussions in Part II of this book.

---

[140] This is explained in much more detail in chs 4–6.

3

Layers of Argumentation Tools and a Fractured Post-911 Narrative

I. Introduction: How Threads of Perception Developed after 9/11

The first chapter of this book addressed the significant impact that certain words, labels or narratives can have on the perception of high-profile matters. Chapter two argued that labels are just one of a number of argumentation tools that can be constructed in a way that is three-dimensional in order to paint a resilient picture in political narratives. In doing so, the chapter elucidated some of the theoretical elements that are employed in this book, while providing a sense of the larger picture around the elements that can make up part of political narratives.

This chapter turns back to the days, months and years after 9/11, to introduce some of the ways in which language changed perceptions about terrorism and specifically about terrorism-related detentions. This is a big subject and certainly not one that can be addressed comprehensively in one chapter. Thus, this chapter argues that one argumentation technique was laid over many of the other tactics used and played a significant role in persuading a receptive public that foundational changes were needed in terms of how terrorism suspects were handled. Chapters four to six then pick up from there, to examine, in greater detail, three specific argumentation techniques that help make up this bigger kaleidoscopic image.

As a general matter, a peculiar form of argumentation structure and a novel form of discourse developed, particularly in the US, after the 9/11 attacks, and this form of argumentation was used to persuade members of the public, the legislative branches and the judiciary that certain threshold changes had occurred, which justified unprecedented governmental action.[1] Much of this discourse process

---

[1] See ch 4 below for a comprehensive discussion of the argument that the 9/11 attacks demonstrated a new threat, such that pre-existing detention structures could be presumptively set aside in some cases; see also Piotr Cap, *Legitimisation in Political Discourse: A Cross-disciplinary Perspective on the Modern US War Rhetoric* (Newcastle, Cambridge Scholars Press, 2006) 2 (noting that 'a consistent pattern of rhetoric was developed in the aftermath of the attacks on the World Trade Center, aiming to justify

occurred in the aftermath of a shocking and horrific terrorist attack, when there was a widespread perception of imminent danger and of an ongoing emergency. As mentioned elsewhere in this book, the imminence of this threat was enhanced by the fact that millions of people watched it happen on live television. Some of the political discourse was reasonable, but some was not.

The argumentation techniques used had varying degrees of success with the intended audiences, and this success changed as time passed, as the initial fear subsided and as events like the military action in Iraq affected public perceptions of the US government and others. Different people were thus at different places, at different times in terms of persuasion. These distinctions were especially pronounced relating to terrorism detentions because of the dramatic shifts that happened very quickly early on, and within members of particular audiences, in particular countries and across different countries. Over time, a certain fracturing of the terrorism-detention narrative emerged, in which people had varying beliefs over issues that, before 9/11, might have been argued to have been more settled. The idea of a fractured narrative is used to describe a situation in which different people received the political narratives differently. The chapters that follow delve into much greater detail on some of the specific argumentation tools that were used.

This piecemeal development of the political narrative, which is certainly not confined to this event, played a role in creating inconsistencies in resulting legal enactments. This is why the approach described in the preceding chapter—of deconstructing the narrative and then reconstructing it through the lens of effective argumentation techniques—has potential. Thus fractured, the narrative led to fragmented practices, again within individual countries and as compared across national jurisdictions. These fragmented practices are explored more in chapters four to six.

II. Manufacturing Confusion: Euphemisms Played a Key Role in Influencing Public Perception[2]

A discussion of the post-9/11 American political narrative would not be complete without including the overarching and substantial role played by euphemisms.

---

military retaliation on account of the apparent imminence of danger facing the American citizens. To this day, the most salient premise of the White House rhetoric has been the construal of the terrorist threat as existing within the US borders. Unlike in the past, when America was going to *foreign* wars in Korea, Vietnam, or recently, Kosovo, the war has come 'home').

[2] 'Manufacturing confusion' is a play on the words 'manufacturing consent', as used in such works as Edward S Herman and Noam Chomsky, *Manufacturing Consent: The Political Economy of the Mass Media* (New York, Pantheon Books, 1988).

Euphemisms are discussed here because they figured in every layer of the narrative set forth by the US government, so their impact was diffused, unlike other techniques, which might have been more specific or more limited in terms of their aim or impact. This technique was therefore layered over the other argumentation techniques that were used.

A euphemism is a relatively small tool in the bigger scheme of a public narrative. However, it can be powerful if the euphemism is used successfully to create a desired impression about something.[3] Euphemisms are typically words used to politely describe something for which a more blunt explanation would be unpleasant or where the underlying subject matter is unpleasant. As Orwell explained:

> In our time, political speech and writing are largely the defence of the indefensible. Things like the continuance of British rule in India, the Russian purges and deportations, the dropping of the atom bombs on Japan, can indeed be defended, but only by arguments which are too brutal for most people to face, and which do not square with the professed aims of the political parties. Thus, political language has to consist largely of euphemism, question-begging and sheer cloudy vagueness. Defenceless villages are bombarded from the air, the inhabitants driven out into the countryside, the cattle machine-gunned, the huts set on fire with incendiary bullets: this is called *pacification*. Millions of peasants are robbed of their farms and sent trudging along the roads with no more than they can carry: this is called *transfer of population* or *rectification of frontiers*. People are imprisoned for years without trial, or shot in the back of the neck or sent to die of scurvy in Arctic lumber camps: this is called *elimination of unreliable elements*. Such phraseology is needed if one wants to name things without calling up mental pictures of them.[4]

As used here, the discussion of euphemisms implies, as Orwell does in his essay, the intentional use of a different word or words to cover the truth of what is actually being described, not to make the description more palatable, but to actually hide the truth.[5] This technique is commonly used in political discourse, where '[o]fficials who seek to push or disregard the limits of legal and legitimate behavior are often inclined to euphemize'.[6]

The use of euphemisms by a government is not, of course, new. There were, however, peculiar strategic qualities to the vocabulary that the US government developed after 9/11, and the crisis circumstances under which these new terms were advanced meant that certain euphemisms quickly became embedded in popular understandings. Distinctive terms were created, obviously to gain public

---

[3] See generally RW Holder, *How Not to Say What You Mean: A Dictionary of Euphemisms* (Oxford, Oxford University Press, 2007).

[4] George Orwell, 'Politics and the English Language' (first published London, Horizon, 1946), reprinted numerous times; see www.orwell.ru/library/essays/politics/english/e_polit/.

[5] See Lisa Hajjar, 'An Assault on Truth: A Chronology of Torture, Deception, and Denial' in Julie A Carlson and Elisabeth Weber, *Speaking about Torture* (New York, Fordham University Press, 2012) 19 (discussing different layers of euphemism employed by the US government in describing the extensive torture programme that it was building).

[6] ibid 19 (citations omitted).

buy-in to planned initiatives that would have faced strong opposition before the attacks. This is important not just to illustrate that some of the linguistic techniques used after the attacks were intentional, and even arguably dishonest, but also to explain the impact that this strategy had on different audiences.

In addition to hiding some of what it wanted to do behind euphemisms, the US government also used terms that bore some resemblance to familiar legal terms, but were actually not quite the same, in an attempt to confuse people about the legal justification for certain actions. Manufacturing confusion appears to have been a specific narrative strategy and the euphemism approach illustrates this intention.

Peculiar terminology emerged after the 9/11 attacks that had not previously been used, and that terminology seems to have been intentionally created to persuade those listening that the Executive Branch could do things that never would have been tolerated otherwise.[7] This terminology often involved highly simplistic characterisations of complex issues. If a government—often the US government— wanted to obfuscate something, it would sometimes simply call it something else. The rules were deemed to be different in the 'post-9/11 world' and, to underscore this, this particular phrase became embedded in popular lexicon to advance this belief and to convey that security was paramount.[8]

Sometimes, these euphemisms meant that an inaccurate term was substituted for an accurate term. Shortly after 9/11, for example, then-US Attorney General John Ashcroft announced the arrests of hundreds of terrorists. It turned out that these 'terrorists' were actually immigrants, none of whom ever faced a successful terrorism conviction.[9] However, calling them terrorists muted opposition.

At other times, terms were made up that were new, which helped underscore the idea that it was a new world with new rules. The 9/11 attacks were called an act of war, and war was declared not on a state or even on a particular entity, but on an ideology—a 'War on Terror'. While the US had previously declared a similar war against a thing in its 'War on Drugs', the War on Terror was used as a pretext for actual war measures. Beyond the declaration, the circumstances under

---

[7] See, eg, Mark Falcous and Michael Silk, 'Manufacturing Consent: Mediated Sporting Spectacle and the Cultural Politics of the "War on Terror"' (2005) 1(1) *Journal of Media and Cultural Politics* 59 (discussing the types of public language sent out by the Bush Administration after the 9/11 attacks, in a comparative context with other events).

[8] See, eg, Jessica Bliss, The Tennessean, 'Coming of Age in Post-9/11 World' *USA Today* (11 September 2014) www.usatoday.com/story/news/nation/2014/09/11/coming-of-age-in-post-911-world/15474695/ (focusing on the experiences of people too young to clearly remember the events of 9/11); Liz Mineo, 'Lessons from a Post-9/11 World' *Harvard Gazette* (12 April 2016) news.harvard. edu/gazette/story/2016/04/lessons-from-a-post-911-world (discussing the experience of a Harvard law graduate who advocates for torture survivors). This expression even appeared in an episode of *Gilmore Girls*, in which a Yale campus guide says: 'And it's a post-9/11 world, so your ID's [sic] are important. You'll be asked for it a lot, so always have it, always, always.' Daniel Palladino, 'The Lorelais' First Day at Yale' *Gilmore Girls Transcript*, crazy-internet-people.com/site/gilmoregirls/pages/s4/s4s/67.html.

[9] See Karen Gullo, 'Ashcroft Discusses New Powers' *Associated Press* (25 October 2001) www.washingtonpost.com/wp-srv/aponline/20011025/aponline195409_000.htm.

which this new war was announced are important. It first arose in an emotionally charged speech by then-President Bush on national television, nine days after the 9/11 attacks. The discursive parameters began to form then, as the world was told they were with us or were with the terrorists.[10] Although high emotion, grief, fear and anger were the underpinnings to this declaration, these factors were not later used, in calmer times, to go back and criticise the declaration of war.

The practical implications of this declaration were seemingly boundless. Asserting that a war was underway, for instance, opened the door for the US President to invoke war powers as Commander in Chief under the US Constitution, powers which were not otherwise available to him.[11] Of course, such a war has the potential to continue indefinitely, so the expanse of presidential power brought about through this declaration cannot be overstated.

Similarly, by convincing people that a war was ongoing, political figures were more easily able to justify to the public when they avoided the national criminal justice systems in cases in which they wanted to hold people, but did not wish to be constrained by constitutional fair trial standards. Torture was no longer torture. It was 'enhanced interrogation' and thus was not the problem that torture was, even though enhanced interrogation and torture were the same thing.[12] 'Waterboarding' became a term that was popularly understood, but it was presented not as torture, but as a less serious technique that was not terrible or even all that problematic for the victim, which is simply not true.[13] Vestiges of this impression can be seen today, as Trump has repeatedly advocated for the reintroduction of waterboarding, saying it is not torture and that it works.[14]

---

[10] President George W Bush, 'Address to a Joint Session of Congress and the American People' *The White House* (20 September 2001) georgewbush-whitehouse.archives.gov/news/releases/2001/09/20010920-8.html. This either/or philosophy was repeated numerous times over the coming years, representing a perspective that those not joining the US in its Global War on Terror were actively supporting the enemy. This is a strong statement and could be difficult to ignore in many ways by countries that had positive relations with the US and an interest in continuing to have such a strong relationship. For a montage of similar statements by the US President, see, 'With Us or against Us', *YouTube*, www.youtube.com/watch?v=-23kmhc3P8U. For a discussion on the use of 'us versus them' rhetoric as a legitimising tool, see John Oddo, 'War Legitimation Discourse: Representing "Us" and "Them" in four presidential addresses' (2011) 22 *Discourse & Society* 287 (assessing speeches by US Presidents Franklin D Roosevelt and George W Bush that are characterised as 'call(s) to arms'); see also ch 6 below.

[11] See US Constitution, Art II, s 2 (saying '[t]he President shall be Commander in Chief of the Army and Navy of the United States, and of the Militia of the several States, when called into the actual Service of the United States').

[12] See generally Jared Del Rosso, *Talking about Torture: How Political Discourse Shapes the Debate* (New York, Columbia University Press, 2015); see also Senate Select Committee on Intelligence, *Committee Study of the Central Intelligence Agency's Detention and Interrogation Program* (updated for release: 3 April 2014), 4 (including a Foreword by US Senator Dianne Feinstein, the Chairman, concluding that CIA detainees were tortured, a conclusion repeated throughout the report).

[13] See Senate Select Committee on Intelligence, above, n 12.

[14] See, eg, Max Greenwood, 'Trump: Waterboarding isn't Torture' *The Hill* (26 January 2017) thehill.com/policy/national-security/316435-trump-waterboarding-isnt-torture.

The war declaration allowed the US government to persuade many people that the existing criminal justice paradigm was presumptively invalid—not for all or even for most cases—but definitely for particular cases. The government was thus spared the need to establish the necessity and validity of its use of the prison at Guantanamo Bay to house those it called 'enemy combatants', even though a number of the people detained there were picked up far from any battlefield and even though the term 'enemy combatant' really did not exist in international law or domestically before the US government simply began using it.[15] The concepts of 'war' and 'terrorism' were conveniently mingled, so those 'enemy combatants' were sometimes called 'terrorists', and the two concepts were thus seen as one in the public consciousness. This created considerable confusion and helped to cloak the US government's actions in removing these people from the realm of constitutional trial standards or international human rights norms.[16]

People held indefinitely with no trial were often simply given this new label of 'enemy combatant', sometimes expressed as 'unlawful enemy combatant', and this somehow made it acceptable for a government to indefinitely detain them, often in secret, or on secret charges, or on no charges and/or based on secret evidence. 'Enhanced interrogation' was somehow acceptable for people who were given this fabricated designation. If people were kidnapped and sent overseas to be tortured, this was not called 'kidnapping'; it was called 'extraordinary rendition', which somehow did not sound so bad and, indeed, sounds a bit technical and thus is perhaps more readily accepted.[17]

When the President wanted to make up new courts, free from the evidentiary constraints of the US Constitution and international law, he simply did so, and he gave them a glossing of legitimacy by calling them 'Military Commissions', which created the false impression that these bodies were the same as other military courts used in the past. In truth, however, these fabricated courts were created simply to apply questionable practices that avoided many mandatory conventions relating to fairness of trials.[18]

The use of euphemisms was sprinkled throughout the various layers of argumentation presented by the US government after 9/11. Beyond that, broader, overarching argumentation tools were used relating to specific points being advanced.

---

[15] See Peter Jan Honigsberg and Erwin Chemerinsky, *Our Nation Unhinged: The Human Consequences of the War on Terror* (Berkeley, University of California Press, 2009) 5, 8 (critiquing the use of this term, among many other things, to create confusion with terms that actually do exist under international law and to give a veneer of legitimacy that does not truly exist); see also generally David Rose, *Guantanamo: America's War on Human Rights* (New York, The New Press, 2004).

[16] See, eg, NPR Staff, 'Are Terrorists Criminals or Enemy Combatants?' *NPR* (21 September 2010) www.npr.org/templates/story/story.php?storyId=129941946 (describing these issues as 'complex ethical and legal questions').

[17] See Honigsberg and Chemerinsky, above, n 15, 5, 10 (critiquing this characterisation of what was an exceptionally brutal practice).

[18] See ch 6 below, in which the differences between these military commissions and legitimate courts are discussed at some length.

III. Forward-Looking Threat-Based Discourse Perpetuated Already Rattled Nerves and Made Governmental Initiatives More Persuasive in the US

Another trend of post-9/11 political discourse was a tendency certainly to focus on the attacks, but more often to focus on the assertion that other attacks were imminent. Punishment for those responsible, while discussed, was not the focus so much as an urgent need to prevent future attacks. This type of language has been studied as an effective entry point into controlling the narrative of the present and the past, as well as the future.[19] Patricia Dunmire describes the unknown future as a powerful tool for the exploitation of political commentary, commenting that 'the future represents an ideologically significant site in which dominant political actors and institutions can exert political power and control'.[20] The US appears to have pursued a form of discourse that can be traced back to Aristotle, in which the speaker asserts the power to do something, while simultaneously establishing 'expediency' or 'harmfulness' of the argued necessary action.[21]

It was not necessarily just the 9/11 attacks themselves that were used to justify shifts in detention paradigms, but a sense that greater, unknown threats loomed on the horizon and that there were significant, unknown, bad entities plotting the next strike. Hand in hand with this sense of imminent threat was the assertion that extraordinary actions were necessary to thwart these potential future threats.[22]

The link between altered detention practices and this new threat was often established through representations by national governments that they had the ability to stop future horrors if they were only given the means to do so. Patricia Dunmire describes this as 'agentive' discourse, because it suggests that 'social actors are seen as highly effective agents who can bring about effects on future events'.[23] Dunmire notes, for example, that, in the US, the 'agentive' power of two entities—the US and its enemies—is laced throughout post-9/11 governmental discourse.[24] She examines this issue in relation to the way in which the US government justified the war in Iraq. She has written about examples of this type of discourse in this context, including language such as that relating to '[s]hadowy

---

[19] See generally Patricia L Dunmire, *Projecting the Future through Political Discourse: The Case of the Bush Doctrine* (Amsterdam, John Benjamins Publishing Co, 2011).

[20] Patricia L Dunmire, '"Emerging Threats" and "Coming Dangers"' in Adam Hodges and Chad Nilep (eds), *Discourse, War and Terrorism* (Amsterdam, John Benjamins Publishing Company, 2007) 19.

[21] ibid 21.

[22] See ch 4 below for an extensive discussion of the argued need to make changes in existing criminal justice detention paradigms.

[23] Dunmire, above, n 20, 23 (internal citations omitted).

[24] ibid 24. This binary—the sort of 'us' versus 'them' language often employed in the wake of 9/11—will be deconstructed in ch 5 and briefly in ch 6 below.

networks of individuals' that can easily cause suffering.[25] An example of the use of future dangers to justify pre-emptive war included this notion:

> Given the goals of rogue states and terrorists, the U.S. can no longer solely rely on a reactive posture as we have in the past. The inability to deter a potential attacker, the immediacy of today's threats, and the magnitude of potential harm that could be caused by our adversaries' choice of weapons do not permit that option. We cannot let our enemies strike first.[26]

While Dunmire's study relates specifically to the discourse used by the US government to justify the invasion of Iraq, it is apparent that such forward-looking, threat-based discourse was the underpinning for a range of exceptional measures, certainly including extraordinary detention scenarios.

Thus far, this book has considered a range of argumentation tools that have been used, particularly by the US government, to create a desired narrative around terrorism. Yet, it almost goes without saying that Perelman and Olbrechts-Tyteca's point about the persuasion of particular audiences would mean that these types of tools would have varying degrees of success on different audiences at different times. These differences could occur for many reasons and, at each stage, an argumentation tool could persuade some people, while failing to persuade others. A tool could also even persuade the same people at one point in time, while fading in persuasiveness at another time. After 9/11, particularly in the US, this led to a certain fracturing both of the narrative around terrorism and of the practices relating to terrorism detentions. To conclude the general discussion relating to political narratives, the next section lays out an example of such a fractured narrative.

IV. A Fractured Narrative Arose After 9/11, as Demonstrated by One Conversation between Representatives of Branches of the US Government

At this point, it may be useful to present an example of the way that the post-9/11 US narrative fractured regarding terrorism detentions. The focus of Part II of this book is on fragmented practices, but the fractured narrative that undergirded these practices caused structural cracks that played a part in the ultimate fragmenting of legal practices. The following example sets the stage for the discussion in Part II.

In choosing the case of Umar Farouk Abdulmutallab as an example of a fractured narrative, a couple of factors were important. This exchange described

---

[25] Dunmire, above, n 20.
[26] ibid 25.

here was the best example found of a publicly available argument about the disposition of a particular case, with the conversation taking place over a fairly compact period of time. It is not an example of the most fragmented detention practice, as Abdulmutallab was ultimately processed through the traditional criminal justice system.[27] Rather, it is an example of a fragmented narrative, in which those participating in the conversation made certain baseline assumptions about what they could do with a terrorism suspect, and these starting assumptions did not correlate with each other.

The conversation shows that, by the time of this incident, an assumption had arisen among some governmental officials that the criminal justice system was merely optional in the disposition of this terrorism suspect in US custody. Rather, some assumed that other options, such as detention at Guantanamo Bay, were equally viable alternatives, simply at the government's discretion. This conversation simply would not have happened before 9/11.

As a preliminary note, the conversation demonstrates a larger fracturing of the narrative when this incident is compared to another one that happened not long afterwards. Abdulmutallab was not a US citizen, which was a foundational reason why the difference of opinion described below happened.[28] There was no comparable debate when Faisal Shahzad tried to set off a car bomb in Times Square in New York in May 2010, because, unlike Abdulmutallab, Shahzad is a US citizen.[29] The example below thus shows that the assumptions of parallel, equally available alternatives were only applied to non-citizens accused of terrorism, even where their conduct might be similar to that of citizen terrorism suspects. While there have been calls to strip citizenship from US citizens convicted of terrorism offenses, the US has not followed places like the UK, and briefly Canada, in their legislation allowing for such citizenship stripping absent other factors, like fraud in naturalisation. However, the discourse addressing the issue of citizenship stripping shows a continued assumption that terrorism and citizenship are linked and is explored in chapter five.[30]

---

[27] See United States Department of Justice, 'Umar Farouk Abdulmutallab Indicted for Attempted Bombing of Flight 253 on Christmas Day' (6 January 2010) www.justice.gov/opa/pr/umar-farouk-abdulmutallab-indicted-attempted-bombing-flight-253-christmas-day.

[28] ibid (noting that Abdulmutallab was a Nigerian national).

[29] See 'NY Bomb-Plot Suspect "Faces Terrorism Charge"' *BBC News* (4 May 2010) news.bbc.co.uk/2/hi/americas/8660370.stm; however, see Ryan Grim, 'Faisal Shahzad Arrest: Lieberman Proposes Taking away Citizenship of Suspected Terrorists' *Huffington Post* (4 May 2010) www.huffingtonpost.com/2010/05/04/faisal-shahzad-arrest-lie_n_562834.html (indicating some conversations, at least, in the days after Shahzad's arrest about stripping him and other terrorism suspects of US citizenship). The issue of the role of citizenship in the fracturing of the narrative will be discussed in more depth in ch 5 below.

[30] See ch 5 below; see, eg, Jordain Carney, 'Cruz: Strip Citizenship from Americans Who Join Terrorists' *The Hill* (14 February 2017) thehill.com/blogs/floor-action/senate/319571-cruz-strip-citizenship-from-americans-who-join-terrorist-groups (explaining the background on the proposal, the Expatriate Terrorist Act, 115th Congress, 1st Session (2017)) (not enacted).

For the purposes of this section, some background facts are useful. On 25 December 2009, Umar Farouk Abdulmutallab, who came to be known in the popular media by the unfortunate nickname of the 'Underwear Bomber', or alternatively as the 'Christmas Day Bomber' or 'Underpants Bomber', was flying to the US from Amsterdam. During the flight, he tried to set off explosives that were hidden in his pants. A group of passengers and members of the flight crew successfully subdued him before the explosives could be detonated.[31] This incident was clearly minor in terms of the physical damage it caused, but reports suggested that, had his attempt been successful, it could have destroyed the plane and killed everybody on board. The attempt triggered a strong governmental response on national security and led to some incongruous debates. After the attempted attack, a number of security measures were instituted, which initially included not allowing international passengers into the US to have any personal items in their laps or to leave their seats for an hour before landing.[32] These measures were later eased up in some of these respects.[33] The current, controversial use of full-body scanners at airports is widely attributed to a response to Abdulmutallab's actions.[34]

---

[31] 'Underwear Bomber Abdulmutallab Sentenced to Life' *BBC News* (16 February 2012) www.bbc.co.uk/news/world-us-canada-17065130; Brenda Bowser Soder, 'Abdulmutallab Life Sentence Demonstrates Strength of Federal Courts in Terrorism Cases' *Human Rights First* (16 February 2012) www.humanrightsfirst.org/2012/02/16/abdulmutallab-life-sentence-demonstrates-strength-of-federal-courts-in-terrorism-cases (noting, as of that date, that the federal courts had significantly more prosecutions than the Military Commissions with six, all of which were being critiqued as lacking legitimacy); United States Department of Justice, Office of Public Affairs, 'Press Release: Umar Farouk Abdulmutallab Sentenced to Life in Prison for Attempted Bombing of Flight 253 on Christmas Day 2009' (16 February 2012) www.justice.gov/opa/pr/2012/February/12-ag-227.html.

[32] See US Department of Homeland Security, 'Secretary Napolitano Announces New Measures to Strengthen Aviation Security' (2 April 2010) www.dhs.gov/ynews/releases/pr_1270217971441.shtm (announcing 'enhanced' security measures for people travelling into the US, which replaced the 'emergency' measures implemented after the attempted attack on 25 December 2009 and were purportedly developed after international consultations, including the United Nations International Civil Aviation Organization); White House, *Surface Transportation Security Priority Assessment* (March 2010) www.whitehouse.gov/sites/default/files/rss_viewer/STSA.pdf, at 8–13 (outlining the goals of the revised security measures and describing them as ensuring a 'secure and resilient transportation network, enabling legitimate travelers and goods to move without significant disruption of commerce, undue fear of harm, or loss of civil liberties'); United States Transportation Security Administration, 'TSA Guidance for Passengers on New Security Measures for International Flights to the U.S.' (2 April 2010) www.tsa.gov/travelers/airtravel/guidance_international_flights.shtm.

[33] See Michael S Schmidt and Ron Nixon, 'Airplane Security Debated Anew after Latest Bombing Plot' *New York Times* (10 May 2012) www.nytimes.com/2012/05/11/world/americas/airplane-security-debated-after-latest-bombing-plot.html; Jeffrey Price and Jeffrey Forrest, *Practical Aviation Security*, 2nd edn (Waltham, MA, Elsevier, 2013) 85.

[34] Michael Haggerson, 'Federal Judge Rules Accused Plane Bomber's Hospital Statements Admissible' *Jurist* (15 September 2011) jurist.org/paperchase/2011/09/federal-judge-rules-accused-plane-bombers-hospital-statements-admissible.php.

A. A Conversation: The Legislative Branch[35]

As Abdulmutallab was taken off the plane in Michigan, authorities began to prepare criminal charges against him. He was initially questioned without the traditional *Miranda* admonition, although this was read to him sometime after his arrest. *Miranda* warnings have been made well known through popular culture and the term refers to warnings that suspects are given about their constitutional rights. The admonition originates from a US Supreme Court case, which ruled that:

> The person in custody must, prior to interrogation, be clearly informed that he or she has the right to remain silent, and that anything the person says will be used against that person in court; the person must be clearly informed that he or she has the right to consult with an attorney and to have that attorney present during questioning, and that, if he or she is indigent, an attorney will be provided at no cost to represent her or him.[36]

This sequence of events stirred considerable outrage among some US law-makers. For instance, then-Senate Minority Leader Mitch McConnell, joined by other US senators, sent a widely discussed letter to then-US Attorney General Eric Holder.[37] The letter was signed by several members of the US Senate, including John McCain, the Republican presidential candidate in 2008.[38] The tone of the letter implies a certain carelessness on the part of the US government in its handling of the arrest, including concern about the government's decision not to 'thoroughly interrogate Abdulmutallab' and adding:

> We remain deeply troubled that this paramount requirement of national security was ignored—or worse yet, not recognized—due to the administration's preoccupation with reading the Christmas Day bomber his *Miranda* rights.

> Apparently there was little, if any, coordination among key components of the administration's national security apparatus on how to treat Umar Farouk Abdulmutallab.

---

[35] In describing this as a conversation, compare Peter Hogg and Allison Bushell, 'The Charter Dialogue between Courts and Legislatures' (1997) 35 *Osgoode Hall Law Journal* 75 (one of a series of articles published about the so-called 'dialogue theory' in Canadian constitutional law, which is a metaphor for exchanges across branches of government. The metaphor of the dialogue has been considerably challenged in Canada and it does not easily translate to the US system of law-making and judicial review because of differences in structure in terms of the separation of powers from that of the Canadian government); see also the critiques in Peter Hogg, Allison Bushell et al, '*Charter* Dialogue Revisited—Or "Much Ado about Metaphors"' (2007) 45 *Osgoode Hall Law Journal* 1 (response by the original authors and others to the ongoing critique of the dialogue metaphor among academics and courts, including the Supreme Court of Canada).

[36] See *Miranda v Arizona*, 384 US 436 (1966).

[37] Kasie Hunt, 'Republicans Rip Eric Holder on Miranda Rights for Underwear Bomber' *Politico* (27 January 2010), www.politico.com/news/stories/0110/32073.html. A copy of the original letter can be found at 'Letter to The Honorable Eric H. Holder Jr., Attorney General, United States Department of Justice', (27 January 2010) www.mccain.senate.gov/public/index.cfm/press-releases?ID=7092FD54-D48F-F35D-06EA-14DCC5440143.

[38] 'Letter to The Honorable Eric H. Holder Jr.', above, n 37.

Shockingly, the administration then made the hasty decision to treat him as a civilian defendant—including advising him of a right in a civilian law enforcement context not to cooperate—rather than as an intelligence resource to be thoroughly interrogated in order to obtain potentially life-saving information.[39]

Among a list of specific questions in the letter, one was: 'Why was such a modest amount of time, apparently less than an hour, devoted to questioning Abdulmutallab prior to telling him that he did not have to cooperate?' Presumably the reference to telling him he did not have to cooperate refers to the 'right to remain silent' portion of the *Miranda* admonition.

In a US criminal case, an hour of questioning prior to the reading of *Miranda* rights could, in itself, be deemed a serious defect, as information obtained through such questioning could be inadmissible in court. There is an exception to the *Miranda* requirement for cases involving public safety.[40] As explained below, the senators were apparently not talking about this exception, but were suggesting a larger rule under which *Miranda* warnings could generally be skipped in these cases. The letter suggests that the variation from a typical criminal procedure safeguard was fine, but the senators criticized the government for not deviating from it more, obviously implying that with this terrorism suspect, the government had the option of simply skipping the *Miranda* admonition and other protections entirely.

Moreover, the letter suggests equal options to treat a terrorism suspect as a criminal defendant or as 'an intelligence' resource to be 'thoroughly interrogated in order to obtain potentially life-saving information', thus entirely bypassing the criminal justice system.[41] Actually, the outraged tone of the letter even suggests that the senators did not see disposition through the criminal justice system as an option at all. The letter does not explain what is meant by a 'thorough' interrogation, and a question arises as to whether the senators were referring to the use of torture or, to borrow the euphemism discussed above, 'enhanced interrogation techniques'.[42] However, the fact that McCain signed the letter suggests that this was not the intent, or at least that it was not the intent of all who signed.[43] McCain is well known for opposing the use of torture.[44]

In the end, the delay before the *Miranda* warning was given led to an argument over admissibility of statements that Abdulmutallab made shortly after his arrest. Abdulmutallab argued that the statements were inadmissible because the

---

[39] ibid.
[40] *New York v Quarles*, 467 US 649 (1984).
[41] 'Letter to The Honorable Eric H. Holder Jr.', above, n 37.
[42] See ibid.
[43] See ibid.
[44] See Adam Chandler, 'This is How a Prisoner of War Feels about Torture' *The Atlantic* (9 December 2014) www.theatlantic.com/politics/archive/2014/12/John-Mccain-Speech-Senate-Republican-CIA-Torture-Report/383589 (describing McCain as breaking with his party to praise the recently released CIA torture report).

Miranda warning had not been given and because he was interviewed while on painkillers.[45] A US federal judge who heard the case ruled that national security interests, including the imminent need to determine whether another attack was about to take place, justified the delay, and his statements were ruled admissible.[46] The judge also ruled that the influence of painkillers was not a bar to admissibility, based on evidence from hospital staff.[47]

Presumably, the judge was applying the public safety exception to the *Miranda* admonition. This exception is applied in individual cases and it allows the *Miranda* admonition to be delayed if there is a public safety reason for questioning the suspect to prevent an imminent danger.[48] The public safety exception does not permit all questioning, but only those questions necessary to resolve the imminent safety issue.[49]

The senators' letter did not appear to be referring to this individualised exception, but rather seemed to suggest that the *Miranda* warning simply not be used at all in cases involving terrorism suspects.[50] The senators' letter goes on to note that members of the US Senate wanted answers as to how this 'ill-advised' decision could have been made.[51]

As a preliminary matter, it is important to note the obvious, and apparently unquestioned, presumption underpinning the letter of the US senators—that there is in fact a distinct and parallel system, separate from the US criminal justice system—that could, on the discretion of governmental officials, have been applied to Abdulmutallab. This system, the letter suggests, would have allowed the US to simply decide to avoid its criminal justice system. Moreover, the letter expresses considerable indignation that this apparently parallel system was not used, implying that this parallel system not only exists, but has become the dominant system of choice in certain cases.

B. The Executive Branch

US Attorney General Eric Holder responded to the senators' letter, explaining in some detail the circumstances under which Abdulmutallab was arrested and interrogated, and he explained in a larger sense the policies of the US government in relation to use of the criminal justice system in terrorism cases.[52] Rather than

---

[45] Haggerson, above, n 34.

[46] ibid.

[47] ibid.

[48] See *New York v Quarles*, above, n 40 (the 5:4 decision giving rise to the public safety exception to the *Miranda* rule).

[49] ibid 658–59.

[50] 'Letter to The Honorable Eric H. Holder Jr.', above, n 37.

[51] ibid.

[52] Eric Holder, Office of the Attorney General, 'Letter from U.S. Attorney General Eric Holder to The Honorable Mitch McConnell' (3 February 2010), *United States Department of Justice*, www.justice.gov/cjs/docs/ag-letter-2-3-10.pdf.

beginning from a presumption in favour of the criminal justice system, Holder instead went to lengths to argue in favour of using that system. While not explicitly stated, this starting approach conveys an implicit assumption that it is up to the party advocating for the use of the criminal justice system to establish its appropriateness rather than for those advocating against use of that system to rebut any presumption in its favour. For instance, Holder wrote:

> Those policies and practices, which were not criticized when employed by previous Administrations, have been and remain extremely effective in protecting national security. They are among the many powerful weapons this country can and should use to win the war against al-Qaeda.
>
> ...
>
> I am equally confident that the decision to address Mr. Abdulmutallab's actions through our criminal justice system has not, and will not, compromise our ability to obtain information needed to detect and prevent future attacks. There are many examples of successful terrorism investigations and prosecutions, both before and after September 11, 2001, in which both of these important objectives have been achieved—all in a manner consistent with our law and our national security interests.[53]

Holder went on to explain that when he made the decision to proceed under the criminal justice system, all relevant agencies were aware of his decision and none objected. Specifically, he argued: 'No agency supported the use of law of war detention for Abdulmutallab, and no agency has since advised the Department of Justice that an alternative course of action should have been, or should now be, pursued.'[54]

Holder noted that it had always been the past policy, 'without a single exception', to proceed under the criminal justice system for all suspected terrorists arrested within the borders of the US.[55] He later explained that only two people arrested within the US had been detained under the laws of war. One was Jose Padilla, arrested at Chicago's O'Hare Airport and held for over three years as an unlawful enemy combatant until being transferred to the criminal justice system, where he was ultimately convicted of a conspiracy offense relating to terrorism.[56] Holder explained that in Padilla's case, as in the case of Ali Saleh Kahlah Al-Marri, it was later deemed erroneous not to proceed under the criminal justice system, and those cases were ultimately transferred.[57] As discussed in more detail in chapter four, it was not at all clear that the decision to transfer Padilla's case to

---

[53] ibid.
[54] ibid.
[55] Holder, above, n 52.
[56] See ibid. The circumstances of Padilla's detention are discussed in considerable detail in ch 4 below.
[57] ibid.

the criminal justice system was undertaken as an admission that failing to do so from the beginning was a mistake. On the contrary, the government had no choice in the matter and was scathingly chastised for its conduct in holding the case outside of the criminal justice system.[58]

Holder's letter suggests that arrest within the US was the deciding feature as to when the criminal justice paradigm would be applied to a terrorism suspect. Of course, an arrest outside of the US has not precluded use of that system. A notable example involved the case of John Walker Lindh, known in the media as the 'American Taliban'. Lindh was captured on the battlefield in Afghanistan in November 2001. When it was discovered that Lindh was a US citizen, he was transferred to the US, where he stood trial before a US federal court on a number of criminal charges relating to providing support to a terrorist organisation. Lindh entered a plea agreement and was sentenced to 20 years in prison.[59] Because Lindh was a US citizen, he could not be designated as an 'enemy combatant', and this may explain the disposition of his case.[60] However, Holder did not address the issue of citizenship, but focused instead on place of arrest.

While Holder's introduction strongly suggested that the criminal justice and war paradigm were competing and available structures, Holder appears to have ended with a conclusion that, for those arrested within the US, the criminal justice system was the presumptive option. The letter then continued to detail successful uses of the criminal justice system to prosecute terrorists, with Holder suggesting that more than 300 terrorism cases were successfully prosecuted under Bush's Administration. He specifically described the case of the so-called 'shoe bomber' Richard Reid, a British national whose factual scenario closely resembles that of Abdulmutallab and who was criminally convicted in US federal court.[61]

As to interrogation, Holder again emphasised that Abdulmutallab was arrested within the US and stated that all defendants arrested and interrogated within the US, regardless of whether the cases were terrorism-related or not, were entitled to *Miranda* warnings. Here, Holder appears to have returned to the idea that terrorism is in fact a criminal justice issue and is indistinguishable from other criminal matters in this respect.[62]

Although arguing for the use of the criminal justice system in this case, Holder discussed the issue of war, which had been raised by those objecting to how the

---

[58] See the discussion in ch 4 below.

[59] See *Statement of Facts: USA v John Lindh*, Criminal No 02-37 (ED Va 2002), *US Department of Justice*, www.justice.gov/ag/statementoffacts.htm; Adam Liptak, 'John Walker Lindh's Buyer's Remorse' *New York Times* (23 April 2007) www.nytimes.com/2007/04/23/us/23bar.html?_r=1&ref=johnwalkerlindh.

[60] See *Hamdi v Rumsfeld*, 542 US 507, 587 (2004) (holding that a US citizen could not be detained indefinitely as an enemy combatant/unlawful enemy combatant) (plurality).

[61] See Holder, above, n 52.

[62] ibid.

case was handled. He reiterated the US government's position that it was, in fact, at war, and that:

> [W]e must use every weapon at our disposal. Those weapons include direct military action, military justice, intelligence, diplomacy, and civilian law enforcement. Each of these weapons has virtues and strengths, and we use each of them in the appropriate situations.[63]

After asserting that the US was at war, Holder concluded his letter by suggesting, once again, that the criminal justice system was one of several available tools, instead of assuming that it was the presumptive system, as he wrote:

> The criminal justice system has proven to be one of the most effective weapons available to our government for both incapacitating terrorists and collecting intelligence from them. Removing this highly effective weapon from our arsenal would be as foolish as taking our military and intelligence options off the table against al-Qaeda, and as dangerous. In fact, only by using all of our instruments of national power in concert can we be truly effective. As Attorney General, I am guided not by partisanship or political considerations, but by a commitment to using the most effective course of action in each case, depending on the facts of each case, to protect the American people, defeat our enemies, and ensure the rule of law.[64]

Although this point varied throughout his letter, overall Holder used language that suggested some agreement with the senators' suggestion that the criminal justice system was just one choice among others at the government's discretion. In so doing, he argued that the criminal justice system was an important tool, but did not say it was constitutionally mandated or presumptively adequate. He did, however, suggest that the criminal justice tool was the option of choice for suspects arrested within the US, and he did not distinguish between citizens and non-citizens regarding that point.[65]

Without eliminating the military option, for military circumstances, Holder could have presented the argument in terms of long-standing US constitutional principles, which do not make use of the criminal justice system merely one option among others when somebody is arrested under such circumstances. While this may not be the case in all jurisdictions, before 9/11 it absolutely was accepted as constitutionally mandated in the US. Even while advocating for use of the criminal justice system, Holder clearly accepted the fracturing of the system and the availability of other options for terrorism detentions.

---

[63] ibid.

[64] ibid.

[65] An analysis of this letter exchange can be found in Scott Horton, 'The Holder-McConnell Letter' *Harper's Magazine* (4 February 2010) www.harpers.org/archive/2010/02/hbc-90006481 (arguing that the policies of the Obama Administration on terrorism detentions are virtually indistinguishable from those of the Bush Administration, that the criminal and military models are each equally viable depending on which is most expedient, and that the criminal justice system has proven more effective in terms of successful convictions than the military commissions system—again, advocating in favour of use of the criminal justice system, but in a way that suggests a permissible either/or scenario).

To demonstrate how inconsistent some of the discourse has been, after Holder's detailed explanation of how suspected terrorists captured in the US should be read *Miranda* rights, there were reports of an interview given by President Barack Obama, shortly after he took office, in which he had challenged claims that the US criminal justice system was inadequate to handle terrorism cases. After clarifying that he disagreed with such claims, President Obama added: 'Now—do these folks deserve *Miranda* rights? Do they deserve to be treated like a shoplifter—down the block? Of course not.'[66] Obama's comments appear to parallel those of the senators in the letter to Holder, advancing a notion, which has continued in American discourse, that a constitutionally mandated criminal procedure protection could simply be eliminated for those suspected of terrorism. This goes well beyond the application of the public safety exception that was likely ultimately employed by the court in the Abdulmutallab case and that is employed in individual facts of a given case.[67]

Former US Attorney General Michael Mukaskey stated, along similar lines:

> Holding Abdulmutallab for a time in military custody, regardless of where he is ultimately to be charged, would have been entirely lawful—even in the view of the current administration, which has taken the position that it needs no further legislative authority to hold dangerous detainees even for a lengthy period in the United States.[68]

Mukaskey's comments seem to suggest that not only are there now parallel and equal systems available to a government where terrorism is alleged, but that there is also the option of blending these supposedly parallel systems, depending solely on expediency.[69] This is a significant break from pre-9/11 American constitutional standards.

In a later speech, Holder again reinforced his acceptance of the fractured narrative, suggesting that Military Commissions were an appropriate alternative to the criminal justice system. In discussing the US government's controversial use of targeted killings, he talked about the ongoing 'war' regarding terrorism, specifically describing the particular tools the US government asserts it can appropriately use:

> But federal courts are not our only option. Military commissions are also appropriate in proper circumstances, and we can use them as well to convict terrorists and disrupt

---

[66] Stephen F Hayes, 'Obama Disagrees with Holder on *Miranda* Rights' *Washington Examiner* (5 February 2010) www.washingtonexaminer.com/opinion/columns/OpEd-Contributor/Obama-disagrees-with-Holder-on-Miranda-rights-83587417.html. At one point, Holder said, in a television interview, that the US government was considering seeking to 'revise' the *Miranda* warning for terrorism suspects. Nico Pitney, 'Eric Holder: *Miranda* Rights Should Be Modified for Terrorism Suspects' *Huffington Post* (9 May 2010) www.huffingtonpost.com/2010/05/09/eric-holder-miranda-right_n_569244.html.

[67] See, eg, Carl A Benoit, 'The Public Safety Exception to *Miranda*' *Federal Bureau of Investigation* (February 2011), leb.fbi.gov/2011/february/the-public-safety-exception-to-miranda (explaining the foundational nature of *Miranda* warnings and how the public-safety exception was employed in specific cases, including Abdulmutallab's).

[68] Hayes, above, n 66.

[69] See James D Fry, 'The Swindle of Fragmented Criminalization: Continuing Piecemeal Responses to International Terrorism and Al Qaeda' (Spring 2009) 43(3) *New England Law Review* 377.

their plots. This Administration's approach has been to ensure that the military commissions system is as effective as possible, in part by strengthening the procedural protections on which the commissions are based. With the President's leadership, and the bipartisan backing of Congress, the Military Commissions Act of 2009 was enacted into law. And, since then, meaningful improvements have been implemented.[70]

These remarks serve to further illustrate that Holder had accepted a fracturing of the narrative, which was basically non-existent before 9/11, suggesting that the criminal justice system was optional and that other systems were equally permissible, at least in some cases.

C. The Judicial Branch

While members of the other branches of government argued over the proper system to which Abdulmutallab should be subjected, his case proceeded in US federal court. Ultimately he pleaded guilty to eight criminal charges relating to terrorism and was sentenced to life in prison.[71] The convictions included counts, among others, of conspiracy to commit an act of terrorism, an attempt to use a weapon of mass destruction and attempted murder within the special aircraft jurisdiction of the US.[72]

One other example illustrates the fracturing of the narrative on these issues, specifically in relation to some of the discourse emanating from US courts. There were a number of cases in which members of the judiciary expressed considerable cynicism about the war paradigm as a parallel option for terrorism detentions. One example arose during the sentencing of Richard Reid, the so-called 'shoe bomber', who was arrested after trying to ignite an explosive in his shoe during a flight into the US and who was referenced in Holder's letter as one of the cases in which the criminal justice system was successful.[73] After US District Court Judge William Young sentenced Reid to life in prison, Reid began critiquing US policies,

---

[70] United States Department of Justice, 'Attorney General Eric Holder Speaks at Northwestern University School of Law' (5 March 2012) www.justice.gov/iso/opa/ag/speeches/2012/ag-speech-1203051.html.

[71] For a detailed discussion of the Abdulmutallab case, including links to many of the underlying documents, see Sung Un Kim, 'Federal Court Sentences Attempted Plane Bomber to Life Imprisonment' *Jurist* (17 February 2012) jurist.org/paperchase/2012/02/federal-court-sentences-accused-plane-bomber-to-life-imprisonment.php.

[72] See the indictment: *USA v Abdulmutallab*, Case 2:10-cr-20005-NGE-DAS (ED Michigan 2010); see also Ryan J Reilly, 'Conservatives Quiet after Saying Civilian System Couldn't Handle Underwear Bomber' *TPM Muckraker* (17 February 2012) tpmmuckraker.talkingpointsmemo.com/2012/02/conservatives_quiet_after_saying_civilian_system_couldnt_handle_underwear_bomber.php (listing statements by various government officials, urging the US government to transfer his case to a military commission, in comparison with the near-silence on the issue after his conviction).

[73] See Holder, above, n 52.

suggesting he was a soldier in 'war' with the US. In his response, Judge Young told Reid:

> We are not afraid of any of your terrorist co-conspirators, Mr. Reid. We are Americans. We have been through the fire before. There is all too much war talk here. And I say that to everyone with the utmost respect.
>
> …
>
> You are not an enemy combatant. You are a terrorist. You are not a soldier in any war. You are a terrorist. To give you that reference, to call you a soldier gives you far too much stature. Whether it is the officers of government who do it or your attorney who does it, or that happens to be your view, you are a terrorist.
>
> And we do not negotiate with terrorists. We do not treat with terrorists. We do not sign documents with terrorists.
>
> We hunt them down one by one and bring them to justice.
>
> So war talk is way out of line in this court. You're a big fellow. But you're not that big. You're no warrior. I know warriors. You are a terrorist. A species of criminal guilty of multiple attempted murders.[74]

With this statement, which was widely reported at the time, Judge Young expressly rejected the narrative of war so vigorously advanced by the other branches of government. He also clearly rejected the fractured narrative of multiple paradigms to deal with people accused of acts of terrorism.

D. The Formalising of Parallel Processes

The US government continued to suggest the existence of parallel proceedings, either of which could be selected in a given case. In March 2010, Harold Koh, legal advisor to the US Department of State, made a speech to the American Society of International Law. In the speech, he reiterated comments made earlier by President Obama. He addressed the legalities of a number of controversial processes espoused by the US government and he, too, suggested that the government had essentially an equal choice between whether to pursue cases under the criminal justice system or military commissions. As Holder had in the specific context of the Abdulmutallab case, Koh spoke of the criminal justice system and its effectiveness as if he was making a concession. Instead of suggesting that a presumption existed in favour of that system, he situated it as one of a number of equally

---

[74] 'Reid: "I am at War with Your Country"' *CNN* (31 January 2003) http://edition.cnn.com/2003/LAW/01/31/reid.transcript (containing a partial transcript of the courtroom exchange between Richard Reid and Judge Young); for more information on Richard Reid, see *USA v Reid*, No 02-10013-WGY (United States District Court for the District of Massachusetts 2002).

possible competing options, referring to it as 'effective' rather than as mandatory. Specifically, he said:

> [W]e have a national security interest in trying terrorists, either before Article III courts or military commissions, and in keeping the number of individuals detained under the laws of war low.

> Obviously, the choice between Article III courts and military commissions must be made on a case-by-case basis, depending on the facts of each particular case. Many acts of terrorism committed in the context of an armed conflict can constitute both war crimes and violations of our Federal criminal law, and they can be prosecuted in either federal courts or military commissions. As the last Administration found, those who have violated American criminal laws can be successfully tried in federal courts, for example, Richard Reid, Zacarias Moussaoui, and a number of others.

> With respect to the criminal justice system, to reiterate what Attorney General Holder recently explained, Article III prosecutions have proven to be remarkably effective in incapacitating terrorists. In 2009, there were more defendants charged with terrorism violations in federal court than in any year since 9/11. In February 2010, for example, Najibullah Zazi pleaded guilty in the Eastern District of New York to a three-count information charging him with conspiracy to use weapons of mass destruction, specifically explosives, against persons or property in the United States, conspiracy to commit murder in a foreign country, and provision of material support to al-Qaeda. We have also effectively used the criminal justice system to pursue those who have sought to commit terrorist acts overseas. On March 18, 2010, for example, David Headley pleaded guilty to a dozen terrorism charges in U.S. federal court in Chicago, admitting that he participated in planning the November 2008 terrorist attacks in Mumbai, India, as well as later planning to attack a Danish newspaper.[75]

Koh's comments echo those being made at the time in the US Administration, conceding the legitimacy of the Military Commissions and again suggesting that the use of the criminal justice system was merely optional, being just one of many available tools. These comments, coming especially from the Obama Administration, surprised many people. Obama had campaigned on a promise to close Guantanamo Bay and to restore the Rule of Law to the US. Instead, as this conversation showed, the US government continued to pursue the possibility of avoiding the criminal justice system entirely through means that were highly controversial.

V. Conclusion

This last chapter in this part returns to the days, months and years right after 9/11 to address some of the changes that happened in terms of political language

---

[75] Harold Hongju Koh, 'Speech to the Annual Meeting of the American Society of International Law: The Obama Administration and International Law' *US Department of State* (25 March 2010) www.state.gov/s/l/releases/remarks/139119.htm.

during this time. The first two chapters in this part argued that the use of particular narrative and argumentation tools can significantly change the public perception of particular aspects of anti-terrorism. This chapter began to address the language, and specifically the fractured narratives, that arose after 9/11 through the use of some of these argumentation tools. To look at the overarching changes, the discussion focused on euphemisms, which were particularly prominent in the post-9/11 US government political discourse.

The various argumentation tools used after 9/11 convinced many in the US, including those in government positions, that the pre-existing criminal justice system was not the only, or necessarily even the presumptive, system to be used for terrorism detentions. By late 2009, when Abdulmutallab tried to detonate explosives on a plane on Christmas Day, it was apparent that the pre-existing understanding that the criminal justice system was the presumptive system for dealing with terrorism suspects had been shattered to some extent. Aside from the lingering, and serious, constitutional questions that persist from that fact, the state of detention practices was, as a result, in a state of some disarray. As discussed elsewhere, most cases continued to go through the criminal justice system, but this was no longer a universal assumption for these cases.

No clear alternative standard had emerged other than a general sense, among some people more than others, that there were now parallel, and equally viable, paradigms that could be applied to these cases outside of the criminal justice system, either entirely or in a piecemeal fashion. Avoiding the criminal justice system is problematic in itself, but the ways in which the system was avoided continued to show signs of considerable fracturing, or inconsistency, across governmental branches, within the US, although, as will be explained in the next part, to a lesser extent elsewhere. What was once unified was now in some state of disarray. To be clear, this is not true in all, or even most, cases. The criminal justice system continues to be the dominant paradigm in all of the places discussed. However, the difference is that, for particular cases, governments began to increasingly assert a right to detain terrorism suspects under different paradigms in particular cases. It is this type of claim that is assessed in the next part.

While this part has given some indication of how this occurred, there is much more to it than has been possible to discuss here. In Part II, a different linguistic approach is taken. Rather than focusing on the bigger picture, as much of this part has, the chapters in Part II will draw one thread out of a much bigger picture of discourse tools and will argue that these specific threads, or points of departure, played significant roles in changing long-standing constitutional detention paradigms for terrorism suspects. Since this narrative originally emanated from the US, the most obvious changes happened there, but echoes of those changes were also seen in places like Canada and the UK.

Part II

Fragmented Practices

Part I of this book took apart different layers of political discourse in order to illustrate how these layers can be strategically configured to paint a persuasive narrative. The metaphor of the kaleidoscope showed that these layers are often multi-dimensional and can enhance each other in a seemingly endless array of configurations. Because of the extensive nature of the narratives that can develop and the potential for fracturing in complex narratives, deconstructing these narratives can be challenging. Chapter three addressed some of the strategic forms of language used, especially emanating from the US after 9/11, including an example to show that, eight years after the attacks, there was considerable fracturing of the narrative surrounding the proper disposition of terrorism suspects. These types of examples continue to be laced throughout this next part of the book.

This second part of the book also turns to characteristics of terrorism detention practices as they evolved after 9/11. Again, the focus will begin in the US, the site of the attacks and the source of much of the idiosyncratic narrative after the attacks. This focus will also include relevant changes in detention patterns beyond what happened in the US, also focusing to an extent on Canada and the UK, particularly where these changes appear to have been in response to the 9/11 attacks. This discussion will, of course, recognise that there are systemic and historical differences across the three countries, which factor into the evolution of these practices.

Much of this book so far has focused on political language from Executive branches of governments, with some included from legislative branches. Governmental judicial branches also played a significant role in the way in which post-9/11 narratives and detention practices developed in different places, and their role cannot be overstated. Judicial decisions played a major role in halting some of the fracturing of the post-9/11 narrative by trying to bring these narratives back to fundamental constitutional norms.

One of the earliest, and most powerful, decisions denouncing post-9/11 detention practices came from the UK Law Lords in the so-called *Belmarsh Detainees* case. Nine men, all foreign nationals, were being detained, potentially indefinitely, on suspicion of terrorism involvement.[1] UK citizens could not be

---

[1] See *A and Others v Secretary of State for the Home Department* [2004] UKHL 56 (hereinafter *Belmarsh Detainees* case).

similarly detained because the men were detained under the immigration system. The detentions were loosely based on a claim that the 9/11 attacks meant that there was an imminent risk of terrorist attacks in the UK.[2]

The House of Lords concluded that such indefinite detention without trial under the Anti-terrorism, Crime and Security Act 2001 was incompatible with the European Convention on Human Rights. This decision, issued in late 2004, instantly made international headlines with its memorable quotes. Part of Lord Richard Scott's quote, reproduced below, became especially prominent:

> An individual who is detained under section 23 will be a person accused of no crime but a person whom the Secretary of State has certified that he 'reasonably ... suspects ... is a terrorist' (section 21(1)). The individual may then be detained in prison indefinitely. True it is that he can leave the United Kingdom if he elects to do so but the reality in many cases will be that the only country to which he is entitled to go will be a country where he is likely to undergo torture if he does go there. He can challenge before the SIAC the reasonableness of the Secretary of State's suspicion that he is a terrorist but has no right to know the grounds on which the Secretary of State has formed that suspicion. The grounds can be made known to a special advocate appointed to represent him but the special advocate may not inform him of the grounds and, therefore, cannot take instructions from him in refutation of the allegations made against him. Indefinite imprisonment in consequence of a denunciation on grounds that are not disclosed and made by a person whose identity cannot be disclosed is the *stuff of nightmares*, associated whether accurately or inaccurately with France before and during the Revolution, with Soviet Russia in the Stalinist era and now associated, as a result of section 23 of the 2001 Act, with the United Kingdom. (Emphasis added)[3]

The powerful language in this decision is discussed in more detail in chapter five below. This example is presented here to set the stage for the way that narratives can shift. This one strongly worded set of opinions caused a shift in the way in which the UK approached these detentions and it sent ripples to that effect to other countries as well. Narratives played a role in differences in the way in which practices developed as time passed. As weak narratives make for weak law, strong narratives have the opposite effect. This notion underpins the issues discussed in Part II.

It is impossible to comprehensively discuss all of the controversies that have arisen regarding anti-terrorism detention practices and it is impossible to apply all of the threads of argumentation theory to these practices within the boundaries of one book. Instead, this section proceeds by way of example, drawing on the idea of points of departure, as described by Perelman and Olbrechts-Tyteca, and van Eemeren, and expanded upon in chapter two. Part II of this book demonstrates, through the use of three examples, how problems in points of departure for arguments significantly affected the development of legal norms regarding terrorism

---

[2] ibid.
[3] ibid para 155 (Lord Scott of Foscote).

detentions after 9/11.[4] If problems can be demonstrated through this one thread of argumentation, the inference is that drawing out the many other elements of argument structure would provide many more pathways to assess the validity of the resulting changes. Other controversial points of departure might have served equally well, and these are acknowledged, even where they might not be expressly included in this work. Other controversial aspects of anti-terrorism detention practices might also have served as examples. These are acknowledged, if not included. Finally, this analysis recognises that some argumentation was sound and that some changes might have been appropriate. However, the focus here is on problematic threads that are used to demonstrate the larger critiques of some aspects of changed terrorism detention practices.

---

[4] See Chaim Perelman and Lucie Olbrechts-Tyteca, *The New Rhetoric: A Treatise on Argumentation,* translated by John Wilkinson and Purcell Weaver (Notre Dame, IN, University of Notre Dame Press, 1969); Frans H van Eemeren et al, *Fundamentals of Argumentation Theory: A Handbook of Historical Backgrounds and Contemporary Developments* (Mahwah, NJ, Lawrence Erlbaum Associates, 1996) 103; and see ch 2 above.

4

Hasty Inductive Generalisation: The Problem with the Claim that the 9/11 Attacks Exposed a Need for New Detention Paradigms

I. Crisis Shifts in Long-Standing Detention Paradigms Occurred after the 9/11 Attacks

The first argumentation point of departure that underscored many changes in post-9/11 terrorism detention practices relates to the idea that 'everything changed' on 9/11.[1] This statement does not stand alone for this purpose, but is accompanied by a second, connected and indispensable component, which is that everything changed in a way that required a shift in the presumptions for terrorism detentions. In other words, the idea is that the 9/11 attacks represented a new threat, or exposed an existing threat not previously seen, which allowed governments to treat pre-existing criminal justice systems as presumptively inadequate in particular cases.

Two preliminary points should be made here. There is much academic debate over whether the 9/11 attacks were unprecedented or whether terrorism itself is new or changing. This chapter focuses on the first issue, relating specifically to the 9/11 attacks, and not on the larger question of whether terrorism itself is new, which is a debate that is acknowledged, but is not central to the claims made in this chapter.[2] The point of departure that is criticised in this chapter has two elements

---

[1] See generally Joseph Margulies, *What Changed When Everything Changed? 9/11 and the Making of National Identity* (New Haven, Yale University Press, 2013) 5–6 (disputing the assumed nature of such changes and arguing that the claims that all had changed were not accurate).

[2] See, eg, Ersun Kurtulus, 'The 'New Terrorism' and its Critics' (2011), 34(6) *Studies in Conflict & Terrorism* 22 (explaining the theory and the major arguments for and against the idea of a 'new terrorism'); Thomas R Mockaitis, *The 'New' Terrorism* (Westport, CT, Praeger Security International, 2007) (breaking down several identified 'myths' about the nature of terrorism, particularly in popular understanding since the 9/11 attacks); Walter Lacquer, 'Terror's New Face: The Radicalization and Escalation of Modern Terrorism' (1998) 20(4) *Harvard International Review* 48; Russell Howard and Bruce Hoffman, *Terrorism and Counterterrorism: Understanding the New Security Environment: Readings & Interpretations* (New York, McGraw-Hill Education, 2012); Peter R Neumann, *Old and*

to it, and these two elements must be read in conjunction with each other. This is that 'everything changed' on 9/11 and that whatever changed justified a shift away from the criminal justice paradigm in particular terrorism cases. Even if the first part is conceded—and some aspects of it are—it does not follow that this concession supports the second part, which is that this shift justified a fragmenting of detention practices or a movement away from those pre-existing paradigms.

The second preliminary point is that this argument starts from the contention that the primary mode of dealing with terrorism detentions in most places before 9/11 was the criminal justice system. Military detentions were used in particular war-related matters, but generally were not seen as the dominant paradigm for terrorism detentions before 9/11 in the US, although they had been employed before, in finite capacities, in places like Israel and the UK.[3] Even today, though, most terrorism cases are still handled under national criminal justice systems. The number of cases handled through extraordinary detention regimes is relatively small in relation to the larger world of terrorism detentions. That said, after 9/11, some governments asserted the option of proceeding with terrorism detentions outside of the criminal justice system in particular cases. In doing so, these governments did not run up against a presumption in favour of the criminal justice system, which they had to overcome in order to so proceed, whereas before 9/11, they would have. As will be explained in more detail in this chapter, the specifics of how this played out varied with different jurisdictions, depending on a number of other factors. However, the shift in presumption was unmistakable. This shift is the subject of this chapter's argument.

To explain the title of this chapter, a 'hasty inductive generalisation' is an argumentation fallacy under which 'a person generalizes from a single anecdote or experience, or from a sample that is too small or too unrepresentative to support his conclusion: Too narrow a range of human experience is taken as a basis for reaching a conclusion about all experiences of a given type'.[4] Rather than being based on an in-depth study of terrorism or the effectiveness of the criminal justice system, the shift in presumption regarding the use of the criminal justice system appears to have largely arisen from the significant loss of life and property damage that happened on 9/11. While shocking, these factors were not enough, on their own, to give rise to the idea that pre-existing paradigms could not be trusted.

New Terrorism: Late Modernity, Globalization and the Transformation of Political Violence (Cambridge, Polity, 2009); Alexander Spencer, 'Questioning the Concept of 'New Terrorism' (2006) 8(8) *Peace Conflict & Development* 1; Peter R Neumann, *Old and New Terrorism: Late Modernity, Globalization and the Transformation of Political Violence* (Cambridge, Polity, 2009) (collectively, these sources are called *The New Terrorism Literature*).

[3] See, eg, Kent Roach, *The 9/11 Effect: Comparative Counter-terrorism* (New York, Cambridge University Press, 2011), 245 (discussing the Diplock courts in the UK); Kathleen Cavanaugh, 'The Israeli Military Court System in the West Bank and Gaza' (2007) 12 *Journal of Conflict & Security Law* 197 (Israel); Amos Guiora, *Global Perspectives on Counterterrorism* (New York, Aspen, 2007) (Israel).

[4] Trudy Govier, *A Practical Study of Argument* (Belmont, CA, Wadsworth Inc, 1988) 331.

II. The 'Unprecedented' Nature of the 9/11 Attacks

On 16 September 2001, George W Bush addressed the people of the US about the attacks. He said: 'We haven't seen this kind of barbarism in a long period of time. No one could have conceivably imagined suicide bombers burrowing into our society and then emerging all in the same day to fly their aircraft—fly U.S. aircraft into buildings full of innocent people—and show no remorse. This is a new kind of—a new kind of evil.'[5] The message was clear. What happened on 9/11 was new and everything had changed.

There is considerable controversy over whether the attacks of 9/11 did indeed expose a new kind of threat.[6] This controversy is noted, but does not necessarily have to be definitively resolved here. While much of the discourse supporting changed practices related to a forward-looking risk that had to be averted, it was still mingled with an invocation of the particular horrors of the 9/11 attacks, especially in the early days after the attacks, where they were frequently described as unprecedented and as catastrophic to pre-existing structures. The sense quickly emerged that these unprecedented attacks called for an unprecedented response.[7]

This point of departure is distinct from that expressed in academic literature relating to the so-called 'New Terrorism', which suggests that terrorism is evolving over time and which has been persuasive on many levels.[8] Terrorism is undoubtedly evolving, and it was doing so before the 9/11 attacks, although this is also not an entirely uncontroversial contention. Terrorism certainly continued to evolve after 9/11. Daesh provides a vivid example of the fact that terrorism is not the local matter that it once was deemed to be, and the asserted religious motivation, however inaccurate, gives terrorism a potentially appealing motivation for certain people. However, it does not follow that it is new in a way that justifies specific governmental responses, and the newness of some aspects of terrorism does not

---

[5] George W Bush, 'Remarks by the President upon Arrival: The South Lawn' *White House Archives* (16 September 2001) georgewbush-whitehouse.archives.gov/news/releases/2001/09/20010916-2.html.

[6] For discussions of the arguments about the 'new' nature of the risk exposed or created by the 9/11 attacks, see, eg, 9/11 Commission, 'The Foundation of the New Terrorism' in *The 9/11 Commission Report* at 47–70, www.911commission.gov/report/911Report.pdf; Davis Brown, 'Use of Force Against Terrorism after September 11: State Responsibility, Self-Defense and Other Responses' (2003–04) 11 *Cardozo Journal of International and Comparative Law* 1 (beginning with the statement that the terrorist attack on 9/11 was 'unprecedented in its scope'); Paul Gilbert, *New Terror, New Wars* (Washington DC, Georgetown University Press, 2003).

[7] See, eg, Benjamin Wittes, *Law and the Long War: The Future of Justice in the Age of Terror* (New York, Penguin, 2008) (arguing for a 'new kind of Constitution for the War on Terror' in the US, suggesting that, while the US detention practices shortly after 9/11 may have failed, the US government was correct in asserting that terrorism presents an unprecedented threat in terms of nature and scope). But see International Commission of Jurists, Eminent Jurists Panel on Terrorism, Counter-terrorism and Human Rights, *Assessing Damage, Urging Action* (Geneva, 2009) 12 (arguing that US policies, in particular, after 9/11 had to fail because they were based on the incorrect premise that the attacks were sufficiently unprecedented as to necessitate deviating from the Rule of Law long in place).

[8] See *The New Terrorism Literature*, above, n 2.

support the often-asserted idea that the 9/11 attacks themselves splintered the world into before and after.

In 2015, the Canadian government, in response to several high-profile Daesh (or Daesh-inspired) attacks, proposed sweeping anti-terrorism legislation. This legislation, commonly referred to by its parliamentary designation of Bill C-51, ultimately met with strong public resistance.[9] Famously, two prominent Canadian law professors in the area of national security, Craig Forcese and Kent Roach, were on sabbatical at the time.[10] Their sabbaticals became newsworthy because they immediately sprang into action in opposition to specific aspects of the proposed legislation, and the process through which they acted had a significant, immediate impact on the public narrative surrounding the proposed legislation.[11] In a political atmosphere demanding that the government be seen as tough on terror, Forcese and Roach made the particulars of the proposed legislation accessible to Canadians in a way they otherwise would not have been. Their efforts changed the public narrative on the legislation.[12] They live-blogged objections to particular aspects of the legislation, invited people to contribute, testified about their concerns in Parliament and ultimately wrote a well-received book called *False Security: The Radicalization of Canadian Anti-terrorism*.[13] The title of the book is important from a narrative perspective in using the language typically used to describe terrorists, but applying it to Canadian government responses. Their work showed the importance and persuasive value of adequate nuance in these discussions.

In terms of the point of departure regarding the newness of terrorist threats, this chapter endorses the following point from their book:

> ISIS is a new terrorist threat, one that is somewhat different from Al-Qaida. The United Nations Security Council has labelled the foreign terrorist fighting inspired by ISIS and others a threat to international peace. We think government politicians have overstated (and probably inflated) the risk through their political rhetoric, but the government has a responsibility to protect Canadians from terrorism, and to stop Canadians from terrorism in foreign lands
>
> …
>
> Our concerns are not with these objectives, but with how the new laws purport to achieve these important goals. The means matter; the details matter; proportionality matters. We are concerned that in their design and manner of addressing their legitimate objectives,

---

[9] The designation Bill C-51 is in use in 2017 to refer to completely different legislation. Because the designation became so well known in Canada for the anti-terrorism legislation, that designation will still be used here to refer to the anti-terrorism legislation.

[10] John Geddes, 'Meet the Professors behind the Swift Assault on C-51' *Maclean's* (3 March 2015) www.macleans.ca/uncategorized/two-profs-take-on-the-harpers-anti-terrorism-bill.

[11] ibid.

[12] This statement is based on personal observations of the author, who followed these developments as they happened.

[13] Craig Forcese and Kent Roach, 'Canada's Proposed Antiterrorism Act', *Wordpress*, cdnantiterror-ismlawaudit.wordpress.com/about (calling for a 'crowdsourced' response to Bill C-51); Craig Forcese and Kent Roach, *False Security: The Radicalization of Canadian Anti-terrorism* (Toronto, Irwin Law, 2015).

the new laws make us less free, and will also likely fail to make us safer from real terrorist threats.[14]

Terrorism is absolutely evolving and responses should evolve too. The larger academic area regarding the 'New Terrorism' pre-dates the 9/11 attacks and is distinct from the argument assessed in this chapter in an important way. The changes emanating from the US after 9/11 did not necessarily stem from the arguments of 'New Terrorism' and, had they done so, the responses implemented might have been more thoughtful in nature. The point of departure for changed practices was more finite than that, just that the 9/11 attacks themselves changed everything, and that the need for changed detention paradigms immediately arose from these attacks. While there were certainly some aspects of the 9/11 attacks that may have been unprecedented or that somehow exposed a new threat, it does not necessarily follow that the newness demonstrated there justified the way in which the criminal justice paradigm was simply swept aside in certain cases. As Forcese and Roach noted, it is possible to agree with the larger objective of fighting terrorism, and even to concede that some aspects of terrorism are evolving, while still noting that '[t]he means matter; the details matter; proportionality matters'.[15]

Moreover, nothing suggests that the political figures who advanced the language of change after 9/11 were aware of, much less influenced by, this area of literature on New Terrorism. Instead, their stated claims were more cataclysmic and tied specifically, and sometimes solely, to the 9/11 attacks. The 9/11 attacks were too often viewed in isolation when supporting the conclusion that everything changed, and a more thoughtful approach would have drawn on the considerable available analysis of terrorism and its morphing character.

As Joe Margulies pointed out in his book *What Changed When Everything Changed*: 'We are often told that September 11 "changed everything." But this is a sentiment more repeated than explained.'[16] While there is no doubt that terrorism has been evolving and is different in nature from the local entity it once was, it is not so clear that the 9/11 attacks exposed a new risk that was so different that governments now needed the option of dispensing with the presumptive use of criminal justice systems for certain terrorism suspects.

Assertions that the attacks were unprecedented began immediately after they occurred and may not have been surprising, given the horrific image of terrorists using planes full of civilians as weapons, the high number of casualties, the massive damage to property including buildings with high symbolic value, and the resulting fallout in terms of trauma, financial implications and ongoing threats. As discussed earlier, all of this happened on live television, with millions of people as first-hand witnesses, and this factor set these attacks apart from many others as well.

---

[14] Forcese and Roach, above, n 13, 8.
[15] ibid.
[16] Margulies, above, n 1, 5–6.

The day after the 9/11 attacks, the Ukrainian representative to the UN Security Council was already talking about the need for significant changes in response to the attacks, noting: 'The magnitude of the events was way beyond terrorism as the world had so far known it … With the new technologies and changed nature of the world, a handful of angry people was enough to cause havoc. New definitions and new strategies had [*sic*] to be evolved for those new forms of terrorism.'[17]

Other remarks supported this idea. In a press release announcing the adoption of UN Security Resolution 1368, Sergey Lavrov, of the Russian Federation, was cited as saying that the US 'had come up against an unprecedented act of aggression from international terrorism'.[18] M Patricia Durrant, of Jamaica, said that the attacks 'had plunged the entire world into an unprecedented period of peril, fear and uncertainty'.[19] German Chancellor Gerhard Schröder remarked the day after the attacks '[t]oday we are still horror-struck by an unprecedented terrorist attack on the principles that hold our world together', further suggesting that 'yesterday's terrorist attack demonstrated once again that security in our world is not divisible. It can only be achieved by standing together more closely for our values and by working together to implement them'.[20]

After he established the Military Commissions at Guantanamo Bay in late 2001, Bush wrote, in a memo dated 7 February 2002, of the need for new detention paradigms because of the specific nature of the 9/11 attacks. The memo says:

> [T]he war against terrorism ushers in a new paradigm, one in which groups with broad, international reach commit horrific acts against innocent civilians, sometimes with the direct support of states. Our nation recognizes that this new paradigm—ushered in not by us, but by terrorists—requires new thinking in the law of war, but thinking that should nevertheless be consistent with the principles of Geneva.[21]

Not all, however, so quickly espoused the view that the attacks were unprecedented in a way that mandated unprecedented responses. Five weeks after the attacks, Derrida critiqued some of the language that was already arising as accepted. For instance, he critiqued the type of language—admittedly used throughout this book—that designated the event simply by a date. This, he said, gave rise to certain inferences:

> When you say 'September 11' you are already citing, are you not? You are inviting me to speak here by recalling, as if in quotation marks, a date or a dating that has taken over our public space and our private lives for five weeks now. Something *fait date*, I would

---

[17] Brown, above, n 6 (quoting Statement of Ambassador Valeriy Kuchinsky, Press Release, SC/7143, 'Security Council Condemns "in Strongest Terms" Terrorist Attacks on United States' *United Nations* (2001) www.un.org/News/Press/docs/2001/SC7143.doc.htm (quoting Valery P Kuchinsky).

[18] ibid.

[19] See ibid (paraphrasing remarks of M Patricia Durrant, Jamaica).

[20] German Chancellor Gerhard Schröder, 'Full Solidarity with the United States' *German History Docs* (12 September 2001) germanhistorydocs.ghi-dc.org/sub_document.cfm?document_id=3724.

[21] President George W Bush, 'Humane Treatment of Taliban and al Qaeda Detainees' *The White House* (7 February 2002) www.pegc.us/archive/White_House/bush_memo_20020207_ed.pdf.

say in a French idiom, something marks a date, a date in history; that is always what's most striking, the very impact of what is at least felt, in an apparently immediate way, to be an event that truly marks, that truly makes its mark, a singular and, as they say here, 'unprecedented' event. I say 'apparently immediate' because this 'feeling' is actually less spontaneous than it appears: it is to a large extent conditioned, constituted, if not actually constructed, circulated at any rate through the media by means of a prodigious techno-socio-political machine. 'To mark a date in history' presupposes, in any case, that 'something' comes or happens for the first and last time, 'something' that we do not yet really know how to identify, determine, recognize, or analyze but that should remain from here on in unforgettable: an ineffaceable event in the shared archive of a universal calendar, that is, a supposedly universal calendar, for these are—and I want to insist on this at the outset—only suppositions and presuppositions.[22]

As this debate developed over the years, invocation of past catastrophic attacks was sometimes used to argue that the attacks were not unprecedented.[23] An example is found in the contention by Jennifer Daskal in 2009, arguing against the use of preventive detention in the US, in part based on the fact that the 9/11 attacks were, indeed, not unprecedented in the sense that they required new detention regimes:

[O]ver the past 230 years, the United States has endured two world wars, a lengthy cold war, waves of domestic terrorism, and a civil war that almost broke the nation apart, without passing legislation that would allow the state to detain people for extended periods based on a prediction of future dangerousness.[24]

In many ways, the debates over whether 9/11 was unprecedented appear to have created a cyclical sort of argumentation. Everything is unprecedented in some way and it would be disingenuous to suggest that there were not many unprecedented aspects to the 9/11 attacks. It is the second component of this presumption, the place of the criminal justice system, that is most dominant in having spurred structural changes to detention standards after 9/11. The question should be, if it is asked at all, whether the criminal justice system was adequate to handle the scenario raised by the 9/11 attacks and whether, if it is deemed inadequate, changes could be made within the existing parameters of this system rather than looking to new systems outside of this paradigm. If the attacks were unprecedented, but the existing system was still adequate, no change would be needed. If the attacks were, in fact, precedented in terms of the threat posed, but because of some characteristic of the criminal justice system, it was indeed not adequate to address the threat, then a much stronger argument for change is presented. And, of course, if the attacks were indeed so unprecedented as to support the necessity of avoiding

---

[22] Giovanna Borradori, *Philosophy in a Time of Terror: Dialogues with Jürgen Habermas and Jacques Derrida* (Chicago, University of Chicago Press, 2003) 86.

[23] See, eg, Jennifer Daskal, 'A New System of Preventive Detention? Let's Take a Deep Breath' (2009) 40 *Case Western Reserve Journal of International Law* 561, 562 (noting further that those actions undertaken in those emergency situations were invariably later 'resoundingly repudiated as mistaken experiments that are contrary to the United States' commitment to due process and the rule of law').

[24] ibid.

the criminal justice system, then the argument for change is likely the strongest yet. However, it is not mandatory that the attacks should be found unprecedented, nor is it necessary that finding them to have a precedent means that no changes are warranted.

In other words, the actual question is not really whether the attacks were unprecedented, but whether there was something new about the attacks, or the threat they exposed, which necessitated an assumption that long-standing principles of constitutional fair trial procedures were inadequate, even where these structures were largely maintained during past crises or abandoned to later remorse.[25] A question to consider is whether, indeed, this underlying presumption, even if it could have been valid in the short term after the attacks as an emergency perspective, has become normalised in the Foucault sense and thus woven into the fabric of the normative developments in this area going forward.[26] These two elements of the question cannot be separated, as they are inextricably linked in the way in which the point of departure was created to support the changes made.

III. The 9/11 Attacks Led to a Claim of Presumptive Inadequacy of National Criminal Justice Systems in Certain Cases

Thus, the 9/11 attacks gave rise to the constant spectre of an imminent, future threat, and to the idea that the world was now somehow new. While not always expressly explained, this belief was linked to the idea that the presumption in favour of the use of criminal justice paradigms in terrorism cases was no longer always in place. This conclusion seems not to have been based on an extensive analysis of responses to terrorism elsewhere, at least by the US, either historically or at that time, but more on a quickly assembled assumption relating specifically to the 9/11 attacks, developed somewhat in a vacuum. As one example, President Bush essentially declared war on terrorism in his speech on 20 September 2001 and this narrative, presented nine days after the attacks, set the stage for the US using a varied war paradigm for detention of suspects at places like Guantanamo Bay.[27]

---

[25] See ibid.
[26] See Michel Foucault, *The History of Sexuality*, vol 1, translated by Robert Hurley (New York, Random House, 1978) 89, 144 (discussing normalisation, rather than law, as a basis for power); Chaim Perelman and Lucie Olbrechts-Tyteca, *The New Rhetoric: A Treatise on Argumentation*, translated by John Wilkinson and Purcell Weaver (Notre Dame, IN, University of Notre Dame Press, 1969).
[27] See President George W Bush, 'Address to a Joint Session of Congress and the American People' *The White House* (20 September 2001), georgewbush-whitehouse.archives.gov/news/releases/2001/09/20010920-8.html.

In some cases, it appears as if the fractured narrative surrounding detention practices caused an underlying instability in some of the procedural structures long identified as mandatory in certain national systems of justice. Questions of effectiveness abound. Forcese and Roach called the Canadian response to particular, later terrorist events, through Bill C-51, an 'extreme whack-a-mole response [that] may just produce more moles while managing to whack a lot of things that are not moles'.[28]

This general approach led to a number of specific reactions and to several high-profile shifts in traditional criminal justice procedural standards. Implicit in the stated presumption that the attacks were unprecedented was the idea that the only way to address this unprecedented event was to avoid the pre-existing criminal justice system in particular cases and to build a new detention regime, or modify an existing regime, that would be adequate to address this unprecedented type of risk.

Rumsfeld's comment about 'unknown unknowns', discussed in chapter two above, while giving rise to some parody, also contains an element of truth.[29] Particularly as the 9/11 attacks were happening, and shortly thereafter, there was considerable confusion as to who was responsible, the extent of the plans for attack and how to respond. This confusion was understandable, given the sudden nature of the attacks in the middle of a metropolitan area and the obvious intention of the hijackers to carry out the attacks in a surprise manner. Thus, it is entirely possible that some of the practices critiqued herein might have been more readily justifiable in those early days, when governments did not know the full nature of the threat. The justification, if it can be found, in this scenario, would lie not in whether the attacks were unprecedented or new, but in the unknown, sudden and confusing nature of the threat, particularly at the outset. As time passed, and considerable information became known to various governments about al-Qaeda, this factor may have lessened as a potential justification.

While there may well have been individual or finite circumstances under which there was a valid necessity for extraordinary actions, it cannot simply be assumed, based on generalised statements, that the attacks created a need to build parallel new detention paradigms or to revise non-criminal paradigms to use for terrorism suspects. Generalised statements did not support the argument that those systems already in existence were entirely inadequate, at least for some cases. If, indeed, it could be established that the existing structures were not adequate in a particular instance—and this would have to be established rather than simply stated—the logical next step would seem to be to adapt those structures somehow rather than to simply set them aside entirely in favour of a parallel system. To the extent that a

---

[28] Forcese and Roach, above, n 13, 9.

[29] Donald Rumsfeld, 'DoD News Briefing—Secretary Rumsfeld and Gen. Myers' *US Department of Defense* (12 February 2002), www.defense.gov/transcripts/transcript.aspx?transcriptid=2636.

parallel system might be deemed necessary, logically it should have been seen as a last resort instead of the presumptive first resort it sometimes was.

Aside from the problem underlying the immediate presumption away from the criminal justice system in some of these cases, the inertia then began to favour these revised practices, and it appears to often have become incumbent on those wishing to rely on the criminal justice system to justify doing so. This shift is obvious from the conversation set out in chapter three above regarding Umar Farouk Abdulmutallab, where members of the US Senate demanded an explanation from the Executive Branch as to why the established criminal justice procedures were followed after he was arrested.

This inertia appears to have changed from a presumption in favour of such systems in some cases and instead in favour of the parallel paradigm.[30] It is not claimed that entire national criminal systems were set aside, as they obviously were not. But such systems were often presumptively set aside in relation to certain people to whom even a suspicion of terrorism affiliation was attached.

Predictability, uniformity and presumptions favouring those accused of crimes appeared to destabilise and, in some cases, were replaced by structures that lacked these characteristics. The US Military Commissions initially had procedural safeguards that were so at odds with traditional criminal justice standards that they were repeatedly revised over the ensuing years, as a result of ongoing challenges before the US Supreme Court and responsive legislation. This ongoing revision has created an ongoing and additional pattern of unpredictability for those subject to these fora, in addition to the unpredictability inherent in the very existence of these structures, outside of the constitutionally protected criminal justice system.[31] As some men continue to remain in custody for years after 9/11, with no prospect of any full judicial hearing relating to their detentions, many of the 9/11 detainees seem to share characteristics with Kafka's man from the country,

---

[30] See ch 2 above for a discussion of inertia.

[31] For some of the back-and-forth on terrorism detentions in the US, see the White House, 'President Issues Military Order: Detention, Treatment, and Trial of Certain Non-citizens in the War against Terrorism' *The White House* (13 November 2001) georgewbush-whitehouse.archives.gov/news/releases/2001/11/20011113-27.html (establishing Military Commissions at Guantanamo Bay); *Rasul v Bush*, 542 US 466 (2004) (finding that Guantanamo Bay detainees had standing to seek habeas corpus review in US courts); Detainee Treatment Act of 2005, HR 2863, Title X (establishing procedures for Combatant Status Review Tribunals, limiting appeals from these tribunals and limiting the ability of Guantanamo Bay detainees to seek habeas corpus or any review in US courts, in response to the *Rasul* ruling); *Hamdan v Rumsfeld*, 548 US 557 (2006) (finding that the Military Commissions could not proceed because they lacked proper procedure and violated the Uniform Code of Military Justice and the Geneva Conventions, specifically Common Art 3); Military Commissions Act 2006, Pub L No 109-366, 120 Stat 2600 (17 October 2006), enacting Chapter 47A of title 10 of the United States Code (and amending s 2241 of title 28) (responding to *Hamdan* and establishing revised procedures for the Military Commissions); *Boumediene v Bush*, 553 US 723 (2008) (holding that the detainees at Guantanamo Bay had a right to habeas corpus hearings under the US Constitution); Military Commissions Act 2009, Title XVIII of the National Defense Authorization Act for Fiscal Year 2010, Pub L 111-84, HR 2647, 123 Stat 2190 (enacted 28 October 2009) (clarifying procedures for the Military Commissions and revising some of the more controversial aspects of the 2006 legislation).

who dies waiting for his case to be heard and who never manages to successfully navigate the arbitrary and incomprehensible rules to find justice.[32]

This type of uncertainty is evidenced by the habeas corpus hearings before US federal courts, which resulted from the US Supreme Court's decision in *Boumediene v Bush*.[33] The US government had claimed for years that prisoners at Guantanamo Bay had no recourse under the US Constitution and no protection under international law. It took multiple trips to the US Supreme Court for this to be established, in 2008, to have been wrong. Thus, for the six years it took for this decision to be reached, prisoners were held essentially in legal limbo at Guantanamo Bay, struggling for recognition of recourse that would have already been available if their cases had proceeded under the criminal justice system.

The criminal justice paradigm never stopped being the dominant vehicle for handling terrorism cases, even in places like the US, which went to such lengths to avoid that system in particular cases.[34] Still, alternative dispositions became a significant, and controversial, approach to terrorism detentions in different places. Guantanamo Bay became a prominent focus for the disposition of certain terrorism suspects (or enemy combatants, or unlawful enemy combatants, as these terms were interchanged as if they meant the same thing). As discussed in more detail in chapters five and six below, national immigration systems also served as a launching point for jurisdictions seeking to avoid their own criminal justice systems, certainly initially in the US, but also in places like Canada and the UK. These systems were sometimes used to detain people suspected of terrorism activities, without the procedural safeguards of the criminal justice system, and these practices evolved in different ways in different places, often not for the better.

If the ultimate objective of these 'new' detention paradigms, outside of the criminal justice system, was to detain terrorists and stop this 'new' threat, one questions whether they have been successful, or whether a presumptively valid criminal justice model would have been a more strategic approach. Implicit in the point of departure that drives this chapter is the notion of necessity. Necessity was

---

[32] See ch 2 above for a discussion of Kafka's *The Trial*; see also Andy Worthington, *Guantanamo Files: The Stories of the 774 Detainees in America's Illegal Prison* (London, Pluto Press, 2007) (detailing information about each prisoner who has been held at the US prison at Guantanamo Bay since the 9/11 attacks, all of whom were men).

[33] *Boumediene*, above, n 31; see also ch 6 below for a discussion of the Military Commissions.

[34] See Robert Chesney and Jack Goldsmith, 'Terrorism and the Convergence of Criminal and Military Detention Models' (2008) 60 *Stanford Law Review* 1079; Richard B Zabel and James J Benjamin, Jr, *In Pursuit of Justice: Prosecuting Terrorism Cases in the Federal Courts, Human Rights First* (2008), *Human Rights First*, www.humanrightsfirst.org/wp-content/uploads/pdf/080521-USLS-pursuit-justice.pdf; Richard B Zabel and James J Benjamin, Jr, *In Pursuit of Justice: Prosecuting Terrorism Cases in the Federal Courts: 2009 Update and Recent Developments, Human Rights First*, www.humanrightsfirst.org/wp-content/uploads/pdf/090723-LS-in-pursuit-justice-09-update.pdf (accepting to some extent the delineation of the crime-versus-war binary as a starting point, regardless of whether advocating for or against the dominance of the criminal justice system); Government of the United Kingdom, *Counter-terrorism Strategy (CONTEST)* (12 July 2011) www.gov.uk/government/publications/counter-terrorism-strategy-contest at 50 (stating '[o]ur priority is always to prosecute people suspected of terrorist-related activity in this country').

also cited by the Priest in explaining the Doorkeeper's actions in Kafka's Parable.[35] Necessity cannot be a sole consideration, granting national governments the power to deviate from constitutionally mandated norms. Necessity is also not a justification if the practices do not actually work.

The extraordinary detention approaches created considerable controversy and litigation for a relatively low number of detainees, at least in relation to the numbers who went through the criminal justice system in the same time period. This appeared to be part of a larger trend, in which political figures tried to persuade different audiences that individual liberties, or law itself, interferes with national security.[36]

Of course, the objective may not have been to secure criminal convictions, but, alternatively, to hold people in a preventive manner, not because of past actions, but because of a fear of future actions, which raises different issues. However, the use of the Military Commissions suggests some governmental interest in securing some form of conviction. Moreover, in the US, it has been suggested that one concern with finally bringing many of the Guantanamo detainees before a criminal court would have been the admissibility of evidence obtained through 'enhanced interrogation'.[37] The US government has, in fact, asserted intelligence gathering as an objective of detentions such as those at Guantanamo Bay. Of course, aside from the moral implications of using torture, it fails to meet even the practical test of this basis, since it has been concluded that the US torture programme simply did not produce reliable intelligence.[38] If the 'new' extraordinary detention regimes were deemed necessary to prevent the 'new' threat of terrorism, there is no published evidence to suggest that they accomplished this end, at least not in a systemic matter that would correspond with the systemic nature of some of these altered practices. However, criminal convictions for the 9/11 attacks might have sent this message.

As suggested in the title of this book, many of the post-9/11 detention practices have been fragmented, within particular jurisdictions, across jurisdictions and over time. Still, there are some common themes that can be drawn from many of these practices. The next section explores some of those themes, as partial support for the proposition that new detention regimes were used, or pre-existing

---

[35] See ch 2 above for a discussion of Kafka's *The Trial*.

[36] See chs 5 and 6 below for an in-depth discussion of some of these alternative structures; see also Mark A Drumbl, 'Guantanamo, *Rasul* and the Twilight of Law' (2004–05) 53 *Drake Law Review* 897, 916 (characterising the US approach as a belief that law impairs, rather than advances, national security).

[37] See, eg, ibid.

[38] See Senate Select Committee on Intelligence, *Committee Study of the CIA's Detention and Interrogation Program: Findings and Conclusions* (updated 3 December 2014) www.feinstein.senate.gov/public/_cache/files/a/9/a992171e-fd27-47bb-8917-5ebe98c72764/7889A5C19ACFE837C78C2192B08 76B90.sscistudyfindingsandconclusions.pdf (partially redacted) 2 (concluding that '[t]he CIA's use of its enhanced interrogation techniques was not an effective means of acquiring intelligence or gaining cooperation from detainees').

non-criminal paradigms were expanded, to deal with those suspected of involvement in terrorism.

A. Characteristics of 'Extraordinary Detention' Practices Included Changes Radiating Out from the US

A US-centric approach to some of this discussion does not suggest that US developments are more important than those in other countries, and it certainly does not suggest that the US approach to terrorism overall has greater significance. Rather, as the site of the attacks, the US generated a stronger reaction, which had echoes in how certain other countries responded. There is some debate over the extent of US influence around the world after 9/11. Kent Roach, for instance, has argued against the notion that the US led the charge to change detention practices in specific response to 9/11. He has argued instead that it was the UK that had the most obvious influence on other national jurisdictions in terms of their detention and interrogation structures after 9/11.[39]

Arguably there is truth in both assertions. The US had the most significant narrative influence on other jurisdictions with its 'with us or against us' approach, and with some of the narrative underpinnings discussed especially in chapter five below.[40] However, in ruling on extraordinary detention practices after 9/11, national high courts in Canada and the UK, for instance, seemed more inclined to look to each other than to jurisprudence in the US in addressing the forms of extraordinary detention practices. This could be for many reasons, not the least of which is that the US was the only jurisdiction to expressly adopt its war scenario for terrorism detentions, likely because of constitutional differences that affected the power distribution under a war paradigm.[41] In terms of the forms of altered detention practices, it does appear that the influence may well have largely emanated out of the UK, while the notion of using such practices more generally emanated from the US.[42]

Why the UK would have been so influential can be considered on a number of levels, such as the fact that Canada and Australia shared a common heritage with the UK in terms of their legal systems, more so than the US, as well as the possibility that the UK was simply viewed as having a more sophisticated understanding of how to address the threat of terrorism, based on its long experience dealing with

---

[39] Kent Roach, *The 9/11 Effect: Comparative Counter-terrorism* (New York, Cambridge University Press, 2011) (comparing different national responses to the 9/11 attacks) 13.

[40] See Bush, above, n 27.

[41] See, eg, US Constitution, Art II, s 2 (designating the President as 'Commander in Chief').

[42] See, eg, *Charkaoui v Canada (Citizenship and Immigration)* [2007] 1 SCR 350, 2007 SCC 9 (hereinafter *Charkaoui I*) (the SCC expressly referred to the UK system of using special advocates in antiterrorism cases in which secrecy was being asserted as necessary).

the Irish Republican Army (IRA).[43] In some cases, it also appears that an initial willingness to follow the US led some national leaders to problems back home, where such initiatives were not met with the enthusiasm they often encountered among the populace in the US.[44] An obvious example would be the widespread protests in 2003 when the US invasion of Iraq was imminent.[45] This may relate back to what Perelman and Olbrechts-Tyteca said about subjective values of a particular audience in the effectiveness of persuasion.[46]

B. Trends for Detentions Inside National Borders versus Outside National Borders

The US influence is also most obvious, even in form, when countries were respond-ing to the attacks through actions outside of their own national borders. The UK, Canada and Australia, as examples, joined the US in its invasion of Afghanistan. The UK and Australia also participated in the US invasion of Iraq, suggesting some adherence to the US response to the 9/11 attacks.

In addition, in dealing with detainees captured in these confrontations, it appears that the US was heavily influential, as can be seen by the cooperation of these governments, on varying levels, regarding detention of their citizens at the US prisons, such as at Guantanamo Bay. Arguably, while Australia and the UK ultimately secured the release of their nationals from Guantanamo Bay, Canada in particular demonstrated a willingness to defer to the US in its detention and treatment of Canadian citizen, Omar Khadr—a controversy that continues to the present day.[47] The willingness of Canada's executive to defer to the US entirely on this matter led to a highly unusual showdown with Canada's courts, resulting in rulings of the Supreme Court of Canada, rebuking the Canadian government for its actions, but falling short of ordering it to act on Khadr's behalf.[48]

However, when it came to detainees within their own borders, it appears that many jurisdictions were less inclined to be influenced by the US in terms of form

---

[43] See generally Roach, above, n 39; Victor Ramraj, Michael Hor, Kent Roach and George Williams (eds), *Global Anti-terrorism Law and Policy*, 2nd edn (Cambridge, Cambridge University Press, 2012) (describing anti-terrorism responses in a number of national jurisdictions).

[44] In 2003, for instance, after Canada had joined the US in its invasion of Afghanistan, and the US was indicating it was about to invade Iraq, street protests took place in Canada. Ultimately, Canada did not join the US in its invasion of Iraq. This is based on my personal recollection from Montreal at that time.

[45] This is based on my personal recollection as an American living in Montreal at the time.

[46] See, eg, the discussion of values of a particular audience in ch 2 above.

[47] See Colin RG Murray, 'The Ripple Effect: Guantánamo Bay in the United Kingdom's Courts' (2010) 23(1) *Pace International Law Review* (OC) 15 (discussing Khadr briefly, as well as the status of other Western citizens, including David Hicks of Australia and Moazzam Begg of the UK).

[48] See *Canada (Justice) v Khadr*, 2008 SCC 28; *Canada (Prime Minister) v Khadr*, 2010 SCC 3 (here-inafter *Khadr II*). This second ruling especially involved strong language by the Supreme Court of Canada, but a recommendation, rather than an order, in terms of a remedy, as the Court did not want to intrude on executive authority.

or extent of the changes and that there, as Roach posits, the influence of the UK was much more obvious.[49] In relation to detentions and interrogations of those captured within national borders and accused of terrorism, Roach persuasively asserts that 'British antiterrorism law has had a much greater effect on other countries than American law, much of which is dauntingly complex and idiosyncratic'.[50] Similarities can be seen through such examples as the use of control orders in Australia, implemented in a different manner but nonetheless comparable to those implemented in the UK.[51] Canada's use of immigration detentions initially mirrored those undertaken in the UK, although the UK turned away from this mechanism, initially in favour of a system of control orders. Canada declined to follow the UK's example in this latter respect, but did initiate a system of special advocates for cases involving secret charges or secret evidence, and in its first *Charkaoui* ruling, the Supreme Court of Canada said it was recommending this system based on the UK model.[52]

Beyond this, it is unquestionable that, as Roach points out, US law in this area appears considerably more complex than comparable paradigms in many other countries. However, as discussed throughout this book, this very complexity could be argued to be intentional, as the US manufactured confusion that muted critique.

C. The Crisis Atmosphere Shortly after the Attacks Led to Some Permanent Structural Changes

The area of emergency declarations is a large one and, as discussed in the Introduction, states of emergency are currently common occurrences around the world because of terrorism. This work will not extensively engage with this area because the detention practices that are the focus of this book were not generally established as temporary emergency measures. They were, however, established in a *milieu* of crisis, so the sense of emergency engendered by the attacks was relevant to how detention practices developed. After the attacks, a sense of imminent, future risk was used to persuade audiences that certain changes had to happen, and had to happen quickly, but the changes themselves were not necessarily established with an eye to the temporary, as true emergency measures are.

The US considered al-Qaeda and the Taliban to be threats to national security even before the 9/11 attacks and, in 1999, then-President Bill Clinton declared a national emergency as a result of this perceived threat.[53] Emergency-themed

---

[49] Roach, above, n 39, 13.

[50] ibid.

[51] See generally Law Library of Congress, *Australia: Terrorism Laws: Control Orders* (October 2008).

[52] See *Charkaoui I*, above, n 42. This and other related cases are discussed in more detail in ch 5 below. See also Immigration and Refugee Protection Act, SC 2001, c 27, s 85, 85.1.

[53] See *Executive Order 13129: Blocking Property and Prohibiting Transactions with the Taliban* (4 July 1999) *Avalon Project, Yale Law School*, http://avalon.law.yale.edu/20th_century/t_0012.asp.

discourse, not surprisingly and not unreasonably in the early days, accelerated after 9/11. Some of the resulting extraordinary detention scenarios may not have initially been intended to be systematic, permanent changes.[54] Instead, they likely began as urgent—or perceived urgent—measures to respond to a catastrophic attack. They certainly arose in an atmosphere of crisis.

In the US, Bush declared a formal state of emergency a few days after the 9/11 attacks, and this state of emergency has been renewed regularly.[55] Some of the critique of treating many of the post-9/11 initiatives as emergencies is the idea of an open-ended emergency—a scenario that has been employed elsewhere, such as in Israel in response to the threat of terrorism.[56] In spite of this declaration of emergency, and a great deal of 'emergency'-oriented discourse, few of the initiatives relating to extraordinary detention of terrorists are couched in terms of emergency, temporary provisions.[57]

Emergency language, which was dominant in the early days after 9/11, faded as time passed. Even when such discourse prevailed, there was considerable disagreement expressed as to whether there ever was, in fact, a true emergency situation relating to terrorism in places like the US or Canada. In 2002, David Dyzenhaus and Rayner Thwaites noted:

> Western legal orders are not living in a time of emergency or terror, despite the best efforts of our leaders to tell us otherwise. Additionally, the idea that the way to deal with

---

[54] Compare David Dyzenhaus, 'The Permanence of the Temporary: Can Emergency Powers Be Normalized?' in Ronald Joel Daniels, Patrick Macklem and Kent Roach (eds), *The Security of Freedom: Essays on Canada's Anti-terrorism Bill* (Toronto, University of Toronto Press, 2001), 21.

[55] See *Declaration of National Emergency by Reason of Certain Terrorist Attacks*, 50 USC 34 § 1621 (14 September 2001) (renewed periodically); 'Letter—Continuation of the National Emergency with Respect to Certain Terrorist Attacks' *White House Archives* (30 August 2016) obamawhitehouse. archives.gov/the-press-office/2016/08/30/letter-continuation-national-emergency-respect-certain-terrorist-attacks. The initial declaration, as it appears originally and as renewed, indicates that the President would be invoking a number of federal statutes that grant the President special powers during times of war or national emergency. In addition, the US Congress passed two authorisations, the first being the *Authorization for Use of Military Force*, Pub L 107-40 (18 September 2001) (authorising the use of military force against those responsible for the 9/11 attacks) and the second being the *Authorization for Use of Military Force against Iraq Resolution of 2002*, Pub L 107-243, 116 Stat 1498 (16 October 2002), both granting the President extraordinary military authority in direct response to the attacks. Referring to the state of emergency he declared in September 2001, then-US President George W Bush then issued the military order, which created the initial military commissions at Guantanamo Bay Detention Centre. See 'President Issues Military Order: Detention, Treatment, and Trial of Certain Non-Citizens in the War against Terrorism' *The White House* (13 November 2001) georgew-bush-whitehouse.archives.gov/news/releases/2001/11/20011113-27.html (establishing Military Commissions at Guantanamo Bay) (collectively, these are referred to as *Urgent Sources*).

[56] For a discussion of how common law countries can address emergencies such as the threat of terrorism, see David Dyzenhaus, *The Constitution of Law: Legality in a Time of Emergency* (Cambridge, Cambridge University Press, 2006); for further discussion of the concept of emergencies as they relate to terrorism, see Victor Ramraj (ed), *Emergencies and the Limits of Legality* (Cambridge, Cambridge University Press, 2008).

[57] See Kent Roach, 'Ordinary Laws for Emergencies and Democratic Derogations from Rights' in Ramraj (n 60) 229 (noting '[a]though I am sceptical about whether the post-9/11 debate is really about emergencies, I am not sceptical about the fact that modern society will confront genuine emergencies').

the challenges to the West sharpened by the events of 9/11 is by waging a 'war on terror' was from the beginning and is, evermore, preposterous.[58]

In addition to the formal declaration of emergency, the US Congress passed two authorisations for the use of military force, and President Bush issued a military order, which established the military commission system at Guantanamo Bay.[59] These declarations and orders were issued in quick succession after the attacks, all being in place by November 2001.[60]

As those orders were being set up, the 'USA Patriot Act' was passed by both Houses in the US Congress and was signed into law by President Bush in late October 2001, approximately six weeks after the attacks, despite being a lengthy and complex document, containing amendments to a large number of federal statutes.[61] Among other things, the USA Patriot Act, which contained a number of temporary, sunset provisions, allowed for special detention provisions for immigrants who were of interest to the US government.[62]

Rhetoric by those in positions of power in the US exuded a sense of extreme crisis, which certainly could be supported by the horrific images from the sites of the attacks and from initial uncertainty as to who was responsible for the attacks. When the US government moved quickly to curtail certain constitutional protections for those accused of terrorism, criticism sprang up, which was addressed in stark terms. The following statement by former US Attorney General John Ashcroft, quoted from his book, is an example of how the government responded to those expressing alarms about incursions to constitutional protections:

> Some people in our country seem more concerned about respecting the dignity and privacy of criminals and terrorists than they are about having an airport full of people obliterated, or a completely booked hotel blown to bits. Perhaps they think, Let's not get so upset about attacks on our embassies or military bases. Maybe, they surmise, the terrorists have good reason for attacking us. We have no right to be harassing innocent people in our country. For some people, not even the grotesque images that filled our television screens after al Qaeda's blatant attacks on 9/11 seem enough to wake them out of their utopia feel-good world.[63]

---

[58] David Dyzenhaus and Rayner Thwaites, 'Legality and Emergency: The Judiciary in a Time of Terror' in Andrew Lynch, Edwina MacDonald and George Williams (eds), *Law and Liberty in the War on Terror* (Sydney, Federation Press, 2002), 9.

[59] See *Urgent Sources*, above, n 55.

[60] ibid.

[61] See *Uniting and Strengthening America by Providing Appropriate Tools Required to Intercept and Obstruct Terrorism Act of 2001*, Pub L 107-56, 115 Stat. 272 (2001) (revising various sections of the US Code) (hereinafter the USA Patriot Act). For a more extensive discussion of the extraordinary circumstances surrounding the signing of the USA Patriot Act, see Maureen T Duffy, 'The U.S. Immigrations in the War on Terror: Impact on the Rule of Law' (unpublished Master's thesis, McGill University, 2005) 10–12.

[62] USA Patriot Act (n 61).

[63] John Ashcroft, *Never Again: Securing America and Restoring Justice* (New York, Hachette Book Group USA, 2006) 259.

Beyond that, however, it is apparent that the shock of such a catastrophic attack, coupled with continued threats by representatives of al-Qaeda against a number of other countries, reasonably led those in power in a number of other democracies to consider that they, too, might be at some risk of attack. Obviously, this response was enhanced, and perceived as confirmed by some, by subsequent high-profile attacks in the years following the 9/11 attacks, including, for instance, the anthrax scares in the US, the 2002 attacks in Bali, the 2004 attacks in Madrid, the '7/7' attacks in London in 2005 and the 2008 attacks in Mumbai.[64] Thus, the sense of crisis and the direct response to 9/11 happened in a number of liberal democracies and was by no means limited to the US or to the original 9/11 reactions.[65]

Some years after the attacks, there was some acknowledgement, even by those in positions of power in the US, that a certain haste precluded thoughtful analysis of initial changes in detention standards. For example, in a speech in May 2009, US President Barack Obama made the following comments about the US response immediately after 9/11:

> Unfortunately, faced with an uncertain threat, our government made a series of hasty decisions. I believe that many of these decisions were motivated by a sincere desire to protect the American people. But I also believe that all too often our government made decisions based on fear rather than foresight; that all too often our government trimmed facts and evidence to fit ideological predispositions. Instead of strategically applying our power and our principles, too often we set those principles aside as luxuries that we could no longer afford. And during this season of fear, too many of us—Democrats and Republicans, politicians, journalists, and citizens—fell silent.[66]

However, it appears that there was not necessarily an accompanying shift back to the standards that existed before these 'hasty decisions' were made. Extraordinary detention practices have evolved differently in different places. Some of the more obvious ones, like the detentions and Military Commission trials at Guantanamo Bay, continue in 2017. Such practices have often evolved into familiar, accepted and increasingly permanent changes—normalised if put in Foucault's terms. Not only were there significant changes that took place in the early days after 9/11, expounded upon throughout this book, but, from one year to the next, the parameters of terrorism detention standards have continued to shift as disputes continue between courts and law-makers, as law-makers have reconsidered some of their initial stances as new government leaders are elected and as popular opinion varies. The result has often, in some places, been an internally inconsistent, arguably arbitrary system, under which completely different systems of justice might

---

[64] See N Kaldas, 'Australia and the Changing Terrorist Threat' (2007) 1(1) *Policing: A Journal of Policy and Practice* 61 (explaining that the fears raised by the 9/11 attacks were continuing and subsequently confirmed by further attacks in London, Madrid, Mumbai, Bali and elsewhere).

[65] See generally Roach, above, n 39.

[66] Barack Obama, 'Remarks by the President on National Security: National Archives, Washington, DC' *White House Archives* (21 May 2009) obamawhitehouse.archives.gov/blog/2009/05/21/security-values.

be available to two people accused by the same government of virtually identical conduct. If, indeed, the intent of the changes was to address the underlying, clearly serious allegations regarding terrorist conduct, it seems that the systems employed to do so would be consistent from one person to the next.

Many of the initiatives that were put in place, however 'hasty' those initial decisions may have been, have gained a certain permanence with the passage of time, in some ways perhaps fuelled simply by the fact that they are now familiar. The reactions to some of the actions taken by democratic governments after 9/11 are somewhat more muted years later, when the extremes—such as torture—still elicit strong responses, but the more insidious changes, such as an apparent shift from the presumption of innocence in some cases, have gained a certain familiarity and are thus questioned much less often and much less strenuously than in the early days after 9/11.[67]

It is not entirely clear if that reduced questioning results from a 'slow creep of complacency', which has made the prospect of fully untangling the complex web of initiatives undertaken since 9/11 simply too difficult.[68] As a pragmatic matter, it is simply easier to begin an argument with the existing, familiar set of standards than it is to go back and untangle the various layers of the initiatives undertaken since 9/11. Moreover, the niche of 'terrorism' has created in the minds of many a seemingly permanent state of exception, and there is often little governmental analysis of larger questions, such as what these alterations mean for detention standards in all other criminal cases or what they might mean for the viability of overarching constitutional norms and/or democratic standards. Some argue that, in the wake of 9/11, some traditionally liberal political democracies have shifted their structures in ways more commonly associated with authoritarian regimes, at least in relation to practices surrounding the detention of terrorism suspects.[69] One author characterises the shift as follows:

> [T]he soft and facilitating state was replaced by a strong and intrusive state, and the categorical gap between rights-based democracies and authoritarian polities narrowed worryingly under a declared open-ended state of emergency and the so called 'war on terror'.[70]

The author refers to this as 'democracy without moorings'.[71] It does appear, with the complex set of standards now allowing for 'exceptions' to traditional

---

[67] See, eg, *Canada (Citizenship and Immigration) v Harkat*, 2014 SCC 37 (upholding the highly controversial, and problematic, special advocate regime in Canada. The system was established in the years after the 9/11 attacks as part of the evolution of security-certificate detentions in Canada).

[68] Quoting *Secretary of State for the Home Department (Respondent) v AF (Appellant) (FC) and Another (Appellant) and One Other Action* [2009] UKHL 28, para 84 (Lord Hope of Craigshead) (hereinafter *AF*).

[69] See, eg, Dora Kostakopoulou, 'How to Do Things with Security Post 9/11' (2008) 28 *Oxford Journal of Legal Studies* 317, 318.

[70] ibid.

[71] ibid 319.

constitutional values, as if the foundational structure of some previously fundamental changes may have indeed become less stable, particularly in relation to
pre-existing standards of criminal justice. This shift appears, in many respects,
to have been based on threshold points of departure, the first of which is that the
9/11 attacks were so unprecedented that they exposed the need to develop a new
paradigm of detention and interrogation standards where terrorism is concerned.

IV. Certain Commonalities Emerged across Jurisdictions Regarding Extraordinary Detention Practices

The discourse employed by national governments after 9/11, and in many respects
continuing to the present day, led to various structural shifts. Some shifts were
unique to particular national jurisdictions, while others appeared to be much
more systemic not only across jurisdictions but also across different types of
proceedings. Some changes had structural differences, but appeared to be based
on similarities in terms of the underlying argumentation and assumptions upon
which they were built.

Arguments did continue, of course, in favour of the criminal justice system, but
they often did so under this new structure, in which the governmental changes
seemed to enjoy a presumption in their favour. Like the conversation about
Abdulmutallab from the last chapter, those advocating for exclusive use of the
criminal justice system were increasingly placed in a defensive position. An example is found in the work undertaken by Richard B Zabel and James Benjamin,
in which they documented every criminal prosecution for terrorism in the US
between 2002 and 2006. They considered prosecutions relating to international
terrorism, noting an exceptionally high rate of success in terms of prosecutions
and also in terms of addressing the evidentiary problems that the US government
was citing as an excuse for not proceeding under the criminal justice system.[72]

Zabel and Benjamin's work was, by necessity, framed as a response to the US
government's assertions that the criminal justice system was not adequate to
address issues of international terrorism in all cases. In the introduction, they
note, in response to arguments for a special 'national security' court: 'A premise of
such arguments is that the traditional court system is not well-equipped to handle
international terrorism cases. We aim to explore that premise.'[73]

---

[72] See Richard B Zabel and James J Benjamin, Jr, *In Pursuit of Justice: Prosecuting Terrorism Cases
in the Federal Courts, Human Rights First* (2008), www.humanrightsfirst.org/wp-content/uploads/
pdf/080521-USLS-pursuit-justice.pdf (hereinafter Zabel and Benjamin I); Richard B Zabel and James
J Benjamin, Jr, *In Pursuit of Justice: Prosecuting Terrorism Cases in the Federal Courts: 2009 Update
and Recent Developments, Human Rights First*, www.humanrightsfirst.org/pdf/090723-LS-in-pursuit-
justice-09-update.pdf (hereinafter Zabel and Benjamin II).
[73] Zabel and Benjamin I, above, n 72.

This characterisation of the issue was necessary because of the emerging presumption that the criminal justice system was inadequate, at least for particular cases. Such an argument, before 9/11, would simply not have happened the same way in the US, and the criminal justice system would not have been deemed optional.

If, indeed, the presumption was continuing to favour the criminal justice system, the US government would have been the one required to prove its case to the contrary. Instead, those seeking to continue the exclusive, or at least dominant, use of the criminal justice system had to be the ones to make their case.

Zabel and Benjamin concluded that the criminal justice system alone did not suffice to handle terrorism—mentioning that other options, including things like intelligence and military—were necessary tools.[74] There is, however, a difference between addressing *terrorism* and addressing *terrorism detentions* and *judicial procedure*, and this distinction is often lost in much of this debate. While noting strains on the criminal justice system, Zabel and Benjamin also noted, among other things, that this system is adaptable and has been adapted in practice, commenting that:

> [E]xperience has shown that the justice system has generally remained a workable and credible system. Indeed, the justice system has shown a key characteristic in dealing with criminal terrorism cases: adaptability. The evolution of statutes, courtroom procedures, and efforts to balance security issues with the rights of the parties reveals a challenged but flexible justice system that generally has been able to address its shortcomings.[75]

Beyond the apparent fracturing in terms of the presumption in favour of the criminal justice system, several themes emerge regarding the fragmenting of detention practices. Some of these themes are discussed below.

A. A Shifting away from the Presumption of Innocence: Moving away from the Magna Carta

Predictability is considered a critical component in criminal law, with the notion that a person cannot be deprived of liberty based on a crime that did not exist as of the time of the conduct or under procedures that are not transparent and fair. It is not just the substantive notice that something is a crime that underpins most modern criminal law proceedings, but also the idea of fair judicial process, under which an accused, facing a loss of liberty, understands what needs to be done in order to refute the charges and thus try to avoid incarceration. The fundamental importance of a person's individual liberty has long underscored legal presumptions, which tended to weigh in the detainee's favour, most notably in

---

[74] ibid 2.
[75] ibid.

relation to the presumption of innocence, often either stated or read into national constitutions.[76]

However, recent trends for terrorism suspects have shown an increasing movement towards a presumption of guilt, at least in those cases undertaken outside of the criminal justice system. Under extraordinary detention regimes, the onus has sometimes shifted to the detainee to prove innocence rather than remaining with the government to establish guilt, as explained in the subsequent sections of this chapter below.[77] There is an obvious difference between placing the burden of proof on the state, which has made the accusation and seeks to take punitive action, and placing it on the detainee, who is at an enormous disadvantage in relation to the state in terms of resources and who is facing extreme personal consequences for failure to meet the burden of proof. The spectre of somebody deprived of liberty, perhaps for life, without ever being told the charges against him or having full access to a court with transparent procedures, or even in some cases having access to legal counsel, is no longer just the 'stuff of nightmares' in many places for certain cases.[78]

One theme is that, overall, these pre-existing liberty presumptions have shifted in some cases. The initial, somewhat reflexive reaction in many countries after 9/11 was a tendency to engage in detentions that had the potential to become indefinite, without accompanying criminal charges. As legal challenges inevitably arose to such practices, some initial commonalities among different countries in terms of how they handled these cases began to dissipate, and practices became more fragmented across jurisdictions. In all of these extraordinary cases, the starting presumption was not that the individual should be free or that the individual should be presumed innocent. Rather, it appears instead as if the starting presumption was that the person was guilty, or dangerous, if the objective of the detention was purely preventive. From the starting point of this assumption of guilt or dangerousness, assessments of measures less restrictive than detention began, rather than assessments of whether the person should be deprived of liberty at all. These detentions have the suggestion of being more preventive than punitive, but also of allowing governments to bypass the higher evidentiary burdens required in a criminal proceeding.[79]

For instance, since 9/11, the question of a detainee's right to petition a court to challenge the lawfulness of the detention—known as habeas corpus—has

---

[76] See, eg, US Constitution, amendments 5, 6 and 14; Constitution Act, 1982, Schedule B to the Canada Act 1982 (UK), 1982, c 11, ss 7 and 11 (d).

[77] This critique comes up in most extraordinary detention scenarios, especially where secret evidence is asserted as necessary, including the Military Commissions at Guantanamo Bay, the security certificate regime in Canada, the control orders (now eliminated) in the UK.

[78] Quoting *Belmarsh Detainees* case, above, Part II, n 1.

[79] For an example of the apparent increased acceptance that preventive detentions are inevitable in the fight against terrorism, see Stephanie Cooper Blum, *The Necessary Evil of Preventive Detention in the War on Terror: A Plan for a More Moderate and Sustainable Solution* (Amherst, NY, Cambria Press, 2008).

been hotly debated in the US.[80] This right to petition for habeas corpus is a long-standing principle of freedom stemming from the English common law tradition and, as such, it has had a dominant place in legal systems deriving from the English tradition, such as those considered herein. The significance of this principle was reaffirmed by the UK House of Lords, when assessing post-9/11 domestic terrorism detentions, as follows:

> In urging the fundamental importance of the right to personal freedom, as the sixth step in their proportionality argument, the appellants were able to draw on the long libertarian tradition of English law, dating back to chapter 39 of Magna Carta 1215, given effect in the ancient remedy of habeas corpus, declared in the Petition of Right 1628, upheld in a series of landmark decisions down the centuries and embodied in the substance and procedure of the law to our own day.[81]

Much has obviously been written about the history of Magna Carta, and this history is primarily relevant here only to demonstrate the long-standing relevance of habeas corpus in these legal systems before 9/11 in order to compare with the way habeas corpus rights were affected afterwards. The above quotation presents habeas corpus as a guarantee that has been continuous in the British legal tradition from its inception with Magna Carta. In the US, this traditional common law notion continued after the separation from Great Britain, and it has been so integral that it is referenced in the original US Constitution. Other concepts of individual freedom tend to be contained within the amendments to the Constitution, particularly, but not exclusively, in the Bill of Rights, which includes the first 10 amendments.[82]

While Magna Carta is widely cited for setting forth the notion of habeas corpus, it is not a source of legally binding authority so much as the source of the tradition for this protection. As one author argues, it represents more a set of principles, and he explains that 'the point is not that Magna Carta provides the grounds for a specific legal right but that it stands for or, at least, represents the start of a tradition of understandings about how governments should behave vis-à-vis the citizenry'.[83] Questions certainly arise as to whether, since 9/11, this understanding in countries deriving part of their legal tradition from principles such as those in Magna Carta

---

[80] In the US, much of this debate was put to rest by the landmark ruling of the US Supreme Court in *Boumediene* (above, n 31), although the decision was specifically relating to Guantanamo Bay detainees, and the US government continued to argue that for other detainees held elsewhere, there was no right to habeas corpus review in US courts. See, eg, *Al Maqaleh v Gates*, 604 F Supp 2d 205 (DC Cir 2009) (subsequent case progress omitted for this purpose).

[81] *Belmarsh Detainees* case, part II, n 1, para 36.

[82] See US Constitution, Art I, s 9 ('The Privilege of the Writ of Habeas Corpus shall not be suspended, unless when in Cases of Rebellion or Invasion the public Safety may require it').

[83] David Clark, 'The Icon of Liberty: The Status and Role of Magna Carta in Australian and New Zealand Law' (2000) *Melbourne University Law Review* 34 (this article discusses the ongoing significance of Magna Carta, including the role of habeas corpus in Australian law, assessing that significance as of a time shortly before the 9/11 attacks. The author notes '*Magna Carta* is part of the legal and political legacy of Australia and New Zealand') (citations omitted).

have changed that 'tradition of understandings' about a government's relationship with its citizens.

Executive detentions are not new and they have sometimes been used in the UK in the past in fighting terrorism, but much less so in places like the US and Canada.[84] A question arises as to whether executive detentions, without criminal charges, should be acceptable, at least without a strong showing by the government that it is acceptable in the finite cases in which they are used. That question is especially compelling in those jurisdictions deriving their history from the tradition that includes the principles of Magna Carta. As William Blackstone said:

> Of great importance to the public is the preservation of this personal liberty: for if once it were left in the power of any, the highest, magistrate to imprison arbitrarily whomever he or his officers thought proper ... there would soon be an end of all other rights and immunities ... To bereave a man of life, or by violence to confiscate his estate, without accusation or trial, would be so gross and notorious an act of despotism, as must at once convey the alarm of tyranny throughout the whole kingdom. *But confinement of the person, by secretly hurrying him to gaol, where his sufferings are unknown or forgotten; is a less public, a less striking, and therefore a more dangerous engine of arbitrary government.* (Emphasis added; some language updated to modern form for readability)[85]

Blackstone eloquently laid out the rare scenario under which habeas corpus might be properly suspended, and his words resonate with the general view taken of this right by modern legal systems deriving from the British common law tradition:

> And yet sometimes, when the state is in real danger, even this may be a necessary measure. But the happiness of our constitution is, that it is not left to the executive power to determine when the danger of the state is so great, as to render this measure expedient. For the parliament only, or legislative power, whenever it feels proper, can authorize the crown, by suspending the habeas corpus act for a short and limited time, to imprison suspected persons without giving any reason for so doing ... In like manner this experiment ought only to be tried in case of extreme emergency; and in these the nation parts with it's [*sic*] liberty for a while, in order to preserve it for ever.[86]

In the US before 9/11, suspensions of habeas corpus were rare and generally in response to a perceived emergency—of finite duration and generally repudiated in later, less-crisis-driven times.[87] A famous example involved President Abraham

---

[84] See Derek McGhee, 'Deportation, Detention & Torture by Proxy: Foreign National Terror Suspects in the UK' (2008) 29(1) *Liverpool Law Review* 99 (discussing the 'separate "executive" justice system for dealing with terror suspects in post-9/11 (and post-7/7) UK'); see also David Bonner, *Executive Measures, Terrorism and National Security* (Burlington, VT, Ashgate, 2007) (containing an excellent and comprehensive discussion of Executive detention measures, with a significant emphasis on practices in the UK).

[85] William Blackstone, *Commentaries on the Laws of England* (1765, Book 1) 130–31, *Avalon Project*, *Yale Law School*, www.yale.edu/lawweb/avalon/blackstone/bk1ch1.htm.

[86] ibid.

[87] A notorious example was the detention of people of Japanese origin or descent, including both citizens and non-citizens, in camps during the Second World War because of a presumption of disloyalty. This practice ultimately led, many years later, to a formal apology by the US Government. See *Korematsu v United States*, 323 US 214 (1944).

Lincoln during the US Civil War. Lincoln ultimately sought Congressional approval for this suspension. In addition to this action, he also sought to try civilians suspected of aiding the Confederates before military commissions within the US.[88]

The US Supreme Court responded with one of its most famous decisions, *In re Milligan*. The Court described the type of circumstances that might justify trials, in the US, of American citizens by military commissions. This could conceivably be permissible, the Court said, on a very temporary basis, and only in the physical proximity of a great emergency, '[i]f, in foreign invasion or civil war, the courts are actually closed, and it is impossible to administer criminal justice according to law'.[89] Only then, the Court said, can martial law be implemented, adding that 'as necessity creates the rule, so it limits its duration; for, if this government is continued after the courts are reinstated, it is a gross usurpation of power'.[90]

The threat situation in the US, for instance, since 9/11 seems less onerous than it did during the US Civil War, when President Lincoln reportedly could see enemy troops from the White House windows. Lincoln famously suspended habeas corpus during the Civil War, when the risk to the country was quite obvious. The trend in liberal democracies, after 9/11, has been towards wider-ranging, and more permanent, shifts in fundamental notions relating to habeas corpus than those contemplated during the US Civil War, although most commonly limited to people who are not citizens of the given national jurisdiction. It is unclear whether the US government was mindful of the admonition from *In re Milligan* in the way that it structured limitations on habeas corpus rights relating to terrorism detainees. The modern, terrorism-related Military Commissions are held at Guantanamo Bay, which the US government tried, unsuccessfully, to argue was outside of the jurisdiction of the US. In addition, by definition, those held at Guantanamo Bay are not US citizens, so the suspensions are factually distinguishable from those described in *In re Milligan*. However, this fact does not justify the distinctions in the treatment of detainees in a government's custody and this will be discussed in more detail in chapter five below.

B. Secret Detentions

Another characteristic of the altered detention practices after 9/11 is that traditional notions of procedural fairness have frequently been eroded for those suspected of terrorism. Separate and apart from overarching changes relating to the presumption of innocence, specific components of what have been deemed elements of fair process have also undergone a perceptible shift in some cases. Traditionally, with

---

[88] See *Ex parte Milligan*, 71 US 2 (1866).
[89] ibid 127–28 (citations omitted).
[90] ibid (citations omitted).

certain, express exceptions, the presumption has been for criminal proceedings to be open, with the general idea that such openness helps to ensure fairness.[91]

Secrecy, however, became a major aspect of terrorism detentions after 9/11, usually on the basis that it was necessary for national security reasons. The extent of this secrecy has varied considerably and it has evolved, as do the specific aspects of detentions to which secrecy is claimed to apply. For example, the US stands out among other nations in having sought to keep the very fact of detention a secret— a practice that seems to have been less common in other liberal democracies that altered their practices after 9/11.[92] It was based on that secrecy that, for instance, the Center for Constitutional Rights, in representing the *Turkmen* plaintiffs, a group of 'special-interest' detainees held in the US under its immigration system shortly after 9/11, represented to the Court that it could not identify all the members of the class.[93] This case, consolidated with others, wound its way through the US courts for years. The Supreme Court of the United States ruled generally in favour of the government, for a variety of reasons, in June 2017.[94]

It is now known that, shortly after the 9/11 attacks, the US government ordered that immigration proceedings for the so-called 'special-interest detainees' be held in secret, including an order that the very fact of their detentions be kept secret.[95] This policy became widely known after publication of the 'Creppy Memo', which lays out the parameters of secrecy to be applied to these cases.[96]

The American processes frequently included secretly detaining people overseas as well, often through secret transfers, known as 'extraordinary rendition'.[97] The US has been accused of secret practices that could arguably be characterised as

---

[91] See, eg, Blackstone's admonition against the potential for abuse from secret detentions (Blackstone, above, n 85).

[92] In other liberal democracies, the tendency has been towards an increased assertion of the need to use secret evidence rather than complete secrecy surrounding the fact of detention or the actual proceedings. However, in addition, secret evidence has been an issue within the US. See Daphne Barak-Erez and Matthew Waxman, 'Secret Evidence and the Due Process of Terrorist Detentions' (2009) 48 *Columbia Journal of Transnational Law* 3.

[93] See *Turkmen v Ashcroft*, Class Action Complaint and Demand for Jury Trial, No 02-CV-02307-JG (filed 17 April 2002) (EDNY 2002), complaint and all court filings online: lawcrawler. findlaw.com/scripts/lc.pl?CID=ILC-LawcrawlerHomepage&sites=findlaw.com&sites=findlaw.com& entry=Turkmen.

[94] See *Ziglar v Abbasi et al*, No 15-1358 (2017).

[95] The 'special interest' detainees will be discussed in more detail in ch 5 below.

[96] See Michael Creppy, 'Instructions for Cases Requiring Additional Security' *FindLaw* (21 September 2001), news.findlaw.com/cnn/docs/aclu/creppy092101memo.pdf; Duffy, above, n 65, 7–8, 12–14 (outlining various US government efforts to keep these proceedings secret, including the release, under great pressure, of a partial list of the detainees, with their names and other information redacted); see also generally David Cole, *Enemy Aliens* (New York, New Press, 2005).

[97] See Commission of Inquiry into the Actions of Canadian Officials in Relation to Maher Arar, *Report of the Events Relating to Maher Arar: Analysis and Recommendations* (2006) *Security and Intelligence Review Commission*, www.sirc-csars.gc.ca/pdfs/cm_arar_rec-eng.pdf; Michael C Jensen, 'Torture and Public Policy: *Mohamed v Jeppesen Dataplan, Inc.* Allows "Extraordinary Rendition" Victims to Litigate around State Secrets Doctrine' (2010) 2010(1) *Brigham Young University Law Review* 117.

kidnapping for the purpose of torture, with detention sites in different places, known as 'black sites'.[98]

One example involves the case of Majid Khan. Khan had previously been granted asylum in the US and grew up outside of Baltimore, Maryland.[99] He alleged that, while on a trip to Pakistan in March 2003, he was kidnapped. He further alleges that he was then held in secret by the CIA for three and a half years, during which, he says, he was tortured.[100] Previously classified information that was cleared for release in 2015 corroborates Khan's version of the torture. The information revealed that he had been waterboarded twice; sexually assaulted, including while being hung naked from the ceiling; hung from a wooden beam for days while naked and provided with no food; kept in total darkness for most of 2003; held in solitary confinement for two years; beaten and threatened with beatings, including with a hammer; and hung from a metal bar on order of a doctor at Guantanamo.[101]

Khan said he made self-incriminating statements to end the torture. According to a habeas corpus petition, he was one of 14 'ghost detainees' transferred to Guantanamo Bay in September 2006. The Center for Constitutional Rights sought habeas corpus relief on behalf of Khan, alleging that it is unconstitutional to deny such relief to a long-term resident and immigrant to the US—a factor that distinguishes Khan's case somewhat from those of the other Guantanamo detainees.[102]

Khan's brother, a US citizen, says that he was interviewed repeatedly by the FBI and that he asked about his brother's whereabouts. The family heard nothing of or from Khan for three years after he disappeared, until, they say, a reporter came to their home and told them that President Bush had mentioned Khan's name in a speech on 6 September 2006.[103] The CCR filed the habeas corpus petition on Khan's behalf on 29 September 2006.[104]

---

[98] For cases from the European Court of Human Rights regarding these 'black sites', see *El-Masri v The Former Yugoslav Republic of Macedonia* (13 December 2012), Application No 39630/09; *Al Nashiri v Poland* (24 July 2014), Application No 28761/11; *Husayn (Abu Zubaydah) v Poland* (24 July 2014), Application No 7511/13 (collectively referred to as *Black Site: ECHR Cases*).

[99] Center for Constitutional Rights, '*Khan v. Bush / Khan v. Gates*: Synopsis', *Center for Constitutional Rights*, ccrjustice.org/home/what-we-do/our-cases/khan-v-obama-khan-v-gates-united-states-v-khan. Full pleadings and other related documents, including Khan's Combatant Status Review Tribunal transcript from Guantanamo Bay, are available through this site.

[100] ibid.

[101] Center for Constitutional Rights, Press Release, 'Former CIA Detainee Majid Khan's Torture Finally Public' (2 June 2015) ccrjustice.org/home/press-center/press-releases/former-cia-detainee-majid-khan-s-torture-finally-public.

[102] Center for Constitutional Rights, above, n 99.

[103] ibid.

[104] ibid; see also *Verbatim Transcript of Combatant Status Review Tribunal Hearing for ISN 10020*, *Center for Constitutional Rights*, ccrjustice.org/files/Majid%20Khan%20CSRT%20Transcript.pdf (unclassified and partially redacted, including portions in which he describes the torture allegations).

The White House version of Bush's speech has apparently been removed, but the *Washington Post* published a transcript. Of Khan, Bush said:

> Once in our custody, KSM was questioned by the CIA using these procedures, and he soon provided information that helped us stop another planned attack on the United States. During questioning, KSM told us about another Al Qaeda operative he knew was in CIA custody, a terrorist named Majid Khan. KSM revealed that Khan had been told to deliver $50,000 to individuals working for a suspected terrorist leader named Hambali, the leader of al Qaeda's Southeast Asian affiliate known as J-I … CIA officers confronted Khan with this information. Khan confirmed that the money had been delivered to an operative named Zubair, and provided both a physical description and contact number for this operative.[105]

It is notable that, as of the date of Bush's speech, none of the people to whom he referred had been convicted of any crime. Nonetheless, he referred to Khan, for instance, as a 'terrorist' rather than as an 'alleged terrorist' or a 'suspected terrorist'.[106] Khan's case is unusual in that he was a long-term resident of the US and actually had legal immigration status there. If he had achieved US citizenship, as his brother did, he would not have been eligible for trial by Military Commission or detention at Guantanamo Bay, and that would have been the only factor deciding his fate, regardless of any alleged conduct.[107] It is also somewhat unusual that his whereabouts were kept secret for three years, even from his family, and only ultimately revealed through a speech by the US President. Khan's case provides an example of the extreme nature of secrecy that could sometimes surround even the existence of these detentions. Khan went through a series of complex legal proceedings in the US in challenging his detention, complicated by changes to the law that were occurring regarding Guantanamo Bay.[108] As of July 2017, he remains at Guantanamo Bay.[109]

Controversy exists about the extent to which other nations engaged in prisoner abuse after 9/11. It has not been established that other liberal democracies kept actual detention programs secret, or similarly indulged in secret proceedings for

---

[105] The White House, Office of the Press Secretary, 'Transcript: "President Discusses Creation of Military Commissions to Try Suspected Terrorists"' *Washington Post* (6 September 2006) www.washingtonpost.com/wp-dyn/content/article/2006/09/06/AR2006090601425.html. 'KSM' is a shorthand reference to Khalid Sheikh Mohammed, another Guantanamo detainee, who the Bush Administration has accused of involvement in the 9/11 attacks.

[106] See ibid.

[107] See 'President Issues Military Order', above, n 55 (designating that certain people, excluding US citizens, could be subject to trial by military commission).

[108] Center for Constitutional Rights, above, n 99.

[109] 'The Guantanamo Docket' *New York Times* (18 July 2017 update) www.nytimes.com/interactive/projects/guantanamo/detainees/10020-majid-khan (reproducing a Department of Defense document on Khan, with the following disclaimer: 'These documents include some assertions that cannot be independently verified. Many allegations have been contested by detainees and their lawyers, and some have been undercut by other evidence'). As discussed more in ch 6 below, there are serious legitimacy issues with the Guantanamo Bay Military Commissions and the proceedings before them.

terrorism suspects, much less their torture, in response to 9/11. However, accusations of complicity with the US have emerged. The 'extraordinary rendition' programme functioned with complicity from other governments, as rulings of the European Court of Human Rights have concluded, but this was a US initiative that does not appear to have been similarly undertaken as a primary approach by other countries.[110] Allegations have also been made regarding complicity by allies such as Canada and the UK in the American mistreatment of prisoners.[111]

C. Secret Evidence and Secret Allegations

Disputes over the use of secret, allegedly classified evidence have been more widespread in extraordinary detention cases. This might involve withholding evidence on claims of national security or, in some instances, withholding the actual claims being made against a detainee. Canada, for instance, has encountered considerable controversy for its use of secret evidence in its 'security certificate' proceedings, which began to be used differently after 9/11, and is an issue that continues to generate justified controversy.[112] In the so-called 'Five Eyes' countries—Australia, Canada, New Zealand, the UK and the US—so-called 'closed material proceedings' (CPMs) have increased in use, especially in the UK and Australia.[113] These are broad mechanisms, used in different settings, and can be generally described as 'secretive legal proceedings used to protect national-security-sensitive material, relied upon by the state as evidence when adjudicating individual rights, while restricting both a person's access to that evidence and representation by legal counsel'.[114] These mechanisms evolved from early, supposedly temporary, measures implemented in a more limited context after 9/11. They have been critiqued

---

[110] See *Black Site: ECHR Cases*, above, n 98; however, see Ruth Blakeley and Sam Raphael, 'British Torture in the "War on Terror"' (2017) 23(2) *European Journal of International Relations* 242 (arguing that the British government has not been truthful in saying that it disavowed the use of torture after 9/11 and alleging significant involvement in prisoner abuse, 'operating under the state of exception established by the US executive').

[111] See, eg, Blakeley and Raphael, above, n 110; *Khadr II*, above, n 48 (finding that Canadian officials violated Khadr's Charter rights by participating in his interrogation under conditions of mistreatment at Guantanamo Bay).

[112] See, eg, *Charkaoui I*, above, n 42; *Canada (Citizenship and Immigration) v Harkat*, 2014 SCC 37; Maureen T Duffy and René Provost, 'Constitutional Canaries: The Elusive Quest to Legitimize Security Certificates in Canada' (2009) 40 *Case Western Journal of International Law* 531 (critiquing the Supreme Court of Canada's decision in *Charkaoui* as well as the subsequent revision of the Immigration and Refugee Protection Act to provide for special advocates). Security certificates are discussed in more detail in ch 5 below, but are mentioned here for context on the issue.

[113] For a discussion of these procedures, see David Jenkins, 'The Handling and Disclosure of Sensitive Intelligence: Closed Material Procedures and Constitutional Change in the "Five Eyes" Nations' in Genevieve Lennon and Clive Walker (eds), *Routledge Handbook of Law and Terrorism* (London, Routledge, 2015) 266.

[114] ibid.

as 'departing from the open, adversarial procedures traditionally required by due process ... risk[ing] a secret form of justice that strikes at the liberty-based raison d'être of the liberal state itself'.[115]

i. The Shifting Starting Point: The Extreme Use of Secrecy after 9/11

This issue of the use of classified evidence obviously did not arise just after 9/11. However, the struggle over supposedly competing claims of national security versus a detainee's right to know the case against him is a particular hallmark of many post-9/11 extraordinary detention practices. In some instances, major changes in the crisis days after 9/11 were scaled back, but not returned to where things were before. Within the UK and Canada, for example, the systems of special advocates, supposedly an improvement on highly problematic post-9/11 practices, have endured considerable criticism.[116] A major reason for that in Canada, for instance, is that the special advocate is granted access to evidence that is sealed for national security reasons, but cannot communicate any of that information to the detainee or counsel without judicial permission.[117] This is supposed to be an improvement over simply holding the person, potentially indefinitely, without ever allowing access to the evidence or allegations.[118]

Both scenarios are problematic. An overall erosion from pre-9/11 standards has clearly occurred. Thus, with special advocates, the detainee could still face the possibility of detention, or other restrictions on liberty, based on evidence that the person has never seen and has never been granted the opportunity to refute.[119] This trend in direction, first to the extreme and then back to the just less extreme, has happened on a number of fronts since 9/11.

Concerns have arisen over the years from powerful sources about the ways in which secret evidence, claimed to be classified, is used. The UK House of Lords expressed concern about this scenario, for instance, in one of three decisions issued

---

[115] ibid.

[116] See generally John Jackson, 'The Role of Special Advocates: Advocacy, Due Process, and the Adversarial Tradition' (2016) 20(4) *International Journal of Evidence & Proof* 343 (assessing controversies behind the use of special advocates, with a particular focus on origins of the mechanism in the UK after 9/11 for deportation decisions and expanding from there).

[117] Immigration and Refugee Protection Act, SC 2001, c 27 s 85.4(2); see generally David Jenkins, 'There and Back Again: The Strange Journey of Special Advocates and Comparative Law Methodology' (2011) 42(2) *Columbia Human Rights Law Review* 279; Fiona de Londras, 'Can Counter-terrorist Internment Ever Be Legitimate?' (2011) 33(3) *Human Rights Quarterly* 596 (suggesting that, while there are legitimacy concerns with current detention models, without trial, of terrorists, there could arguably be a model conceived that would have a stronger sense of legitimacy).

[118] See Duffy and Provost, above, n 112.

[119] See generally three cases decided on the same day by the House of Lords in the UK, critiquing particular components of the control order procedures: *Secretary of State for the Home Department v MB (FC)* [2007] UKHL 46, 34–40, 54, 60–77, 82–87 (hereinafter *MB*); *Secretary of State for the Home Department v JJ and Others* [2007] UKHL 45, H 56 (hereinafter *JJ*); *Secretary of State for the Home Department v E and Another* [2007] UKHL 47 (hereinafter *E*) (collectively referred to as the *Three Control Order Cases*).

on the same day in October 2007.[120] While upholding in general, at least as of that date, the control orders in those cases—with the exception of one they deemed to involve overly restrictive conditions—some of the Lords expressed concerns about the use of secret evidence in the special advocate proceedings.[121] Lords Bingham and Brown both pointed out that, due to the serious nature of the liberty deprivations in these cases, procedural fairness is important.[122]

One of the Law Lords quoted from Canada's *Charkaoui I* decision in stating that the controlled person should see the evidence being used against him.[123] Lord Bingham wrote extensively of international authorities, all pointing to the same conclusion—that procedural fairness required that an accused be fully apprised of the evidence being used against him.[124] He quoted from the US Supreme Court case of *Hamdi v Rumsfeld*, for example, where the rights to be heard and to be notified were called 'essential constitutional promises'.[125]

Lord Bingham then discussed why he believed a system using special advocates, who are not allowed to communicate classified evidence to the accused or the accused's counsel, fails to meet the requirements of fundamental fairness:

'The use of an SAA is, however, never a panacea for the grave disadvantages of a person affected not being aware of the case against him.' The reason is obvious. In any ordinary case, a client instructs his advocate what his defence is to the charges made against him, briefs the advocate on the weaknesses and vulnerability of the adverse witnesses, and indicates what evidence is available by way of rebuttal. This is a process which it may be impossible to adopt if the controlled person does not know the allegations made against him and cannot therefore give meaningful instructions, and the special advocate, once he knows what the allegations are, cannot tell the controlled person or seek instructions without permission, which in practice (as I understand) is not given. 'Grave disadvantage' is not, I think, an exaggerated description of the controlled person's position where such circumstances obtain. I would respectfully agree with the opinion of Lord Woolf … that the task of the court in any given case is to decide, looking at the process as a whole, whether a procedure has been used which involved significant injustice to the controlled person.[126]

Lord Brown expressed his reservations more bluntly:

I cannot accept that a suspect's entitlement to an essentially fair hearing is merely a qualified right capable of being outweighed by the public interest in protecting the state against terrorism (vital though, of course, I recognise that public interest to be). On the contrary, it seems to me not merely an absolute right but one of altogether too great

---

[120] *MB*, above, n 119.

[121] The House of Lords also expressed concern about the conditions in one case, which involved a curfew of 18 hours, indicating that was excessively restrictive. *JJ*, above, n 119.

[122] *MB*, above, n 119, paras 24, 90.

[123] ibid para 30 (citation omitted).

[124] ibid paras 24, 90 (citations omitted).

[125] ibid para 30 (quoting *Hamdi v Rumsfeld*, 542 US 507 (2004)).

[126] ibid para 35 (citations omitted).

importance to be sacrificed on the altar of terrorism control. By the same token that evidence derived from the use of torture must always be rejected so as to safeguard the integrity of the judicial process and avoid bringing British justice into disrepute ... so too in my judgment must closed material be rejected if reliance on it would necessarily result in a fundamentally unfair hearing.[127]

The use of secret evidence presents a peculiar problem in terms of analysis. Public statements rarely explain the reason for keeping the evidence secret. Without the evidence being revealed, it is impossible to really accurately assess the need for such processes. Moreover, there is the general suspicion that secrecy tends to raise, which is that somebody seeking to hide something has something to hide. Such a proposition may go too far, as secret evidence is not an unheard-of concept even in traditional criminal proceedings. As mentioned earlier, Canada's Evidence Act, for example, specifically provides procedures for situations in which the Crown asserts that evidence in a trial must be kept secret, often for national security reasons, including procedural safeguards.[128]

While there may be individual circumstances in which the need for secrecy can be established, its widespread application to many of these cases raises some concerns. This accusation has specifically been raised in regard to the US, where it has been claimed, for example, that the government seeks to classify certain information not for national security reasons, but to cover its use of torture.[129] However, without seeing any of the evidence, such claims must remain, to some extent, speculative.

Criticisms both of preventive detention and the use of secret evidence continued to emanate from judicial rulings. In February 2009, the European Court of Human Rights stated, in relation to the so-called 'Belmarsh Detainees: 'The Court does not accept the Government's argument that Article 5 § 1 permits a balance to be struck between the individual's right to liberty and the State's interest in protecting its population from terrorist threat.'[130] Shortly thereafter, in June 2009, the UK House of Lords once again criticised control orders, strongly stating that the scheme of using secret evidence does not allow for fair judicial proceedings.[131] In spite of such strongly worded statements, the practice continues to be asserted as essential in particular cases dealing with terrorism suspects.

---

[127] ibid para 91 (citations omitted).

[128] 'International Relations and National Defence and National Security', in Canada Evidence Act, s 38 RSC, 1985, c C-5.

[129] Such an allegation was made by Majid Kahn, as discussed above. See Scott Shane, 'Detainee's Lawyers Rebut CIA on Tapes' *New York Times* (19 January 2008) www.nytimes.com/2008/01/19/washington/19detain.html?_r=2&scp=2&sq=Guant%E1namo&oref=slogin&oref=slogin (alleging that CIA agents videotaped an interrogation session with him in 2003, in which he alleges he was tortured. The issue arose in part because of the CIA's claims that it did not videotape interrogations after 2002, and an ongoing scandal relating to the apparent destruction of these interrogation tapes).

[130] *A and Others v United Kingdom*, Application No 3455/05, 2009 ECHR (2009).

[131] *AF*, above, n 68.

V. Special Mechanisms that Bypassed the Criminal Justice System Entirely

In the Introduction to this book, it was explained that the discussion herein relates primarily to what is being called 'extraordinary detention' practices. Again, changes have certainly occurred in the criminal justice system, and many of these changes are reasonably subject to critique.[132] That particular critique is not undertaken in this work, however, because there is another way to slice some of the issues, relating to the disposition of terrorism cases undertaken entirely outside of the criminal justice paradigm.

This section addresses the cases of two extraordinary detainees. These cases are unusual in that they involved citizens of the national jurisdictions pursuing the deprivation of their freedom, but they serve as examples of the type of fragmenting of practices that occurred after 9/11. They also serve as examples of particular judges fighting back against governmental attempts to so detain people. It may well be that the vigorous response is related to the fact that those involved were citizens, but this was not made explicit in the cases discussed below.

The first case is that of Jose Padilla, an American citizen who was held by the US government, without trial, for three and a half years as an 'enemy combatant' or 'unlawful enemy combatant'.[133] The second case is that of Joseph Thomas, an Australian citizen who was, in fact, tried before the criminal system in Australia, convicted, had his conviction overturned on appeal and was then subjected to a control order that limited his freedom.

A. The US: Unlawful Enemy Combatants—Example: The Case of Jose Padilla

The Jose Padilla case is arguably one of the strangest examples of an extraordinary approach to a post-9/11 detention in the US. Padilla's detention status was changed more than once and, in each instance, the timing suggested that it was changed specifically to avoid the criminal justice system or to avoid judicial critique. Padilla is a US citizen who was arrested at Chicago's O'Hare Airport in

---

[132] See, eg, Markus D Dubber, 'Citizenship and Penal Law' (2010) 13 *New Criminal Law Review* 190 (discussing differences in how the criminal law might be applied depending on citizenship); see also James Edwards, 'Justice Denied: The Criminal Law and the Ouster of the Courts' (2010) 30(4) *OJLS* 725 (talking about the changing character of criminal law, and the rise of 'ouster offences', which, it is argued, deprives the criminal courts of the ability to adjudicate wrongdoing in particular instances).

[133] Both terms have been used. For consistency, the term 'unlawful enemy combatant' is used in this book.

May 2002, after arriving on a flight from Pakistan.[134] He was initially detained on a material-witness warrant. He filed a challenge to that detention and, before that matter could be decided, US President Bush declared him an enemy combatant and ordered that he be taken into military custody.[135] However, because he is a US citizen, he was held at a prison within the US, which is itself rather unusual, given the US government's long-standing and continuing claims that it was too danger-ous to bring terrorism suspects to the US—one of the arguments used to justify detention centres such as that at Guantanamo Bay.[136]

Padilla was then held with no criminal trial and was still being held in 2004 when the US Supreme Court declined to decide his case on the merits, based on its conclusion that his attorney had named the wrong person in a habeas corpus petition.[137] During the time of his detention, it was widely reported that the US government was accusing him of conspiring to produce a so-called 'dirty bomb' for use in an attack on an American city. The allegations were reported to have been based on statements made by another terrorism-related detainee, Abu Zubaydah, amidst claims that the interrogation of Zubaydah was carried out using torture.[138] The torture of Zubaydah was later confirmed.[139]

Padilla continued to be held as an enemy combatant and his case continued to follow a strange procedural path. In September 2005, a federal appellate court upheld the President's authority to detain Padilla as an enemy combatant, a dis-position that was then appealed to the US Supreme Court. In December 2005, the US government filed an 'emergency' petition before the same appellate court, seeking permission to transfer Padilla to a civilian court for criminal trial and for the order from the previous September to be vacated—with the accompanying suggestion that this would render the pending Supreme Court case moot. The appellate court refused the government's request, forcing the government to seek permission from the US Supreme Court, which granted the request and denied hearing on the case.[140]

In refusing, the appellate court made the frank suggestion that there could be 'in the absence of explanation, at least an appearance that the government may be attempting to avoid consideration of our decision by the Supreme Court'.[141] In the

---

[134] *Rumsfeld v Padilla*, 542 US 426 (2004) (outlining the facts of the Padilla detention to that date); see also Tung Yin, 'Enemies of the State: Rational Classification in the War on Terrorism' (2007) 11 *Lewis & Clark Law Review* 903, 930.

[135] *Rumsfeld v Padilla*, above, n 134, 431 (referring to *Authorization for Use of Military Force*, Pub L 107-40, 115 Stat 224 (18 September 2001).

[136] See Dahlia Lithwick, 'Cowardly, Stupid, and Tragically Wrong' *Slate* (5 April 2011) www.slate. com/articles/news_and_politics/jurisprudence/2011/04/cowardly_stupid_and_tragically_wrong.html (criticising the decision of the Obama Administration to avoid US courts for certain detainees at Guantanamo Bay).

[137] *Rumsfeld v Padilla*, above, n 134.

[138] ibid 430–31.

[139] See *Abu Zubaydah*, above, n 98.

[140] *Hanft v Padilla*, 546 US 1084, 126 S Ct 978 (2006); *Padilla v Hanft*, 547 US 1062, 126 S Ct 1649 (2006).

[141] *Padilla v Hanft*, 432 F 3d 582 (4th Cir 2005).

order refusing the request, the justices came close to accusing the US government of outright dishonesty, including the following remarkable statement:

> The government has held Padilla militarily for three and a half years, steadfastly maintaining that it was imperative in the interest of national security that he be so held. However, a short time after our decision issued on the government's representation that Padilla's military custody was indeed necessary in the interest of national security, the government determined that it was no longer necessary that Padilla be held militarily. Instead, it announced, Padilla would be transferred to the custody of federal civilian law enforcement authorities and criminally prosecuted in Florida for alleged offenses considerably different from, and less serious than, those acts for which the government had militarily detained Padilla. The indictment of Padilla in Florida, unsealed the same day as announcement of that indictment, made no mention of the acts upon which the government purported to base its military detention of Padilla and upon which we had concluded only several weeks before that the President possessed the authority to detain Padilla, namely, that Padilla had taken up arms against United States forces in Afghanistan and had thereafter entered into this country for the purpose of blowing up buildings in American cities, in continued prosecution of al Qaeda's war of terrorism against the United States.

> The announcement of indictment came only two business days before the government's brief in response to Padilla's petition for certiorari was due to be filed in the Supreme Court of the United States, and only days before the District Court in South Carolina, pursuant to our remand, was to accept briefing on the question whether Padilla had been properly designated an enemy combatant by the President.[142]

The Court was careful to note that its comments were based on the timing of the pleadings and on the unexplained disparity between the facts as presented to justify the military detention and those presented in the subsequent criminal indictment, noting that it was in no position to determine if the appearance this raised was based on fact.[143]

As pre-trial preparations began in the newly instituted criminal case, Padilla's lawyers argued that he was mentally unfit to stand trial. Specifically, they argued that he suffered from post-traumatic stress disorder as a result of years of solitary confinement with no court proceedings and, they alleged, as a result of torture by his captors, a claim the US government denied. After a hearing, the court found him fit to stand trial.[144] Padilla was ultimately found guilty on conspiracy charges related to providing support to terrorist organisations and was sentenced to 17 years in prison on 22 January 2008.[145]

---

[142] ibid 584.

[143] ibid 585.

[144] Peter Whoriskey, 'Judge Rules Padilla is Competent to Stand Trial' *Washington Post* (1 March 2007) www.washingtonpost.com/wp-dyn/content/article/2007/02/28/AR2007022801377.html.

[145] Kirk Semple, 'Padilla Sentenced to 17 Years in Prison' *New York Times* (22 January 2008) www.nytimes.com/2008/01/22/us/22cnd-padilla.html?ex=*1358744400*&en=79875802c6ca7fc9&ei=5088&partner=rssnyt&emc=rss.

The government had sought a much higher sentence of 37 years and, when she announced her ruling, the judge noted that there was no evidence linking Padilla, or his co-defendants, to any actual terrorism attack. She compared the crimes for which he was convicted to much more serious crimes, such as that of Terry Nichols, who had been convicted in the Oklahoma City bombing. The judge gave Padilla credit for time served for the three-and-a-half years in which he had been held in military detention.[146] In September 2011, after a series of appeals, a federal appellate court deemed the sentence in Padilla's case to have been too lenient and sent it back to the trial court.[147]

A parallel civil action continued, based on Padilla's claim that he had been tortured while in US custody. In May 2012, a federal appellate court found that John Yoo, who gained some notoriety for his role in creating the 'Torture Memos', had qualified immunity due to his position at the time of the alleged conduct and thus ruled that Padilla could not pursue his lawsuit. The Court based its ruling on the conclusion that it was not entirely clear at the time of the conduct that terrorism-related detainees were entitled to the same constitutional protections afforded to those detained under the criminal justice system. Additionally, while the court conceded without deciding that the treatment of Padilla amounted to torture and that the torture of an American citizen violates the US Constitution, it declined to find that Padilla's treatment was in fact torture, primarily because of ongoing debates at that time relating to the definition of torture.[148] The Court noted that at the time of the alleged conduct:

> Here, of course, the Supreme Court had not, at the time of Yoo's tenure at OLC, declared that American citizens detained as enemy combatants had to be treated at least as well, or afforded at least the same constitutional and statutory protections, as convicted prisoners.[149]

The constant, questionably timed changes in Padilla's detention status do raise a serious question as to whether the government was primarily attempting to hold him indefinitely, but to avoid having to meet fundamental due process to justify the detention. This, as the appellate court previously noted, must remain speculative. What is not speculative, however, is that the US government held Padilla for years under its newly designated status of 'unlawful enemy combatant', asserting that it was not possible to try his case before an Article III Court in the US.[150] The government then completely changed positions, requesting that Padilla's case be transferred to a civilian court and, in the open criminal trial, very few of the allegations that the government had been making publicly about Padilla appeared.

---

[146] ibid.

[147] ibid; *United States v Padilla et al*, No 08-10494 (11th Cir 2011) (finding that the trial court failed to properly apply the 'terrorism enhancement' in sentencing under US Sentencing Guidelines Manual § 3A1.4 (2001)).

[148] *Padilla v Yoo*, 678 F 3d 748 (9th Cir 2012).

[149] ibid.

[150] See US Constitution, Art III (providing for the system of federal courts).

The disparities between the government's accounts before the appellate court, when it argued he was a dangerous enemy combatant who could not be safely put on trial, and its factual allegations in the subsequent criminal filing just a few weeks later raise at least an appearance of improper avoidance of the criminal justice system. The Padilla case illustrates, as did other cases, that the criminal justice system is at least presumptively capable of handling cases of those accused of terrorist acts—evidently including this case, which the US government had long argued was not possible—and that allowing a government to sidestep criminal procedural protections can lead to abuse. If the intention of the government was to detain somebody it suspected was involved with terrorism, the most positive outcome was achieved through the criminal justice system.

B. The UK and Australia: Control Orders—Example: The Case of 'Jihad Jack'

In Padilla's case, although the government was unhappy with the sentence, a criminal conviction was ultimately secured. However, what happens when a government holds a criminal trial for somebody it accuses of terrorism and that person is not successfully convicted? Is there then an option to pursue other means to detain the person?

Australia provided one answer to this question in a scenario upheld by its High Court in *Thomas v Mowbray*. Australia's criminal legislation had been amended to allow for control orders under certain circumstances for those suspected of terrorism-related offences.[151] The case concerned Joseph Thomas, known locally as 'Jihad Jack'.[152] Thomas was arrested in Pakistan in 2003 and was alleged to be in possession of an Australian passport that had been altered, purportedly to conceal some of his travels.[153] He was initially detained, then removed to Australia in June 2003, where he remained free for 17 months, until he was arrested and charged with terrorism-related offences in November 2004.[154] He was initially convicted of receiving funds from a terrorist organisation, as well as of possessing a falsified passport.[155]

On appeal, Thomas successfully argued that he had made incriminating statements under circumstances that were not voluntary and thus that they should not have been admitted at his trial.[156] At his trial, he testified—and the judge accepted

---

[151] *Thomas v Mowbray* [2007] HCA 33 (citations omitted).
[152] See, eg, Tom Allard, 'Jihad Jack Wife's Terror Link' *Sydney Morning Herald* (29 August 2006) www.smh.com.au/news/national/jihad-jack-wifes-terror-link/2006/08/28/1156617275236.html?page=fullpage#contentSwap1.
[153] *R v Thomas* [2006] VSCA 165.
[154] ibid paras 1–2.
[155] ibid para 3.
[156] ibid para 5.

as true—that he was arrested in Pakistan while travelling home to Australia and was taken to a waiting vehicle 'not handcuffed or shackled, but blindfolded and hooded'.[157] The appellate court decision gives further details on the circumstances under which Thomas was questioned. Thomas claims that although he was wearing a hood, he could hear, from the accents, that two of the people interrogating him were Americans, and he says he made false statements out of fear of being sent to Guantanamo Bay or otherwise detained indefinitely.[158] Over time, he says that the interrogation deteriorated to being extremely coercive and that he told the interrogators what he thought they wanted to hear.[159] Alastair Adams, an Australian consular employee, was allowed to see Thomas approximately two weeks after he was captured, and described an exchange with Pakistani officials and Thomas, which suggested that the officials were threatening Thomas with being sent to Guantanamo Bay.[160]

The Court of Appeal's opinion included detailed information on subsequent interviews, including transcripts and accounts by other people, to demonstrate the coercive nature of these interviews.[161] The Court concluded that the evidence of the statements should not have been admitted at trial and reversed the conviction of the lower court.[162]

The Court of Appeal issued its ruling on 18 August 2006.[163] On 27 August, a federal magistrate issued an interim control order for Thomas.[164] Under the control order, Thomas was required:

> [T]o remain at his residence in Williamstown, Victoria, between midnight and 5 am each day unless he notified the Australian Federal Police of a change of address … to report to the police three times each week … to submit to having his fingerprints taken. He was prohibited from leaving Australia without the permission of the police … from acquiring or manufacturing explosives … from communicating with certain named individuals, and from using certain communications technology.[165]

On 2 August 2007, the High Court, in a separate case challenging the validity of the control order (and not considering the underlying criminal case), upheld the control order as valid.[166] The Court noted that the order had been entered in an *ex parte* proceeding and that the specific procedural posture of the case had meant that the control order was in effect longer than was the norm.[167]

---

[157] ibid para 9.
[158] ibid para 10.
[159] ibid paras 16–18.
[160] ibid para 21.
[161] ibid paras 24–61.
[162] ibid para 120.
[163] ibid.
[164] *Thomas v* Mowbray, above, n 151, para 1.
[165] ibid para 2.
[166] See, eg, ibid paras 1–33 (explaining the reasoning of Justice Gleeson for upholding the order).
[167] ibid.

The issues focused on separation of power questions, because of Australia's legal structures, with the majority finding that it was within the power of the Parliament to enact the relevant provision of the Criminal Code, and within the power of the judicial branch to enter such orders. For example, Justice Gleeson noted that a control order is designed to prevent an act of terrorism.[168] He wrote that an interim control order, such as the one before the Court, could only be issued following the request of the Attorney General, based on a belief of 'reasonable grounds that the order sought would substantially assist in preventing a terrorist act or suspect on reasonable grounds that the person in relation to whom the order is sought has provided training to, or received training from, a listed terrorist organization'.[169] Justice Gleeson pointed out that the parties had not argued that it was beyond the authority of the Australian Parliament to provide for control orders in situations where it is deemed necessary to address the risk of terrorism.[170]

Thomas had argued that control orders are inappropriate because they represent a punitive restriction on liberty in a case in which there has been no finding that a crime has been committed. Justice Gleeson found that proposition to be too broad, noting that there are circumstances under which restrictions on liberty can be based on potential future actions, which must thus be carefully delineated. Examples include 'apprehended violence' orders made by judicial officers, which do not involve detention, but which do involve restrictions on liberty.[171]

Justice Kirby wrote a scathing and lengthy dissent, arguing that the portion of the Criminal Code allowing for these control orders was invalid. He began by noting that: 'Terrorism is not a new phenomenon … Conduct sharing features now associated with 'terrorism' has occurred for centuries.'[172] Like the appellate justices in the Padilla case, Justice Kirby raised the concern that the Australian government was improperly sidestepping the criminal justice system. While noting that the application for an interim control order was made within a week of the reversal of the conviction, he observed: 'This sequence of events inevitably gave rise to an appearance, in the plaintiff's case, of action by the Commonwealth designed to thwart the ordinary operation of the criminal law and to deprive the plaintiff of the benefit of the liberty he temporarily enjoyed pursuant to the Court of Appeal's orders.'[173]

Justice Kirby expressed great concern for the majority's upholding of the control-order scheme, writing:

> However, in Australia, judges in federal courts may not normally deprive individuals of liberty on the sole basis of a prediction of what might occur in the future. Without an

---

[168] ibid para 9.
[169] ibid.
[170] ibid para 13.
[171] ibid para 19.
[172] ibid para 158 (citations omitted).
[173] ibid para 182. Shortly afterwards, a new trial was ordered for Thomas.

applicable anterior conviction, they may not do so on the basis of acts that people may fear but which have not yet occurred. Much less may such judges deprive individuals of their liberty on the chance that such restrictions will prevent others from committing certain acts in the future. Such provisions partake of features of the treatment of hostages which was such a shameful characteristic of the conduct of the oppressors in the Second World War and elsewhere. It is not a feature hitherto regarded as proper to the powers vested in the Australian judiciary. In Australia, we do not deprive individuals of their freedoms because doing so conduces to the desired control of others.[174]

Justice Kirby found 'even more novel and offensive to principle' the notion that the legislation allows for a deprivation of liberty, not just based on a fear of future acts by the person controlled, but also on a fear of future acts of others. The government could seek to thwart the feared actions of others by placing the restrictions on a different person—the controlled person.[175] He warned:

To do this is to deny persons their basic legal rights not for what they have been proved to have done (as established in a criminal trial) but for what an official suggests that they might do or that someone else might do. To allow judges to be involved in making such orders, and particularly in the one-sided procedure contemplated by Div 104, involves a serious and wholly exceptional departure from basic constitutional doctrine unchallenged during the entire history of the Commonwealth. It goes far beyond the burdens on the civil liberties of alleged communists enacted, but struck down by this Court, in the Communist Party Case. Unless this Court calls a halt, as it did in that case, the damage to our constitutional arrangements could be profound.[176]

Among what Justice Kirby described as 'offending features' of the legislative scheme are the use of *ex parte* determinations, the 'uniform minimization of rights' and the 'withholding of evidence' from the person so controlled.[177] Justice Kirby raised concerns that it was solely up to the judge to make findings based on this often-secret evidence, and he cited other countries that employ a system of advocates for such determinations.[178]

These two cases provide examples of some of the personal experiences of people subject to extraordinary detention practices. While, again, each contains some features that are arguably unusual, each also involves extensive discretion on the part of the Executive, which caused members of the judiciary to at least raise the concern that the detentions were handled in the way that they were simply because the government was unable or unwilling to proceed under the criminal justice system. Whether this speculation is ever proven to be true, these cases raise enough questions to suggest that a presumption against the use of the criminal justice system, even if only in a few cases, can raise serious problems.

---

[174] ibid para 355.
[175] ibid para 357.
[176] ibid.
[177] ibid para 364.
[178] ibid para 365.

VI. Other Examples of Changes: Torture and Targeted Killings

A. Torture Became a Tool of Extraordinary Detention Practices

Two other practices that do not involve detention per se are discussed in this chapter because they are connected to extraordinary detention practices. As will be discussed further in chapter six below, the US adopted a peculiar 'war' model in relation to terrorism that was not significantly followed by most other national jurisdictions. While a number of US allies did participate in the military actions in Afghanistan and Iraq, thus employing a wartime approach to terrorism in that respect, countries outside of the US did not unilaterally adopt the sort of Military Commission, war-detention scenarios, particularly for those who were not captured on the battlefields of Afghanistan and Iraq. It is partially for this reason that the 'war' approaches of the US are discussed separately in chapter six below. The issue of torture has been touched upon in a couple of places in this book and it is also discussed here in order to illustrate that this was a distinctive part of post-9/11 extraordinary detention practices. As discussed in chapter three above, these tactics were used without an overt admission that they constituted torture.

While asserting that it did not torture prisoners, the US government went to considerable lengths to justify its 'enhanced interrogation' tactics.[179] Much is now known about the fact that the US did, indeed, engage in widespread torture of terrorism detainees who were held outside of the criminal justice system.[180] Considerable effort was expended by the US government to find ways to torture people, but to simultaneously avoid any legal or political fallout for doing so. In what have come to be known as the 'Torture Memos', government officials produced legal opinions as to what constituted torture, which was, in part, necessitated because of a US federal statute calling for serious penalties for government officials ordering or engaging in acts of torture.[181] These memos have gained considerable notoriety, as they essentially represent a way to paint torture with a veneer of legality that it never had.

---

[179] Jeremy Waldron, 'Torture and Positive Law: Jurisprudence for the White House' (2005) 105 *Columbia Law Review* 1681.

[180] See Senate Intelligence Committee, *Senate Intelligence Committee Study on CIA Detention and Interrogation Program* (updated 3 April 2014) www.feinstein.senate.gov/public/index.cfm/senate-intelligence-committee-study-on-cia-detention-and-interrogation-program.

[181] See *Crimes and Criminal Procedure: Torture*, 18 USC §§ 2340–40A; see also, eg, John Yoo, Deputy Assistant Attorney General, Department of Defense, 'Memorandum for William J. Haynes II, General Counsel, Department of Defense' *George Washington University* (9 January 2002) www.gwu.edu/~nsarchiv/NSAEBB/NSAEBB127/02.01.09.pdf; Alberto R Gonzales, 'Decision re: Application of the Geneva Convention on Prisoners of War to the Conflict with Al Qaeda and the Taliban' *George Washington University* (25 January 2002) www.gwu.edu/~nsarchiv/NSAEBB/NSAEBB127/02.01.25.

Jeremy Waldron undertakes a shift of the kaleidoscope on this issue when he argues that one reason why the arguments over torture heightened after 9/11 is that the starting point of the analysis changed. Torture, he argues, had a different status before 9/11, as a 'legal *archetype*', an absolute ban that was symbolic of societal values renouncing the use of 'brutality' in legal systems. Where torture is instead treated as just another legal rule or another tactical option, it loses that stature and is subject to erosions such as that evidenced by the 'Torture Memos', in which degrees of permissible mistreatment are argued.[182] Waldron summarises this argument by saying:

> I argue that the prohibition on torture is not just one rule among others, but a legal archetype—a provision which is emblematic of our larger commitment to non-brutality in the legal system. Characterizing it as an *archetype* affects how we think about the implications of authorizing torture (or interrogation methods that come close to torture). It affects how we think about issues of definition in regard to torture. And it affects how we think about the absolute character of the legal and moral prohibitions on torture.[183]

Waldron's characterisation is useful. His presentation immediately shifts the issue, so what may otherwise have had indicators of a logical argument, when torture is viewed as simply another legal rule, may have a different appearance when the starting point of the discussion is the idea that the prohibition on torture is an absolute and not just another rule. His method of argumentation thus has similarities to the overall methodology espoused by people like Perelman and Olbrechts-Tyteca, with the point of departure being shifted to bring about an entirely different view of the issue.

   This book does not attempt to necessarily present the voluminous commentary on the issue of torture so much as to include it as an example in which the notion that everything changed after 9/11 led to an acceptability of ideas that, before 9/11, were absolutely renounced. In the case of torture, this illustration is rather vivid, as this was one issue on which there was previously considerable consensus among countries that included the US. While the US never accepted the label of 'torture' for its 'enhanced interrogation' methods, it is obvious that, instead, it undertook a semantic exercise, which significantly narrowed the idea of what would constitute torture beyond its pre-9/11 meaning.

   One of the 'Torture Memos' explains, among other things, the President's authority in times of war, specifically referencing the war against al-Qaeda, and suggests that under those exceptional circumstances, the statute that banned torture in the US was presumptively unconstitutional. Thus, the language of the memo mirrors the underlying point of departure critiqued in this chapter that 9/11 changed the world in ways that required new approaches to detention and

---

pdf; Jay S Bybee, 'Memorandum for Alberto R Gonzales Counsel to the President' *US Department of Justice* (1 August 2002) dspace.wrlc.org/doc/bitstream/2041/70964/00355_020801_001display.pdf (portions redacted).

[182] Waldron, above, n 179.
[183] ibid 1681.

interrogation. It says 'we conclude that, under the current circumstances, necessity or self-defense may justify interrogation methods that violate Section 2340A'.[184] Thus, the obvious suggestion is that, after 9/11, something was presumptively different, and new detention and interrogation parameters were now necessary as a result.[185]

B. The Evolution Continues: Targeted Killings

This chapter focuses heavily on language espoused closer to the time of the attacks, with the objective of following these discursive threads to see what they became in terms of normative standards. One practice that gained prominence, expanding several years after the attacks, regards the US-asserted legal justification for the use of targeted killings in its fight against terrorism. While not a new controversy globally, the issue is new in many ways for the US, or has been over the past few years. The practice gained prominence under the Obama presidency and it was arguably used to replace bringing new detainees to Guantanamo Bay, which Obama was trying to close.

In a speech in 2010, Harold Koh, in his capacity as Legal Advisor to the Department of State, argued that targeted killings were legal in the 'armed conflict' against al-Qaeda, justified, he said, under international law and by the *Authorization for Use of Military Force* passed by the US Congress shortly after the attacks. He listed the common objections to the practice, generally refuting each with a statement that principles governing armed conflicts governed and permitted the practice. Specifically, he noted:

> As recent events have shown, al-Qaeda has not abandoned its intent to attack the United States, and indeed continues to attack us. Thus, in this ongoing armed conflict, the United States has the authority under international law, and the responsibility to its citizens, to use force, including lethal force, to defend itself, including by targeting persons such as high-level al-Qaeda leaders who are planning attacks. As you know, this is a conflict with an organized terrorist enemy that does not have conventional forces, but that plans and executes its attacks against us and our allies while hiding among civilian populations. That behavior simultaneously makes the application of international law more difficult and more critical for the protection of innocent civilians. Of course, whether a particular individual will be targeted in a particular location will depend upon considerations specific to each case, including those related to the imminence of the threat, the sovereignty of the other states involved, and the willingness and ability of those states to suppress the threat the target poses.[186]

---

[184] Bybee, above, n 181.

[185] See Werner GK Strizke et al (eds), *Terrorism and Torture* (New York, Cambridge University Press, 2013) (containing an interdisciplinary set of perspectives on the link between the condemned behaviours of terrorism and state-sponsored torture).

[186] Harold Hongju Koh, 'Speech to the Annual Meeting of the American Society of International Law: The Obama Administration and International Law' *US Department of State* (25 March 2010) www.state.gov/s/l/releases/remarks/139119.htm.

Koh's speech, as a representative of the US government, shows some variance from some of the positions he took before assuming that position, when he was writing as an academic at Yale, and provides a (perhaps unintentional) example of the way in which discourse and argumentation can change depending on who is presenting the case or on whose behalf one speaks.[187]

The targeted-killing controversy gained additional prominence after the US targeted a US citizen, Anwar al-Aulaki, killing him through a CIA drone strike in Yemen after alleging that he was an al-Qaeda operative.[188] Eric Holder, the US Attorney General at the time, made a speech in which he outlined a justification for the use of such killings. In his speech, Holder repeatedly referred to al-Aulaki as a terrorist or al-Qaeda operative, even though no judicial proceeding had ever established any such connection. Moreover, much of the controversy arose over the fact that al-Aulaki was a US citizen, suggesting that there would be less dispute, at least within the US, if non-citizens were targeted.[189] In referring to the Due Process Clause of the US Constitution, Holder asserted that: 'The constitution guarantees due process, not judicial process.'[190] His statement contradicted more than 200 years of constitutional jurisprudence in the US as to the meaning of due process, and it is unclear whether it was simply an inappropriate statement or whether it signalled an additional shift in the US approach to judicial process in terrorism cases. The issue of targeted killings raises the question of whether the death penalty, already a controversial issue in the US, is now to be applied without even the benefit of any judicial process, on the President's discretion. In the case of al-Aulaki, the question is unavoidable.

While the practice itself is not new, aspects of it were. The fact that al-Aulaki was a US citizen, along with statements made by US officials justifying the attacks, caused the issue to gain prominence in the public discourse. Legal attempts to intervene before the strike that killed al-Aulaki were ultimately unsuccessful, with

---

[187] See, eg, Harold Hongju Koh, 'Foreword: On American Exceptionalism' (2003) 55 *Stanford Law Review* 1479 (among other things, criticising the US Administration for its flat presentation of issues without nuance and encouraging the US to pursue an approach that rejects 'double standards' and adhere to traditional ideals and legal principles); Harold Hongju Koh, 'The Law under Stress after September 11' (2003) 31 *International Journal of Legal Information* 317 (based on remarks delivered in 2002).

[188] His name is typically spelled 'al-Awlaki' in the popular media. In legal pleadings relating to his case and that of his son, the name is spelled 'al-Aulaki', so that spelling is adopted herein, even though that is not always the spelling used throughout the case. See Ryan Patrick Alford, 'The Rule of Law at the Crossroads: Consequences of Targeted Killing of Citizens' (2011) 4 *Utah Law Review* 1203, fn 3 (explaining the differing translations of the name from Arabic).

[189] Associated Press, 'US Attorney General Justifies 'Targeted Kill Programme" *The Guardian* (5 March 2012) www.guardian.co.uk/world/2012/mar/05/attorney-general-targeted-kill-programme.

[190] ibid; see US Constitution, amendment 5 ('No person shall be held to answer for a capital, or otherwise infamous crime, unless on a presentment or indictment of a Grand Jury, except in cases arising in the land or naval forces, or in the Militia, when in actual service in time of War or public danger; nor shall any person be subject for the same offense to be twice put in jeopardy of life or limb; nor shall be compelled in any criminal case to be a witness against himself, nor be deprived of life, liberty, or property, without due process of law; nor shall private property be taken for public use, without just compensation').

a US court refusing to hear the case on its merits because it was a 'political question' and granting a government motion to dismiss in December 2010.[191] Al-Aulaki was killed in a drone strike on 30 September 2011.[192]

While the targeted killing of a US citizen evoked an especially strong response, some of this response appears to have muted in the US as time has passed. However, the experience intensified for al-Aulaki's family. His 16-year-old son, Abdulrahman al-Aulaki, also a US citizen, was also killed in Yemen two weeks after the strike that killed his father.[193] In February 2017, it was reported that al-Aulaki's eight-year-old daughter, Nawar, was killed in a joint American-UAE raid in Yemen.[194]

The debate relating to the US's use of targeted killing has some of its own distinctive discourse characteristics. The fact that a US court refused to hear the case before al-Aulaki was targeted for death is disturbing. Judicial approval would not, necessarily, legitimise the action; quite the contrary. But the absence of such review opened the door for completely unchecked Executive discretion on such a major action. A question arises as to whether courts showed reluctance to hear these cases because the idea of targeted killing is such an extreme, and intuitively so at odds with fundamental values relating to fair judicial process, that courts do not want to be in the position of having to approve such actions and thus to be complicit. Conversely, they may also not want to be in the position of blocking them if doing so really would result in a terrorist attack. This conversation is far from resolved and is certain to continue.[195]

In 2014, the US government lost a legal battle, brought by the *New York Times* and the American Civil Liberties Union, which were seeking release of a memo, known to exist, that detailed the government's legal case for the targeted strike against al-Aulaki. It released a redacted version of the memo.[196] The basic justification that the US government provided was that it had evidence that al-Aulaki

---

[191] *Al-Aulaqi v Obama*, Civil Action No 10-1469 (JDB), Memorandum Opinion (DC Cir 2010) www.ccrjustice.org/files/2010.12.07_Al-Aulaqi%20Decision_0.pdf.

[192] Center for Constitutional Rights, 'Al-Aulaqi v. Panetta: Synopsis', www.ccrjustice.org/ourcases/current-cases/al-aulaqi-v-panetta.

[193] *Al-Aulaqi v Panetta*, No 12-cv-_____ (US Dist. DC filed 18 July 2012) (original complaint) www.ccrjustice.org/files/July-18-2012-Nasser-Al-Aulaqi-Complaint.pdf.

[194] Ryan Browne, 'Daughter of Anwar al-Alwaki Reported Killed in Yemen Raid' *CNN* (1 February 2017) www.cnn.com/2017/01/31/politics/yemen-raid-daughter-al-qaeda-leader/index.html.

[195] For some critique regarding targeted killing see, eg, Vincent-Joël Proulx, 'If the Hat Fits, Wear it, if the Turban Fits, Run for Your Life: Reflections on the Indefinite Detention and Targeted Killing of Suspected Terrorists' (2005) 56(5) *Hastings Law Journal* 801; Jeremy Waldron, 'Can Targeted Killing Work as a Neutral Principle?' (2011) NYU School of Law, Public Law Research Paper No 11-20, ssrn.com/abstract=1788226; Claire Finkelstein, Jens David Ohlin and Andrew Altman (eds), *Targeted Killings: Law and Morality in an Asymmetrical World* (Oxford, Oxford University Press, 2012) (containing a chapter by Waldron similar to the aforementioned paper). For a further discussion of the controversy over judicial review in targeted killing, see ch 6 below.

[196] See Charlie Savage, 'Justice Department Memo Approving Targeted Killing of Anwar al-Awlaki' *New York Times* (23 June 2014) www.nytimes.com/interactive/2014/06/23/us/23awlaki-memo.html (containing the court ruling and a copy of the redacted memo, written over a year before al-Aulaki was killed. Another American, Samir Khan, was also killed, but was not, according to the US government, targeted).

was continuing to engage in a terrorist group, representing a continuing and imminent threat to the US, and that it was not feasible to try to capture him.[197] More than one memo was written. According to the *New York Times*, when the authors of the original memo saw a law blog discussing the legal definition of murder as including an American killing another American overseas, they went back and revised the memo to argue that the statute did not apply.[198]

VII. Conclusion

What emerges from these and many other examples is a sense that significant changes were frequently hastily implemented in the days after the 9/11 attacks, not just in the US but also in a number of national jurisdictions. These changes related only to certain types of detainees, but often went to the very heart of what had been considered fair judicial proceedings, the right to be heard by a competent authority, the right to be apprised of any allegations, the right to challenge detention, the right to know the evidence to be produced, the right to counsel and even the right not to be executed without some form of judicial process. The changes may have varied from place to place, both in form and extent, but change happened in a number of national jurisdictions, apparently based on the belief that 'everything changed' after the 9/11 attacks and that these changes required the use of alternative detention paradigms for particular terrorism cases. If, indeed, national jurisdictions felt the need for such change, the trend was to seek means of detaining people entirely outside of the criminal justice system or, alternatively, to pull away to the extent possible from pre-existing criminal justice procedural protections, often on the back of this presumption, which does not appear to be as solid as such a significant change would suggest.

As time passes and people become accustomed to the changes, many of these changes have gained characteristics of the permanent. This tendency carries with it some dangers of its own, as long-standing, foundational constitutional norms are abandoned, although to varying degrees. While it is not suggested that such abandonment is ever justified, it is especially disturbing to see it happen with so little calm reflection or backward-looking analysis. If, indeed, everything did not change after 9/11, then the building of new regimes, or expanding of parallel regimes, seems to have been a costly endeavour with too little to show in terms of benefits. Even if everything changed, the dependent condition that these changes

---

[197] ibid.

[198] Charlie Savage, 'Court Releases Large Parts of Memo Approving Killing of American in Yemen' *New York Times* (23 June 2014) www.nytimes.com/2014/06/24/us/justice-department-found-it-lawful-to-target-anwar-al-awlaki.html (citing/linking to Kevin Jon Heller, 'Let's Call Killing al-Awlaki What it is—Murder' *Opinio Juris* (8 April 2010) opiniojuris.org/2010/04/08/lets-call-killing-al-awlaki-what-it-is-murder).

mandated the building or enhancing of detention paradigms outside of the criminal justice system has never been established. Given the significantly greater success of the criminal justice system in handling cases since 9/11, this claim even seems to have been refuted. Moving forward as if this point of departure had been established is deeply problematic.

For certain cases, the presumption now favours these new regimes and, constitutional provisions notwithstanding, many national jurisdictions have simply accepted this new presumption with surprisingly little protest. Rather, the mere assertion of a future threat has been adequate in many cases. This type of assertion was accepted as adequate support for changes in the early days after 9/11 and it remains adequate today in some respects. In spite of some internal disputes about the specifics, the overarching idea that the criminal justice system can sometimes be avoided where terrorism is alleged has been accepted in some places, and forward-looking terrorism responses simply include this acceptance.

While the context was somewhat different, Lord Hope's words, reiterating the importance of the Rule of Law and procedural fairness, still ring true:

> The consequences of a successful terrorist attack are likely to be so appalling that there is an understandable wish to support the system that keeps those who are considered to be most dangerous out of circulation for as long as possible. But the slow creep of complacency must be resisted. If the rule of law is to mean anything, it is in cases such as these that the court must stand by principle. It must insist that the person affected be told what is alleged against him.[199]

In a speech made in August 2010, US Supreme Court Justice Anthony Kennedy responded to a question about the use of Military Commissions instead of Article III Courts in the US by saying that US courts are perfectly capable of trying these cases.[200] A similar view was expressed by John G Coughenour, the judge who presided over the trial of convicted 'Millennium Bomber' Ahmed Ressam. Coughenour wrote an op-ed in the *New York Times* in which he said:

> The case against Mr. Ressam demonstrates that our courts can protect Americans from terrorism. Through the commendable efforts of law enforcement authorities in 1999, Mr. Ressam was captured before he was able to carry out his plan to bomb the airport. For two years after his conviction, thanks in part to the fairness he was shown by the court, Mr. Ressam provided intelligence useful to terrorism investigations around the world, as German, Italian, French and British authorities were willing to attest.

> After a fair and open trial in which Mr. Ressam was convicted by a jury of his peers, I stated at sentencing that 'we have the resolve in this country to deal with the subject of terrorism, and people who engage in it should be prepared to sacrifice a major portion

---

[199] *AF*, above, n 68, para 84.
[200] Associated Press, 'Supreme Court Justice Kennedy Says Most Terrorism Cases Should Be Tried in Civilian Courts' *Fox News* (19 August 2010) www.foxnews.com/us/2010/08/19/supreme-court-justice-kennedy-says-terrorism-cases-tried-civilian-courts.

of their life in confinement'. Mr. Ressam now sits in a federal prison, and his punishment has the imprimatur of our time-honored constitutional values.[201]

Where a government seeks to avoid criminal courts for these cases, the pre-9/11 discursive presumption favoured the use of the criminal justice system, and deviation from these courts, if it was ever allowed, would only occur on a government showing of truly extraordinary circumstances. However, the discourse used after the 9/11 attacks appears to have given rise to a presumption against the criminal justice system when a government asserts necessity to avoid that system, and it appears to have arisen on a false premise that the 9/11 attacks somehow fragmented the validity of the criminal justice system, at least for some cases.

This is a moment when going back, deconstructing the narratives that led to these fragmented practices and reconstructing them in a more supportable way would prove useful. Given the prevalent nature of terrorism in the world today, going backward in this way could produce a more productive, constitutionally supported way of going forward.

[201] John G Coughenour, 'How to Try a Terrorist' *New York Times* (1 November 2007) www.nytimes.com/2007/11/01/opinion/01coughenour.html.

5

False Premise: Non-citizens as the Terrorist 'Other'

I. Many Post-9/11 Detention Changes Sprang from the False and Simplistic Idea that Terrorists were Non-citizens

This chapter turns to another argumentation point of departure, the most prevalent and most obvious one underscoring extraordinary detention practices in a number of places. Simply stated, the point of departure was that terrorists are non-citizens, or, alternatively, that non-citizens are terrorists, which has a wider sweep in terms of who is presumptively labelled a terrorist. Chapter one went into great detail about a narrative that was advanced in 2017 by US President Donald Trump, which emphasises terrorist incidents in which the perpetrators claim to act on behalf of Islam and which de-emphasises those incidents in which the perpetrator is not Muslim or in which the victims are Muslim. Much has been written about the tendency by national jurisdictions to paint people who are Muslim as more likely to be terrorists. It comes up in many different scenarios, such as in widespread accusations of profiling at airport security.[1]

However, when it comes to extraordinary detention practices, the parameters are a bit different, with citizenship often serving as an explicit argumentation point of departure as extraordinary detention practices were implemented after 9/11. It is not that citizenship was not an issue before 9/11, but it was a dominant feature in the particular changes that came about after 9/11. Yet, all non-citizens were not the same, and a non-citizen who was Muslim was much more likely to be subject to extraordinary detention practices than one who was not. The difference was that the citizenship distinction was explicit, and the distinction based on being Muslim, or having a national origin from a largely Muslim country, was generally less explicit and even outright denied in some instances.[2]

---

[1] See, eg, Charu A Chandrasekhar, 'Flying While Brown: Federal Civil Rights Remedies to Post-9/11 Airline Racial Profiling of South Asians' (2003) 10 *Asian American Law Journal* 215.

[2] See, eg, President George W Bush, 'Address to a Joint Session of Congress and the American People' *The White House* (20 September 2001) georgewbush-whitehouse.archives.gov/news/releases/2001/09/20010920-8.html (discussed in some detail later in this chapter).

Governments were more open about the 'them-versus-us' approach when it came to non-citizens of a given national jurisdiction. There were many reasons for this, as will be explored in more depth in this chapter. This distinction permeates all of the extraordinary detention practices discussed throughout this book. However, the disparate impact of these practices on people who were Muslim is undeniable. While not admitted so openly, it is clear that a subordinate point of departure to the one regarding citizens is that Muslims were deemed more likely to be terrorists, and this insidious association gained traction over the ensuing years. This process set the stage for the type of blatant anti-Muslim political discourse in 2017, which was described in chapter one.

A 'false premise' is, just as it sounds, a point of departure for an argument that is simply not true.[3] Trudy Govier explains that: 'If a premise is false and you have the basis for showing that it is false, you will not accept it and the argument in which it appears will fall down on the ... condition of argument adequacy.'[4] The generalised point of departure that terrorists are non-citizens, the Other, was clearly false. And yet, even to the present day, governments assert a right to deviate from constitutional norms for the detention of terrorism suspects based on this false premise.

Targeting non-citizens has an intuitive appeal for some governmental officials because citizens can thus be assured that the action will happen to 'them' in order to protect 'us'. It stands to reason that people are more likely to agree to rights deprivations for others than for themselves. The approach also appeals to a certain xenophobia that always seems to lie under the surface, especially in times of heightened fear. Non-citizens also cannot vote, so the political fallout for politicians advancing this assumption is likely to be minimised.[5] Citizens, of course, can vote and could object to such practices through voting. Do they do so though?

In Canada, one example of this type of persuasion was a statement made in Parliament by then-Canadian Minister of Public Safety Stockwell Day, as revisions to the security certificate legislation, later successfully enacted, were being debated in 2008:

> I would encourage all colleagues to set aside partisanship to realize that the security certificates have been proven not to threaten the individual rights and freedoms of Canadians. As a matter of fact, the security certificate cannot even be applied against a Canadian citizen. It can only be used on foreign nationals or those who are not Canadian citizens.[6]

---

[3] Trudy Govier, *A Practical Study of Argument* (Belmont, CA, Wadsworth Inc, 1988) 86.

[4] ibid.

[5] See generally David Cole, *Enemy Aliens* (New York, New Press, 2005) (pointing out that non-citizens cannot vote and thus make easier targets).

[6] 142 39th Parl Deb, HC 2nd Session (2008) No 041 1340, *Parliament of Canada*, www.ourcommons.ca/DocumentViewer/en/39-2/house/sitting-41/hansard (this quote was included in the following article: Maureen T Duffy and René Provost, 'Constitutional Canaries: The Elusive Quest to Legitimize Security Certificates in Canada' (2009) 40 *Case Western Reserve Journal of International Law* 531, 547).

Since targeting non-citizens is simply easier and less politically risky, it can also be used as a door for advancing a form of normalisation and expansion of measures, sometimes referred to as 'mission creep'.[7] Mission creep is a term used in the military to describe a 'gradual, unauthorized broadening of the original mission'.[8] Once a particular extraordinary detention practice has been normalised against non-citizens, it can be seen as less shocking if it is later expanded to citizens. This phenomenon is seen in a number of extraordinary detention scenarios, including the introduction of control orders in the UK, the contemplation of military detentions of US citizens in the controversial 2012 US National Defense Authorization Act and the targeting of a US citizen for a drone strike in the case of Anwar al-Aulaki.[9] In the years after 9/11, citizenship has also been a continuing dividing line, as seen in the use of citizenship stripping in some places for those suspected of terrorism involvement. This chapter focuses on discourse in the years immediately following, and sometimes preceding, 9/11, but does so cognisant of the fact that much of the same type of discourse continues to dominate political narratives in 2017.[10] It is therefore of continuing and prominent importance. First, some of the othering language is addressed, and then examples of particular, resulting fragmented practices are presented.

A. Particular Characteristics of this Point of Departure: The Terrorist 'Threat' from Non-citizens and 'Second-Class' Citizens

The preceding section divided the ideas of citizenship and national origin/religion for the purpose of this point of departure because the two components played out in somewhat different ways. These elements, however, were intertwined in the argumentative underpinnings to how extraordinary detention practices ultimately developed. In some ways, the concept of citizenship, certainly within the US, but arguably in places like Canada and the UK as well, changed after 9/11. Where, before 9/11, citizens were legally viewed in many ways based on their formal citizenship status, after the attacks, this narrative fractured and citizenship developed perceived tiers. Some citizens came to be seen as second-class citizens.[11]

---

[7] See Elizabeth L Hillman, 'Mission Creep in Military Lawyering' (2011) 43(3) *Case Western Reserve Journal of International Law* 565, 567.

[8] ibid.

[9] See David Anderson QC, 'Control Orders in 2011: Final Report of the Independent Reviewer on the Prevention of Terrorism Act 2005' *Terrorism Legislation Reviewer* (2012) terrorismlegislationreviewer.independent.gov.uk/wp-content/uploads/2013/04/control-orders-2011.pdf; National Defense Authorization Act for Fiscal Year 2012, HR 1540 (2012) (subsequent history omitted and controversy continues); see the discussion on al-Aulaki in ch 4 above.

[10] See ch 1 above.

[11] See Craig Forcese, 'A Tale of Two Citizenships: Citizenship Revocation for "Traitors and Terrorists"' (2014) 39(2) *Queen's Law Journal* 551 (persuasively critiquing Canada's citizenship revocation legislation, which was subsequently revised).

Citizenship came in some ways to be viewed in terms of allegiance, within the US in particular, as evidenced by the palpable swell of national loyalty after the 9/11 attacks. Citizens who showed such allegiance, or at least who were seen as doing so, were perceived as 'us', while those who did not, or even those who criticised actions taken by the US government, especially in response to the attacks, encountered considerable hostility.[12] A compact example is found in the scenario involving the Dixie Chicks described in chapter two above. A more prominent example can be seen in the way in which national governments respond to certain cataclysmic events.

This reflection of citizenship, or of being one of 'us' as related to perceptions of allegiance, evokes ideas of the othering of those of Japanese descent, whether citizens of the US or Canada, or not, after the attack on Pearl Harbor during the Second World War. Extraordinary detention was deemed acceptable based on perceived loyalty, and this perception of loyalty was based entirely on national origin. Conduct was not relevant and entire families, including children, were torn from their homes and placed in internment camps. Citizens entitled to procedural fairness clearly did not include those of Japanese origin, according to those governments, because they were treated as the Other and as a national security risk, even when they were citizens. Non-citizens of Japanese origin were obviously treated as the Other as well. Perceived loyalty was based on blatant racism, with a presumption that those of Japanese origin were presumptively disloyal and thus could be deprived of their liberty and incarcerated solely because of their national origin. This approach was upheld during this time by the US Supreme Court in the now-notorious *Korematsu* decision.[13] This ultimately led, many years later, to the US and the Canadian governments formally apologising and paying reparations to the victims.[14] This infamous example demonstrates the ways in which views of citizenship can fracture after a cataclysmic event.

The detentions during the Second World War of those of Japanese descent took place on a large scale, and it was explicitly enunciated that civilians, even including children, were being detained solely on national origin.[15] After 9/11, on the other hand, detentions were not so extensive and all people who had those immutable characteristics were not detained. This made it easier for those responsible to deny that they were doing this, even in the face of evidence that they were.

---

[12] See ch 2 above.

[13] *Korematsu v United States*, 323 US 214 (1944); *Korematsu v United States*, 584 F Supp. 1406 (ND Cal 1984) (vacating Korematsu's conviction, 40 years later); see also Susan Kiyomi Serranot and Dale Minami, '*Korematsu v United States*: A Constant Caution in a Time of Crisis' (2003) 10 *Asian Law Journal* 37.

[14] See Civil Liberties Act of 1988, 50a USC ss 1989b et seq (acknowledging the wrongdoing in the relocation and internments and granting reparations to Japanese-American citizens interned during the Second World War); 'Internment of Japanese Canadians' *Canadian Encyclopedia* (22 September 1988) www.thecanadianencyclopedia.ca/en/article/internment-of-japanese-canadians (containing the video of the speech during which Prime Minister Brian Mulroney apologised and which explains the reparations plan).

[15] Kiyomi and Minami, above, n 13.

Before 9/11, one of the largest terrorist attacks within the US occurred in Oklahoma City. The form of othering seen during the Second World War and after 9/11 did not occur after this attack. There were several perpetrators, with perhaps the most prominent being Timothy McVeigh, an American citizen who supposedly undertook the attack as revenge for the deaths after the siege in Waco, Texas.[16] He was a member of the National Rifle Association, Caucasian, of varying religious beliefs, but originally Catholic, and he took the Catholic sacrament of the anointing of the sick before he was executed.[17]

After the Oklahoma City attack, citizenship and othering did not become the issues they were in the other instances. A catastrophic attack, with significant loss of life, including horrific images of children killed at their daycare centre, resulted in a criminal investigation, trials and sentences. There was no significant questioning of whether the criminal justice paradigm worked. Caucasian, Catholic male US citizens or non-citizens with these attributes were not singled out for 'special' investigation and detention. In many ways, the Oklahoma City and 9/11 differences fell along the lines of what was deemed 'domestic' terrorism and what was 'international' terrorism. The intuitive instinct to undertake othering may arise more readily when the attack triggering the reaction is not carried out by somebody who would normally be perceived as 'us' in terms of at least citizenship and immutable characteristics. Thus, all terrorists are not constructed in the narrative in the same way. However, a question arises as to whether the distinctions among terrorism, along the lines of citizenship, religion or national origin, have a real connection to the objective of stopping terrorism or whether they serve as a convenient political stepping stone for desired governmental changes.

This presumption of 'the Other' as a relevant factor in national responses, particularly to 9/11, has been heavily discussed in a wide range of literature, either through the use of the theoretical concept of the Other or through more traditional language regarding discrimination or equality.[18] In this chapter, however,

---

[16] Jinee Lokaneeta, 'Revenge and the Spectacular Execution: The Timothy McVeigh Case' (2004) 33 *Studies in Law, Politics, and Society* 331.

[17] ibid.

[18] For example, I participated in a conference in Szczecin, Poland, in September 2012 ('Who is "Us" and Who is "Them" after 9/11—Reflections on Language, Culture and Literature in Times of Ideological Clashes', *University of Szczecin*, www.us.szc.pl/main.php/usandthem2011), which brought together academics from a wide range of disciplines to explore this phenomenon after 9/11. Existing works in law, English philology, linguistics, history, literature, film studies and even music were presented, addressing this issue, which has been widely discussed across a range of disciplines and a range of geographical borders. For other examples of works exploring the conception of the Other relating to terrorism post-9/11, see Frédéric Mégret, 'From "Savages" to "Unlawful Combatants": A Postcolonial Look at International Humanitarian Law's "Other"' in Anne Orford (ed), *International Law and its 'Others'* (Cambridge, Cambridge University Press, 2006); Ryszard Kapuscinski, *The Other* (Krakow, Verso, 2008); Randa A Kayyali, 'The People Perceived as a Threat to Security: Arab Americans since September 11' *Migration Policy Institute* (1 July 2006) www.migrationinformation.org; Arab-American Discrimination Committee, *Report on Hate Crimes and Discrimination against Arab Americans: The Post-September 11 Backlash: September 11, 2001–October 11, 2002, Arab-American Discrimination Committee*, www.adc.org/PDF/hcr02.pdf; Anthea Roberts, 'Righting Wrongs or Wronging Rights?

the issue is considered in a somewhat different manner from much of the post-9/11 anti-terrorism literature. The manner of development of this iteration of 'the Other' is not a stark creation of the 9/11 attacks, but rather is a more circular concept that has been ongoing, back and forth, between the involved entities for years and that was ongoing well before the attacks.[19] The attacks themselves represented a cataclysmic part of this vicious cycle, and the responses may have developed as they did in part because of the constantly escalating nature of this phenomenon. Rather than representing solely a post-9/11 creation, the othering scenario after 9/11 was arguably also really an escalation of this ongoing cycle and was not necessarily different in nature from prior perceptions. The difference was that the 9/11 attacks accelerated the political narratives that led to particular extraordinary detention practices.

The form of othering that involves national origin, religion and sometimes gender, which can be identified early in the post-9/11 responses, appears to continue, on some level, to the present. Muslims, particularly those from countries that have large Muslim populations, continue to disproportionately represent those being othered as terrorists. The so-called Muslim ban, described at length in chapter one, is an example of this. None of the people affected by this ban have been individually identified as terrorists. Instead, a larger presumption has arisen that people from these places are more likely to be terrorists and sweeping measures are implemented to support that presumption. In that instance, though, it is not

The United States and Human Rights Post-9/11' (2004) 15(4) *European Journal of International Law* 721; Office of the United Nations High Commissioner for Human Rights, *The Rights of Non-citizens* (2006) www.ohchr.org/Documents/Publications/noncitizensen.pdf; Daniel Moeckli, *Human Rights and Non-discrimination in the War on Terror* (Oxford, Oxford Publishing, 2008) (assessing post-9/11 measures in the US, the UK and Germany, and concluding that there was evidence of discrimination based on national origin and citizenship); see generally David Dyzenhaus (ed), *Civil Rights and Security* (Farnham, Ashgate, 2009); Annette Becker, 'Between "Us" and "Them"' in Adam Hodges and Chad Nilep (eds), *Discourse, War and Terrorism* (Amsterdam, John Benjamins Publishing Co, 2007) 161 (noting that '[p]olitical discourse is about taking sides. This becomes particularly apparent at times when a war, or a nation's active participation in a war, is at stake'); Amaney A Jamal, *Race and Arab Americans before and after 9/11: From Invisible Citizens to Visible Subjects* (Syracuse, Syracuse University Press, 2008); Detroit Arab American Study Team, *Citizenship and Crisis: Arab Detroit after 9/11* (New York, Russell Sage Foundation, 2009); see also generally Ana Maria Salinas de Frias et al (eds), *Counterterrorism: International Law and Practice* (Oxford, Oxford University Press, 2012); David Brotherton and Philip Kretsedemas, *Keeping out the Other: A Critical Introduction to Immigration Enforcement Today* (New York, Columbia University Press, 2008); Clark Butler, *Guantanamo Bay and the Judicial-Moral Treatment of the Other* (West Lafayette, IN, Purdue University Press, 2007); Ruth Bienstock Anolik and Douglas L Howard, *The Gothic Other: Racial and Social Constructions in the Literary Imagination* (Jefferson, NC, McFarland & Co, 2004); Anthony Burke, *Beyond Security, Ethics and Violence: War against the Other* (New York, Routledge, 2007); Jürgen Habermas, *The Inclusion of the Other: Studies in Political Theory* (Boston, MIT Press, 2000); Rayner Thwaites, *The Liberty of Non-citizens: Indefinite Detention in Commonwealth Countries* (Oxford, Hart Publishing, 2014).

[19] See, eg, Simon Reeve, *The New Jackals: Ramzi Yousef, Osama Bin Laden and the Future of Terrorism* (Boston, Northeastern University Press, 1999) (a pre-9/11 book discussing some already prominent figures in the world of 'Islamic terrorism'. The use of the word 'jackal' is pejorative in a way that may have racial implications, as a jackal is an animal found in Asia and Africa).

just males who are heavily affected. The mission creep has extended the practices to include everybody from those nations. Eliminating a perceived discrimination against one gender has simply extended discrimination to a larger pool of non-citizen others.

The initial justification—that some of these measures were appropriate because they only applied to non-citizens—was built on an argumentation point of departure that terrorists were non-citizens. From this false premise, some aspects of extraordinary detention then extended to citizens, under the guise of eliminating discrimination against non-citizens. Therefore, instead of correcting the problem, such extensions actually just extended the problem to a larger group of people. This is the 'mission creep' described above. Citizenship itself eroded, with the emergence of certain people treated as second-class citizens. In relation to the concept of the Other, there were several sub-levels of fracturing of the post-9/11 narrative and resulting detention practices.

There has been an increasing shift in the focus within the world of anti-terrorism detentions. After 9/11, the overwhelming focus was on international terrorism. In such a scenario, it is more intuitively reasonable to consider factors such as citizenship because, almost by definition, the terrorist threat is envisioned as originating from the outside. In recent years, however, the discourse has increasingly turned towards an inclusion of domestic terrorism, but with a focus that is apparently influenced by the post-9/11 anti-terrorism paradigms. As this internal focus continues and as national governments continue to apply post-9/11 structures and approaches to domestic terrorism, the potential is that the application of many of these types of extraordinary measures could increasingly include citizens of the national jurisdiction in question. If, however, these strategies have foundational problems, the solution to this inconsistency might not be to extend them to domestic detention, but rather to reconsider whether they were appropriate even in terms of international terrorism.

The stereotypical presumption of the terrorist Other as a Muslim male is an enduring, false image. Chapter four discussed the argumentation point of departure that gave rise to a justification to employ new detention regimes. This chapter focuses on the argumentation point of departure that most often shaped the specific forms of these new regimes. The notion of the terrorist as the non-citizen Other arose in more than one place, but, over the years, for many reasons, the forms of detention structures based on that point of departure fragmented, both within individual jurisdictions and across jurisdictions. Thus, while there may be consistency in the underlying argumentation points that were used for persuasion for these regimes, there is considerable fragmenting that arose in their specific forms.[20]

---

[20] See Thwaites, above, n 18, 3–4 (mentioning the 'deep divergence' across judicial rulings in different jurisdictions relating to indefinite detention of non-citizens after 9/11).

B. The Other: Stereotypes and Lack of Nuance

Much of the political discourse since 9/11, not just emanating from the West or the US, but also from groups claiming to act on behalf of Islam, has painted an 'us' against 'them' scenario in stark terms, often without the nuance that would more accurately describe the situation. In a speech at Cairo University in 2009, for instance, US President Barack Obama assumed such a rift in saying: 'I consider it part of my responsibility as president of the United States to fight against negative stereotypes of Islam wherever they appear ... But that same principle must apply to Muslim perceptions of America.'[21]

The obvious implication, of course, is that the two groups exist in separate, non-overlapping groups and that they think as one entity and have a single, unified belief system, which is diametrically opposed to that of the other. Even in this speech, in decrying the use of stereotypes, Obama himself appears to engage in the most blatant form of stereotyping.

It is, of course, not uncommon for political discourse to present scenarios in stark, non-nuanced terms, most particularly in times of perceived emergency or danger.[22] Piotr Cap has written, from a linguistics perspective, about this phenomenon in developing theories relating to 'legitimisation' and 'proximisation' in political discourse, specifically in relation to US government discourse after 9/11. His emphasis is on the discourse surrounding the justification of the invasion of Iraq, but he writes of the larger discursive environment after 9/11, noting that while there is a history of this type of discourse in the US in times of war, it had a new dimension after 9/11:

> Although following the [*sic*] WWII the legitimization of each consecutive military involvement has drawn on the simplistic dichotomy of 'us' and 'them', the latter party usually symbolizing some kind of adversarial or plainly evil ideology that could potentially jeopardize the American system of beliefs and values or, in the long run, threaten the lives of the American people, it was not until after 2001 that the ideologies of evil and terror could be claimed, by analogy, to have already been operating within the American territory.[23]

Moreover, the idea of presenting an enemy (or perceived enemy) in stereotypical terms, or simply presenting another culture that way, has long been recognised and discussed in various academic disciplines, such as in Edward Said's formulation

---

[21] Laura Meckler and Jay Solomon, 'Obama Chides Israel, Arabs in His Overture to Muslims' *Wall Street Journal* (4 June 2009) online.wsj.com/article/SB124409999530984503.html.

[22] See, eg, Becker, above, n 18, 161; see also David Haugen (ed), *National Security: Opposing Viewpoints* (San Diego, Greenhaven, 2007) (collecting issues from various people, with opposing perspectives presented on certain questions, including some relating to the limitations of civil rights in the name of national security); Glenn Greenwald, *A Tragic Legacy: How a Good vs. Evil Mentality Destroyed the Bush Presidency* (New York, Three Rivers Press, 2007) 8, 14, 26–32; see also ch 6 below.

[23] Piotr Cap, *Legitimisation in Political Discourse: A Cross-disciplinary Perspective on the Modern US War Rhetoric* (Newcastle, Cambridge Scholars Press, 2006) 2.

of the Other in *Orientalism*.[24] In the particular case of the 9/11 attacks, such a formulation seemed expedient when the US government initially faced immediate pressure to identify those responsible. When it emerged, shortly after the attacks, that the perpetrators were 19 non-US nationals, most of whom were from Saudi Arabia and some of whom were in the US on visas that had been obtained under questionable circumstances, the characteristics of the terrorist 'Other' began to formulate in the discourse and responses.[25] That was solidified when Osama bin Laden's al-Qaeda network was identified as the entity responsible for the attacks.

II. The Claimed Need to Protect 'Us' from 'the Other'

There is great political power in being able to paint a one-dimensional, purely evil enemy when trying to persuade an audience that change is needed. Dora Kostakopoulou said it well when she proposed that this stark framing of these issues may have created what she calls a 'cognitive filter' through which argued changes are then viewed, noting:

> [U]nder the 'war on terror' construction, politics is reduced to a simplistic and, in my opinion, flawed opposition between 'us' and 'them', which, in turn, lends further support for the emergence of a politics and laws of fear. The political realm is not only permeated by the Schmittean exclusionist discourse of friend v foe and the 'enemy' becomes stereotyped, but dissidents and opponents are also seen as traitors or outsiders, at best. In this 'duality trap', the institutional context of political violence is bracketed under the veil of simplistic explanations rooted in cultural differences or in envy and hostility towards American democracy and prosperity, such as 'they hate us because we elect our leaders'. By framing risks, such as international terrorism, as a 'clear and present danger to the existence of our civilization' or as a question of societal survival, and not as an issue of risk management, national executives manage to loosen the grip of the normal checks and balances that have underpinned the constitution and rule of law on executive decision making.[26]

This idea of creating a simplistic enemy from a complex situation for political reasons is threaded through many areas in the field of law and has been, for instance, discussed at length in recent years in relation to the securitisation of immigration.[27] The Other involves a relatively well-known and long-standing

---

[24] See Edward Said, *Orientalism* (London, Vintage Books, 1978).

[25] See 9/11 Commission, *The 9/11 Commission Report*, www.911commission.gov/report/911Report.pdf.

[26] Dora Kostakopoulou, 'How to Do Things with Security Post 9/11' (2008) 28 *Oxford Journal of Legal Studies* 317, 319, 322.

[27] See, eg, Delphine Nakache, 'The "Othering" Process: Exploring the Instrumentalization of Law in Migration Policy' (DCL Thesis, McGill University Faculty of Law, 2008, unpublished); Mégret, above, n 18.

theoretical concept, which has been examined and revised by a range of scholars, such as Georg Hegel, Jean-Paul Sartre, Jacques Derrida, Emmanuel Levinas and Edward W Said.[28] Generally speaking, the Other has been defined in many different ways, depending on the analysis being undertaken. For example, it can be defined as a way in which one group views and treats another group, typically based on defining characteristics deemed to set the 'other' group apart from the one viewing them. The notion of the Other is not necessarily always viewed in a negative light and has been, in some cases, characterised as a means of establishing one's own identity. Thus, for instance, in establishing parameters of citizenship, the perspective of the Other might be a basis for determining who belongs within one national group and who might belong in another.[29]

It is the conceptualisation of the Other as an exclusionary tool between two groups that is of particular, although not exclusive, interest in this work, especially as articulated by Said in his definitive book *Orientalism* and expounded upon in later works.[30] Said considers the phenomenon of the Other in terms of the need by one group to denigrate another. More specifically, he does so in relation to tensions between the 'West' and the 'East'—a tension that can arguably be said to underlie some aspects of the modern fight against terrorism, and one that makes the application of his theories to the terrorism scenario especially compelling.

Under Orientalism, those primarily in Europe, or the former colonial powers, view those in the East, or those who were under their former colonial rule, as the exotic 'Orient'. The designation comes with a bundle of qualities, which have little basis in reality, but instead serve as a simplistic characterisation of the East, created in the West, to preserve its self-perception of superiority. Said explains it as follows:

> Orientalism is never far from what Denys Hay has called the idea of Europe, a collective notion identifying 'us' Europeans as against all 'those' non-Europeans, and indeed it can be argued that the major component in European culture is precisely what made that culture hegemonic both in and outside Europe: the idea of European identity as a superior one in comparison with all the non-European ideas about the Orient, themselves

---

[28] See, eg, Ernesto Laclau and Chantal Mouffe, *Hegemony and Socialist Strategy: Towards a Radical Democratic Politics* (London, Verso, 1985) 129 (describing how things are viewed in relation to their opposite); see also generally Jacques Derrida, *Théorie d'ensemble* (Paris, Seuil, 1968).

[29] For some more in-depth discussions of more recent permutations of the notion of the Other, see Desmond Manderson, 'The Care of Strangers' *SSRN*, papers.ssrn.com/sol3/papers.cfm?abstract_id=1515424; Desmond Manderson, *Proximity, Levinas, and the Soul of Law* (Montreal, McGill-Queen's University Press, 2007); Desmond Manderson (ed), *Essays on Levinas and Law: A Mosaic* (New York, Palgrave Macmillan, 2008). While not necessarily contributing to an academic understanding of the issue, a popular-culture reference to this concept can be found in the film *The Others* starring Nicole Kidman—a thriller very loosely based on Henry James' work *The Turn of the Screw*. The film changes many elements of that original story and appears to demonstrate that the idea of the Others as separate and distinct may be misleading, and that, in fact, what we perceive to be characteristic of the Others may actually be a reflection of a reality in ourselves.

[30] See Said, above, n 24; Edward W Said, *Covering Islam: How the Media and the Experts Determine How We See the Rest of the World* (New York, Vintage Books, 1997).

reiterating European superiority over Oriental backwardness, usually overriding the possibility that a more independent, or more sceptical, thinker might have had different views on the matter.[31]

One wonders, for instance, if Said's type of idea of the self-perceived superiority of the West in relation to the East was a factor in the ease with which citizenship and national origin—primarily singling out those from largely Muslim countries or the 'East'—were underlying notions in national responses after the 9/11 attacks. It is well beyond the scope of this book to undertake a comprehensive analysis of the many theoretical writings on this concept of 'the Other', at least in its broader sense. However, the configuration of the issue as a negative, as stated by Said, gives an important underpinning to the success of the point of departure that terrorists are non-citizens, and especially non-citizens who are Muslim. To be persuaded by this argumentation point is to believe that the world of terrorism, specifically since 9/11, has been dominated, from all sides, by an amorphous, dangerous, probably Muslim, probably non-citizen, shadowy 'Other'. As Frédéric Mégret defines the Other, it can be seen as the '"Other" at times barely mentioned, sometimes indirectly so, but which haunts the very beginnings and evolution of the laws of war. It is their dark alter ego, the "uncivilized", "barbarian", "savage" from which the laws seek to distance themselves'.[32] Because this Other is perceived as so dangerous, the usual laws can be more easily argued to be inadequate or otherwise unworkable, and extraordinary measures gain an aura of legitimacy when applied to this Other. Thus, the point of departure identified in chapter four—that the nature of the 9/11 attacks requires the building of new detention paradigms—supports the point of departure set forth in this chapter, which is the false premise that terrorists are Others, non-citizens, probably Muslim. The points of departure do not exist in isolation, but build upon one another to make the cohesive whole of the argument presented to support changes in detention structures.

III. The Othering before and after 9/11 was Directed between Organisations Like Al-Qaeda and those Claiming to Represent the West, Each Accelerating it against the Other

The 9/11 attacks, as well as a number of subsequent attacks, were attributed to al-Qaeda, which was run by Osama bin Laden, who, until his death, seemed to have been perceived as a larger than life, purely evil entity. The long-stated purpose of al-Qaeda had been the creation of a Holy War, sometimes called *Jihad*, against

---

[31] Said, above, n 24, 7.
[32] Mégret, above, n 18.

the US in particular and sometimes stated to be against Westerners in general.[33] It is undeniable that the 9/11 attacks were intended to inflict horrific loss of life and economic hardship on the US, and that the intended victims, on that day at least, were Americans.

The concept of the Other cannot be fully deconstructed without an assessment of the way in which this concept may have driven the actual 9/11 attacks themselves, as well as numerous attacks before and after.[34] Said conceived of the 'Other' as a concept expounded by the former colonial West towards the formerly colonised East. He described the construction of the Orient as a technique to allow for a reflection not so much on actual characteristics of the Orient, but as a way of reinforcing Western identity, reflecting back on the West in such a way as to create an image of what it means to be the West in contrast to these Others.[35]

In the underpinnings of the 9/11 attacks themselves, at least as viewed through public statements attributed to al-Qaeda, this type of reflection, somewhat in reverse, is often explicit. Bin Laden, until his death, engaged in othering of the West and most particularly, although, not exclusively, the US. This was not so much done to define characteristics of the US, but to try to create a particular, albeit false, identity of Islam in the minds of Muslims. Therefore, this discussion of othering of the West usefully focuses on particular statements that bin Laden made, in particular before the 9/11 attacks.

Al-Qaeda statements, including two 'fatwas' bin Laden issued in the 1990s, refer to the West and, most particularly the US as 'Crusaders'.[36] This term was obviously not chosen by accident, but was intended to evoke reactions similar to those raised when recalling the actual Crusades, in which soldiers from the West, claiming to

---

[33] See Fawaz A Gerges, *The Rise and Fall of Al-Qaeda* (Oxford, Oxford University Press, 2011) (describing the history of al-Qaeda, including its role in what he argues to be a false narrative of the organisation as an imminent danger in the US).

[34] Said, above, n 24. Some scholars would object to characterising the portrayal of the West, or of the US, by bin Laden as othering, as there is a line of thought that suggests that this can only be directed towards those perceived as the minority or those that have been the subject of persecution. Thus, the West could other the formerly colonised East, but characterisations directed at the West that involve stereotyping and similarly sweeping assumptions would not be deemed othering. This type of limitation is often seen in feminist scholarship. See, eg, Simone de Beauvoir, *The Second Sex*, translated by HM Parshley (London, Penguin Books, 1947, translated 1953, 1972, 2005). This book rejects this notion, suggesting that the idea of 'the Other' can have different implications in different factual circumstances and that any generalised characterisation of a group, based on immutable characteristics, as 'them' for the purpose of negative conduct can constitute othering, at least in line with Said's perspective of the Other as a reflection back upon ourselves.

[35] Said, above, n 24.

[36] See, eg, Osama bin Laden, 'Declaration of War against the Americans Occupying the Land of the Two Holy Places', www.actmemphis.org/usama-bin-laden-1996-declaration-of-war-against-the-americans.pdf (an original translation by PBS is no longer available online); Osama bin Laden, 'Jihad against Jews and Crusaders', fas.org/irp/world/para/docs/980223-fatwa.htm (collectively referred to as the *Bin Laden Fatwas*); see also Michael Scheuer, *Osama Bin Laden* (Oxford, Oxford University Press, 2011) 6.

act on behalf of Christianity, invaded Muslim countries, with the express intention of conversion. The term was clearly a binary 'us' versus 'them' narrative.

In defending his call for attacks against civilians, bin Laden frequently said that targeting civilians was appropriate because the US has a long history of oppressing and killing civilians in Muslim nations, and thus retaliation was justified. In his statements, he painted the West, often interchangeable with the US and sometimes including Israel, as attempting to assert hegemonic control over Muslim nations and thus deserving of retaliation, while at other times characterising attacks on American civilians as self-defence.[37]

In so doing, bin Laden painted the 'West' in stark terms, in a sort of mirror image of the phenomenon described by Said. Said's focus was on the way in which the West characterised the East, with an eye to deconstructing what he perceived as inaccurate, simplistic and stereotypical notions. Bin Laden-type rhetoric would thus shine a mirror back from the East onto the West, characterising it as oppressive, but attempting to suggest that this oppression justified a war-like response by the East as revenge. Thus, bin Laden inverted and then expanded Said's type of othering in suggesting that actions by the US government, Israel or the West—however he put it at any given moment—rendered those of American, Israeli or Western culture as worthy targets for killing and as somehow less deserving of life. In so doing, bin Laden demonstrated othering in its most egregious form, using generalisations and simplistic stereotypes to dehumanise those he characterised as the Other—including Americans and anybody deemed to be 'their allies'. For instance, in his 1998 Fatwa, he said:

> The ruling to kill the Americans and their allies—civilians and military—is an individual duty for every Muslim who can do it in any country in which it is possible to do it, in order to liberate the al-Aqsa Mosque and the holy mosque [Mecca] from their grip, and in order for their armies to move out of all the lands of Islam, defeated and unable to threaten any Muslim. This is in accordance with the words of Almighty God, 'and fight the pagans all together as they fight you all together', and 'fight them until there is no more tumult or oppression, and there prevail justice and faith in God'.[38]

Just as Obama did in his 2009 speech described above, bin Laden painted Muslims and Americans as two separate groups. This lack of nuance and simplistic description is typical of inaccurate and othering narratives.

Shortly after the 1998 Fatwa was issued, in 1999, bin Laden made a statement, broadcast on Al Jazeera, that American civilians were, in fact, soldiers because they paid taxes to the US government.[39] The obvious conclusion from this is that

---

[37] *Bin Laden Fatwas*, above, n 36.

[38] Bin Laden, 'Jihad against Jews and Crusaders', above, n 36.

[39] 'Timeline of al-Qaida Statements (June 10, 1999 Statement)' *MSNBC*, www.msnbc.msn.com/id/4686034/ns/world_news-hunt_for_al_qaida/t/timeline-al-qaida-statements/#.T71it3lYvDM; see also 'Building an Organization, Declaring War on the United States' in 9/11 Commission, *The 9/11 Commission Report*, www.911commission.gov/report/911Report.pdf.

he was saying that American civilians were not civilians and thus could be killed under his model of holy war. This attempt to put a factual support under his othering rhetoric is itself simplistic and overbroad, attempting to link conduct of the intended targets with his calls to kill them.

It is clear that the 9/11 attacks were intentionally directed at civilians and that the intention was to kill those civilians solely based on the fact that they were American. Of course, many people who were not American died on 9/11 as well, and a number of the people murdered were Muslim, thus undermining the intent of creating an act that was a stark action by Muslims against Americans. Nonetheless, the discourse of al-Qaeda leading up to the attacks, and after the attacks, suggested the possibility that the 9/11 attacks were a violent manifestation of othering, directed from the 'Muslim' East to the 'American' West.[40] Of course, the reality was much more complicated than that, on both sides, but this characterisation of the attacks appears to have reflected a foundational motive.

In his denunciations of US actions in places like Saudi Arabia and Palestine, bin Laden arguably engaged in different levels of othering. Calling for attacks on Americans represents an outward form of othering, characterising 'them' as evil and dehumanising them based on characteristics he attributed to them. At the same time, in calling for Muslims to unite and in citing asserted wrongdoing in places like Palestine and Saudi Arabia, bin Laden publicly represented that he spoke on behalf of Muslims, and he implied a unified way of thinking among large numbers of people who he claimed to represent. In so doing, he was falsely othering moderate Muslims in simplistic and stereotypical terms. This, in turn, later served to fuel the process of othering against predominantly Muslim countries. Bin Laden sought to portray a situation in which Muslims were under siege by Americans or by the West.

In some aspects of national responses to 9/11, it is tragically apparent that bin Laden achieved this objective, and some of the extraordinary detention practices in particular gave rise to a belief among some that Muslims were under attack. This othering has continued and vestiges of it can be seen in some of Daesh's more recent actions, such as dressing its Western victims in orange, to represent the colours worn by prisoners at Guantanamo Bay, before brutally killing them.[41] The cycle has many levels and is seemingly endless.

---

[40] See Hugo Slim, *Killing Civilians: Method, Madness, and Morality in War* (New York, Columbia University Press, 2008); Quintan Wiktorowicz and John Kaltner, 'Killing in the Name of Islam: Al Qaeda's Justification for September 11' (2003) 10(2) *Middle East Policy Council Journal* 76 (citing 'A Statement from Qaidat al-Jihad Regarding the Mandates of the Heroes and the Legality of the Operations in New York and Washington').

[41] See Diane Feinstein, 'Let's Finally Close Guantanamo' *New York Times* (4 November 2015), www. nytimes.com/2015/11/05/opinion/lets-finally-close-guantanamo.html (noting that it is 'no coincidence' that Daesh dresses hostages in uniforms that resemble the Guantanamo Bay prison uniforms, before brutally killing them).

IV. The Cycle of Othering that Led to the 9/11 Attacks Continued in Some of the National Responses to the Attacks

Thus, the 9/11 attacks themselves arguably represented a stark form of othering, as do those other terrorist attacks in which civilians are intentionally targeted based solely on their national origin, religion or other immutable characteristics. In some ways, certain national governments reacted with a mindset that too closely resembled that of the terrorists themselves, thus perpetuating the problems involved in other-based violence. The othering undertaken by a number of national governments was a response to a perceived othering directed at them— a disproportionate, misdirected response at times, but a response nonetheless. In order to really understand the underpinnings of what many countries did after 9/11, it is critical to understand how these governments, and their populations, perceived this othering and to recognise that while the parameters of some of the responses may have been problematic, they did not occur in a vacuum. A notion of Americans, or Westerners, as the 'Other' was an underpinning to the attacks themselves, and a reactionary, reversed othering underscored many aspects of the responses. The two undertakings did not mirror each other, but it is undeniable that they occurred and, in both cases, they involved actions based on wide generalisations and characterisation of people based on immutable characteristics.

In traditional warfare, othering is an inherent component.[42] However, the parameters of these Others tend to be easily defined, as wars often pit one national government against another or alternatively involve the increasingly common scenario of civil war, which, while bearing some similarities to terrorism, still tends to entail conflicts that can be identified in terms of location and parties. Thus, the enemy and locus of conflict are more easily identified in many ways. In the case of terrorism, particularly terrorism that is not state-sponsored, the 'enemy' may be less easy to identify, but can be just as deadly, if not more so.

A. 11 September 2001

Recounting the actual events of the 9/11 attacks would not be useful, as that story has been told countless times, and any reader of this book will be familiar with what happened that day. The World Trade Center had previously been bombed in 1993, and significant security and other upgrades had been made in response.[43]

---

[42] See, eg, generally Cole, above, n 5 (discussing enemy alien legislation in the US relating to times of war).

[43] *9/11 Commission Report*, above, n 25, 280.

Some people reported that the changes made after the 1993 attacks made it possible for them to escape the buildings on 9/11, although there were numerous problems identified later in terms of what people were told in advance and as the attacks unfolded.[44]

It is now well known that the attacks were perpetrated by 19 men, most of whom were from Saudi Arabia and all of whom purported to act on behalf of al-Qaeda and in the name of Islam.[45] None of the perpetrators of the attacks was a US citizen and questions were later raised about the legal basis for admitting some of them to the country.[46] They had come to the US before the attacks and some of them had participated in flight training at schools in the US, apparently to prepare for hijacking the planes and flying them into the intended targets.[47]

It is also known that 2,977 people died that day, or in the years after, and many more were physically in the area, especially in New York, during the attacks.[48] On an average day, approximately 50,000 people worked in the Twin Towers and there were roughly 140,000 people who visited daily.[49] Thousands more were in the immediate vicinity, both in New York and in Washington DC.[50] As the attacks unfolded, false rumours abounded as to other attacks, with one false report indicating that Camp David had been attacked.[51]

Considerable confusion surrounded the attacks that day, as it was unknown who was attacking or the full extent of their targets. As rumours of missing planes and potential targets abounded, the downtown areas, or at least governmental offices, in many American cities were evacuated. Thus, the sense of imminent and personal threat expanded well outside of New York City, Washington DC and Pennsylvania. News coverage of the attacks continued around the clock for several days, with the constant public message that the attacks happened because somebody wanted to kill Americans.[52]

---

[44] ibid 281.

[45] ibid 214–41.

[46] ibid.

[47] ibid.

[48] ibid 311. The number stated varies across sources. *The 9/11 Commission Report* is considered the authoritative source, listing the toll at 2,973. The Medical Examiner's Office has attributed four subsequent deaths to the results of inhaling the toxic fumes near the World Trade Center. See 'September 11, 2001: Background and Timeline of the Attacks' *CNN* (8 September 2016) www.cnn.com/2013/07/27/us/september-11-anniversary-fast-facts/index.html (including an additional four casualties, based on four people who died later, and whose deaths were ruled to be homicide as a result of the attacks).

[49] '9/11 in Numbers' *The Guardian* (18 August 2002) www.theguardian.com/world/2002/aug/18/usa.terrorism.

[50] This included Secretary of Defense Donald Rumsfeld, who was in the Pentagon when the plane hit. After feeling the impact, Rumsfeld reportedly ran to the crash site to help people there. *The 9/11 Commission Report*, above, n 25, 37.

[51] This rumour apparently incorrectly related to United Airlines Flight 93, which crashed in Pennsylvania, after passengers tried to overcome the hijackers. See Eric Draper, 'We're the Only Plane in the Sky' *Politico* (September 2016) www.politico.com/magazine/story/2016/09/were-the-only-plane-in-the-sky-214230.

[52] Many of the statements in this section are based on my own recollections.

The immediate, and obvious, response in the US was a surge of national patriotism. By the late afternoon on 9/11, spontaneous shows of patriotism were evident, such as in widespread displays of American flags. In the days after the attacks, newspapers carried full-page pictures of the flag, usually with a message saying 'United We Stand', an expression that became a sort of mantra, appearing in various places, including on signs and in windows of businesses and homes.[53]

In addition to a collective sense of danger, brought about by the manner of the attacks and the confusion that followed, the events of that day were, again, further personalised simply by virtue of the fact that millions of people saw the second plane hit on live television, as well as seeing the Towers collapse. Millions who were not physically close to New York City watched live as the horrific events unfolded, including the distressing sight of people jumping or falling out of the buildings, and the buildings collapsing with thousands of people trapped inside.

In some ways, 9/11 played out in slow motion, giving an unusual opportunity to hear the voices of the victims before the crashes, as some made phone calls from the various planes and from the World Trade Center after the crashes, as numerous calls were made by people trapped in the buildings.[54] Many of these calls were recorded and subsequently released to the public, thus creating a sense of horror in hearing the victims' voices and of immediacy to the events.[55] These factors, combined, were somewhat distinctive to 9/11, and the reaction that followed was certainly influenced by a sense among many of having been eyewitnesses to the horrors of that day.

Therefore, the shock of 9/11, both within the US and beyond, was not simply because of the catastrophic loss of life or the loss of Towers that had enormous symbolic value, but because of various unusual factors that served to personalise the attacks. Even as news accounts continued shortly after the Towers fell, CNN, which was presenting live coverage of the attacks, was running taglines across the bottom of the screen, asking for people who were fluent in specific languages, including Arabic and Farsi. As people within the US tended to close ranks against

---

[53] This is based on my recollections.

[54] See, eg, '91 E-mails from Ground Zero' *American Lawyer* (2001) www.americanlawyer.com/ id=900005522968/91-EMails-From-Ground-Zero?slreturn=20170625162558 (including e-mails beginning shortly after the attacks of people trying to track down co-workers); 'Chilling Final Words of Those Who Died inside the Twin Towers on 9/11' *The Mirror* (11 September 2009) www.mirror.co.uk/ news/uk-news/chilling-final-words-of-those-who-417979 (alleging that more than 1,000 calls were made in the 10 minutes after the first plane struck, adding that some people reached their loved ones and that others left messages); Ed Vulliamy, 'The Real Story of Flight 93' *The Guardian* (2 December 2001) www.guardian.co.uk/world/2001/dec/02/september11.terrorism1 (including the reported last words of Todd Beamer, 'Let's roll', as heard over the phone when passengers joined forces to try to attack the hijackers).

[55] See Maria Godoy, 'Sept. 11 Tapes: Sounds of Horror, Chaos, and Valor' *NPR* (16 August 2006) www.npr.org/templates/story/story.php?storyId=5658516; see also Jules and Gedeon Naudet, *9/11* (a graphic documentary made by two French brothers who happened to be producing a film about a firefighting unit near the World Trade Center as the attack unfolded and who captured the events of that day, including both planes hitting the Towers, and detailed, disturbing scenes from inside and around the World Trade Center as the day progressed).

the horrors of the attacks and as they were repeatedly told they were potential targets as Americans, a sense of a lack of personal security arose. Symbols of standing united against this outside threat abounded. US governmental statements, including this issuing of calls for those who could speak Arabic and Farsi, created a parallel reaction in terms of looking outward to who the perceived enemy was. Even before the end of that day, the seeds had been planted for who would be considered 'us' and who would be considered 'them'.

B. The Early Internal Reaction to 9/11

One obvious effect of the attacks was to make the danger of sudden and violent death seem imminent, and incidents in the days after the attacks, such as the anthrax scares, did little to reassure people. The 9/11 attacks have been so excessively discussed that, in many ways, the actual trauma they caused has tended to get lost, as is normal in relation to so many other catastrophic historical events, both before and after. But it is this sense of national trauma that is important to recognise, as it was an underpinning of the response that emanated out of the US.

Moreover, although the attacks occurred in the US, the sense of imminence expanded well outside its borders, as nationals of a number of countries were killed and as al-Qaeda statements suggested that other Western nations were likely to be targets. The sense of an imminent threat may not have been as great outside of the US in the early days after 9/11, but it was nonetheless there. As a personal example, I was in Montreal a couple of weeks after the attacks. We got caught in an unusual traffic jam and a visibly distressed woman in the car next to us rolled down her window and asked if there had been a terrorist attack.

Othering, with the mirror-image type effect described by Said, involves two levels, both internal and external. A sense of internal identity is needed to reflect out onto the perceived Other, as it is this sense of contrast that is the underpinning for this process. The specifics of what happened on 9/11 set the stage for both levels of othering.

In the early days after the attacks, American flags were extremely prominent in the US. Seemingly every car had a clip-on American flag and wherever one went, enormous flags were prominent. Patriotic music ran on the radio in the first few days after the attacks, in place of normal programming. For days, 24-hour news coverage showed the horrors of the aftermath of the attacks, full of graphic accounts of body parts in the area and interlaced with heart-wrenching scenes of people looking for their loved ones. On 13 September 2001, I heard, on a popular music station, a song from the Second World War called 'Praise the Lord and Pass the Ammunition', one of many songs that had a call-to-arms tone that were played in those days. The song was originally written in 1942 as a response to the attacks by the Japanese military on Pearl Harbor.[56] The initial response within the US, and

---

[56] See Frank Loesser, 'Praise the Lord and Pass the Ammunition', 1942.

the unusual swell of patriotism, arguably represented a form of recoiling inward immediately after the attacks. It did not take long for this reaction to then turn around and to recoil back outward.

Patriotism and shock quickly gave way to a sense that some dramatic response was needed. As described in chapter four, the language after the attacks immediately suggested that this was a 'new' form of terrorism, which, given the horrific nature of what so many people had watched or experienced live, or heard through victim phone calls, was not treated as controversial.[57] However, with the calls for those speaking Arabic and Farsi, which ran as early as the day of the attacks, as well as quick statements by the US government that it was the notorious al-Qaeda network that was responsible for the attacks, the pulling together mentality that dominated in the US began to be mirrored with an image of who the terrorists were. Thus, the 'othering' took on another dimension.

C. 'Nous sommes tous Américains'[58]

The sense of internal unity, of a national identity, that Americans apparently experienced shortly after the attacks in some ways emanated outside of the US borders, as allegiances seemed clear in the face of such horrific attacks. As the Federal Aviation Administration closed US airspace on 9/11, many planes were rerouted to Canada. People, unable to get back to the US, were stranded, and many people in Canada opened their homes to those travellers. People in Vancouver took in approximately 8,500 people and those in the small town of Gander, Newfoundland took in another approximately 6,500 people.[59]

Right after the attacks, there was an immediate international outpouring of condemnation, as well as sympathy for Americans. Condolences poured in from around the world. Flags flew at half-mast in Canada.[60] The US National Anthem was played at the Changing of the Guards at Buckingham Palace in the UK. A famous editorial ran in France's *Le Monde* on 13 September 2001, with a headline that read 'Nous sommes tous Américains' ('We are All Americans').[61]

Thus, again, the initial response was a form of othering that involved turning inward, and formulating a sense of unified identity within the US and, to some extent, with the US from outside of its borders. At the same time, while expressing unity with the US, some national jurisdictions reacted with a sense that they too could be potential targets, just as the US was. The image of such destruction in a

---

[57] See *The 9/11 Commission Report*, above, n 25.
[58] 'Nous sommes tous Américains' *Le Monde* (13 September 2001) www.lemonde.fr/idees/article/2007/05/23/nous-sommes-tous-americains_913706_3232.html.
[59] See 'Obama Thanks Canada for Aid on 9-11 in Letter to PM' *CTV News* (9 September 2011) www.ctvnews.ca/obama-thanks-canada-for-aid-on-9-11-in-letter-to-pm-1.694716.
[60] This is based on my recollection.
[61] *Le Monde*, above, n 58.

busy urban centre, which did not generally experience such attacks, arguably sent shockwaves across a number of national jurisdictions in terms of the potential within their own borders as well. The reaction quickly shifted from shock to a call for a response. And in responding, this early unifying reaction was used in somewhat of a mirror fashion, setting the stage for a classic 'us' versus 'them' binary in the discourse and in the responses.

D. 'They Hate Our Freedoms'[62]

On 20 September 2001, President Bush made a televised speech to a joint session of the US Congress, in which he spoke about the fact that Americans were targeted, and he purported to answer the question of why 'they' hated 'us'. In so doing, he appears to have laid the discursive groundwork for at least part of what would develop as the Global War on Terror, and he signalled a shift from internal othering to outward-looking othering, in which he painted Americans and 'the enemy' in stark terms and characterised the coming fight clearly as one of good versus evil. Because of the circumstance of when it was given and how it was received, this speech laid a narrative groundwork for much of the subsequent response to terror, supporting a shift in the othering cycle, which was now shifting back to looking outward from the US.

Bush began by essentially establishing that Americans are good and that the 'others' who are the terrorists, are clearly evil. It is not surprising that people who could inflict the horrors of the 9/11 attacks would be portrayed as evil, but this binary was presented in more global terms. For example, he said:

> Americans are asking, why do they hate us? They hate what we see right here in this chamber—a democratically elected government. Their leaders are self-appointed. They hate our freedoms—our freedom of religion, our freedom of speech, our freedom to vote and assemble and disagree with each other.[63]

Having laid down a characterisation of 'us' as defenders of freedom and democracy, President Bush then identified 'them'. He presented information available at that point as to the identity of the attackers of 9/11:

> The evidence we have gathered all points to a collection of loosely affiliated terrorist organisations known as al Qaeda. They are some of the murderers indicted for bombing American embassies in Tanzania and Kenya and responsible for bombing the USS Cole.

> Al Qaeda is to terror what the Mafia is to crime. But its goal is not making money, its goal is remaking the world and imposing its radical beliefs on people everywhere.

---

[62] Bush, above, n 2.
[63] ibid.

The terrorists practice a fringe form of Islamic extremism that has been rejected by Muslim scholars and the vast majority of Muslim clerics; a fringe movement that perverts the peaceful teachings of Islam.

The terrorists' directive commands them to kill Christians and Jews, to kill all Americans and make no distinctions among military and civilians, including women and children. This group and its leader, a person named Osama bin Laden, are linked to many other organisations in different countries, including the Egyptian Islamic Jihad, the Islamic Movement of Uzbekistan.

There are thousands of these terrorists in more than 60 countries.

They are recruited from their own nations and neighborhoods and brought to camps in places like Afghanistan where they are trained in the tactics of terror. They are sent back to their homes or sent to hide in countries around the world to plot evil and destruction. The leadership of al Qaeda has great influence in Afghanistan and supports the Taliban regime in controlling most of that country. In Afghanistan we see al Qaeda's vision for the world. Afghanistan's people have been brutalized, many are starving and many have fled.[64]

Thus, Bush began using the language of warfare that came to underscore much of the 'War on Terror', which is discussed at greater length in chapter six below. At the same time, the pre-existing criminal justice system approach can be seen in this language, such as in referring to the terrorists as 'murderers' or comparing terrorists to the Mafia. It is apparent that, at this point of the speech, Bush was drawing on criminal justice concepts in making an analogy. Thus, in US discourse terms, this speech represents a sort of bridge between the criminal justice approach to terrorism detentions that was dominant before 9/11 and a beginning of a shift towards treating terrorism, in loose terms, as a form of warfare. Another discursive element that arose in this speech is the notion that killing women is tantamount to killing children, which raises a number of gender-related issues. Aside from ignoring the fact that, in the US, women increasingly serve in the military, it also perpetuates an outdated notion that women are to be equated with children in terms of helplessness, and thus suggesting that it is somehow more wrong to kill them than it is to kill men. This element of Bush's speech is not further discussed herein, except to note that it presents yet another layer of othering.

Using absolute, unequivocal language, Bush made demands in relation to Afghanistan and the Taliban, but he also used language creating an obvious distinction between the Taliban, al-Qaeda and terrorists, and those more generally of the Muslim faith, noting, for instance:

The Taliban must act and act immediately.

They will hand over the terrorists or they will share in their fate. I also want to speak tonight directly to Muslims throughout the world. We respect your faith. It's practiced

---

[64] ibid.

freely by many millions of Americans and by millions more in countries that America counts as friends. Its teachings are good and peaceful, and those who commit evil in the name of Allah blaspheme the name of Allah.

...

The terrorists are traitors to their own faith, trying, in effect, to hijack Islam itself.[65]

The speech began to present a roadmap, suggesting that terrorists intent on destroying the US were hiding in large numbers of countries around the world. 'They' were everywhere.

The speech clearly drew on the sense of national unity that arose after the attacks—not surprisingly, as it was given only nine days after they occurred. It also characterised the events of 9/11 and of the upcoming fight against terror in terms that clearly left no room for middle ground and clearly defined who was right and who was wrong. This fight, according to Bush, was all about the American identity that had emerged as so dominant since the attacks. It was about defending freedom itself: 'Tonight, we are a country awakened to danger and called to defend freedom. Our grief has turned to anger and anger to resolution. Whether we bring our enemies to justice or bring justice to our enemies, justice will be done.'[66] In cementing the idea of the Other as enemy, Bush made it very clear that there were only two sides, 'us' and 'them', and that there was no room for disagreement:

> We will starve terrorists of funding, turn them one against another, drive them from place to place, until there is no refuge or no rest. And we will pursue nations that provide aid or safe haven to terrorism. Every nation, in every region, now has a decision to make. *Either you are with us, or you are with the terrorists* ... From this day forward, any nation that continues to harbor or support terrorism will be regarded by the United States as a hostile regime. (Emphasis added)[67]

Echoing the language of the Other as savage, which appears in many ways to fit into the long-standing models of the Other, Bush characterised the fight in terms of who was civilised and who was not:

> This is not, however, just America's fight. And what is at stake is not just America's freedom. This is the world's fight. This is civilization's fight. This is the fight of all who believe in progress and pluralism, tolerance and freedom.

> We ask every nation to join us. We will ask, and we will need, the help of police forces, intelligence services, and banking systems around the world. The United States is grateful that many nations and many international organizations have already responded—with sympathy and with support. Nations from Latin America, to Asia, to Africa, to Europe, to the Islamic world. Perhaps the NATO Charter reflects best the attitude of the world: *An attack on one is an attack on all.*

---

[65] ibid.
[66] ibid.
[67] ibid.

The civilized world is rallying to America's side. They understand that if this terror goes unpunished, their own cities, their own citizens may be next. Terror, unanswered, cannot only bring down buildings, it can threaten the stability of legitimate governments. And you know what—we're not going to allow it. (Emphasis added)[68]

As of that date, as the so-called 'War on Terror' began, the lines had been clearly delineated as to who was friend and who was foe, and no discursive room had been left for a middle ground. At least initially, and within the US, this tone gained wide popular acceptance.

After this speech, Bush's approval rating within the US soared to approximately 90 per cent.[69] While it is speculative as to the reason, the timing suggests that the attacks, and this speech, caused this surge. No doubt it was aided by the internalisation Americans undertook after the attacks and by a cultural belief that Americans should support the President in times of national danger. It is, however, especially striking in this instance, when Bush had been elected less than a year earlier under highly controversial circumstances, losing the popular vote, but winning the Electoral College, and after a contentious battle over a recount in Florida, which decided the election. During his inauguration in January 2001, just eight months earlier, a planned walk in a public space had to be cancelled because of the actions of more than 20,000 protestors, including people who threw bottles and eggs at the motorcade. The protests were called the largest since Richard Nixon's inauguration in 1973, during the protests to the Vietnam War.[70]

V. The 'Other' Moves Forward as a Foundation for Extraordinary Terrorism Detention Practices

In chapter four, the discussion focused on the point of departure that the 9/11 attacks were 'unprecedented', or certain variations on that presumption, such as the notion that they were different in a way that required significant changes to various legal regimes, including detention standards. This point of departure, of course, does not stand in isolation, but is interlaced with the other narrative

---

[68] ibid.

[69] See Gallup Polls, 'Presidential Approval Ratings', www.gallup.com/poll/116500/presidential-approval-ratings-george-bush.aspx (showing President Bush's approval rating jumping from 51 per cent on 7 September 2001 to 86 per cent on 14 September 2001 and peaking at 90 per cent on 21 September 2001, the day after his speech).

[70] See Ron Kampeas, 'Inauguration Protests Largest since Nixon in '73' *CJ Online* (21 January 2001) cjonline.com/stories/012101/new_inaugprotests.shtml#.WXfSXtPyvBI.

For a discussion of the circumstances surrounding President Bush's election, see *Bush v Gore*, 531 US 98 (2000) (*per curiam*) (ruling in favour of George W Bush that a vote recount, ordered by the Florida Supreme Court, was unconstitutional).

techniques, and the undercurrent point of the non-citizen terrorist Other is an important part of that overall narrative.

In using the general idea of the attacks being unprecedented, the follow-up step was often to use the concept of the Other to single out people for the revised detention regimes that were allegedly necessitated by the unprecedented nature of the attacks or to otherwise undertake policies that caused certain groups to be disproportionately represented among those detained. In so doing, the second point of departure, of the terrorist as the non-citizen Other, played into who would encounter these altered practices.

Across various jurisdictions, non-citizens were significantly more vulnerable to revised practices than were citizens, although this was an initial trend that has changed more recently in some places, resulting in some particular fragmentation in practices, both within some jurisdictions and across certain jurisdictions. As discussed further in the following sections, the characteristics of a perceived Other can morph over time.

Carla Ferstman linked some of these points of departure, although not specifically calling them points of departure, in the following way:

> There is a tendency to view terrorism as the most severe challenge to humankind's existence in our time; as an unprecedented and exceptional challenge. The fear of the unprecedented ill of terrorism tends to govern policy-makers' responses to it. Labeling the challenge as 'exceptional' or 'unprecedented' has dramatized the fight against terrorism as having absolute priority, and has served to legitimate exceptional policies, practices, executive measures and laws. This has led to a series of justifications in the name of terrorism, justifications which have been applied mainly against non-citizens—minorities, immigrants, asylum-seekers and refugees, and which have been said to be more effective in undermining personal security than any terrorist attack.[71]

While the specifics morphed and began to vary from one place to another, in the early days after the attacks, the terrorist Other was portrayed as having certain characteristics—a non-citizen, Muslim, male and/or of a national origin in a country that is predominantly Muslim. As researchers at New York University have argued:

> [T]he construction of a terrorist 'Other' has conflated notions of race, ethnicity, religion, national origin, gender, and political views, effectively racializing Islam, Muslims, and Muslim religious practice as radically threatening to U.S. national security interests. Muslim men have been constructed as particularly dangerous.[72]

---

[71] Carla Ferstman, 'The Human Security Framework and Counterterrorism: Examining the Rhetoric Relating to "Extraordinary Renditions"' in Alice Edwards and Carla Ferstman, *Human Security and Non-citizens: Law, Policy and International Affairs* (Cambridge, Cambridge University Press, 2010) (citations omitted) 535.

[72] Center for Human Rights and Global Justice, *Targeted and Entrapped: Manufacturing the 'Homegrown Threat' in the United States* (New York, New York University School of Law, 2012) chrgj. org/documents/targeted-and-entrapped-manufacturing-the-homegrown-threat-in-the-united-states (this report addresses more recent changes to so-called 'home-grown' terrorism investigations in the US, which utilise concepts of the Other as terrorist that emerged in the early days after 9/11).

National jurisdictions that utilised extraordinary detention practices in response to 9/11 did so through two primary mechanisms. Each involved utilising a system that allowed for a claim, at least, that non-citizens could be treated differently. The US, as discussed throughout this chapter, declared a 'War on Terror', under which it claimed that it could hold non-citizens outside of a criminal justice, or really even a war, paradigm. Places like Canada and the UK, on the other hand, held non-citizens outside of the criminal justice paradigm primarily through use of their immigration systems, under a growing phenomenon known as the securitisation of immigration.

A. A 'War on Terror'

Bush's 20 September 2001 speech represented a dividing line in terms of reactions to the attacks. While the dominant reaction within the US before that was a form of closing of ranks, as evidenced by the 'United We Stand' mantra, the reaction unequivocally turned back outward, from a focus on a unified US identity to a unified outward response, turning on the perceived perpetrators of the attacks and on those who might undertake such attacks in the future. As the attacks were unusual in their enormity and level of destruction, so too were the responses. The Other had been explicitly identified as members of identified terrorist groups, but which, Bush bluntly stated, could include anybody who did not join the US in its fight against terror. The ultimate view of who was the terrorist Other ultimately expanded well beyond bin Laden and the al-Qaeda network, and factors aside from conduct were sometimes used to target people.

Again, in establishing its War on Terror, the US government initially used language suggesting that all Muslims were not to be treated as potential terrorists. However, the impact of extraordinary detention practices created as part of the War on Terror fell almost exclusively on those who were Muslim, making many people cynical that Muslims were not being targeted. Possibly inadvertently, Bush enhanced this impression by using, on at least two occasions, language suggesting that the US was involved in a 'crusade' against terrorism.[73] A few days after the attacks, he said that 'this crusade, this war on terrorism is going to take a while'.[74] His use of the word raised serious concerns, with one author saying at the time:

> [T]here is growing anxiety here [in Europe] about the tone of American war rhetoric …
> President Bush's reference to a 'crusade' against terrorism, which passed almost unnoticed by Americans, rang alarm bells in Europe. It raised fears that the terrorist attacks could spark a 'clash of civilizations' between Christians and Muslims, sowing fresh winds

---

[73] See the discussion of bin Laden's use of this word for strategic reasons (above, n 36 and accompanying discussion).

[74] George W Bush, 'Remarks by the President upon Arrival' *The White House* (16 September 2001) georgewbush-whitehouse.archives.gov/news/releases/2001/09/20010916-2.html.

of hatred and mistrust ... 'We have to avoid a clash of civilizations at all costs', French foreign minister Hubert Vedrine said on Sunday. 'One has to avoid falling into this huge trap, this monstrous trap' which he said had been 'conceived by the instigators of the assault'.[75]

Even then, bin Laden's othering narrative was recognised and alarms were being raised that the US should not play into that narrative in its response. Various commentators warned the US not to use stark language that gave the impression of a 'clash of civilizations'.[76] For example, one political analyst warned: 'The same black and white language he uses to rally Americans behind him is just the sort of language that risks splitting the international coalition he is trying to build ... This confusion between politics and religion ... risks encouraging a clash of civilizations in a religious sense, which is very dangerous.'[77] Another writer later said:

> Crusade. I remember a momentary feeling of vertigo at the President's use of that word, the outrageous ineptitude of it. The vertigo lifted, and what I felt then was fear, sensing not ineptitude but exactitude. My thoughts went to the elusive Osama bin Laden, how pleased he must have been, Bush already reading from his script.
>
> ...
>
> Osama bin Laden was already understood to be trying to spark a 'clash of civilizations' that would set the West against the whole House of Islam. After 9/11, agitated voices on all sides insisted that no such clash was inevitable. But crusade was a match for jihad, and such words threatened nothing less than apocalyptic conflict between irreconcilable cultures. Indeed, the President's reference flashed through the Arab news media. Its resonance went deeper, even, than the embarrassed aides expected–and not only among Muslims. After all, the word refers to a long series of military campaigns, which, taken together, were the defining event in the shaping of what we call Western civilization. A coherent set of political, economic, social and even mythological traditions of the Eurasian continent, from the British Isles to the far side of Arabia, grew out of the transformations wrought by the Crusades. And it is far from incidental still, both that those campaigns were conducted by Christians against Muslims, and that they, too, were attached to the irrationalities of millennial fever.[78]

Although Bush's aides had claimed the word was not used intentionally, Bush used it again in February 2002, even after the backlash from his prior use of the word. In complimenting Canada for joining the US-led invasion of Afghanistan,

---

[75] Peter Ford, 'Europe Cringes at Bush "Crusade" against Terrorists' *Christian Science Monitor* (19 September 2001) www.csmonitor.com/2001/0919/p12s2-woeu.html.

[76] See Richard Bonney, *False Prophets: The 'Clash of Civilizations' and the Global War on Terror* (Oxford, International Academic Publishers, 2008), 294 (reproducing numerous such statements).

[77] Ford, above, n 75.

[78] James Carroll, 'The Bush Crusade' *The Nation* (2 September 2004) https://www.thenation.com/article/bush-crusade (referring to the fact that the Crusades began not long after the year 1000 and thus in a time period when a millennium brought fears of a catastrophe. Similarly, he notes, the 9/11 attacks, and the aftermath, happened shortly after the year 2000, when millennium fears had also arisen).

he said: 'They stand with us in this incredibly important crusade to defend free-dom, this campaign to do what is right for our children and our grandchildren.'[79] Whether intended or not, Bush was mirroring the language that bin Laden had used to try to convince people that the US was persecuting Muslims.[80] Beyond that, post-9/11 American rhetoric was laced with Christian-based religious references, which could only have underscored this perceived religious battle for some.[81]

This was in spite of pains taken elsewhere to characterise this as a war on terror, not a war on Islam. While the issue of a war against an ideology is discussed more in chapter six below, it is also relevant for the purpose of this chapter. Calling the response a war, aside from triggering constitutional powers for the President, built upon this sense that this was a fight between the US and 'them'. In a tradi-tional war situation, the enemy would typically be people who are not citizens, and actions taken would be designed to keep citizens safe. The American-declared 'War on Terror' was arguably different from previously seen conflicts, in that it was an asserted declaration of war against an ideology, and the proposed enemy could therefore be from a wide range of national jurisdictions, regardless of the official stance of the national jurisdiction of their origin. In practice, this meant that those targeted in this War on Terror, and particularly through revised deten-tion practices, were indeed from a wide range of national jurisdictions, but were overwhelmingly Muslim and male. The US has, for instance, detained a number of people who are nationals, not of an enemy nation, but of its allies in its military operations as part of the War on Terror.[82] Moreover, while this book is referring to Bush's speech as a declaration of war, this is true in narrative terms only. The US Constitution provides the mechanism for a formal declaration of war, a power that rests not with the President, but with Congress.[83]

The US pursuit of the war paradigm was unique in some respects among responses of other national jurisdictions and, although few jurisdictions spe-cifically followed all of the US war measures undertaken after 9/11, most who

---

[79] George W Bush, 'President Rallies the Troops in Alaska' *The White House* (16 February 2002) georgewbush-whitehouse.archives.gov/news/releases/2002/02/20020216-1.html.

[80] See Peter Waldman and Hugh Pope, '"Crusade" Reference Reinforces Fears War on Terrorism is against Muslims' *Wall Street Journal* (21 September 2001) www.wsj.com/articles/SB1001020294332922160.

[81] See, eg, Jackson Lears, 'How a War Became a Crusade' *New York Times* (11 March 2003) www.nytimes.com/2003/03/11/opinion/how-a-war-became-a-crusade.html (op-ed, around the time of the Iraq invasion).

[82] For example, the US detention of Omar Khadr, a Canadian citizen, at Guantanamo Bay has been the subject of a long-term controversy in Canada. See, eg, *Canada (Prime Minister) v Khadr* 2010 SCC 3 (Khadr was captured by the US at the age of 15 in Afghanistan and controversially detained in Guantanamo Bay. Canada was an ally in the US invasion of Afghanistan).

[83] United States Constitution, Art I, s 8, cl 11 ('[Congress shall have Power] To declare War, grant Letters of Marque and Reprisal, and make Rules concerning Captures on Land and Water'). The US Congress never issued such a declaration, although it did issue an *Authorization for Use of Military Force*, which has been interpreted as giving the President broad authority in relation to the War on Terror. See *Authorization for Use of Military Force*, PL 107-40, 18 September 2001, 115 Stat 224).

responded to the attacks were, in some respects, influenced by the US approach. This influence did not generally extend to enacting similar wartime measures, but did have an apparent influence on how certain domestic detentions were handled. Some countries did join the US in its military actions in Afghanistan and Iraq, as part of the so-called 'Coalition of the Willing'. However, the sometimes elaborate structures the US put in place for detaining people caught in its 'War on Terror' represented a revised version of a traditional war-dominated approach that, ultimately, was primarily American.[84]

Kent Roach characterises much of the US response to 9/11 as 'Executive Power and Extra-Legalism'.[85] Indeed, in classifying its post-9/11 responses as 'war' measures, it is apparent that the US government was undertaking a shift in power in favour of the Executive. Executive detentions are not unprecedented, but they are rare in the US and are always controversial when used, in part because of constitutional constraints.[86] Under the US Constitution, the President is Commander in Chief of the military and thus when acting through this authority can claim more extensive powers than can typically be claimed under ordinary circumstances.[87] Roach combines this factor with the notion of 'extra-legalism', which is an effective combination, as the US arguably expanded its claimed detention authority beyond the pre-existing legal parameters and under circumstances that caused many to criticise it for attempting to act outside of the law.[88]

The fact that places like Guantanamo Bay can only be used for detaining people who are not US citizens, as explained below, suggests that conduct, on its own, does not trigger the use of some of these revised detention standards, but that instead the form of detention and proceeding can vary significantly depending on where the person accused falls on the continuum of the terrorist Other. In seeking to legitimate its wartime detention structures, the US employed discourse that came to be characteristic of its 'War on Terror' and tended to present a discursive basis for justifying the treatment of some people as the Other. A US citizen suspected of terrorism, for instance, will never face potentially indefinite detention at Guantanamo Bay, even if that citizen has undertaken identical conduct to those who are held there.

---

[84] See Matthew A Baum, 'The Iraq Coalition of the Willing *and* (Politically) Able: Party Systems, the Press, and Public Influence on Foreign Policy' (2013) 57(2) *American Journal of Political Science* 442 (arguing that a more robust media tended to reduce the willingness to contribute troops to the invasion of Iraq).

[85] Kent Roach, *The 9/11 Effect: Comparative Counter-Terrorism* (New York, Cambridge University Press, 2011) 161–235.

[86] For a discussion of Executive detentions in the UK, where they have been used more in the past, see Dominick McGoldrick, 'Security Detention: United Kingdom Practice' (2008) 40(3) *Case Western Reserve Journal of International Law* 507.

[87] See US Constitution, Art II, s 2.

[88] See Roach, above, n 85, 161–235.

i. The Guantanamo Bay Military Commissions for 'Certain Non-citizens'[89]

The controversy over the designation of certain people as 'unlawful enemy combatants' largely emanated from the US, as other national jurisdictions generally did not follow suit in attempting to make such special designations under enhanced war powers brought about through the War on Terror.[90] The US has not asserted that US citizens can be detained at extraordinary detention centres like Guantanamo Bay or that they can be brought before the Military Commissions there. The bulk of US extraordinary detention practices were explicitly aimed at non-citizens. Bush's Military Order, which established the Military Commissions at Guantanamo Bay, only applied to 'certain non-citizens', as was made explicit even in the title of the document.[91] In this, and in how the US handled immigration detentions shortly after 9/11, the message was clear and explicit that terrorists were non-citizens. While the US never seriously tried to argue that citizens should be held at Guantanamo Bay, some attempts have been made to expand extraordinary detention to citizens, through the kind of mission creep described above.

The US President has been argued to have the authority to declare certain detainees as unlawful enemy combatants in large part because of a joint Congressional enactment, undertaken shortly after the attacks. This joint resolution, known as the *Authorization for Use of Military Force* (AUMF), was passed by Congress on 14 September 2001—the same day on which memorial services relating to the attacks were ongoing in the US and around the world. Bush signed the resolution on 18 September.[92]

Drawing on the language of the attacks having been unprecedented, discussed above in chapter four, as well as delineating the attacks as against US citizens and the need to protect citizens being a priority, the AUMF contained the following introduction:

> Whereas, on September 11, 2001, acts of treacherous violence were committed against the United States and its citizens; and

> Whereas, such acts render it both necessary and appropriate that the United States exercise its rights to self-defense and to protect United States citizens both at home and abroad; and

---

[89] Quoting 'President Issues Military Order: Detention, Treatment, and Trial of Certain Non-citizens in the War against Terrorism' *The White House* (13 November 2001) georgewbush-whitehouse.archives.gov/news/releases/2001/11/20011113-27.html (establishing Military Commissions at Guantanamo Bay).

[90] Compare Shiri Krebs, 'Lifting the Veil of Secrecy: Judicial Review of Administrative Detentions in the Israeli Supreme Court' (2012) 45 *Vanderbilt Journal of International Law* 639 (discussing a similar detention regime in Israel, written by a former advisor on legal matters to Chief Justice Dorit Beinisch, President of the Israeli Supreme Court). Israel's administration detention system is discussed more in ch 6 below.

[91] 'President Issues Military Order', above, n 89.

[92] AUMF, above, n 83.

> Whereas, in light of the threat to the national security and foreign policy of the United States posed by these grave acts of violence; and

> Whereas, such acts continue to pose an unusual and extraordinary threat to the national security and foreign policy of the United States; and

> Whereas, the President has authority under the Constitution to take action to deter and prevent acts of international terrorism against the United States ...[93]

The resolution itself includes rather broad authorisation language:

> The President is authorized to use all necessary and appropriate force against those nations, organizations, or persons he determines planned, authorized, committed, or aided the terrorist attacks that occurred on September 11, 2001, or harbored such organizations or persons, in order to prevent any future acts of international terrorism against the United States by such nations, organizations or persons.[94]

This authorisation, while brief, continues to be cited as authority for a number of exceptional measures regarding terrorism detentions and other matters. It was used as a foundational document in a number of US extraordinary detention practices in the years after 9/11. In fact, Obama opposed the controversial detention provisions in the proposed National Defense Authorization Act 2012 (NDAA), arguing that the US government already had that detention authority under the AUMF and that codifying this authority in new legislation would be an admission by the US government that the extraordinary measures already taken under the AUMF were not already legally permitted. Rather than expanding detention authority, as many had argued it would, Obama argued that it would in fact limit detention authority or, worse, constitute an admission that extraordinary detention measures after 9/11 were not legally supported.[95]

As mentioned above, in the years after 9/11, initial attempts to use the authorisation to detain US citizens as unlawful enemy combatants were unsuccessful. One case involved Jose Padilla (this is discussed at length in chapter four above).[96] After years of judicial rulings relating to the US government's assertion that Padilla was an unlawful enemy combatant, the US government voluntarily withdrew this designation and, instead, simply prosecuted Padilla in an Article III criminal proceeding.[97]

A second case involved Yaser Hamdi. Hamdi was born in Louisiana to parents from Saudi Arabia, so he held dual citizenship, as the US Constitution confers

---

[93] ibid.

[94] ibid.

[95] See NDAA, above, n 9; Ateqah Khaki, 'Senate Rejects Amendment Banning Indefinite Detention' *American Civil Liberties Union* (11 November 2011) www.aclu.org/blog/national-security/senate-rejects-amendment-banning-indefinite-detention.

[96] See ch 4 above.

[97] See ch 4 above; Art III refers to the US Constitution, which contains a provision establishing the US judicial system.

citizenship on those born within the US.[98] He was captured in Afghanistan and held briefly at Guantanamo Bay before the US government determined that he was a citizen and transferred him to military detention within the US.[99] In pleadings filed before the US Supreme Court, which included numerous *amicus* briefs, there was much discussion of his citizenship status, including arguments that he had renounced his citizenship by taking up arms against the US, and one party arguing that he was never a citizen, based on disagreements over the interpretation of the relevant provision in the US Constitution.[100] The US government did not seek to return Hamdi to Guantanamo Bay, but did assert that he was an unlawful enemy combatant and could be held as one in military detention within the US.[101]

The US Supreme Court accepted Hamdi's status as a citizen in its ruling, while addressing the question of governmental powers regarding the detention of a citizen under such circumstances. Lower court rulings had previously raised numerous concerns about the quality of the evidence against Hamdi, apart from his status and how he could be detained. He was ultimately held for three years.[102]

The Supreme Court ruling was a plurality decision. A majority found that the designation and military detention of Hamdi was permitted under the AUMF previously passed by Congress, but because he was a citizen, he was entitled to certain procedural protections.[103] As a general matter, the Court did not question the use of a wartime paradigm and, indeed, as Hamdi was purportedly arrested on a battlefield in Afghanistan, this issue presented less controversy in his case than in others. The decision is known for, among other things, reasserting the importance of the separation of powers in the US, with Justice Sandra Day O'Connor famously writing: 'We have long since made clear that a state of war is not a blank check for the President when it comes to the rights of the Nation's citizens.'[104]

Justice Scalia's dissenting opinion is noteworthy when looking at some of these detentions in terms of the non-citizen Other, as he drew a strong and unyielding line between the rights that must be accorded under the US Constitution to US citizens, in contrast to his thoughts, on the same day, in relation to a companion case, *Rasul v Bush*, involving non-citizen detainees at Guantanamo Bay.[105] Part of

---

[98] *Hamdi v Rumsfeld*, 542 US 507 (2004) (plurality); see also US Constitution, amendment XIV ('All persons born or naturalized in the United States, and subject to the jurisdiction thereof, are citizens of the United States and of the State wherein they reside').

[99] *Hamdi*, above, n 98, 510.

[100] ibid.

[101] ibid (again, the Court refers to the asserted status as that of an 'enemy combatant'. The term 'unlawful enemy combatant' is used for the sake of consistency).

[102] ibid; see also Ben Herzog, 'Revocation of Citizenship in the United States' (2011) 52(1) *European Journal of Sociology* 77, 78.

[103] *Hamdi*, above, n 98, 507.

[104] ibid 536.

[105] ibid; see *Rasul v Bush*, 542 US 466 (2004) (Scalia, J dissenting) (the first in a series of rulings relating to the parameters of habeas corpus rights for those held at Guantanamo Bay. Rasul had been released before the US Supreme Court decided his case. Justice Scalia, in a dissenting opinion, argued that the court had no jurisdiction to hear a claim by a non-citizen held outside of the territorial

the distinction was based on Hamdi's status as a US citizen and part on the fact that he was being held within the US, so his concerns regarding territorial jurisdiction outside of the US, which were prominent in his *Rasul* dissent, were not evident in his *Hamdi* dissent.

Regarding Hamdi, Justice Scalia cited Blackstone to write: 'The very core of liberty secured by our Anglo-Saxon system of separated powers has been freedom from indefinite imprisonment at the will of the Executive.'[106] Justice Scalia conceded the legitimacy of the wartime paradigm, but went to great lengths to distinguish between enemy aliens and enemy citizens, noting that the detention of enemy combatants until the end of hostilities was common practice: 'That is probably an accurate description of wartime practice with respect to enemy aliens. The tradition with respect to American citizens, however, has been quite different. Citizens aiding the enemy have been treated as traitors subject to the criminal process.'[107]

While Justice Scalia's critique of the detention was limited solely to Hamdi's status as a citizen and to his presence within the US, he addressed the arguments that had suggested that the US Constitution did not apply to times of crisis, noting:

> Many think it not only inevitable but entirely proper that liberty give way to security in times of national crisis that, at the extremes of military exigency, *inter arma silent leges*. Whatever the general merits of the view that war silences law or modulates its voice, that view has no place in the interpretation and application of a Constitution designed precisely to confront war and, in a manner that accords with democratic principles, to accommodate it.[108]

The US government chose not to pursue further action against Hamdi, instead entering a deal in exchange for his release. This deal demonstrated the importance of the citizen/non-citizen divide. Hamdi was required to renounce his American citizenship, agree not to return to the US for ten years and refrain from travelling to a number of listed countries. With that agreement, Hamdi was sent to Saudi Arabia. He also had to agree not to sue the US for how he was treated.[109] After his

---

jurisdiction of the US). The US Supreme Court ultimately decided that detainees there did have a right to habeas corpus review of their detentions under the US Constitution in *Boumediene v Bush*, 553 US 723 (2008), which resulted in a large number of habeas corpus petitions being heard in US federal courts, as well as a number of detainees being ordered released from Guantanamo Bay.

[106] *Hamdi*, above, n 98.

[107] ibid 559.

[108] ibid 579.

[109] Ben Herzog, 'Revocation of Citizenship in the United States' (2011) 52(1) *European Journal of Sociology* 77, 78; see also Abigail D Lauer, 'Note: The Easy Way Out? The Yaser Hamdi Release Agreement and the United States' Treatment of the Citizen Enemy Combatant Dilemma' (2006) 91 *Cornell Law Review* 927 (arguing that the Hamdi agreement was an easy solution in his case, but presented problems for other cases in which the US government might wish to designate a citizen as an unlawful enemy combatant). A question arises as to whether, should Hamdi challenge the renunciation of his citizenship in the future, he would be successful. A US citizen may renounce citizenship, but must do so voluntarily, and it is unclear how circumstances like this might be viewed by a US court in the future.

return to Saudi Arabia, he gave an interview, in which he said he was innocent of the allegations brought by the US.[110]

Ali Saleh Kahlah Al-Marri, a legal US resident but not a US citizen, was also initially held as an unlawful enemy combatant. A federal appellate court panel first ruled in his favour, then reheard the case before the entire court. It ruled that the AUMF allowed the President to declare an alien, even one living lawfully within the US, an unlawful enemy combatant.[111] This conclusion was troubling for a number of reasons, including that Al-Marri was arrested in the US and not anywhere near a battlefield. Although the US Supreme Court granted certiorari, the change of government in 2009 stopped the legal proceedings. The Obama Administration transferred Al-Marri's case to a federal court in the US, and Al-Marri pleaded guilty to charges involving conspiracy and providing material support to a terrorist organisation. It is therefore unknown whether the US Supreme Court would have allowed for the deprivation of due process for a non-citizen, legal resident of the US, arrested and held in the US, after a presidential declaration that he was an unlawful enemy combatant.[112]

Ultimately, the US limited the type of 'mission creep' described above, mostly because the Courts opposed extending extraordinary detentions to citizens, but did not necessarily similarly uphold the rights of non-citizens. The US did not meet the same level of resistance when applying these tactics to non-citizens, although of course there has been some resistance. Generally, however, the non-citizen terrorist Other gained dominance in US extraordinary detention practices.

Nevertheless, an obvious exception is found in the targeted killing of Anwar al-Aulaki, a US citizen, whose case is discussed in chapter four, above.[113] When al-Aulaki's two children were later killed in subsequent raids, both killings were dismissed by the US government. Abdulrahman al-Aulaki was 16 when he died with his 17-year-old cousin and other civilians. The US government described

---

See generally *Hamdi*, above, n 98; *Afroyim v Rusk*, 387 US 253 (1967) (holding that US citizens may not be deprived of their citizenship involuntarily); *Vance v Terrazas*, 444 US 252 (1980) (holding that a US citizen must have acted with an evidenced intent to relinquish citizenship to have it revoked). An open question at the time of Hamdi's deal was also whether the US government would try to detain him again, as a non-citizen, but to date this has not happened.

[110] 'Hamdi Voices Innocence, Joy about Reunion' *CNN* (14 October 2004) www.cnn.com/2004/WORLD/meast/10/14/hamdi/.

[111] *Al-Marri v Pucciarelli*, 534 F 3d 213 (4th Cir 2008) (containing the notation that it was vacated and remanded by the Supreme Court for dismissal as moot, 6 March 2009).

[112] See Bruce Miller, 'No Virtue in Passivity: The Supreme Court and Ali Al-Marri' (2011) 33(3) *Western New England Law Review* 697, 753.

[113] The killings of al-Aulaki's two children in later incidents has not been established as targeted against them. See Charlie Savage, 'Justice Department Memo Approving Targeted Killing of Anwar Al-Awlaki' *New York Times* (23 June 2014) www.nytimes.com/interactive/2014/06/23/us/23awlaki-memo.html?_r=0 (containing a copy of the original, redacted memo, in which the US asserted that the AUMF gave it the authority to target an American citizen for death); see also Glenn Greenwald, 'Obama Killed a 16-Year-Old American in Yemen. Trump Just Killed His 8-Year-Old Sister' *The Intercept* (30 January 2017) theintercept.com/2017/01/30/obama-killed-a-16-year-old-american-in-yemen-trump-just-killed-his-8-year-old-sister (discussing the circumstances of the killing of al-Awlaki's children).

those killed as 'collateral damage'.[114] There was originally some public opposition to the targeted killing of US citizens. Stephen Colbert, a comedian, famously said on his show that '[d]ue process just means there's a process that you do'.[115] However, the outcry was generally muted and short-lived, and the Obama Administration never admitted any wrongdoing.

The Obama Administration had been planning a later raid in Yemen and, when Trump took office, he elected to follow through on the plan. When the US killed eight-year-old Nora al-Aulaki, Trump lamented the death of a US service member and the injuries of others. He said nothing about Nora or the 30 civilians, including children, who died. Nora was shot in the neck and bled to death over a period of two hours.[116] As explained in the Introduction, targeted killing is not a detention practice, but it is included in the description of such practices, since it involves the ultimate deprivation of liberty without any judicial process.

Another exception to the exclusion of citizens from extraordinary detention practices arose in the highly controversial NDAA. This legislation contained a provision expanding governmental power to hold people in military detention in the US. Specifically, the Act includes citizens within that expanded detention power, as demonstrated by combining relevant provisions and reading them together.[117]

The legislation allows for '(1) [d]etention under the law of war without trial until the end of the hostilities authorized by the Authorization for Use of Military Force'.[118] This section lists activities that would allow for detention of somebody under its provisions, including:

(1) A person who planned, authorized, committed, or aided the terrorist attacks that occurred on September 11, 2001, or harbored those responsible for those attacks.

(2) A person who was a part of or substantially supported al-Qaeda, the Taliban, or associated forces that are engaged in hostilities against the United States or its coalition partners, including any person who has committed a belligerent act or has directly supported such hostilities in aid of such enemy forces.[119]

The legislation also has a section that applies to 'foreign Al Qaeda terrorists' and specifically exempts US citizens and lawful resident aliens from its provisions.[120] While this exemption is included in the section relating to 'foreign Al Qaeda terrorists', it is not included in the previous section quoted above.[121] This failure to

---

[114] Greenwald, above, n 113.

[115] ibid.

[116] ibid.

[117] NDAA, above, n 9; see also Oona Hathaway et al, 'The Power to Detain: Detention of Terrorism Suspects after 9/11' (2013) 38(1) *Yale Journal of International Law* 123 (delineating different types of detentions for which the US claimed authority after 9/11 for those suspected of involvement in terrorism).

[118] See NDAA, above, n 9, s 1021(c)(1).

[119] ibid s 1021(b).

[120] ibid s 1022.

[121] ibid ss 1021, 1022.

exclude US citizens from these particular provisions led to a court action, in which the plaintiffs sought an injunction from enforcement.[122]

The plaintiffs included reporters, who feared that their activities in pursuing stories might be viewed as an activity supporting al-Qaeda and the Taliban, pursuant to section 1021 of the NDAA, as well as activists who expressed concern that their expressive activity might be deemed to fall under this provision. Noam Chomsky and Daniel Ellsberg were among the plaintiffs. Those pursuing the action were US citizens.[123]

A US federal judge ultimately issued a permanent injunction on the enforcement of section 1021(b)(2) of the NDAA quoted above. The US government filed for—and was granted—an emergency stay by the Second Circuit Court of Appeals, which ultimately overturned the preliminary injunction entered by the District Court, ruling that the plaintiffs lacked standing.[124] The Supreme Court of the United States denied certiorari in 2014.[125] Given the important issues to be determined through this case, the Supreme Court's decision was disappointing at best.[126]

Thus, the US had been left with some limitations, but has also made some inroads, in attempted expansions of some of its extraordinary detention measures beyond non-citizens. This type of expansion has encountered greater resistance than that associated with its measures against non-citizens suspected of terrorism. The cases discussed here convey a conclusion that the measures should not be expanded to citizens because they are already deeply problematic when used on non-citizens.

ii. Use of National Immigration Systems, outside of Criminal Justice Systems, to Detain Terrorism Suspects: The Securitisation of Immigration[127]

Although the war paradigm was in many ways a quirk of the US response, a more prominent and widespread reaction involved a number of jurisdictions using their national immigration systems as primary tools in the fight against terrorism. The securitisation of immigration is a process that has been discussed at

---

[122] *Hedges v Obama*, 12 Civ 331 (KBF) (SDNY 2012).

[123] ibid.

[124] *Hedges v Obama*, No 12-3176 and 12-3644 (2d Cir 2013).

[125] *Hedges v Obama*, No 13-758 (certiorari denied).

[126] See Jim Caton, 'The Importance of Hedges v Obama' *Legal Reader* (3 December 2015) www.legalreader.com/the-importance-of-hedges-v-obama (laying out the various important issues left unresolved after the Supreme Court's refusal to hear the case).

[127] Some small portions of this section were published previously in an earlier form, which has evolved since then. For this section, some material is loosely drawn from two publications: Duffy and Provost, above, n 6; and Maureen T Duffy, '"The Slow Creep of Complacency": Ongoing Challenges for Democracies Seeking to Detain Terrorism Suspects' (2010) *Pace International Law Review* 42.

great length in various academic writings.[128] The othering aspect of using a non-criminal process, which by definition can only include non-citizens as its subjects, is obvious.[129] This avenue of detention underscores the point of departure in this chapter: that terrorists are non-citizens or that non-citizens are terrorists. Moreover, while national jurisdictions normally have some level of procedural protections for those detained under immigration systems, they are lower than those afforded to detainees under the criminal justice system.

The idea of othering immigrants, or non-citizens, is not new and is not a solely post-9/11 phenomenon. Even the idea of different standards for non-citizens within the criminal justice system has a precedent. Gunther Jakobs developed an idea, corollary to what is discussed here, called 'enemy criminal law', in which non-citizens who are deemed to be enemies of the state are treated differently when accused of wrongdoing, and where procedural differences such as greater possibility for preventive detentions and other abridged procedural protections are deemed acceptable.[130] Rather than the pretextual use of the immigration system (or the rules of war) to focus on non-citizens, enemy criminal law allows for a differential use of the criminal justice system based on citizenship. The idea of enemy criminal law has been compared to the American notion of 'unlawful enemy combatants'.[131] A key difference is that enemy criminal law refers to variations in the criminal justice system, while the idea of unlawful enemy combatants is drawn from the laws of war. Each idea suggests that something about this 'enemy' absolves the government of a requirement to adhere to the procedural protections of the paradigm from which the proceedings are drawn, based on citizenship.[132]

This example demonstrates that much can be critiqued about the treatment of non-citizens under criminal law paradigms as well. However, in a number of instances, national governments have avoided the criminal justice system entirely, even where that system had also been altered to better advantage the governments in some instances. Immigration detentions have figured significantly in that trend. So, while this is not solely a post-9/11 phenomenon, it is a dominant characteristic in post-9/11 extraordinary detention practices.

---

[128] See, eg, Philippe Bourbeau, *The Securitization of Migration: A Study of Movement and Order* (New York, Routledge, 2011); Dace Schlenz, *Did 9/11 Matter? Securitization of Asylum and Immigration in the European Union in the Period from 1992 to 2008* (Oxford, Refugees Study Center, 2010); Didier Bigo, 'Is Otherness a Question of Security or a Question of Freedom?' and François Crépeau, 'Protecting Migrants' Rights: Undocumented Migrants as Local Citizens' in François Crépeau and Colleen Sheppard, *Human Rights and Diverse Societies: Challenges and Possibilities* (Newcastle upon Tyne, Cambridge Scholars Publishing, 2013).

[129] See generally Nakache, above, n 27 (considering in depth the 'othering' of migrants).

[130] See Gunther Jakobs, 'On the Theory of Enemy Criminal Law' (2010) 7 *Augsburger Studien zum Internationalalen Rechert* 167 (translation); see also Carlos Gómez-Jara Díez, 'Enemy Combatants versus Enemy Criminal Law: An Introduction to the European Debate Regarding Enemy Criminal Law and its Relevance to the Anglo-American Discussion on the Legal Status of Unlawful Combatants' (2010) 11(4) *New Criminal Law Review* 529–561.

[131] Gómez-Jara Díez, above, n 130.

[132] ibid.

Sometimes, the greater ease in detaining people under the immigration system fuelled the narrative, giving governments a vehicle through which to thus assure citizens that they were rounding up terrorists. This happened in the US in the early days after 9/11. Although the US quickly changed its emphasis to war-like detentions, there were also immigration detentions that fit this model. The US designated some people from particular countries as 'special-interest' detainees and publicly announced the arrest of 'terrorists', even though none of the 'special-interest' detainees was ever successfully prosecuted for a terrorism-related offence and most were deported after sometimes-secret detention hearings.[133] The following statement from then-US Attorney General John Ashcroft, referring to these special-interest detainees, demonstrates this connection:

> Within days of the September 11 attacks, we launched this anti-terrorism offensive to prevent new attacks on our homeland. To date, our anti-terrorism offensive has arrested or detained nearly 1,000 individuals as part of the September 11 terrorism investigation. Those who violated the law remain in custody. Taking suspected terrorists in violation of the law off the streets and keeping them locked up is our clear strategy to prevent terrorism within our borders.[134]

What Ashcroft does not note in his comments is that the suspicion of law violations usually involved some form of immigration violation. However, the implication is that the violations relate to terrorism. The 'suspected terrorists' were in fact immigrants, designated for 'special' status not based on suspicions relating to their conduct, but on the basis of their age, national origin and gender.[135]

The US post-9/11 immigration detentions were somewhat unique in that the government openly admitted that it was targeting males over the age of 16 from a list of designated countries, most of which were in predominantly Muslim countries (Cuba and North Korea were also included). While most of the 9/11 terrorists allegedly came from Saudi Arabia, that country was not one of those listed in the US Federal Register as being subject to 'special-interest' screening.[136] The Trump Executive Orders regarding travel, which were discussed at length in chapter one above, has been compared to the special-interest detention programme implemented after 9/11. A significant difference is that the 'special-interest' programme listed some countries that are not predominantly Muslim, such as North Korea and Cuba, and it did not involve a complete ban on entry to the US, as the Trump Executive Orders did. Of course, it also happened in a different environment, in

---

[133] See Cole, above, n 5.

[134] Maureen T Duffy, 'The US Immigrations in the War on Terror: Impact on the Rule of Law' (unpublished Master's thesis, McGill University, 2005) (quoting John Ashcroft, 'Prepared Remarks for the US Mayors Conference' *US Department of Justice* (25 October 2001) www.justice.gov/archive/ag/speeches/2001/agcrisisremarks10_25.htm).

[135] *The September 11 Detainees: A Review of the Treatment of Aliens Held on Immigration Charges in Connection with the Investigation of the September 11 Attacks* (June 2003) c 4, *US Department of Justice Office of the Inspector General*, www.usdoj.gov/oig/special/0306/index.htm.

[136] ibid.

response, however misguided, to a significant crisis, and Trump's Executive Orders did not appear in such an environment. The special-interest detentions were also intentionally undertaken in many cases in secret.[137] However, the Trump Executive Orders were undertaken in an extremely public manner and, as discussed at length in chapter one above, the surrounding public statements caused the Trump Administration some problems as the cases have wound their way through the courts.[138]

Immigrants, it seemed, were seen as presumptive terrorists in the aftermath of 9/11 or, at least, in relation to the special-interest detainees, immigrants of specific, explicitly designated national origins were treated as presumptive terrorists.[139] It has been estimated that 5,000 men, whose national origins overwhelmingly represented countries in the Middle East, were detained under the various iterations of the special-interest detentions. Most were ultimately deported. While the immigration detentions in the US were arguably more widespread than those in other countries, they garnered considerably less attention, no doubt eclipsed by the simultaneous war measures that the US was undertaking.

Also in the US, The Immigration and Naturalization Service ceased to exist as a separate department and was, instead, included under the new, larger Department of Homeland Security, with the obvious inference being that immigration was a matter of homeland security.[140] The much-discussed and highly controversial USA Patriot Act also contained revisions to detention requirements for immigration cases, but the provisions, while controversial, provided more protections for detainees than the procedures actually followed by the US government in the early days after 9/11.[141] In spite of the heavy use of its national immigration system, the lack of litigation and recent developments have meant that much of this area has gone unnoticed, even within the US.

Much more prominent national discussions occurred in jurisdictions like Canada and the UK about the use of their national immigration systems to detain

---

[137] See Michael Creppy, 'Instructions for Cases Requiring Additional Security' *FindLaw* (21 September 2001) news.findlaw.com/cnn/docs/aclu/creppy092101memo.pdf (containing instructions for secret proceedings); Duffy, above, n 134, 7–8, 12–14 (outlining various US government efforts to keep these proceedings secret, including the release, under great pressure, of a partial list of the detainees, with their names and other information redacted); see also generally *Cole*, above, n 5; see also ch 4 above, section IV.

[138] This discussion is current as of late June 2017. See *Executive Order 13769, Protecting the Nation from Foreign Terrorist Entry into the United States*, (27 January 2017) 82 Federal Register 8977 (hereinafter *Trump Executive Order I*); Executive *Order 13780, Protecting the Nation from Foreign Terrorist Entry Into the United States*, (16 March 2017) 82 Federal Register 13209 (superseding *Trump Executive Order I*) (hereinafter *Trump Executive Order II*); see also, eg, *State of Washington; State of Minnesota v Trump et al*, No 17-35105 (9th Cir 2017); *State of Hawaii et al v Trump*, No 17-15589) (9th Cir 2017); *International Refugee Assistance Project v Trump*, No 17-1351 (4th Cir 2014) (each upholding a lower court's injunction on one of the Executive Order travel bans); see also ch 1 above, section IV.

[139] See *Cole*, above, n 5; Duffy, above, n 134.

[140] See Homeland Security Act (2002) Pub L 107-296, 116 Stat. 2135.

[141] See Duffy, above, n 134 (for a detailed discussion of the circumstances surrounding the signing of the USA Patriot Act).

people, potentially indefinitely, on suspicion of being terrorists. In some cases, the actual detention may end, but the person continues to be subject to serious limitations on personal freedom for indefinite periods of time. In the years after 9/11, the national high courts in Canada and the UK addressed almost identical provisions and practices for the use of national immigration systems, but, when assessing whether such practices were discriminatory, they came to very different conclusions. Each country looked to the practice of the other country in assessing these types of detentions. A look at the different reasoning they employed is therefore instructive.

a. The UK and the Belmarsh Detainees[142]

As was the case for most aspects of extraordinary detentions after 9/11, the national high courts played a significant role in determining whether immigration status could serve as a primary basis for determining whether a person could be detained indefinitely as a suspected terrorist. The major UK decision was issued first. The Supreme Court of Canada referred to this decision with approval in its own initial ruling, but it did not reach the same conclusion, that is, that singling people out for extraordinary detention was discriminatory when presumptively only applied to non-citizens. In a larger sense, the disparity in the ways in which the courts viewed this specific issue illustrates the extent to which each deemed othering, based on citizenship, to be acceptable.

The UK House of Lords addressed this issue in its 2004 *Belmarsh Detainees* case. The detainees in the UK were being held under immigration legislation, pending deportation, for a suspicion of affiliation with terrorism-related activities. None of them had been charged with any criminal activities. The deportation could not be effected because there was a credible risk that the detainees would be tortured on return to their home countries. At the same time, the British government argued that they could not be released, as this would pose a risk to national security.[143]

The House of Lords largely rejected the position of the British government, often through the use of forceful language that made international headlines. One basis for some of their opinions was that to apply these detention standards to non-citizens, but not to citizens was both discriminatory and was, according to one Law Lord, simply illogical.

Lord Bingham noted that, by definition, the immigration system created a distinction between nationals and non-nationals, but that it did not necessarily follow that this distinction could be applied when the immigration system was being used for what was primarily a security matter.[144] In an exposition of his view of the Rule of Law, published a few years after the *Belmarsh Detainees* case

---

[142] *A (FC) and Others (FC) (Appellants) v Secretary of State for the Home Department (Respondent)* [2004] UKHL 56 (hereinafter *Belmarsh Detainees* case).

[143] ibid paras 1–3.

[144] ibid paras 67–68.

and shortly before his death, Lord Bingham identified a number of factors that are necessary for an action to be arguably compliant with the rule of law, including 'equality before the law'. He quoted US Supreme Court Justice Robert Jackson as saying 'there is no more effective practical guaranty against arbitrary and unreasonable government than to require that the principle of law which officials would impose upon a minority must be imposed generally'.[145]

In his decision in the *Belmarsh Detainees* case, Lord Scott, who was quoted in the Introduction to Part II for his famous 'stuff of nightmares' quote, also noted that the European Convention on Human Rights:

> [D]oes not justify a discriminatory distinction between different groups of people all of whom are suspected terrorists who together present the threat of terrorism and to all of whom the measures, if they really were 'strictly necessary', would logically be applicable. If those who are suspected terrorists include some non-Muslims as well as Muslims, it would, in my opinion, be irrational and discriminatory to restrict the application of the measures to Muslims even though the bulk of those suspected are likely to profess to be Muslims. Some might well not be professed Muslims. Similarly, it would be irrational and discriminatory to restrict the application of the measures to men although the bulk of those suspected are likely to be male. Some might well be women. Similarly, in my opinion, it is irrational and discriminatory to restrict the application of the measures to suspected terrorists who have no right of residence in this country. Some suspected terrorists may well be home-grown.[146]

Lord Scott's last comment relating to 'home-grown' terrorists appeared to have been prophetic when, several months later, three of four men who carried out suicide bombings in London in July 2005 turned out to be British nationals.[147] Other terrorism suspects have been British nationals too, as was, allegedly, Khalid Mohamed Omar Ali, who was arrested near Parliament on suspicion of planning an attack.[148]

Turning back to the *Belmarsh Detainee* case, Lord Nicholls wrote that the discriminatory nature of the Belmarsh detentions was sufficiently compelling to provide a basis for judicial intervention even on a national security measure, where, normally, Parliament would enjoy greater leeway. In fact, he said that Parliament undermined the entire scheme because it failed to provide for a means of similarly detaining nationals suspected of terrorism:

> The difficulty with according to Parliament the substantial latitude normally to be given to decisions on national security is the weakness already mentioned: security

---

[145] Tom Bingham, *The Rule of Law* (London, Penguin Group, 2010) 59 (quoting *Railway Express Agency Inc v New York*, 336 US 106 (1949)).

[146] *Belmarsh Detainees* case, above, n 142, para 158.

[147] See McGoldrick, above, n 86, 513 (noting additionally that by the end of 2007, eight UK nationals were subject to control orders); see also Dominic McGoldrick, 'Terrorism and Human Rights Paradigms: The United Kingdom after 11 September 2001' in Alexis Keller and Andrea Bianchi (eds), *Counterterrorism: Democracy's Challenge* (Oxford, Hart Publishing, 2008) 111.

[148] Vikram Dodd and Alice Ross, 'Westminster Terrorism Suspect is 27-Year-Old British National' *The Guardian* (28 April 2017), www.theguardian.com/uk-news/2017/apr/28/westminster-terror-attack-suspect-named-khalid-mohammed-omar-ali.

considerations have not prompted a similar negation of the right to personal liberty in the case of nationals who pose a similar security risk. The government, indeed, has expressed the view that a 'draconian' power to detain British citizens who may be involved in international terrorism 'would be difficult to justify'. But, in practical terms, power to detain indefinitely is no more draconian in the case of a British citizen than in the case of a non-national. There is no significant difference in the potential adverse impact of such a power on (1) a national and (2) a non-national who in practice cannot leave the country for fear of torture abroad.[149]

Although the British government was not bound by the ruling of the House of Lords, the decision received considerable attention, both within the UK and internationally, and the government did enact new legislation in response to the ruling.[150] After the decision, a system of control orders was implemented in the UK, which themselves were subject to considerable critique. Unlike the detention scenario under which the Belmarsh Detainees were held, control orders could be applied to citizens and non-citizens and involve varying forms of limitations on actions, which were often similar to house arrest.[151] Special Advocates could be appointed to represent the interests of the detainees where secrecy of evidence was asserted, but were limited in that they were allowed to view secret evidence under certain circumstances, yet could not disclose to the person who was subject to the control order what the evidence includes without permission.[152]

Once this type of abridged procedural protection was expanded beyond non-citizens, opposition grew. As has been said elsewhere in this chapter, opposition from citizens, who can vote, is likely to have a greater impact than that from non-citizens, and citizens themselves are more likely to object to a restriction of their own liberties. In early 2012, the UK replaced its control order regime with Terrorism Prevention and Investigation Measures (TPIMs), which involve less restriction on liberty and more surveillance of those subject to the TPIMs.[153] TPIMs have had more than one iteration in terms of the restrictions allowed.[154]

Some insight into the controversy many of these undertakings provoked can be seen in relation to control orders, which, unlike many other extraordinary

---

[149] *Belmarsh Detainees* case, above, n 142, para 83.

[150] Anderson, above, n 9.

[151] McGoldrick, above, n 86; Bingham, above, n 145, 149–50 (quoting former Chief Justice Arthur Chaskalson of South Africa, who expressed concern about control orders, which can involve significant restrictions on personal liberty and can be so onerous that people find it impossible to comply and are then prosecuted for non-compliance).

[152] See generally three cases decided on the same day by the House of Lords in the UK, critiquing particular components of the control order procedures. *Secretary of State for the Home Department v MB (FC)* [2007] UKHL 46, paras 34–40, 54, 60–77, 82–87 (hereinafter *MB*); *Secretary of State for the Home Department v JJ and Others* [2007] UKHL 45, para 56 (hereinafter *JJ*); *Secretary of State for the Home Department v E and Another* [2007] UKHL 47 (hereinafter *E*) (collectively referred to as the *Three Control Order Cases*).

[153] See Anderson, above, n 9.

[154] See Counter-Terrorism and Security Act 2015 (expanding the restrictions that can be permitted under TPIMs and creating what is sometimes called TPIMs Mark II).

detention regimes, tended to involve some form of house arrest rather than imprisonment. As the UK was moving away from control orders, the independent reviewer, charged with reviewing national anti-terrorism laws, said of them:

> The purely preventative aim of the control order system, its separation from the criminal justice process, its application to home citizens and the length of time for which an individual could be subject to it ... placed it towards the more repressive end of the spectrum of measures operated by comparable western democracies.[155]

In relation to the number of prosecutions under the criminal justice system for terrorism offences, the number of times control orders or TPIMs have been used is relatively small.[156] It would, however, be a mistake to dismiss their significance for that reason. First, even one person subjected to diminished procedural fairness is still significant. Second, part of the danger is the ability of a government to employ these measures, whether they actually do so or not. As with many other extraordinary detention measures, there are conflicts over the measures themselves, as well as over the possibility of governmental abuse. If one accepts that it is unacceptable to so detain people or to limit their freedoms in this manner, without the procedural protections allowed under the criminal justice system, then the existence of these governmental powers is problematic regardless of how often they are employed. Not all accept that at all, of course. Even the Independent Reviewer of Terrorism Legislation has said that, in limited cases, and with some changes, TPIMs can be useful for disrupting terrorist plots.[157] However, the Reviewer has made suggestions for improvements. While some have been acknowledged by the government, others, such as the need for court oversight, have been opposed.[158]

Indeed, evidence suggests a recent uptick in the use of TPIMs in the UK.[159] In October 2016, the Home Office announced that six people were subject to them, which was an increase in their use compared to the preceding few years.[160] In 2014, it had appeared that TPIMs were falling out of use, or 'withering on the vine' as the Independent Reviewer of Terrorism Legislation had noted, with one person subject to a TPIM order.[161] After multiple, horrific terrorist attacks in the UK in London and Manchester in 2017, UK Prime Minister Theresa May has publicly argued for an enhanced power to detain terrorism suspects where there is sufficient evidence to know they are a threat, but not enough evidence to criminally prosecute them. This statement, whether intentional or not, was unusual in

---

[155] Anderson, above, n 9.
[156] ibid.
[157] David Anderson QC, 'TPIMs in 2014' *Independent Reviewer of Terrorism Legislation* (March 2015) terrorismlegislationreviewer.independent.gov.uk/tpims-in-2014-march-2015.
[158] ibid.
[159] Alan Travis, 'Six People are Subject to TPIMs, Home Office Reveals' *The Guardian* (26 October 2016) www.theguardian.com/uk-news/2016/oct/26/six-people-are-subject-to-tpims-home-office-reveals.
[160] ibid.
[161] Anderson, above, n 157.

that it was a governmental admission that an extraordinary detention mechanism was a tool that governments wanted because they could not prove their cases in a criminal proceeding. May expressed strong resolve to introduce such legislation, saying: 'If human rights laws stop us from doing it, we will change those laws so we can do it.'[162] There is currently talk of reviving previously proposed legislation to enhance the powers under TPIMs.[163]

b. Canada and the Security Certificate Problem

The Supreme Court of Canada (SCC) dealt with similar detentions under its 'security certificate' regime. The controversies over those detentions have developed quite differently in Canada than they have in the UK, even though the SCC expressly cited to the 2004 *Belmarsh Detainee* case when initially ruling on the constitutionality of security certificates in *Charkaoui* in 2007.[164] While the UK House of Lords had found a security detention regime which applied only to non-citizens discriminatory in the UK, the SCC did not find such a scheme to be discriminatory in Canada.

After 9/11, Canada had changed its immigration legislation to, among other things, increase the pool of people who could be detained under its security certificate regime. Technically, as in the Belmarsh scenario, these detentions were pending deportation, were undertaken under the immigration system and thus could not be used for Canadian citizens. Those detained under the security certificate regime have been held without any criminal proceeding, based on allegations of involvement with terrorism. Information regarding the specifics of those allegations is often withheld from the detained person. In practice, for a number of people who could not be deported because of a fear of torture in the receiving countries, this regime has meant that detentions sometimes went on for years, varied at times with house arrest or other deprivations of liberty outside of outright detention. Those who have been subject to security certificates have struggled to defend themselves outside of the criminal justice system, where secret evidence continues to be permitted, although altered somewhat by the introduction of special advocates.[165]

The narrative point of departure at issue in this chapter—that non-citizens were terrorists—is evident in the way in which this issue has played out in Canada. The SCC ruled differently on the issue of discrimination against non-citizens than

---

[162] Helen Fenwick, 'Explainer: What's the Difference between TPIMs and Control Orders?' *The Conversation* (7 June 2017) theconversation.com/explainer-whats-the-difference-between-tpims-and-control-orders-79068 (explaining what the government is likely seeking in terms of expanded detention powers).

[163] ibid (discussing the proposed Enhanced Terrorism Prevention and Investigation Measures Bill 2012, which may be revived).

[164] *Charkaoui v Canada (Minister of Citizenship and Immigration)* 2007 SCC 9.

[165] Duffy and Provost, above, n 6 (citations omitted, but containing a more detailed critique of this sequence of events).

the House of Lords did in the *Belmarsh Detainees* case, distinguishing the House of Lords' decision on the basis that British law explicitly entertained the possibility of indefinite detention for non-nationals only, while, they said, indefinite detention was not the issue under Canadian law. While it is true that the language being considered by the *Charkaoui* Court, in Canada's Immigration and Refugee Protection Act, did not expressly mention indefinite detention, the factual scenarios before the Court clearly suggested that this was a possibility. The Court itself noted the plight of Hassan Almrei, one of the three named parties, who was still detained and who did not know 'when, if ever, he would be released'.[166]

In fact, the Law Lords' opinions had not really focused on the length of detention, but focused instead on the issue of discrimination. It was this disparity between detentions for those suspected of terrorism based on citizenship more than the potential length of the detentions that was dispositive. This distinction is important because the Law Lords generally found the entire detention scheme to be invalid, largely based on this part of its ruling. As described above, Lord Bingham had pointed out in the *Belmarsh Detainees* case that it was normal for immigration law to create a distinction between nationals and non-nationals, but was not so when the immigration system was being used for what was primarily a security matter.[167] In *Charkaoui*, the SCC simply found that the immigration system always distinguishes between nationals and non-nationals, and did not acknowledge the issue of the system being used more for a security than an immigration purpose.[168]

The SCC, in failing to find its similarly problematic scheme discriminatory, left the overarching system in place, choosing to address some of the underlying procedural problems rather than acknowledging that the entire system was flawed. Even as to those procedures, the SCC pointed, with approval, to the special advocates system that was then already under considerable critique in the UK.[169]

In its 2007 ruling in *Charkaoui*, the SCC invited a government response that focused only on procedural specifics and not the larger human rights implications of this entire detention scheme. The Court's suggestion that the security detention had not become disconnected from the deportation process seems to have unquestionably accepted a legislative scheme that was almost identical to that considered by the House of Lords, and that had clearly been seen as having become unhinged from the deportation process.[170]

To provide some context, it is possible that the SCC's ruling as to the discrimination issue differed from that of the UK House of Lords in the *Belmarsh Detainees* case because of another undercurrent that is not necessarily related to national security. The *Charkaoui* case was decided in the midst of a series of

---

[166] ibid; *Charkaoui*, above, n 164, para 13.
[167] *Belmarsh Detainees* case, above, n 142, paras 67–68.
[168] *Charkaoui*, above, n 164, paras 129–31.
[169] ibid; see generally the *Three Control Order Cases* discussed in ch 4 above (see also above, n 152).
[170] See the SCC's discussion of this issue; *Charkaoui*, above, n 164, paras 129–31.

rulings by the SCC, which significantly altered the test to be met to establish a Charter section 15 claim and which have narrowed section 15 to such an extent that some have suggested that it is now riddled with obstacles that make it difficult to succeed under this provision.[171]

Regardless of why the SCC ruled as it did, its failure to find the detention scheme in *Charkaoui* to be discriminatory meant that the system continued. The SCC did find problems under section 7 of the Charter and gave Parliament a year to remedy the problem. The result was a system of special advocates, modelled on that employed in the UK and a subject of ongoing controversy.[172] There have been additional rulings on security certificates since the 2007 *Charkaoui* decision, but this decision has ruled out the possibility of challenging the regime as a whole, and these decisions have focused more in internal procedural issues in the regime.[173]

In the years following the 2007 *Charkaoui* decision, two of the named parties, Adil Charkaoui and Hassan Almrei, were ultimately granted rulings quashing their security certificates for different reasons. Both men remain in Canada and are now free from the restrictions under which they were placed on their release from detention.[174] Mahmoud Jaballah had a finding in 2016 that his security certificate was unreasonable. The government is appealing this ruling.[175]

The five men at the centre of the post-9/11 controversy are sometimes called 'The Secret Trial 5' and they were the subject of a documentary by that name, describing the extreme personal impact of the security certificate regime on them and on their families.[176] As of mid-2017, Mohammed Harkat, for example, has been subject to a security certificate for almost 15 years, without ever having been charged with a crime. In 2014, a unanimous SCC ruled that the special advocate regime, which was added to Canada's immigration legislation, after the 2007 *Charkaoui* decision, was constitutionally valid.[177] This ruling cleared the way for

---

[171] See, eg, Jennifer Koshan, 'Redressing the Harms of Government (In)action: A Section 7 versus Section 15 Charter Showdown' (2013) 22(1) *Constitutional Forum* 31 (discussing trends in the decisions regarding equality and how such claims have been increasingly difficult to successfully pursue, possibly because of the Court's approach); see generally Colleen Sheppard, *Inclusive Equality: The Relational Dimensions of Systemic Discrimination in Canada* (Montreal, McGill-Queen's University Press, 2010). In *Charkaoui*, the SCC never expressly applied the s 15 analysis, determining instead that the matter did not fall within the purview of s 15. See *Charkaoui*, above, n 164; see also Rayner Thwaites, 'Discrimination against Non-citizens under the Charter: *Charkaoui* and Section 15' (2008) 34 *Queen's Law Journal* 669 (persuasively arguing that the *Charkaoui* decision upheld indefinite detention for non-citizens, unlike many other works, which argue, less persuasively, that this decision basically struck down Canada's security-certificate regime).

[172] See Immigration and Refugee Protection Act, SC 2001, c 27, ss 85–85.1 (IRPA).

[173] As discussed throughout this section. This status has a corollary in Australia, which has been widely criticised for the harshness of its detention policies regarding non-citizens. See Thwaites, above, n 18, 37–118.

[174] ibid 279–82 (describing the events around both releases).

[175] Jim Bronskill, 'Ottawa Appeals Ruling to Nix Security Certificate in Jaballah Terror Case' *Globe and Mail* (12 August 2016) www.theglobeandmail.com/news/national/ottawa-appeals-decision-to-nix-security-certificate-in-jaballah-terror-case/article31390715.

[176] Amar Wala and Noah Bingham, *The Secret Trial 5* (Documentary, 2014).

[177] *Canada (Citizenship and Immigration) v Harkat* 2014 SCC 37.

Harkat's deportation, which he continues to challenge, arguing that there is a risk that he will be tortured in his native Algeria.

While court proceedings continued, Harkat remained under various conditions over the years, including detention, restrictive house arrest and then other conditions such as being required to wear a GPS device, to abstain from using the Internet or mobile phones, to have somebody in the house with him at all times and to check in weekly with the Canada Border Services Agency.[178] Some of these conditions have been lifted over the years. His wife, Sophie Harkat, has spoken publicly about the hardships that this situation has placed on their family. For a significant time, Sophie was required to supervise her husband in their home, which caused great stress, including seriously restricting her in her ability to work. In the film *The Secret Trial 5*, she spoke of how they were forced to miss having children because of the uncertainty.[179]

Harkat himself has expressed considerable distress both at the restrictive terms under which he is living and at the ongoing risk that he will be deported to Algeria. After the 2014 SCC decision, he said that the Canadian government should send him to Algeria 'with a box', because he said the Algerian government was going to torture and kill him.[180] Although the Canadian government has repeatedly asserted, over the past 10 years, that Harkat is a 'sleeper agent' for al-Qaeda, it has never charged him with a criminal offence. Harkat has publicly asked the government to criminally charge him in order to give him the opportunity to mount a defence.[181]

Even the way in which Harkat's latest SCC case progressed says something about the bizarre nature of being faced with a security certificate. The SCC heard oral arguments in Harkat's case in two parts, on 10 and 11 October 2013. The first hearing, on 10 October, was open to the public and was live-streamed on its website. For the second hearing, the SCC took the extraordinary step of holding the hearing in secret, going so far as to refuse to disclose even the time or the location of the hearing, except for reports that the case was not being held at the Supreme Court.[182] An announcement appeared on its website and for those on the SCC mailing list, after the argument happened, saying it had happened.[183] One issue

---

[178] See *Harkat and the Minister of Citizenship and Immigration et al*, 2013 FC 795 (lifting some of the conditions of Harkat's supervision, including removing the GPS device and allowing limited use of a mobile phone).

[179] *The Secret Trial 5*, above n 176.

[180] Andrew Duffy, '"Send Me with a Box": Harkat Says He'll Be Killed if Returned to Algeria' *Ottawa Citizen* (15 May 2014) ottawacitizen.com/news/national/send-me-with-a-box-harkat-says-hell-be-killed-if-returned-to-algeria.

[181] See Jeff Sallot, 'Not a Security Risk, Harkat Says, Seeking Charges or Freedom' *Globe and Mail* (10 July 2006) www.theglobeandmail.com/news/national/not-a-security-risk-harkat-says-seeking-charges-or-freedom/article1105868.

[182] See *Minister of Citizenship and Immigration et al v Mohamed Harkat et al*, No 34884, Docket, Order of 2 August 2013, *Supreme Court of Canada*, www.scc-csc.gc.ca/case-dossier/info/dock-regi-eng.aspx?cas=34884. The webcast of the 10 October hearing can be viewed online at www.scc-csc.gc.ca/case-dossier/info/webcast-webdiffusion-eng.aspx?cas=34884.

[183] I received this announcement.

before the SCC in that proceeding was the constitutionality of the special advocate regime and the secrecy surrounding the evidence used. Thus, the SCC's decision to hold the oral arguments in secret, the content of which has never been disclosed, was unusual indeed.[184]

At the time of writing this book, Harkat continues to fight deportation to Algeria, arguing that he will be tortured if he is sent there.[185] To provide some context, the US often held off on returning Guantanamo Bay detainees to Algeria, once cleared for release, out of fear that they would be tortured there. One detainee described the choice between staying at Guantanamo Bay and being returned to Algeria as 'dancing between fires'.[186]

VI. Conclusion: The False Premise of the Non-citizen Terrorist Other, which was Dominant in Post-9/11 Responses, Remains Foundational in Different Ways in Different Countries

Terrorism, by its nature, involves othering. The 9/11 attacks clearly involved an escalation of an ongoing form of othering, in which bin Laden wrongly claimed to act on behalf of Islam, identified Americans as fair targets and tried to start a form of culture war between Americans, or the West, and Muslims, who were portrayed as the East. Much of the dynamic after 9/11 has had echoes of Said's concept of Orientalism, although sometimes in reverse, and it is a seemingly endless cycle. Clearly Daesh is following a similar strategy.

After 9/11, extraordinary detention practices emerged from a number of national jurisdictions, which established non-citizens as the terrorist Other or suggested that terrorists were non-citizens. The US pursued this false point of departure in two ways: first through the use of its immigration system and then through the way in which it detained 'unlawful enemy combatants' through its war paradigm. In places like the UK and Canada, this false premise emerged as an undergirding to the way they initially used their immigration systems to detain non-citizens on security grounds. While the idea of citizenship was the explicit basis for this othering, those held under these regimes were generally Muslim

---

[184] *Harkat*, above, n 177.

[185] Debra Black, 'Mohamed Harkat Girds Himself for Another Fight to Stay' *The Star* (2 August 2016) www.thestar.com/news/immigration/2016/08/02/mohamed-harkat-girds-himself-for-another-fight-to-stay.html; see also *Mahjoub v Canada (Citizenship and Immigration)*, 2017 FCA 157 (dismissing an appeal of the Federal Court's finding that the security certificate in this case is 'reasonable').

[186] See Centre for Constitutional Rights, 'Abdul Aziz Naji: Algerian Guantanamo Refugee in Need of Protection' *CCR Justice*, ccrjustice.org/sites/default/files/assets/files/Abdul%20Aziz%20Naji%20-%202pages.pdf.

and male.[187] It is clear that these false premises that emerged after 9/11 still under-score certain governmental actions, as the controversies over Trump's Executive Orders on travel, discussed at length in chapter one above, demonstrate.

As described in this chapter, and throughout this book, extraordinary detention practices evolved in some places, and there was a fragmenting of these practices, depending on many factors.[188] One factor appears to have been how resoundingly a government rejected the false premise of the non-citizen as terrorist. Thus, in the UK, after a formidable response from the House of Lords, security immigration detentions yielded to other mechanisms that could equally be applied to citizens. This 'mission creep', as described earlier in this chapter, had its own problems, as a flawed practice is not better if applied to more people and discrimination is just one issue with these practices. Moreover, the initial acceptance of some of these practices for non-citizens opened the door for expanding them, albeit in varied form, to citizens, when they might not have been tolerated at all if they had ini-tially been applied directly to citizens. Once the practices extended to citizens, they became increasingly less draconian, and the inference is that citizens, who have more obvious political power, are likely to be less amenable to widespread rights deprivations when they are the subject of these deprivations.

In Canada, the SCC had a much more tolerant response to the government detaining people under different standards in security cases involving non-citizens. Based on that dichotomy, security certificates continue to be used for some people, and there has not been a comparable expansion of such measures to citizens in Canada. The outcome has been a truly Kafkaesque scenario for some of the people subject to security certificates for 15 years or more. If the intention is to stop terrorists, it is hard to justify only using this scheme for non-citizens. It is also hard to justify using it for so long, with, in the couple of Secret Trial 5 cases still pending, no clear end in sight. This is especially so when a government has made no attempt to proceed on criminal charges, permitting a full defence, for all of that time. It is difficult to imagine citizens tolerating the detention, or house arrest, or other limitations on freedom, without charge or trial, of their fellow citizens for 15 years or longer. That said, now that the idea of the security certificate regime, and that particular use, has normalised, perhaps it will seem less shocking if the mission creep seen in the UK begins. That is not the recommendation here, of course, because, again, the discrimination issue is just one of the problems with this regime.

---

[187] See Simon Rogers, 'Guantánamo Bay Detainees: The Full List' *The Guardian* (25 April 2011) www.guardian.co.uk/world/datablog/2011/apr/25/guantanamo-bay-detainees-full-list (containing a link to a spreadsheet they created from the raw data that was declassified, relating to approximately 800 detainees, who were overwhelmingly Muslim and male).

[188] For an in-depth discussion of different practices across different jurisdictions, see Kent Roach (ed), *Comparative Counterterrorism Law* (Cambridge, Cambridge University Press, 2015); Roach, above, n 85; Victor Ramraj et al (eds), *Global Anti-terrorism Law and Policy*, 2nd edn (Cambridge, Cambridge University Press, 2012).

The importance of citizenship in terms of the narrative of the terrorist Other has continued in recent years in a new form, with the emergence of citizenship stripping for those accused of association with terrorism in a number of countries.[189] This practice has been described as a response to Daesh and the problem of people going overseas to join them.[190] As a general matter, there are few actions that can result in citizenship stripping, and traditionally it tended to only happen in situations in which there is, for instance, fraud in the procurement of the citizenship.[191] Stripping citizenship because of alleged involvement in terrorism is a dramatic governmental response, with wide-ranging repercussions for the person who loses citizenship. The clear implication of this trend is that if a terrorist is a citizen, the person can be othered by stripping them of that citizenship, thus adding them to the group of non-citizen Others and, in some places, subjecting them to at least the possibility of extraordinary detention practices where those practices still apply only to non-citizens.[192]

Beyond the concerns about othering, the practice has been subject to other controversies and, in Canada, it was described by Roach and Forcese as a 'desperate and inefficacious measure to fight terrorism'.[193] Canada had briefly enacted legislation allowing for the stripping of citizenship from dual citizens for suspected terrorism, spying or treason, but a change of government brought about a repeal of this particular provision after a couple of years.[194]

Moreover, those who face just the possibility of having citizenship stripped, even if it does not actually happen, are still placed in a sort of Other category. The term 'second-class citizen' suggests that some people are more citizens than others, and it seems to apply to this scenario.[195] In the UK, there has been considerable controversy because the government has asserted that it can strip citizenship even from those who have only one citizenship, legally rendering them stateless.[196]

---

[189] See Sangeetha Pillai and George Williams, 'Twenty-First Century Banishment: Citizenship Stripping in Common Law Nations' (2017) 66(3) *International and Comparative Law Quarterly* 521 (explaining in depth changes to citizen-revocation laws in Australia, the UK and Canada).

[190] See ibid; see also Audrey Macklin, 'Citizenship Revocation, the Privilege to Have Rights and the Production of the Alien' (2014) 40(1) *Queen's Law Journal* 1, 21; Forcese, above, n 11.

[191] Forcese, above, n 11.

[192] See Sangeetha and Pillai, above, n 189; see also David Anderson QC, 'Citizenship Removal Resulting in Statelessness' *Independent Reviewer of Terrorism Legislation* (April 2016) www.gov.uk/government/uploads/system/uploads/attachment_data/file/518120/David_Anderson_QC_-_CITIZENSHIP_REMOVAL__web_.pdf (discussing the controversy in the UK, particularly in cases in which the national only has one citizenship and would be stateless if stripped of that one citizenship).

[193] Kent Roach and Craig Forcese, 'Why Stripping Citizenship is a Weak Took against Terrorism' *Globe and Mail* (3 March 2016) www.theglobeandmail.com/opinion/why-stripping-citizenship-is-a-weak-tool-to-fight-terrorism/article29003409.

[194] See Government of Canada, 'Backgrounder: Bill C-6 Receives Royal Assent' (19 June 2017) www.canada.ca/en/immigration-refugees-citizenship/news/2017/06/bill_c-6_receivesroyalassent0.html (comparing the legislation as enacted under the prior government with the new provisions).

[195] See British Columbia Civil Liberties Association, 'It's Official: Second-Class Citizenship Goes into Effect' (3 June 2015) bccla.org/2015/06/its-official-second-class-citizenship-goes-into-effect (responding to Canada's short-lived citizenship-stripping legislation).

[196] Anderson, above, n 192.

In March 2017, the European Court of Human Rights upheld the stripping of the citizenship of a dual citizen from Sudan, facilitating any continued citizenship stripping in the UK.[197] In Canada, the short-lived legislation that allowed for such stripping of citizenship only applied to dual citizens, but it raised the inference that dual citizens were somehow lesser, or second-class, citizens.[198] Either scenario is problematic.

Whatever form it takes, it is apparent that the point of departure for many post-9/11, and continuing, changes to terrorism detention practices is the idea of the non-citizen terrorist Other. It is equally apparent that the recent rise of Daesh has some connection with the view promulgated by its leaders that there is a war for fundamental identity between Islam and the West, and the mirror image of this message underscores some of the response to Daesh. While both premises are, or should be, understood as clearly false, they continue to dominate as the world moves forward in relation to responses to terrorism. Reviewing the problematic role in post-9/11 narratives, and the corresponding legal changes, could be one way of changing in order to travel in a better direction. Proceeding on a false premise in responding to terrorism strongly suggests, among many other things, that the resulting responses simply will not work.

---

[197] *K2 v United Kingdom*, Application No 42387/13 (ECHR, 2017) (regarding the stripping of citizenship from a dual Sudanese-British national who was living in the UK and which happened while he was out of the country).

[198] See, eg, British Columbia Civil Liberties Association, above, n 195.

6

False Dichotomies in the Narrative: The 'Either/or' Dilemma

I. Binary Language in the Post-9/11 Narrative and How it Precluded Nuance that Might Have Led to Better Responses

Chapters four and five dealt with argumentation points of departure, an argumentation tool in which a starting narrative is the foundational point for how an argument develops. The specific points of departure used in those chapters—one relating to the need to build new detention regimes in response to unprecedented attacks and the other insinuating that terrorists are non-citizens (or that non-citizens are terrorists)—have served as foundational arguments by governments seeking to change terrorism detention practices in response to 9/11. However, the point of departure used as the basis for chapter five regarding non-citizens serves multiple argumentation functions. Indeed, as argued in chapter five, it constitutes a false premise and thus is flawed as an argumentation strategy. It also serves as a point of departure regrading the terrorist Other, a foundation for some of the changes in terrorism detention practices.

However, it plays another argumentation role in its presentation form as a point of departure as a binary, an either/or statement that phases out levels of nuance. When a binary is presented in such stark terms, it leaves little room for disagreement and it makes a particular choice seem absolute, so it can be an effective, but not necessarily accurate, argumentation tool. If rephrased a bit, the point of departure could be described as 'us versus them', with 'us' being citizens and 'them' being non-citizens. Unstated but implied, of course, is that 'we' are good and 'they' are evil. Also unstated, but clearly present, has been the idea that the struggle is one of 'us' against Muslims. The overwhelming presence of Muslim males in extraordinary detention scenarios makes this conclusion impossible to avoid. Governments justify this on the basis of the othering undertaken by groups like al-Qaeda and Daesh, which wrongly claim to act on behalf of Islam. The implication is clearly that those who are in that group of non-citizen Muslim males are somehow different, so the constitutional protections relating to fair trials somehow do not apply to them when a government seeks to detain them.[1]

---

[1] This cycle is discussed at length in ch 5 above.

Before elaborating on the use of such binaries to support extraordinary detentions, some beginning definitions are necessary. A 'binary' can be defined in mathematical terms, but, for this purpose, it is used in the sense of a 'binary opposition',
which can be described as:

> [T]he system by which, in language and thought, two theoretical opposites are strictly
> defined and set off against one another but simultaneously arranged, somewhat
> paradoxically, in pairs. These pairs are not unlike those which might be generated by a
> psychoanalytical word-association test and are manifest in obvious combinations:
>
> — Life/Death
> — Day/Night
> — Sun/Moon
> — Apollonian/Dionysian
> — Culture/Nature
> — Reason/Passion[2]

To explain the chapter title, a 'false dichotomy' is a statement that presents two
options as an either/or scenario, which falsely suggests that these two options are
the only two available and that the stark framing of these either/or options is the
only way, or even the true way, to see them.[3] It is much easier to persuade an audience if one can present only two clear choices, one portrayed as obviously good
and the other portrayed as evil. Nuance in an argument makes persuasion less
easy. The focus in this chapter, then, is not always on the substance of a statement
or point of departure, but also on the form of the argumentative points presented.
Examples demonstrate situations that politicians presented as stark binaries, when
the reality was or is actually much more nuanced. If legal changes were accepted
based on a false dichotomy, then that is another basis for questioning the validity
of the change.

In the case of the binary discussed in chapter five, had the 'us' versus 'them'
narrative simply been framed as a contrast of innocent civilians versus terrorists,
the choice would have been obvious, and it would have more accurately explained
the situation that plays out repeatedly involving terrorism. The problem was not
necessarily the use of a binary itself, but the form of the binary used, in which the
points contrasted with each other were too broad and generalised, and thus captured groups of people who were not necessarily really part of the binary. These
groups, although presented as opposing groups, were not always opposing groups
at all. Therefore, some of the post-9/11 narratives were built on a foundation of
false dichotomies.

---

[2] Greg Smith, 'Binary Opposition and Sexual Power in 'Paradise Lost'' (1996) 27(4) *Midwest Quarterly* 383.

[3] Trudy Govier, *A Practical Study of Argument* (Belmont, CA, Wadsworth Inc, 1988) 330; see also Esther D Reed (ed), *Civil Liberties, National Security and Prospects for Consensus: Legal, Philosophical and Religious Perspectives* (Cambridge, Cambridge University Press, 2012) (containing a collection of essays, from a philosophy perspective, dealing with the 'false dichotomy' of the notion that civil liberties must be traded off to enhance security).

Binaries are often intentionally used to demonise a group seen as an enemy and, in those instances, it is almost always a deceptive argumentation tool. Such rhetoric underscored Hitler's rise to power, in which he selected particular groups to demonise. In his notorious work, *Mein Kampf*, Hitler wrote, for example: 'If, with the help of his Marxist creed, the Jew is victorious over the other peoples of the world, his crown will be the funeral wreath of humanity and this planet will, as it did thousands of years ago, move through the ether devoid of men.'[4] Millions of people were murdered on the back of this narrative.

The idea of 'us' versus 'them' has, at its core, a dehumanisation of 'them', not just suggesting that they are different, but somehow implying that they are less human and a danger to those constructed as 'us'. As Hitler sought to portray Jewish people as somehow a risk to the 'us' he constructed, dehumanisation is otherwise a significant part of the rhetoric underpinning wars, genocide and an endless range of other human rights abuses. Thus, the Tutsis in Rwanda were targeted for genocide with rhetoric describing them not as human beings, but as 'cockroaches'. This narrative arose after a colonial history, in which the Hutus had been mistreated as the constructed inferior Other.[5]

Obviously, the examples of the Nazis and the Rwandan genocide are extreme examples. However, they demonstrate the violence that can emerge from abusive uses of a binary that demonises one group, and they demonstrate some of the differing pathways through which the false dichotomy of the Other arose. The examples are used not particularly as comparisons to the matters discussed in this book, but to extrapolate rhetoric that appears in this particular form to its potentially devastating conclusions, thus demonstrating a significant problem from binaries in general and from this type of binary in particular.

The narratives of 'us' versus 'them' normally tend to be more insidious than in these examples. While, in the early days after 9/11, governments denied that they were targeting people who were Muslim, even within the sub-group of the non-citizens they did admit to targeting, there was a disparate impact on people who were Muslim in extraordinary detention regimes. As time passed and the process of normalisation occurred, Donald Trump emerged as an American President who openly demonises people who are Muslim.[6] Thus, the political discourse that dominated in the early years after 9/11 continues to be relevant, as it has evolved into a more blatant form of discriminatory discourse in this context. It also continues to serve as the foundation for how legal norms develop, as demonstrated

---

[4] Jewish Virtual Library, 'Adolf Hitler: Excerpts from Mein Kampf', *Jewish Virtual Library*, www.jewishvirtuallibrary.org/excerpts-from-mein-kampf#1 (this source was intentionally cited out of an unwillingness to directly cite to Adolf Hitler for this statement, even though it is his writing).

[5] See Daniel Rothbart and Tom Bartlett, 'Rwandan Radio Broadcasts and Hutu/Tutsi Positioning' in Fathali M Moghaddam et al (eds), *Global Conflict Resolution through Positioning Analysis* (New York, Springer, 2008) 227 (discussing how the rise of identity politics gave momentum to an increase in violence against those whose identity was seen as inferior and harmful).

[6] See the discussion of the narrative denying the targeting of non-citizen Muslims in ch 5 above and of Trump's commentary relating to Muslims in ch 1 above.

by the controversy over the Executive Orders regarding travel, which are known in popular discourse as a 'Muslim ban' or a 'travel ban' and were discussed at length in chapter one above.

In its 2016–17 annual report, Amnesty International wrote about the continuing tendency for governments to use the narratives of 'us' versus 'them' and of the toll that such narratives were taking on fundamental human rights:

> 2016 saw the idea of human dignity and equality, the very notion of a human family, coming under vigorous and relentless assault from powerful narratives of blame, fear and scapegoating, propagated by those who sought to take or cling on to power at almost any cost.
>
> …
>
> Donald Trump's poisonous campaign rhetoric exemplifies a global trend towards angrier and more divisive politics. Across the world, leaders and politicians wagered their future power on narratives of fear and disunity, pinning blame on the 'other' for the real or manufactured grievances of the electorate.[7]

Although the 'us' versus 'them' binary is a commonly used narrative tool and was not unique to the post-9/11 political discourse, it was nonetheless a dominant feature of the particular narrative that was constructed after the attacks to justify extraordinary detention regimes. It was not, however, the only binary that was dominant in the post-9/11 political discourse. Other binaries undergirding the discourse regarding terrorism have been identified.[8]

Returning to the metaphor of the kaleidoscope, this chapter shifts the post-9/11 narrative to look at this different dimension of argumentation strategy. This different layer supplements, although arguably at a different level, the argumentation strategies already discussed in this book. Like the labels discussed in chapter one, governments also layered binary statements through various levels of the narratives they were advancing. In so doing, they often painted complicated situations as a simplistic choice between one option or another. This strategy helped to frame the issues to achieve their desired ends, and it went a long way towards persuading receptive audiences that particular changes were necessary in the fight against terrorism. This chapter proceeds with some examples of this binary discourse and how it led to particular changed understandings of terrorism detention practices.

One useful aspect of the kaleidoscope metaphor is that it can be used to demonstrate that the post-9/11 political argumentation strategies are not linear, but that, rather, different elements can be considered on different levels, and intersecting with each other in different ways and at different points, in a more

---

[7] Amnesty International, *The State of the World: A Global Pushback against Human Rights* (2016–17) www.amnesty.org/en/latest/research/2017/02/amnesty-international-annual-report-201617, 12, 15.

[8] See Fergal F Davis and Fiona de Londras, 'Counter-terrorist Judicial Review: Beyond Dichotomies' in Fergal F Davis and Fiona de Londras (eds), *Critical Debates on Counter-terrorist Judicial Review* (Cambridge, Cambridge University Press, 2014), as posted on *SSRN*, papers.ssrn.com/sol3/papers. cfm?abstract_id=2356021.

three-dimensional structure. In so doing, these configurations can produce new ways of looking at objective facts. Each of the argumentation tools discussed in this book can have that effect, on its own, but part of what this chapter demonstrates is that there are seemingly endless ways in which different tools can be used and combined. Beyond the 'us' versus 'them' binary already discussed, this chapter proceeds with three examples of 'binary' discourse, which have different aspects and vary in relation to each other, which helped to advance argued changes regarding terrorism detention practices after 9/11. Different levels of binaries were common in post-9/11 narratives regarding the need to change terrorism detention practices in a particular way.

The reader may think, after reading these examples, that there is so much more that could be said about them. That is undoubtedly true. It is not intended that these examples definitively resolve the issues they address. They involve the subject of extensive debates that have been ongoing for years. Rather, they were chosen for this chapter because they are complex situations that were presented in post-9/11 political discourse in highly simplistic, false dichotomy terms, in order to persuade a receptive audience. For each, the binary is presented with some discussion to illustrate how ineffective the binaries were in describing the complex reality of the situation. The objective is therefore to criticise the form of speech used, with the additional suggestion that this flawed political discourse was an underpinning for changes that occurred in terrorism detention practices in particular places. As the political discourse was flawed, so were many of the practices that flowed from that discourse.

II. Incommensurability in Binary-Based Discourse: The False Dichotomy of Balancing Liberty and Security Dominated after 9/11

A. 'Balance?'

Possibly one of the most frequently stated governmental propositions since 9/11 is the idea that liberty and security must be balanced.[9] For this purpose, the terms 'liberty' and 'security' are chosen simply because they are most commonly used, but variations are also common, in which security or safety is more broadly articulated as a factor to balance against individual rights. As an example of this kind of discourse, in 2008, British Home Secretary Jacqui Smith commented

---

[9] See, eg, Paul Reynolds, 'Balancing Liberty with Security' *BBC News* (23 October 2008) news.bbc.co.uk/2/hi/7687091.stm (quoting various government officials and others on this issue); Jeremy Waldron, 'Security and Liberty: The Image of Balance' (2003) 11(2) *Journal of Political Philosophy* 191.

that: 'The Prevention of Terrorism Act 2005 strikes the right balance between safeguarding society and safeguarding the rights of the individual.'[10]

The Prevention of Terrorism Act 2005, to which Smith referred, provided the authority for control orders, a form of extraordinary detention that was introduced after the House of Lords issued the *Belmarsh Detainee* ruling in 2004, and, as explained more in chapter five, above, were subsequently replaced by TPIMs.[11] This balance language echoes language employed in other places, such as in the Supreme Court of Israel, which noted, regarding legislation allowing for extraordinary detention in terrorism cases: 'Such legislation must reflect the necessary balance between security needs and the liberty of the individual in the territory.'[12]

A competing argument regarding the 'balance' between liberty and security suggests that this manner of presenting this ideal might be misleading. Kenneth Roth, on behalf of Human Rights Watch, said that the best way to ensure security is to safeguard human rights—that the two are not contrary, opposing values, but, rather, both objectives can be enhanced without sacrificing one for the other. As an example of his point, Roth pointed to Spain's response to terrorism, not just in relation to 9/11, but also to other attacks, including the Madrid bombing in 2004. Unlike countries like the US, Canada, the UK and Australia, Spain did not develop parallel detention paradigms and continued to respond exclusively to terrorism detentions through a criminal justice, prosecution approach.[13] Thomas Hammarberg, the then Human Rights Commissioner for the Council of Europe, echoed Roth's sentiments relating to the balancing of these values, saying: 'As for the "balance" concept, I avoid the word. Human rights and civil liberties should apply in all situations. Rights are most relevant when there is a threat or a crisis.'[14]

The formulation of this binary cannot necessarily be expressly linked to changed detention practices, but it is used so often in political statements, and was used so often after 9/11, that it is reasonable to infer that it helped to support changes that, by their nature, infringed on individual liberties in the name of enhanced security. While the binary sounds logical at first, it is problematic when explored in more depth. What does it mean to 'balance' these two values? The literal idea of balance evokes an image of a scale, in which the weights of each must be the same to achieve an outcome in which the two elements are at an equal level with each

---

[10] See Reynolds, above, n 9 (pointing out that the word 'balance' was important in different respects and quoting Bush as saying: 'This war is more than a clash of arms—it is a decisive ideological struggle, and the security of our nation is in the balance').

[11] See ibid; Prevention of Terrorism Act 2005 c 2 (UK).

[12] See *Marab v IDF Commander*, Supreme Court Sitting as the High Court of Justice (18 April 2002, 28 July 2002), para 21 (citing to the Fourth Geneva Convention for the proposition that certain individual rights can be set aside on the basis of necessity to enhance security in times of war).

[13] Reynolds, above, n 9. This difference in response was pointed out by Lord Hoffmann in the *Belmarsh Detainees* case: *A (FC) and Others (FC) (Appellants) v Secretary of State for the Home Department (Respondent)* [2004] UKHL 56, para 96.

[14] Reynolds, above, n 9.

other on the scale, much like the image of the scales of justice in law. However, it is unlikely that this is what 'balance' means in the statement of this binary.

Beyond the issue of what notion of 'balance' is accepted, it is also implicit in this discussion that this balance, or what was needed to find the balance, somehow shifted after the 9/11 attacks. Arguably, the true argument was that individual liberties and security were opposites, and that one must be diminished to enhance the other, and that the one to be diminished must always be liberty in the name of security. The objective was not really to 'balance' anything, but to diminish one to give dominance to the other. Thus, the image evoked is not of a scale, with two equal sides, but of a scale in which one side significantly outweighs the other. The objective is not to achieve equality between the two values, but to assert that one value must be diminished in order to strengthen the other.

This relates back to the idea from chapter four suggesting that there was something specific about the 9/11 attacks that necessitated building new detention regimes. The implication is that the emphasis had shifted away from individual liberties in favour of security and that this change was necessary to find the newly revealed point at which 'balance' could again be achieved. Along the same lines, if broad language is used, suggesting that there must be 'balance' between these two values, then it is easier to comfort people in the belief that there is a proper 'balance' to be found, that individual liberties are still being respected as much as possible and that the changes are the least intrusive necessary to keep them safe. In other words, this binary suggests that all that is happening is a recalibration to address this 'new' threat and that once this recalibration is done, all will again be well, balanced and fair on both fronts.

Jeremy Waldron has addressed the potentially misleading use of the notion of 'balance' in this scenario by saying:

> [W]hat are we implying when we say the balance has shifted? Is it just a matter of our having thought of a new reason, or of new facts having given rise to new reasons, which weigh more on one side than the other? That we can make sense of: there is now (say, since September 11, 2001) something new to be said on one side of a familiar debate and nothing new to be said on the other. But 'balance' also has connotations of quantity and precision, as when we use it to describe the reconciliation of a set of accounts or the relative weight of two quantities of metal. Where is the warrant for our reliance on this quantitative imagery when we say that the new consideration not only adds something to the debate but 'outweighs' all considerations on the other side?[15]

Thus, Waldron suggests that those advancing this point might basically mean that denying all liberty would be the safest route, but that liberty is so cherished that, to maintain it, some element of risk is accepted, beyond the idea of no risk at all.[16] He notes: 'But even with the adjustments in civil liberties … no one feels as secure as before: so everyone has to be a little braver for the sake of the modicum of liberty

---

[15] Waldron, above, n 9, 192–93.
[16] ibid.

that is left.'[17] He argues, for a number of reasons, that it is important to challenge the rhetoric surrounding the image of 'balance' in this context.[18]

B. Liberty versus Security: The Assumption of Commensurability

Aside from what is meant by the use of the word 'balance' and how it is understood in the popular mind, there is another question raised by this binary. It is simply assumed that liberty and security are comparable, but opposing, values and that, by definition, diminishing one enhances the other. Some scholars suggest that the sequence of placement in the binary gives an indication as to which element is deemed dominant over the other. Even where the order is not dispositive, the suggestion in a binary is that one of the competing values is more important than the other.[19] While the implication is probably intended to be that liberty dominates, the reality is that liberty is always argued as having to be sacrificed in the name of security.[20]

A question also arises as to whose liberty and whose safety are at issue. This question presents an example of how the binaries discussed in this book, as well as the many other argumentation tools set forth in the book, can overlap, or were used in conjunction with each other. Although these tools are separated out for the purpose of analysis, these different tools were combined in different ways to produce the post-9/11 narrative. The clear implication—to make this binary acceptable to an audience of voters—is that limitations will be placed on 'their' liberty to ensure 'our' safety, and the 'us' versus 'them' binary discussed above has a central role in the issues raised by this binary. The concepts in the different argumentation tools operate in conjunction with one another.

Certainly, those who lost their liberty, such as the victims of the extraordinary rendition torture programme, were made less safe by that loss of liberty.[21] Nothing has demonstrated that other people were made more safe because certain people were detained without criminal procedure protections, especially since criminal procedure mechanisms were consistently still available. Those detained were absolutely not more safe. A more accurate description of these values might be that the liberty of some is argued to be necessarily diminished to enhance the

---

[17] ibid 194.

[18] ibid.

[19] ibid 197 (citing J Rawls, *A Theory of Justice*, revised edn (Cambridge, MA, Harvard University Press, 1999) 36–40 (lexical priority), 214–20 (priority of liberty in this binary)).

[20] See David M O'Brien, 'Detention and Security versus Liberty in Times of National Emergency' in Mary L Volcansek and John F. Stack (eds), *Courts and Terrorism: Nine Nations Balance Rights and Security* (New York, Cambridge University Press, 2011) (also, generally, see the other essays in the collection, with the overarching theme relating to this 'balance').

[21] See generally Commission of Inquiry into the Actions of Canadian Officials in Relation to Maher Arar, *Report of the Events Relating to Maher Arar* (2006) (detailing the events surrounding the 'extraordinary rendition' and torture of Canadian citizen Maher Arar).

safety of others. While there are some inroads into personal liberty that have more widespread impact, the bulk of extraordinary detention practices after 9/11 had an impact on a finite subset of individuals and, if increased security was indeed the goal, then this related to the security of other people.

Clearly, it is not as straightforward as the binary suggests. The concept of 'incommensurability' suggests the lack of a common measure.[22] Thus, if one option is presented as, by definition, ruling out the other, there is an assumption that the two options have indicia of commonality that allows for reduction to some form of common denominator. Some suggest that this concept relates more to comparability, such as that found in the well-known metaphor of comparing apples to oranges. Incommensurability, however, suggests more than a comparison, but suggests that the two concepts considered have been placed on a form of metaphoric scale, with one element on one side and the other element on the other, and that any change made to the first, by definition, affects the weight of the second. This goes beyond comparison and suggests a level of inter-relatedness that makes the two not just comparable, but somehow inextricably linked and, to some extent, mutually exclusive or, conversely, mutually constitutive.[23]

There are different lines of thought in relation to the notion of incommensurability. Ruth Chang draws a distinction between comparability and incommensurability, arguing '[l]et us henceforth reserve the term "incommensurable" for items that cannot be precisely measured by some common scale of units of value', which, she argues, is not the same thing as simply not being subject to comparison.[24] However, if this conclusion is accepted, then, by definition, it is not possible to achieve 'balance' between liberty and security, which, on its face, suggests being 'precisely measured by some common scales of units of value'.[25]

Items might be compared to each other even if they cannot necessarily be reduced to a common denominator. James Griffin has written that commensurability does not, in fact, suggest that the two items asserted to be commensurable are equal, but that one of the items asserted to be commensurable must, by definition, be formulated in a way that requires that one actually dominates over the other. This notion, which he refers to as 'trumping', suggests that realising one concept means, by definition, that the other cannot be realised, suggesting that the second value is less important.[26]

---

[22] Clint Shinn, 'Difference, Incommensurability, Decision' (2009) 2(1) *Emergent Australian Philosophers* 1 (arguing that it is possible, within the political sphere, to understand difference without those differences becoming incommensurable).

[23] See Ruth Chang (ed), *Incommensurability, Incomparability, and Practical Reason* (Cambridge, MA, Harvard University Press, 1997); see also Ruth Chang, 'Against Constitutive Incommensurability or Buying and Selling Friends' (2002) 11(2) *Social, Political, and Legal Philosophy* 33.

[24] Chang, *Incommensurability*, above, n 23, 2.

[25] See ibid.

[26] See James Griffin, *Well-Being: Its Meaning, Measurement and Importance* (Oxford, Clarendon Press, 1986) 83.

If one is to accept the connection between these two concepts, what is being described is more like a sliding scale, in which liberties are removed to enhance an argument for safety. Once removed, liberties are rarely returned, even when the situation may seem safer. A beginning problem in this particular binary is that both concepts—liberty and security—are extremely broad and include many things. A measure with a small impact on liberty, but a high demonstrable value in curbing security risks may seem reasonable. A measure that has a massive impact on liberty, but little or no demonstrable impact on safety might similarly be obviously unacceptable. Where the arguments for 'balance' arise is in those situations in which a government asserts that it has to make a significant incursion into individual liberty and that there is a notable improvement in security when it does so. When critiquing controversial national security legislation in Canada, known as Bill C-51, Kent Roach and Craig Forcese described it as yet another piece of legislation granting 'new powers with definite civil liberties costs incurred for doubtful security gains'.[27] This is not an unusual critique of post-9/11 extraordinary detentions either, and it suggests that this simplistic binary may, in its very simplicity, be hiding the truth behind an issue that is really quite complex.[28]

C. 'Balancing' Security against a Range of Individual Rights: The Problem of Sweeping Generalisations

It is this notion of commensurability that raises questions when assertions are made that a proper balance must be struck between liberty and security.[29] In the US, Benjamin Franklin was often quoted in the post-9/11 debates as having said: 'They who can give up essential liberty to obtain a little temporary safety deserve neither liberty nor safety.'[30] It could well be argued in different instances that

---

[27] Kent Roach and Craig Forcese, 'Renewed Bill C-51 Questions: Balancing National Security with Civil Liberty' *Globe and Mail* (17 October 2016) www.theglobeandmail.com/opinion/renewed-bill-c-51-questions-balancing-national-security-with-civil-liberty/article32393193.

[28] For a detailed discussion of this and other concerns with the 'balance' metaphor, see Stuart Macdonald, 'Why We Should Abandon the Balance Metaphor: A New Approach to Counterterrorism Policy' (2008) 15 *ILSA Journal of International and Comparative Law* 95.

[29] For various permutations and some critiques of this binary, see, eg, David Cole and Jules Lobel, *Less Safe, Less Free: Why America is Losing the War on Terror* (New York, New Press, 2007); David Dyzenhaus (ed), *Civil Rights and Security* (Burlington, VT, Ashgate, 2009); Kent Roach, 'Must We Trade Rights for Security? The Choice between Smart, Harsh or Proportionate Security Strategies in Canada and Britain' (2006) 27 *Cardozo Law Review* 2157; Joseph Nye, 'Balancing Liberty and Security' *Huffington Post* (26 December 2005) www.huffingtonpost.com/joseph-nye/balancing-liberty-and-sec_b_12896.html; John Kleinig et al, *Security and Privacy: Global Standards for Ethical Identity Management in Contemporary Liberal Democratic States* (Canberra, ANU Press, 2011).

[30] After 9/11, variations on this quote, widely attributed to Benjamin Franklin, circulated to criticise the dominant aspects of the post-9/11 paradigm. The version quoted here is widely believed to be the original, published in Franklin's memoirs. See Benjamin Franklin and William Temple Franklin, *Memoirs of the Life and Writing of Benjamin Franklin, LL.D.* (London, William Coburn, 1818), 270 (containing this quotation).

they are actually connected, but that enhancing individual liberties also enhances security.

In some respects, this binary might be more persuasive if broken down from the broad, generalised framing it often has in the political discourse. Rights are never absolute. If a person commits a crime, societal safety, among other motivations, would justify, after a fair trial, imprisoning that person. However, it is much more difficult to justify sweeping deprivations of individual liberties on equally sweeping claims of enhancing security.

Stuart Macdonald, in characterising the critiques of this metaphor, points out that differences of opinion on where this balance lies may not necessarily be because of a diminished view of the importance of liberty, but may be because of different understandings of what each element on the two sides of the balance actually entails.[31] In fact, he points out that, after 9/11, many actually argued that civil liberties should not be undermined, because this would be to hand the terrorists a victory.[32]

Lord Hoffmann raised a similar idea in the *Belmarsh Detainees* case, as he wrote about the risks raised by the UK government's detention policies, noting:

> The real threat to the life of the nation, in the sense of a people living in accordance with its traditional laws and political values, comes not from terrorism but from laws such as these. That is the true measure of what terrorism may achieve. It is for Parliament to decide whether to give the terrorists such a victory.[33]

For this and other reasons, the European Court of Human Rights rejected the 'balance' metaphor in its review of the Belmarsh detentions, noting: 'the Court does not accept the Government's argument that Article 5 § 1 permits a balance to be struck between the individual's right to liberty and the State's interest in protecting its population from terrorist threat.'[34] Christopher Michaelson argues that the two values are not 'mutually exclusive', but rather are 'mutually enforcing'.[35]

The idea of balancing values that are argued to be competing is not a new notion in constitutional law and theory. It is a concept that has been subject to considerable critique in other contexts.[36] This critique plays out differently in different places. Canada's Constitution Act, 1982, for example, allows for such balancing, protecting certain rights under the Charter 'subject only to such reasonable

---

[31] Macdonald, above, n 28, 98.
[32] ibid.
[33] *Belmarsh Detainees* case, above, n 13, para 97.
[34] *A and Others v United Kingdom*, Application No 3455/05 2009 ECHR (2009).
[35] Christopher Michaelson, 'Balancing Civil Liberties against National Security? A Critique of Counterterrorism Rhetoric' (2006) 29(2) *University of New South Wales Law* 1, 3–4.
[36] See Robert Alexy, 'Constitutional Rights, Balancing, and Rationality' (2003) 16(2) *Ratio Juris* 131, 134–40 (containing critiques of balancing in regard in individual rights under national constitutions, with a particular focus on the German Constitution); Jürgen Habermas, *Between Facts and Norms: Contributions to a Discourse Theory of Law and Democracy*, translated by William Rehg (Boston, MIT Press, 1996) (arguing that allowing for balancing in relation to constitutionally mandated individual rights undermines the structure of those rights).

limits prescribed by law as can be demonstrably justified in a free and democratic society'.[37] The need for proportionality, however, is intended to still give proper deference to individual rights under the Constitution.[38] Importantly, the government, in order to justify the infringement of an individual right, has the burden of establishing the justification and must do so under a fairly stringent test that requires a showing of facts relating to that infringement.[39] Implicit in the idea that individual rights can be infringed, based upon certain societal interests, is the notion that protecting society also protects the rights of those so protected. Thus, liberty and security are not so clearly on opposing sides of the proverbial scale, which also undermines the usefulness of this particular binary.[40]

Such balancing is not explicitly permitted in all national constitutions.[41] In the US, for instance, there is no provision that is comparable to section 1 of Canada's Constitution Act, 1982. However, the idea of societal interests is built into the way in which constitutional rights are interpreted.[42]

The problem arises with broad metaphors, which are not necessarily explicitly linked to particular governmental actions, but which still serve as the political justification for sweeping changes.[43] A clear example arises in extraordinary detention scenarios such as those presented at Guantanamo Bay, where an entire new detention paradigm was built on the back of generalised assertions, such as the need to balance liberty and security. The detainees there do not have a presumption in favour of their individual rights. Indeed, one of the primary problems with that detention centre has been the extreme difficulty detainees have faced trying to have their cases heard at all before US courts, and a seeming shift of the presumption away from the presumption of innocence seen in criminal proceedings.[44] Such an abridgement of rights, taken in relation to more than just one particular

---

[37] See Constitution Act, 1982, Schedule B to the Canada Act 1982 (UK), 1982, c 11, s 1.

[38] See, eg, *R v Oakes* [1986] 1 SCR 103; *Alberta v Hutterian Brethren of Wilson Colony*, 2009 SCC 37, [2009] 2 SCR 567; *R v Keegstra* [1990] 3 SCR 697. Debates sometimes arise where two rights are seen to be competing with each other, as to whether one dominates over the others, as the extent of rights is generally limited where it intrudes on the rights of another. See *R v NS*, 2012 SCC 7 (outlining a series of steps to be followed in addressing such an assertion of competing rights). Compare Alexy, above, n 36 (discussing the view that the German Constitution addresses the issue of balancing with a proportionality requirement, which is intended to still give a certain dominance to individual rights).

[39] This is commonly called the *Oakes* test, although there are elements to it beyond those laid out in the *Oakes* decision. See *Oakes*, above, n 38.

[40] Macdonald, above, n 28, 97.

[41] For a discussion of how this issue of societal interests factors into the interpretation of individual rights in the UK, see, eg, generally Andrew Ashworth, *Human Rights, Serious Crime, and Criminal Procedure* (London, Sweet & Maxwell, 2002).

[42] See, eg, *Hamdi v Rumsfeld*, 542 US 507 (2004) (discussing the interconnection between societal security interests and individual liberties of a citizen held as an 'unlawful enemy combatant').

[43] See Stuart Macdonald, 'The Unbalanced Imagery of Anti-terrorism Policy' (2008) 18 *Cornell Journal of Law and Policy* 519 (critiquing the use of this type of metaphor to address what is actually a subject that is more complex than the metaphor can capture).

[44] See *Boumediene v Bush*, 553 US 723 (2008) (ruling that the US Constitution allowed prisoners detained at Guantanamo Bay to have habeas corpus hearings before US courts, culminating approximately six years of attempts to obtain these hearings by those detained there).

detainee and based on broader assertions of liberty, is different in nature from those balancing considerations undertaken in situations such as through the use of section 1 of the Charter in Canada.

In the post-9/11 context, there has been a range of variations on this larger 'balance' assertion, with the one fairly consistent factor being that 'security' is 'balanced' against some individual right ideal, whether it is liberty, privacy, governmental transparency or perhaps the right to a fair hearing, and that this justifies sweeping structural changes, rather than serving as an interpretation tool in a particular scenario.[45] Security in this context is usually used to refer to 'national security', which, in turn, does not necessarily refer to all things deemed necessary for public safety, but has been used more narrowly since 9/11 to refer to anti-terrorism or counter-terrorism.[46] In fact, 'security' can refer to many things outside the terrorism context, such as military security, economic security, environmental security, food security or the success of anti-criminal initiatives, with one example being the fight being undertaken in Mexico relating to drug cartels.[47] However, extraordinary detentions of the sort described in this book are not generally similarly legitimised by liberal democracies, at least as of the writing of this book, in relation to these other 'security' issues. This broader assertion of balance has been used as a sweeping theoretical underpinning through which states seek to legitimise extraordinary detentions specifically where they have asserted that the detainee has some connection to terrorism.

The balance binary, so frequently employed since 9/11, is therefore flawed for many reasons, including the fact that each element of the seemingly simple binary actually contains complexities that are ultimately hidden in the argument, because of the misuse of simplifying, binary language. Stuart Macdonald writes:

> The balance metaphor's image of a set of scales fails to capture the complexity of the task of analysing counterterrorism policy. One of the principal reasons for this is that it assumes a shared understanding of what each pan of the metaphorical scales represents, and so fails to engage with the variety of perspectives individuals hold on what the demands of security and liberty actually are, and on how these demands would best be met ... The presentation of security and liberty as binary opposites epitomized by the image of a set of scales thus has a certain political appeal. Nonetheless, the balance metaphor is inadequate as an analytical framework.[48]

---

[45] See Nicola McGarrity and Edward Santow, 'Anti-terrorism Laws: Balancing National Security and a Fair Hearing' in Victor Ramraj, Michael Hor, Kent Roach and George Williams (eds), *Global Anti-terrorism Law and Policy*, 2nd edn (Cambridge, Cambridge University Press, 2012) ch 6 (characterising some of this debate when it arises regarding elements of a fair proceeding).

[46] See Helga Haftendorn, 'The Security Puzzle: Theory-Building and Discipline-Building in International Security' (1991) 35 *International Studies Quarterly* 3.

[47] See, eg, President Barack Obama, 'National Security Strategy' *The White House* (May 2010) www.whitehouse.gov/sites/default/files/rss_viewer/national_security_strategy.pdf (describing the 'war' against al-Qaeda as only one of many areas in which national security is an issue).

[48] Macdonald, above, n 28, 143, 145.

Macdonald points out the risk of using imagery in 'complex and emotionally-charged debates'.[49] He also notes that this metaphor addresses the wrong question. The metaphor's focus on increasing security fails to address the problems that arise from disproportionate levels of public fear.[50]

An effective metaphor explains something that might otherwise be confusing. The metaphor of balance, presented as a simplistic binary between liberty and security, may have been intended to help in understanding. In practice, however, it can have the opposite effect, basically to oversimplify complex issues and provide a sort of cover for governmental actions that may not, at all, fit into the binary as presented.[51] The metaphor of 'balance' between liberty and security, particularly in the post-9/11 world, may sound comforting, but it is not based on reality and it cannot stand as an argumentation foundation for making decisions on legal standards.

III. The Paradigm Fractures: The Misleading American Crime-or-War Detentions Debate

In chapter three above, a conversation regarding the so-called 'Underwear Bomber' was used to demonstrate that, among some US officials, the narrative as to terrorism-detention structures had fractured, with some thinking that the case should be handled under the traditional criminal justice paradigm and with others thinking that it should be handled under a war detention model. The war-versus-crime paradigm also arose in chapter four above when discussing some of the characteristics of post-9/11 detention models. It came up, yet again, in chapter five above as a strong underpinning to the differential detention regime used for non-citizens perceived as the terrorist Other. As mentioned elsewhere in this book, the same narrative facts can serve different purposes in deconstructing the post-9/11 narrative, and different components of this argumentation played out in different ways, and in conjunction with each other in varying forms, similar to the multi-dimensional picture in a kaleidoscope.

This debate is therefore also important in this chapter, because it represents a different level of binary argumentation that was sometimes used to address,

---

[49] Macdonald, above, n 43, 539.

[50] ibid.

[51] For further critiques of rhetoric of balance between civil liberties and security, see generally David Cole and James Dempsey, *Terrorism and the Constitution: Sacrificing Civil Liberties in the Name of National Security*, 3rd ed (New York, New Press, 2006); Lucia Zedner, 'Securing Liberty in the Face of Terror: Reflections from Criminal Justice' (2005) 32(4) *Journal of Law and Society* 507; Daniel Farber (ed), *Security v. Liberty: Conflicts Between Civil Liberties and National Security in American History* (New York, Russell Sage, 2008).

in simplistic terms, what was actually quite a complex debate. This binary was different from those previously addressed in this chapter. It was a largely US form of argumentation, which was not really adopted, in the detention debates, by other national jurisdictions. Within the US, it had some peculiar characteristics as well. It was presented as an either/or scenario between the criminal justice system and a system of wartime detentions, in situations that suggested that both were equal, competing options, and that this was a settled matter when that was not at all the case.[52]

Although the war-versus-crime binary was often used to describe the disposition of terrorism suspects after 9/11, it is important to say at the outset that most terrorism cases, including within the US, have continued to be handled under the criminal justice system.[53] Moreover, if successful convictions are an indicator of success of that system—and that is by no means assumed, particularly in jurisdictions with a presumption of innocence—it is apparent that the fight against terrorism has encountered considerably more success in traditional criminal courtrooms than it has under the various forms of extraordinary detentions.[54] Various statistics produced to mark the tenth anniversary of the attacks support this proposition. For instance, the US Department of Justice (DOJ) noted, in 2011, that the criminal justice system had been successful in the years since 9/11, and various sources reported, as the 10-year anniversary of 9/11 approached, that between 35,000 and 38,000 terrorism suspects had been convicted worldwide through criminal justice systems.[55] The DOJ report indicated:

> Over the past decade, the department has successfully and securely used the criminal
> justice system to convict and incarcerate hundreds of defendants for terrorism and

---

[52] See Note, 'Responding to Terrorism: Crime, Punishment, and War' (2002) 115(4) *Harvard Law Review* 1217 (presenting an early argument about the lack of logic in responding to the 9/11 attacks with a war model and comparing this to criminal-justice responses to earlier terrorist attacks); Jeremy Elkins, 'The Model of War' (2010) 38(2) *Political Theory* 214.

[53] See Richard B Zabel and James J Benjamin, Jr, *In Pursuit of Justice: Prosecuting Terrorism Cases in the Federal Courts, Human Rights First* (2008) www.humanrightsfirst.org/wp-content/uploads/pdf/080521-USLS-pursuit-justice.pdf (hereinafter Zabel and Benjamin I) (studying, then updating in 2009, a comprehensive review of anti-terrorism cases prosecuted in US courts); Richard B Zabel and James J Benjamin, Jr, *In Pursuit of Justice: Prosecuting Terrorism Cases in the Federal Courts: 2009 Update and Recent Developments, Human Rights First*, www.humanrightsfirst.org/wp-content/uploads/pdf/090723-LS-in-pursuit-justice-09-update.pdf; United States Department of Justice, 'Ten Years Later: The DOJ after 9/11: Protecting America through Investigation & Criminal Prosecution', www.justice.gov/911/protect.html (listing examples of successful prosecutions both in relation to international and 'home-grown' terrorism); see also Martha Mendoza, 'Since 9/11, at Least 35,000 Terrorism Convictions Worldwide' *Denver Post* (3 September 2011) www.denverpost.com/nation-world/ci_18822690 (describing a freedom of information request that found 35,117 terrorism convictions in 66 countries since 9/11 and explaining that some convictions were for abusive enforcement of terrorism laws by governments).

[54] ibid, all sources; see also Kent Roach, 'The Criminal Law and its Less Restrained Alternatives' in Ramraj, above, n 45.

[55] See, eg, Mendoza, above, n 53.

terrorism-related offences that occurred both in the United States and overseas, including plots targeting both civilian and military targets. These post-9/11 terror prosecutions have proceeded without any terror defendant escaping federal custody or terrorist retaliation against a judicial district.[56]

Another area in which criminal justice systems have arguably proven superior to extraordinary detention regimes is in curbing governmental abuse. In Canada, a terrorism conviction was thrown out when it was determined that the government had undertaken extensive efforts to persuade the defendants to commit an act of terrorism, amounting to entrapment.[57] That said, there has also been criticism that terrorism prosecutions in some places have involved abusive governmental tactics to stifle dissent.[58]

The US suggestion was that terrorism detentions after 9/11 were being addressed under one of these paradigms—criminal justice or the war paradigm. However, as will be argued in this section, what actually happened was quite different. Most terrorism cases in the US continued to be processed through the criminal justice system. A much smaller number of cases began to be handled through a new, sort of hybrid, regime that arose, in which the US drew some elements from the criminal justice system and some from traditional war paradigms, but in which the approach was really not fully contained within either pre-existing paradigm. It was this particular binary that arguably led to the parallel detention structures seen at Guantanamo Bay, the policies allowing for torture, and the claim that a system of Military Commissions could simply replace pre-existing Article III courts in the US, which oversee criminal prosecutions in matters regarding terrorism.

When sending those people who it designated as unlawful enemy combatants to Guantanamo Bay and its Military Commissions, the US asserted, basically, that it could not proceed at all within the criminal justice paradigm, but also that the wartime paradigm did not quite work either. The entire structure of the Military Commissions is based on a US assertion that those detained at Guantanamo Bay are 'enemy combatants' or 'unlawful enemy combatants', and thus that the laws of war do not apply to them.[59] While using language that has many of the hallmarks of being relevant to wartime, the US appears, in fact, to have laid out a new

---

[56] United States Department of Justice, above, n 53.

[57] *R v Nuttall*, 2016 BCSC 1404.

[58] See, eg, Mendoza, above, n 53 (describing cases uncovered around the world, in response to Associated Press Freedom of Information requests, which showed that some people were prosecuted for terrorism as part of abusive governmental use of such systems to stifle peaceful protest).

[59] See *Hamdan v. Rumsfeld*, 548 US 557 (2006) (clarifying that the Geneva Conventions do apply to the detainees at Guantanamo Bay and finding that the Military Commissions, in their then form, violated the US Uniform Code of Military Justice (UCMJ), 10 USC ß801 et seq (2000 ed and Supp III) and Common Art 3 of the Geneva Conventions); see also Fionnaula Ni Aolain and Oren Gross (eds), *Guantanamo and Beyond: Exceptional Courts and Military Commissions in Comparative Perspective* (Cambridge, Cambridge University Press, 2013) (containing an excellent array of essays considering the use of special courts, including military commissions).

detention paradigm, which does not quite fit either the criminal justice or the war-time detention regimes. For instance, the US asserts the right to hold detainees in its War on Terror, potentially indefinitely, as related to the idea of prisoners of war, who are held until the end of hostilities. At the same time, the US has established the Military Commissions, which try the detainees in a way that is similar to, but by no means identical to, that undertaken in criminal proceedings.

An overlap between wartime actions and criminal detentions is not completely unprecedented, as evidenced in criminal prosecutions, for instance, of those accused of war crimes.[60] However, the model under which two similarly situated detainees could go through different systems, based largely on an Executive decision, is a new fracturing of these paradigms that has continued with some modifications in the US since the early days after 9/11.

Other jurisdictions that responded to the 9/11 attacks did not adopt this war-based paradigm in their detention practices, although, as discussed in chapter five above, they sometimes targeted non-citizens through other extraordinary detention measures. This difference even on this particular approach resulted in a certain fragmenting of terrorism detention practices across jurisdictions. For example, Sir Ken McDonald QC, the former Director of Public Prosecutions in the UK, said of the 7/7 attacks and in critique of government officials who were saying otherwise:

> London is not a battlefield. Those innocents who were murdered on July 7, 2005 were not victims of war. And the men who killed them were not, as in their vanity they claimed on their ludicrous videos, 'soldiers'. They were deluded, narcissistic inadequates. They were criminals. They were fantasists. We need to be very clear about this. On the streets of London, there is no such thing as a 'war on terror', just as there can be no such thing as a 'war on drugs'.
>
> The fight against terrorism on the streets of Britain is not a war. It is the prevention of crime, the enforcement of our laws and the winning of justice for those damaged by their infringement.[61]

In addition, Indonesia responded to the 2002 Bali attacks through criminal justice measures relating to detentions. The Indonesian government did not declare a war on terror, although it did use the military at times to respond to regional terrorism.[62] Umar Patek, captured in late 2011, was convicted by an Indonesian court for his role in carrying out the Bali attacks and was sentenced to 20 years in

---

[60] Tribunals such as the International Criminal Court operate in this purview. See Rome Statute of the International Criminal Court, 17 July 1998, 2187 UNTS 90, entered into force 1 July 2002.

[61] Clare Dyer, 'There is No War on Terror: Outspoken DPP Takes on Blair and Reid over Fear-Driven Legal Response to Threat' *The Guardian* (24 January 2007) www.guardian.co.uk/politics/2007/jan/24/uk.terrorism (speech to the Criminal Bar Association).

[62] See Kent Roach, *The 9/11 Effect: Comparative Counter-Terrorism* (New York, Cambridge University Press, 2011) 143–58 (describing and giving context to Indonesia's more moderate response after 9/11 and to the Bali attacks).

prison in June 2012.[63] Perhaps because of its history, Indonesia pursued a more moderate approach than that espoused by the US—enacting new anti-terrorism legislation in 2002, but through a democratic process and resisting the war model espoused by the US.[64]

The outcome for Patek is in contrast to that for Khalid Sheikh Mohammed, long claimed by the US to have been the 'mastermind' behind the 9/11 attacks. Mohammed has been detained at Guantanamo Bay since 2003, has never faced a criminal court, was tortured, including being waterboarded 'at least 183 times', and has a case pending before a Guantanamo Bay Military Commission that has not reached a final disposition as of the writing of this book.[65]

The controversy over the legitimacy of the actions undertaken by the US aside, cases such as these suggest a difference in terms of efficacy of approaches. Like the 9/11 attacks, the Bali attacks were claimed to have been undertaken by al-Qaeda, and a criminal prosecution was clearly possible and resulted in a significant sentence.

Mohammed, by contrast, can likely never be brought before a criminal proceeding in the US, in part because, presumably, his statements, elicited under torture, would not be admissible. Instead, almost 17 years after the 9/11 attacks, his legal proceeding before a Military Commission has not concluded. Even when it does, legitimacy questions will remain if he is convicted, because of the nature of his detention, the nature of the Military Commissions and the now-undisputed fact that he was tortured. An ongoing problem for some terrorism prosecutions is also the fact that information is often gained as intelligence, which does not clearly translate into admissible evidence for a criminal proceeding, or is deemed protected, and this may motivate governments to try to hold people without a criminal proceeding.[66] If one of the objectives of a prosecution is punishment, or some sense of justice for the victims, survivors and loved ones, the Military Commissions have failed to achieve these objectives.

The Guantanamo detainees are all accused, although often not charged even before the Military Commissions, with some form of past action that involved

---

[63] Rudy Madanir and Hilary Whiteman, 'Indonesian Court Sentences Bali Bomber to 20 Years in Jail' *CNN* (21 June 2012) www.cnn.com/2012/06/21/world/asia/patek-bali-bombing-verdict/index. html.

[64] Roach, above, n 62, 143–58.

[65] Spellings of his name vary. Senate Select Committee on Intelligence, *Committee Study of the Central Intelligence Agency's Detention and Interrogation Program* (updated for release 3 April 2014) 85; Office of Military Commissions, *9/11: Khalid Shaikh Mohammed et al, Office of Military Commissions*, www.mc.mil/CASES.aspx (direct links do not appear to specific cases, but the case of Khalid Shaikh Mohammed is hyperlinked on the referenced site).

[66] See Kent Roach, 'The Unique Challenges of Terrorism Prosecutions: Towards a Workable Relation Between Intelligence and Evidence', *Report of Inquiry into the Investigation of the Bombing of Air India Flight 182*, vol 4, 297–98 (Ottawa, Government of Canada, Minister of Public Words and Government Services, 2010) (discussing the issue of intelligence versus evidence).

either terrorism or taking up arms against the US. This belief is manifest in the entire structure of the Military Commissions, which are pseudo-criminal bodies before which detainees are charged with some form of past action, tried and, if convicted, given some form of sentence.[67]

Thus, the objective is based on a notion of punishment for a past action, and implicit in that is the prevention of future offences—ideals that are actually more consistent with traditional criminal justice systems than with typical war-time detentions. Perhaps cognisant of this gap, the potential crimes before the Military Commission contain 'offences' that are called war crimes. Some of these have been invalidated before US courts, once the cases reach the courts on appeal from the Military Commission system, because they were fabricated offences that did not exist in domestic or international law before the creation of the Military Commissions, which was generally after the events giving rise to the charges occurred.[68]

There is no question that modern warfare has changed. Some scholarship since 9/11 has focused on whether the 9/11 attacks, and the responses, demonstrate that the war paradigm itself has shifted.[69] Other scholarship has also suggested that the emergence of new forms of enemies suggests that traditional battlefields—and thus accepted laws of war—no longer operate in the same manner.[70] Both questions are valid and important, and they also suggest that the issues raised here and in other scenarios are far too complex to be reduced to a simple binary.

---

[67] See, eg, *United States of America v Khadr: Charge Sheet* (2007) www.defense.gov/news/Apr2007/ Khadrreferral.pdf (containing list of charges against Canadian citizen Omar Khadr, described as an 'alien unlawful combatant', all stemming from Khadr's alleged actions in Afghanistan in 2002); US Department of Defense, 'Military Commissions: Fairness, Transparency, Justice: About Us', *Military Commissions*, www.mc.mil (describing the military commissions and noting '[a]n alien unprivileged enemy belligerent who has engaged in hostilities, or who has purposefully and materially supported hostilities against the United States, its coalition partners or was a part of al Qaeda, is subject to trial by military commission under the Military Commissions Act of 2009'); see also Kent Roach, 'Guest Blog: Omar Khadr, KSM and Military Commissions', *International & Transnational Criminal Law*, rjcurrie.typepad.com/international-and-transna/2012/05/guest-blog-omar-khadr-ksm-and-military-commissions.html (noting that 'Military commissions as conducted at Guantanamo represent a new paradigm that fall outside the traditional laws of war and crime').

[68] See, eg, *United States of America v Hamdan*, No 11-1257 (DC Cir 2012) (overturning Hamdan's 'conviction' before a Military Commission because the offences with which he was charged did not exist in international law at the time of the incidents alleged, and such crimes could not be prosecuted retroactively).

[69] See, eg, Dyzenhaus, above, n 29; and Roach, above, n 29.

[70] See, eg, Frédéric Mégret, 'War and the Vanishing Battlefield' (2012) 9(1) *Loyola University Chicago International Law Review* (arguing that some of the deconstruction of the concept of the 'battlefield', dominant since 9/11, is eroding the normative force of laws relating to warfare); Keith Spicer, *Sitting on Bayonets: America's Endless War on Terror and the Paths to Peace* (Createspace, 2012); Ali Khan, *A Theory of International Terrorism: Understanding Islamic Militancy* (The Hague, Martinus Nijhoff Publishers, 2006) (arguing that the ontology after 9/11 regarding Islamic militancy is being used to justify a number of human rights violations, including the 'War on Terror').

On some levels, it appears that the crime-versus-war binary is more a matter of public presentation than a reflection of reality. In fact, this appears to represent, to an extent, a false narrative, as the most controversial detention structures under the US 'war' paradigm do not represent wartime detentions, even under the US's own representations. Rather, the Military Commissions, and detentions such as those at Guantanamo Bay, appear to represent a third line of detention structure, drawing some elements from the criminal justice paradigm, some from the war-time paradigm and not entirely fitting into either category.[71]

A. Declaration of War, Abandonment of War Rhetoric and Resurrecting the War Rhetoric

Wartime language emerged early after the attacks on a number of fronts, and initially not only in the US. For example, on 12 September 2001, the UN, in Security Council Resolution 1368 (2001), strongly condemned the terrorist attacks and used terminology relating to the right of self-defence, describing the terrorists as a 'threat to international peace and security'.[72] While calling for the accountability for those responsible for the attacks, the Resolution also reiterates the right of 'individual and collective self-defence'.[73]

The US has sent some confusing signals over the years as to whether it considered itself to be at war. Much can be said to criticise the idea of a war against terrorism. Conflicts undertaken in Afghanistan and Iraq bear more of the hallmarks of a traditional war scenario than does the overarching 'War on Terror', which could be invoked to detain people as unlawful enemy combatants even when those people were not apprehended on a battlefield.[74] The inconsistent nature of this discourse suggests its importance in legitimating certain actions.

The 'War on Terror' and the 'Global War on Terror' were terms used consistently during the administration of then-President George W Bush, who obviously introduced the idea in the US after 9/11. Shortly after President Barack Obama's inauguration, his administration signalled that it would abandon the war discourse and war approaches that had been employed by the prior administration.

---

[71] See Roach, above, n 62; see also the Military Commission Table, reproduced below.
[72] Security Council Resolution 1368, UN SCOR, 4370th mtg, UN Doc S/RES/1368 (2001).
[73] ibid.
[74] See, eg, the discussion of Jose Padilla's case in ch 4 above, who was arrested in Chicago, and the cases of the Algerian Six, arrested in Bosnia after a court proceeding acquitting them of terrorism-related charges. See Almir Maljević, 'Extraordinary Renditions: Shadow Proceedings, Human Rights, and "the Algerian Six": The War on Terror in Bosnia and Herzegovina' in Marianne Wade and Almir Maljevic (eds), *A War on Terror? The European Stance on a New Threat, Changing Laws and Human Rights Implications* (New York, Springer, 2009) 261.

On his first day in office, Obama issued an executive order, instituting a study of Guantanamo Bay, with the objective of closing the prison camp within a year.[75] Commentary from that time suggests a belief that this phase of US policy was about to end, perhaps not completely, but to a large extent regarding the war rhetoric.[76] As this was ongoing, high-level governmental officials, most notably Secretary of State Hillary Clinton, indicated that the use of the expression 'war on terror' was going to be abandoned. Reporters in Europe had noted, early in the Obama Administration, that the US government had stopped using the term, and when Clinton was asked about it, she said: 'The administration has stopped using the phrase and I think that speaks for itself.'[77]

In November 2009, the US government announced that some detainees from Guantanamo Bay would be tried in US federal courts, while others would be held potentially permanently at the detention centre, creating some confusion over the status of those remaining detainees. The most prominent of the announced trials in the US—that of Khalid Sheikh Mohammed, discussed above, who was accused of being the mastermind behind 9/11—did not, in fact, ultimately take place there. Mohammed is currently facing a proceeding before a Military Commission at Guantanamo Bay, after a significant backlash erupted in response to the possibility of him being sent to the US to stand trial.[78]

In spite of early signals under Obama that the government would abandon the war rhetoric espoused shortly after the attacks, it is increasingly apparent that much of that rhetoric, and this hybrid line of approach at Guantanamo Bay, will continue. In 2010, for example, a highly controversial Military Commission proceeding went forward against Omar Khadr, a Canadian citizen who was captured by US forces in Afghanistan when he was 15 years old, seeming to nullify Obama Administration's early promises that the Military Commission and Guantanamo Bay detentions would cease.[79]

---

[75] Barak Obama, 'Executive Order 13492—Review and Disposition of Individuals Detained at the Guantanamo Bay Naval Base and Closure of Detention Facilities', *Government Printing Office* (22 January 2009) www.gpo.gov/fdsys/pkg/CFR-2010-title3-vol1/pdf/CFR-2010-title3-vol1-eo13492.pdf.

[76] See, eg, Greg Miller, 'Obama Preserves Renditions as Counter-terrorism Tool' *Los Angeles Times* (1 February 2009) articles.latimes.com/2009/feb/01/nation/na-rendition1 (noting '[t]he CIA's secret prisons are being shuttered. Harsh interrogation techniques are off-limits. And Guantanamo Bay will eventually go back to being a wind-swept naval base on the southeastern corner of Cuba').

[77] 'Clinton: New Team Not Using "War on Terror" Term' *USA Today* (2009) www.usatoday.com/news/washington/2009-03-30-global-war_N.htm.

[78] See Office of Military Commissions, *9/11: Khalid Shaikh Mohammed et al*, *Office of Military Commissions*, www.mc.mil/CASES.aspx.

[79] For background on the Khadr case, see Maureen T Duffy, 'Between a Rock and a Hard Place: An Unjust Ending to an Unjust Process for Omar Khadr' *ABlawg* (27 October 2010) ablawg.ca/2010/10/27/between-a-rock-and-a-hard-place-an-unjust-ending-to-an-unjust-process-for-omar-khadr (criticising the entire process leading to Khadr's 'guilty' plea before the Military

After Anwar al-Aulaki was killed in a targeted strike in Yemen, the Obama Administration further signalled that the war rhetoric was continuing, and it has continued ever since. In March 2012, US Attorney General Eric Holder gave a speech in which he defended the US government's targeted killing programme. He said:

> I'm grateful for the opportunity to join with you in discussing a defining issue of our time—and a most critical responsibility that we share: how we will stay true to America's founding—and enduring—promises of security, justice and liberty.

> Since this country's earliest days, the American people have risen to this challenge—and all that it demands. But, as we have seen—and as President John F. Kennedy may have described best—'In the long history of the world, only a few generations have been granted the role of defending freedom in its hour of maximum danger.'

> Half a century has passed since those words were spoken, but our nation today confronts grave national security threats that demand our constant attention and steadfast commitment. It is clear that, once again, we have reached an 'hour of danger'.

> We are a nation at war. And, in this war, we face a nimble and determined enemy that cannot be underestimated.[80]

This war rhetoric was echoed the next month, when a US official acknowledged that the US was undertaking a programme of targeted killing against suspected terrorists, justified, he argued, by the *Authorization for Use of Military Force* issued shortly after the attacks.[81] Increasingly, at least for the US, the war discourse is showing signs of becoming a permanent feature of its anti-terrorism initiatives. Obama left office without closing the Guantanamo Bay prison, and the Military Commissions are still operating. Obama did reduce the number of prisoners there and did not send new prisoners.[82] Trump has made statements suggesting

---

Commission); Maureen T Duffy, 'A "Convicted Terrorist" by Any Other Name' *ABlawg* (13 May 2015) ablawg.ca/2015/05/13/a-convicted-terrorist-by-any-other-name (critiquing the media for often unquestioningly accepting the terminology used to describe Khadr, which is generally inaccurate and prejudicial).

[80] US Department of Justice, 'Attorney General Eric Holder Speech on Targeted Killing of U.S. Citizens: Full Transcript' *Public Intelligence* (6 March 2012) publicintelligence.net/attorney-general-eric-holder-speech-on-targeted-killing-of-u-s-citizens-full-transcript.

[81] John O Brennan, Assistant to the President for Homeland Security and Counterterrorism, 'The Ethics and Efficacy of the President's Counterterrorism Strategy', Speech at the Woodrow Wilson International Centre (2012) www.youtube.com/watch?v=cM4mCEXi5v4; Mark Mardell, 'White House in First Detailed Comments on Drone Strikes' *BBC News* (1 May 2012) www.bbc.co.uk/news/world-us-canada-17901400 (explaining that the US is in a 'war' with the Taliban and al-Qaeda, and explaining the US's reasons for arguing that targeted killings are lawful under the laws of war).

[82] See, eg, Carole Rosenberg, 'Guantanamo by the Numbers' *Miami Herald* (25 October 2016, updated 10 June 2017) www.miamiherald.com/news/nation-world/world/americas/guantanamo/article2163210.html (one of a series of articles by *Miami Herald* reporter Carol Rosenberg, in which, among other things, she has kept track of the movements of prisoners and resulting tallies at Guantanamo Bay).

that he will expand use of the detention centre and he has also vowed to bring back torture at the prison.[83] The war rhetoric is clearly in the US to stay, at least for now.

B. War versus Crime or a Third, Hybrid Paradigm?[84]

As the war rhetoric became dominant in the discourse again, the question continues as to whether detentions such as those at Guantanamo Bay actually fit under a wartime paradigm as suggested in much of the political narrative. Some effort has been made by the US government to suggest that the Military Commissions are not terribly different from either the criminal law or wartime paradigms, and it appears that the detention scenario at Guantanamo Bay borrows elements from each paradigm.

As an example, the US Office of Military Commissions posted a table purporting to compare the three 'legal systems', consisting of the criminal justice system (Article III courts), traditional courts martial and the Military Commissions undertaken at Guantanamo Bay, and advancing the notion that the three are quite similar. This appears to be an attempt to show that the Military Commissions are comparable to the other proceedings in terms of fairness, and it is a clear attempt to infuse this notion into the political narrative. Similarities to the pre-existing paradigms are emphasised and differences are not always mentioned.

An introduction to the table mixes some of the language of the old and of the new, noting that the Military Commissions were born of 'military necessity' and that they are a form of military tribunal, then noting that the history of military commissions goes back, in varying forms, to the days of the Revolutionary War. This presentation of the Military Commissions as part of a long tradition dating back to the early days of the US strongly communicates a position that these structures are not new. However, the same introduction implies that there is something new about these particular Military Commissions when it notes that they were created out of military necessity, which is described as the underpinning of the commissions. The following portion of the table illustrates this attempt to show

---

[83] Phil Mattingly and Kevin Liptak, 'First on CNN: GOP Senators Push Trump on "Expansion" of Guantanamo Bay' *CNN* (13 February 2017) http://edition.cnn.com/2017/02/13/politics/guantanamo-bay-senator-letter/index.html (giving a sense of the state of political commentary on the issue as of early 2017).

[84] The binary is presented in its most simple form, but there are acknowledged, additional layers of binaries that could be discussed as well. See, eg, René Provost, 'Asymmetrical Reciprocity and Compliance with the Laws of War' in Benjamin Perrin (ed), *Modern Warfare: Armed Groups, Private Militaries, Humanitarian Organizations, and the Law* (Vancouver, UBC Press, 2012) 17 (discussing the dangers of current arguments about reciprocity in warfare relating to compliance with international humanitarian law and suggesting a legal pluralistic approach as a means of enhancing compliance with these laws, particularly in more recent, irregular forms of warfare).

that the Military Commissions are really not all that new in relation to pre-existing criminal proceedings and military hearings, and illustrates some of the factors used to compare these entities:[85]

RULE OR PROCEDURE	Military Commissions	Courts-Martial	Article III Court
Basic Procedural Protections			
Accused is presumed innocent until proven guilty	✓	✓	✓
Prosecution bears the burden of proof	✓	✓	✓
Guilt must be proved beyond a reasonable doubt	✓	✓	✓
Trial must take place without undue delay	✓	✓	✓

Where the Military Commissions differ, most notably in terms of evidence rules, from criminal proceedings or traditional courts martial, the presentation still suggests that they are not significantly different. The table is too long to reproduce here in its entirety, but it compares certain procedural issues, such as the right to counsel or the admissibility of hearsay evidence, again suggesting that the three systems are comparable and in some cases, such as in the allowance of free legal counsel regardless of ability to pay, even going so far as to suggest that the Military Commission provides better protection for detainees, at least than Article III courts:[86]

RULE OR PROCEDURE	Military Commissions	Courts-Martial	Article III Court
Defense counsel at no cost, regardless of ability to pay more info	✓	✓	
Defense counsel at no cost for indigent accused	✓	✓	✓
May hire counsel at no cost to the government more info	✓ Subject to certain limitations	✓	✓
Attorney client privilege is honored	✓	✓	✓

---

[85] Reproduced portion of the full table, which can be found at Office of Military Commissions, 'About Us: Legal System Comparison' (2012), *Military Commissions: Fairness, Transparency, Justice*, www.mc.mil/ABOUTUS/LegalSystemComparison.aspx (this reproduction is an earlier version of the table, which has been changed only in terms of design, not substance. This earlier version was chosen to use here for greater readability on reproduction. Formatting has been adjusted for the purpose of continuity with the book style).

[86] ibid.

It is unlikely that the people held at Guantanamo Bay (some since 2002) who were tortured, kept isolated from the world and often fighting vigorously to have their cases heard in Article III courts would agree with this presentation of the three proceedings as essentially comparable. There is certainly room to challenge some of the representations made here about the Military Commissions.

This table also, maybe not intentionally, contradicts the US war rhetoric by making it clear that the Military Commissions are not military courts in the traditional sense at all. Rather, the US has established a third line of proceedings, sort of a hybrid, which draws some elements from courts martial used in the military (but varies from those) and draws some elements from the criminal justice system (but varies from those as well).

The political narrative that was used to persuade a receptive audience of the need for these extraordinary detention mechanisms, involving the war-versus-crime binary, does not quite reflect the true state of affairs. The fractured narrative, apparent on a number of levels in this particular discourse, appears to have given rise to an entirely new system of 'justice' for some people in some cases.[87] The issue of prosecutions before the Military Commissions is by no means settled, as former detainees continue to raise challenges. Thus, this debate and the underpinnings of argumentation that led to the creation of the Military Commissions remain highly relevant.

Currently, Ali Hamza Ahmad Suliman al-Bahlul is seeking review before the Supreme Court of the United States for his 'conviction' before the Military Commission. He seeks relief based on the assertion, already accepted in some lower courts, that the crime of which he was 'convicted' did not exist in international or domestic law at the time of the actions giving rise to the charges.[88] This will have obvious implications for the relatively few other cases that have completely proceeded through the Military Commission system, including the high-profile case of Omar Khadr, the 15-year-old Canadian citizen whose 'guilty plea' before the Military Commission was surrounded by extremely disturbing circumstances that undermined its legitimacy.[89]

However, what is clear is that the claim of a choice between war courts or traditional criminal courts in terrorism cases has been advanced through political

---

[87] See *Bowden Institution v Khadr*, 2015 SCC 26 (the third Supreme Court of Canada decision in Khadr's favour, which reflects the significant problems that arose after Khadr was repatriated to serve his Military Commission sentence in Canada, and the Canadian courts had to try to figure out how these non-criminal offenses compared to Canada's actual crimes. Khadr's 'conviction' before the Military Commission is currently on appeal in the US and similar appeals are proceeding for other former detainees).

[88] Mark Gollom, 'Khadr's War Crimes Appeal Could Hinge on Bin Laden Propagandist's Case' *CBC News* (21 July 2017) www.cbc.ca/news/world/omar-khadr-appeal-war-crimes-case-al-bahlul-1.4214566 (containing statements from Omar Khadr's American lawyer, suggesting that another case, which the former detainee is asking the Supreme Court of the United States to hear, could be dispositive in invalidating questionable 'war crimes' charges brought against Guantanamo Bay Military Commission defendants, including Omar Khadr).

[89] ibid; Duffy, 'Between a Rock and a Hard Place', above, n 79.

commentary as a false dichotomy, when the very structuring of the Guantanamo Bay Military Commissions demonstrates that the US has really created a hybrid tribunal, with elements favourable to the government selected from the pre-existing paradigms and with terminology designed to confuse a public audience that seems to still be highly receptive to persuasion on this issue. Whether the courts will be so persuaded remains to be seen.

IV. Terrorism Detentions: 'Everything Old is New Again'[90]

This third example contains a binary that is different still from the ones previously discussed in this chapter. It relates primarily to detention changes in the US and it draws on past practices, or continuing practices, in other national jurisdictions. The main difference between this binary and those previously discussed is that this binary has been less stated and was more implied. Thus, while not expressly stated as an argumentation basis for altering terrorism detention practices, like the other binaries discussed, the things that actually were said and done made it clear that this binary was part of the fabric of the post-9/11 political discourse regarding terrorism detentions.

As discussed at length in chapter four above, one of the points of departure for the post-9/11 political discourse was that something about the 9/11 attacks was different in a way that required the building of new terrorism-detention paradigms. That chapter detailed some of the characteristics of changes that were made to terrorism-detention practices after 9/11. These changes were new within the particular jurisdictions being discussed. It was this aspect of 'newness' for detention practices that was part of the point of departure in chapter four, as national jurisdictions sought to persuade different audiences that the terrorism-detention practices they had been using had to be changed. Thus, the changes were internal within those national jurisdictions.

The binary discussed in this section takes part of that argumentation point and views it from a different dimension, again similar to what happens when one turns a kaleidoscope. Like many of the argumentation tools discussed throughout this book, this binary could also have been discussed in relation to the point of departure underscoring chapter four. It is used here, instead, because of the fact that it has a binary orientation, with some tension between the idea of 'new' paradigms and 'old' ones. It is somewhat different from the point of departure in that chapter,

---

[90] This title is inspired by Peter Allen and Carole Bayer Sager, 'Everything Old is New Again' (song), *Continental American* (1974).

which looks to the argued need to build new detention regimes or regimes that are new to that particular national jurisdiction. This point, by contrast, acknowledges that while these paradigms may have been new to the national jurisdictions that used them after 9/11, they are not new when viewed more globally. It is this aspect of that picture that is expanded for consideration here.

While detention practices undoubtedly had indicia of newness within the national jurisdictions that changed them after 9/11, it does not necessarily follow that the practices were changed in a vacuum and were new in their entirety. Looking outside of the US, it becomes apparent that some of these 'new' practices were actually 'old' practices undertaken in other jurisdictions. Thus, this problematic argumentation feature is set forth as the 'old-versus-new' binary, and it is included even if it was not expressly stated, because the implication was significant to how detention practices may have changed.

While it is apparent that places like the US drew on practices from other countries, the US government did not appear to generally include this fact in its attempts to persuade the public of the need for new regimes. It cannot be definitively established, of course, that the US looked to other national practices in developing its own approaches to terrorism detention and interrogation. However, the existence of long-standing, and very similar, paradigms in those other places makes it clear that they must have.

Acknowledging that influence on the public might have been deemed unwise for US government officials at that time, when international law was being lambasted, popular sentiment suggested closing borders, and there was a certain derision directed out from the US, especially towards countries that did not join the US efforts. The ridiculous 'Freedom Fries' issue is an example of how popular sentiments were leaning.[91] If there had been much public discussion of the US looking to other nations to build its strategies, that might have backfired in such an atmosphere. Such an acknowledgement might also have undermined the claim that was being made at the time that the 9/11 attacks were different, specifically necessitating the building of 'new' regimes, as discussed in detail in chapter four above. If, in fact, the government had publicly said that it was adopting long-standing approaches from other jurisdictions, that point of departure would have been rendered less credible.

---

[91] See, eg, Jens David Ohlin, *The Assault on International Law* (Oxford, Oxford University Press, 2015); Robert J Delahunty and John Yoo, 'Against Foreign Law' (2005) 29 *Harvard Journal of Law & Public Policy* 291 (arguing that international and foreign law cannot be used to interpret US constitutional law and speculating as to why some judges use these resources); Sean Loughlin, 'House Cafeterias Change Names for "French" Fries and "French" Toast' *CNN* (12 March 2003) www.cnn.com/2003/ALLPOLITICS/03/11/sprj.irq.fries (discussing the notorious change to items on the Congressional cafeteria menu to express anger against the French for refusing to join in with the invasion of Iraq. The word 'French' was substituted with 'Freedom'); see ch 5 above.

Moreover, there would, of necessity, also have to be discussion of how those structures played out elsewhere, what worked, what did not and what lessons could be internalised as the US especially built its own 'new' detention paradigms. If, however, this influence was not acknowledged, then these 'new' structures would look much more experimental in nature, with a certain amount of trial and error tolerated. It is obvious, from things like the torture memos and the initial claims that no international or US constitutional law applied to the Guantanamo detainees, that the US was looking for ways to sidestep existing legal structures. Arguably, it would be easier to do so if the existence of similar structures elsewhere, and the lessons learned there, were not acknowledged. Comparing US actions to these 'old' practices reveals a new layer of critique to the regimes that the US built after 9/11. Thus, in order to examine this post-9/11 binary, it is useful to look back before the attacks, and outside of the US, to particular ways that certain jurisdictions dealt with terrorism detention and interrogation.

While the declaration of a War on Terror after 9/11 is arguably idiosyncratic to the US, the use of wartime, emergency or executive powers to undertake extraordinary detention actions is certainly not merely a post-9/11 US phenomenon, but has been used before in different ways in different places. The 'new' response by the US to the 'new' threat exposed by the 9/11 attacks was not necessarily new in many respects, but was arguably a reconfiguration of approaches taken in other jurisdictions with past experiences in fighting terrorism. That, in turn, suggests that the US was not building a new paradigm in response to a new threat, as it claimed to be doing, but was drawing on ideas from other jurisdictions in its quest to avoid existing detention paradigms in the US.

A. Extraordinary Detentions

This book does not try to address all variations on historical administrative, or extraordinary, detentions. It proceeds by example to make the point, and none of the discussions of the different scenarios are intended to be comprehensive. A number of examples could be considered, such as the aforementioned detentions of those of Japanese descent by the US and Canada during the Second World War, the 'emergency' detentions undertaken by Canada during its October crisis, or Lincoln's suspension of habeas corpus during the US Civil War. Those detention scenarios obviously vary greatly among them, but they show that there has been historical controversy across a number of fronts regarding detentions that are outside of a criminal justice model. Another factor that must be considered in reading this section is that, as discussed earlier in this book, the idea of Executive detentions are more familiar in some places than in others, and thus that post-9/11 changes may seem more shocking in some places than in others. However, for the purposes of this section, the focus is more on a comparison of historical practices with those undertaken by the US in its 'War on Terror'. Examples are given below.

i. The UK: Extraordinary Detentions during 'the Troubles'

An estimated 3,300 people were killed and 40,000 injured in terrorist attacks in the UK relating to Northern Ireland over a number of years.[92] In the early 1970s, approximately 2,500 people were detained under emergency regulations.[93] In his comparative analysis of anti-terrorism measures around the world, Kent Roach notes the similarities between the measures taken in the UK during the Troubles with Northern Ireland and anti-terrorism measures employed in former British colonies, such as Singapore, Malaysia and Palestine, after that time.[94] While this book argued in chapter four above that it was the US, and not places like the UK, that most heavily influenced anti-terrorism narratives after the 9/11 attacks, Roach persuasively argues that the UK had a greater influence around the world in terms of the form of these responses. Although the US war-like detentions appear to be quite different from how the UK and other nations responded to 9/11, there is much to suggest that the US responses were, in fact, influenced by past practices in the UK, among others.

A separate stream of anti-terrorism initiatives developed in former British colonies in the years before 9/11, as Roach argues, and it is additionally notable that India's policies appear to be part of this stream of influence.[95] This is a rather ironic development, as the UK's own approach to terrorism detentions after 9/11 appeared to be less influenced by what it did during the Troubles with Northern Ireland than the response implemented by the US was.[96]

The situation in the UK regarding Northern Ireland differed from the 9/11 attacks, in that the UK situation involved an ongoing pattern of violence over a protracted period of time.[97] As the violence continued, the pattern of extraordinary

---

[92] Roach, above, n 62, 244 (citing *Countering International Terrorism: The United Kingdom's Strategy*, Cmnd 6888, July 2006).

[93] ibid.

[94] ibid 244 45.

[95] ibid; see also Derek P Jinks, 'The Anatomy of an Institutionalized Emergency: Preventive Detention and Personal Liberty in India' (2000) 22 *Michigan Journal of International Law* 311, 313; Ujjwal Kumar Singh, 'Mapping Anti-terror Legal Regimes in India' in Ramraj, above, n 45 (describing India's 60-year history with terrorism, and the provision in the Indian Constitution allowing for preventive detention); Sudha Setty, 'Comparative Perspectives on Specialized Trials for Terrorism' (2010) 63 *Maine Law Review* 131 (addressing the then-heated controversy about creating special terrorism courts in the US by discussing such bodies in the UK, Israel and India).

[96] See Helen Fenwick and Gavin Phillipson, 'UK Counter-terror Law Post-9/11: Initial Acceptance of Extraordinary Measures and the Partial Return to Human Rights Norms' in Ramraj, above, n 45 (arguing that the UK chose a different route in fighting terrorism after 9/11 than the political route espoused earlier relating to Northern Ireland); compare Jessie Blackbourn, 'International Terrorism and Counterterrorist Legislation: The Case Study of Post-9/11 Northern Ireland' (2009) 21 *Terrorism and Political Violence* 133 (arguing that UK Prime Minister Tony Blair distinguished counter-terrorism in relation to Northern Ireland from that involving international terrorism after 9/11, following an 'accommodation' model regarding Northern Ireland and a 'suppression' model relating to international terrorism).

[97] See Stephen J Schulhofer, 'Checks and Balances in Wartime: American, British and Israeli Experiences' (2004) 102(8) *Michigan Law* Review 1906, 1931–33 (providing a detailed account of the pattern of violence relating to the IRA, as well as the development of the UK government responses).

detentions evolved in response. Examples that evoke the responses, especially in the US after 9/11, are included in this chapter.

ii. Administrative Detentions in Israel before 9/11

Commonalities can also be found with some of the approaches in Israel relating to terrorism detentions. Israel is well known for having faced a long-standing issue with terrorism and its anti-terrorism initiatives date back to the days of the British Mandate.[98] Terrorist attacks resulted in more than 300 deaths during the 1990s and over 1,000 deaths between 2000 and 2011.[99] The Israeli government reports that between 2015 and August 2017, 55 people were killed and 812 people were injured in terrorist attacks.[100]

It would be beyond the scope of this book to attempt to exhaustively describe Israel's anti-terrorism structure, as it is long-standing and complex. Rather, elements of this scheme that provide examples comparing these endeavours with those undertaken by the US after 9/11 are used.[101]

Early on, a variety of factors led to a perceived need to enact legislation to address what was perceived to be an ongoing emergency situation regarding terrorism.[102] Israel's Defence (Emergency) Regulation 1945 allowed for a number of extraordinary measures, including the power 'to demolish houses, decide on administrative detentions and deportations, and administer criminal justice before a military rather than an ordinary civilian court'.[103] Anti-terrorism provisions evolved over time.

Daphne Barak-Erez, formerly Dean of the Faculty of Law at Tel Aviv University and now a member of the Israeli Supreme Court, suggests that a criminal justice-versus-prevention binary is critical to understanding Israel's anti-terrorism mechanisms.[104] Like all of the national jurisdictions discussed herein, Israel has

[98] See Roach, above, n 62, 244–58 (discussing the UK's anti-terrorism initiatives before 9/11), 100–29 (describing pre-9/11 anti-terrorism initiatives in Israel); Daphne Barak-Erez, 'Israel's Anti-terrorism Law: Past, Present, and Future' in Ramraj, above, n 45, 597–620].

[99] Roach, above, n 62, 100 (citing statistics from the Israeli Ministry of Foreign Affairs); see also Claude Klein, 'On the Three Floors of a Legislative Building: Israel's Legal Arsenal in Its Struggle Against Terrorism' (2006) 25(5) *Cardozo Law Review* 2223 (for a detailed discussion of the evolution of Israel's anti-terrorism initiatives).

[100] Israel Ministry of Foreign Affairs, 'Wave of Terror 2015–2017', mfa.gov.il/MFA/ForeignPolicy/Terrorism/Palestinian/Pages/Wave-of-terror-October-2015.aspx.

[101] For a more comprehensive discussion of Israel's anti-terrorism regime, see, eg, David Kretzmer, *The Occupation of Justice: The Supreme Court of Israel and the Occupied Territories* (Albany, State University of New York Press, 2002).

[102] See Barak-Erez, above, n 98; Stephanie Cooper Blum, 'Preventive Detention in the War on Terror: A Comparison of How the United States, Britain, and Israel Detain and Incapacitate Terrorist Suspects' (2008) *Homeland Security Affairs* 1, 3, 8–11; Yigal Mersel, 'Judicial Review of Counter-terrorism Measures: The Israeli Model for the Role of the Judiciary during the Terror Era' (2006) 38 *New York University Journal of International Law and Politics* 67.

[103] Barak-Erez, above, n 98, 598; for another comprehensive discussion of the history, see Klein, above, n 99.

[104] Barak-Erez, above, n 98, 601.

criminal penalties for various acts related to terrorism, but prevention is a significant factor in its overall anti-terrorism legal regime. Administrative detentions are used in Israel as preventive measures to detain people who the government fears may engage in acts of terrorism in the future.[105] In 1979, Israel enacted the Emergency Powers Detention Law, which replaced the administrative detention provisions in the Defence (Emergency) Regulation and allows for preventive detention where the Minister of Defence has 'reasonable cause' to believe the person should be detained for reasons of 'state security or public security'.[106] The detention must be reviewed by a President of a District Court within 48 hours, with subsequent reviews every three months.[107] The evidence that forms the basis for the detention may be withheld from the detainee, but heard by the President of the District Court outside of the presence of the detainee if the President finds that disclosure would be detrimental to 'state security or public security'.[108] The law is only in effect when a state of emergency has been declared, but a state of emergency has been renewed continuously since 1948.[109]

The Basic Law: Dignity and Liberty, enacted in 1992, allows for judicial review of statutes, but does not apply retroactively, so it cannot be used in relation to the Emergency Powers Detention Law of 1979.[110] It can, however, be applied to the Internment of Unlawful Combatants Law, which was enacted in 2002.[111] This law, unlike many of its predecessors, does not require the issuance of an emergency for the law to apply, suggesting greater permanence in more recent legislation in this area.[112] Unlawful combatants are non-citizens 'who have directly or indirectly participated in hostilities against Israel or are members of forces that do so and who are not, as regular soldiers, entitled to prisoner of war status'.[113]

Roach points out that this third category resembles that followed by the US at Guantanamo Bay, suggesting that neither the laws of war or the criminal justice paradigm apply completely to anti-terrorism under this approach.[114] The similarities are striking and they cannot be attributed to coincidence. A difference is that the US, for its own reasons, has been reluctant to openly adopt a detention paradigm based entirely on prevention, even though, in practice, it is doing

---

[105] ibid.
[106] Roach, above, n 62, 117 (citing 36 LSI 89; an English translation of this law is available at (1990) 21 *Columbia Human Rights Law Review* 510).
[107] Barak-Erez, above, n 98, 602 (quoting s 6(c) of the Detentions Law).
[108] Roach, above, n 62, 119.
[109] Amnesty International, *Starved of Justice: Palestinians Detained without Trial by Israel* (2012) www.amnesty.org/en/library/asset/MDE15/026/2012/en/d33da4e1-b8d2-41fe-a072-ced579ba45c7/mde150262012en.pdf; Roach, above, n 62, 117.
[110] Barak-Erez, above, n 98, 600–01 (discussing 1992, SH 1391).
[111] ibid (also noting that in the Unlawful Combatants Decision, Crim A 6659/06 *A v Israel* (not published, 2008), the Supreme Court reviewed the Internments of Unlawful Combatants Law under the Basic Law and found it to be constitutional).
[112] ibid, 600, fn 10.
[113] Roach, above, n 62, 119.
[114] ibid.

exactly that. Security certificates in Canada and TPIMs in the UK also have a clear preventive aspect to them. Between 2000 and 2010, the Supreme Court of Israel considered 322 cases of administrative detention. None of these cases resulted in a release order, and the Court did not repudiate the use of secret evidence in any of them.[115]

iii. Special Tribunals for Terrorism Cases

The evolution of the US model for the Military Commissions has not quelled critiques of the Commissions based on questions of legitimacy. Talk of specialised terrorism courts seems to have lessened within the US, but the Military Commissions continue, although they have been used for a relatively small number of the cases of detainees being held at Guantanamo Bay. The US government has indicated that they will continue, under what it suggests are more 'fair' proceedings set forth in the Military Commissions Act of 2009.[116] However, the idea of separate courts for terrorism is not at all new and special courts have been used, and were used before 9/11, in a number of jurisdictions.

a. Diplock courts in the UK

The UK has used specialised courts for terrorism in the past. Roach describes an evolution of these detentions in the UK, noting that regulations relating to Northern Ireland initially allowed for indefinite detention of those suspected of acting in a way adverse to peace. Lord Diplock, after whom the Diplock courts were named, conceded that many held under this structure were held under evidence that was not sufficient. However, he commented that it was not possible to proceed under the criminal justice system, because of the continuing threat of terrorist attacks.[117] Although the UK did not declare a 'war' on terrorism, it appears that similar binaries regarding the criminal justice system were used and that there too, the criminal justice system was presumptively deemed to be inadequate. Roach describes an evolution under which initial objections to the manner of proceeding on detentions led to some additional procedural safeguards, which linked the detentions more explicitly to the threat of terrorism. People could be detained if suspected of involvement in terrorism. Yet, even with procedural safeguards added, Roach

---

[115] Shiri Krebs, 'Lifting the Veil of Secrecy: Judicial Review of Administrative Detentions in the Israeli Supreme Court' (2012) 45 *Vanderbilt Journal of International Law* 639 (addressing an empirical study of these decisions, written by a former advisor on legal matters to then-Chief-Justice Dorit Beinisch, President of the Israeli Supreme Court).

[116] See the Military Commissions Act 2009, Title XVIII of the National Defense Authorization Act for Fiscal Year 2010, Pub L 111-84, HR 2647, 123 Stat 2190 (enacted 28 October 2009).

[117] Roach, above, n 62, 245 (citing Lord Diplock, *Report of the Commission to Consider Legal Procedures to Deal with Terrorist Activities in Northern Ireland*, Cmnd 5185, 1972, paras 32 and 33).

notes that people could still be detained based on secret evidence and hearsay.[118] He explains:

> Even under the improved procedures, however, the commissioners and detention appeal tribunal relied on secret evidence and hearsay testimony. The hearsay was often provided by testimony from Special Branch officers about allegations from unnamed and perhaps unreliable informers or statements extracted from the detainee. Because so much secret evidence was considered, detainees often did not know the details of the allegations against them.[119]

Thus, many of the same controversies that surrounded the Diplock courts can be analogised to those surrounding the US Military Commissions, both in relation to the overarching need and legitimacy of such bodies and in relation to the asserted need to proceed with abridged rules in relation to procedure.

b. Military Courts in Israel

Looking to Israel, the process by which special courts were created to address the threat of terrorism can, again, be analogised to the approach taken by the US after 9/11. Like the US, Israel created military courts to address terrorism detentions, specifically after the 1967 Six-Day War, to try Palestinians suspected of terrorist attacks against Israel.[120] Israeli citizens, by contrast, are tried in the civil system for matters relating to terrorism.[121] The military courts have some vestiges of criminal proceedings, such as the right to habeas corpus review, but they involve limitations in other procedural respects. The Israeli Defense Forces have discretion to determine whether a Palestinian suspected of a terrorism-related matter is tried before a civilian court or a military court.[122]

Again, this system has some generalised analogies to the US Military Commissions at Guantanamo Bay.[123] The dichotomy in terms of process relating to citizens and non-citizens suggests, first, that terrorists are more likely to be non-citizens and, second, that it is acceptable to deprive non-citizens of procedural protections, while not doing the same with regard to citizens. Israel has also followed, with some differences, a quasi-military model in its procedural approaches to terrorism detentions, but only in some cases, with a parallel system of criminal

---

[118] ibid.

[119] ibid.

[120] Setty, above, n 95, 158; see also Kathleen Cavanaugh, 'The Israeli Military Court System in the West Bank and Gaza' (2007) 12 *Journal of Conflict & Security Law* 197; Amos Guiora, *Global Perspectives on Counterterrorism* (New York, Aspen, 2007).

[121] Setty, above, n 95, 158.

[122] ibid (explaining in depth the procedural differences between a military court and a civilian proceeding, as well as the various critiques of the use of these special courts).

[123] See generally Sudha Setty, 'The United States' in Kent Roach (ed), *Comparative Counter-terrorism Law* (Cambridge, Cambridge University Press, 2015) 49 (discussing the US system of addressing terrorism detentions).

justice ongoing for other cases. The similarities to the US post-9/11 approach are, again, striking.

The use of special courts, a military model in the case of Israel and a presumptive rejection of the criminal justice model in relation to the Diplock courts all bear similarities to changes in the US after 9/11. If nothing else, an assessment of the legitimacy of special terrorism courts would be more complete by looking to the experiences of jurisdictions that have implemented them before. A determination of what works and what does not in such a regime would obviously benefit from a close examination of other jurisdictions with similar experiences. Instead, the US gave the impression that it was building 'new' regimes and learning as it went along. Such an impression appears disingenuous.

iv. Targeted Killings

Targeted killings have been discussed previously in this book, particularly in relation to assertions by the US government that this practice is legitimate and necessary.[124] As explained earlier, while targeted killing is not specifically a detention practice, it is a more extreme form of deprivation of liberty, more extreme even than detention, which the US has asserted to be legal, specifically since 9/11. It is therefore relevant to this discussion. This tactic to deal with alleged terrorists has been used, rather controversially, by Israel for some time, and it appears that the US may have borrowed this tactic from the Israeli legal arsenal.

Targeted killings have been used by Israel against those considered to be active terrorists, and where the government involved argues that less harmful measures cannot be taken. Generally, the latter condition relates to the fact that the target is not physically present in Israel or within reach of the Israeli military through other means.[125] The normative structures surrounding this practice are considerably more structured than in the US, and the Israeli Supreme Court has ruled that, provided certain conditions are met, targeted killings may be permissible.[126] In laying out the issue, the Court placed the issue of terrorism in context, noting:

> In February 2000, the second *intifada* began. A massive assault of terrorism was directed against the State of Israel, and against Israelis, merely because they are Israelis. This assault of terrorism differentiates neither between combatants and civilians, nor between women, men, and children. The terrorist attacks take place both in the territory of Judea, Samaria, and the Gaza Strip, and within the borders of the State of Israel. They are directed against civilian centers, shopping centers and markets, coffee houses and restaurants. Over the last five years, thousands of acts of terrorism have been committed

---

[124] See the discussion of the US programme for targeted strikes in chs 4 and 5 above.

[125] Barak-Erez, above, n 98, 610.

[126] ibid; HCJ 769/02 *The Public Committee against Torture in Israel v The Government of Israel* (not published, 2006) (in English), elyon1.court.gov.il/files_eng/02/690/007/A34/02007690.a34.pdf (hereinafter *Targeted Killings Decision*).

against Israel. In the attacks, more than one thousand Israeli citizens have been killed. Thousands of Israeli citizens have been wounded. Thousands of Palestinians have been killed and wounded during this period as well.[127]

The Court then discussed the arguments of the parties, including the argument that innocent civilians are frequently killed in these strikes.[128] It concluded that targeted killings could nonetheless be permissible if the military established a number of things, and a rather heavy burden of proof is placed on the military. Rather than determining that targeted killing, in the larger sense, is justified, the Court indicated that cases needed to be assessed on their individual merits.[129]

While the public disclosure of the US government using targeted killings in certain cases, and the publicity over the killings of Anwar al-Aulaki and, arguably, Osama bin Laden may represent an expanded public phase in the US fight against terrorism, the concept is not new at all. It appears, in this respect, that the US has been influenced by Israel, where targeted killings have been more prominent and are arguably more ingrained into the normative scheme. Israel's experience, beyond giving some indicators as to the usefulness of these strikes, as well as some underpinning arguments as to their legitimacy, also addresses an emerging debate arising from the US practice as to whether judicial oversight would serve to legitimate these strikes.[130] While not definitively answering this question, it is propounded herein that many of the extraordinary detention measures employed after 9/11 have structural similarities to undertakings elsewhere and that turning to the experiences of these other jurisdictions has arguably influenced many of the decisions made after 9/11 in relation to appropriate responses.

V. Conclusion: Deconstructing the Binaries

The examples chosen for this chapter demonstrate that, beyond substance, the form of the presentation of an argument can have a significant impact on its persuasiveness. The discussion of these examples was not intended to be

---

[127] *Targeted Killings Decision*, above, n 126, para 1.

[128] ibid.

[129] ibid; for an additional discussion of the legal framework of the Israeli targeted killing policy, see Orna Ben-Naftalit and Keren R. Michaeli, '"We Must Not Make a Scarecrow of the Law": A Legal Analysis of the Israeli Policy of Targeted Killings' (2003–04) 36 *Cornell International Law Journal* 233. For an early, very useful discussion of the legal framework being developed in the US, see William C Banks, 'Targeted Killing and Assassination: The US Legal Framework' (2003) 37(3) *University of Richmond Law Review* 667.

[130] See Amos Guiora, 'Israeli Legal Expert: Lack of Judicial Oversight in Targeted Killings a "Recipe for Disaster"' *Gale* (2013) go.galegroup.com.ezproxy.lib.ucalgary.ca/ps/i.do?p=AONE&u=ucalgary&id =GALE|A318265561&v=2.1&it=r&sid=summon&authCount=1 (criticising the way in which targeted killings were developing in the US); Martin Flaherty, 'The Constitution Follows the Drone: Targeted Killings, Legal Constraints, and Judicial Safeguards' (2015) 38(1) *Harvard Journal of Law and Public Policy* 21.

comprehensive, nor could it be. It was also not intended to resolve what are frequently complex controversies. Instead, the intent was to show that these are matters that cannot be accurately portrayed by the simplistic binaries that were often advanced, or implied, to support them.

Where governments seek to change long-standing constitutional protections for detainees, in terrorism or in any other context, a generalised assertion that they are balancing security and liberty is, at best, a structurally questionable foundation for the claim. It cannot, in fact, be an accepted presumption that liberty and security are contradictory and opposing values, such that one must be diminished to enhance the other. Moreover, such a presumption of balance, while arguably sometimes valid when applied to individual facts of individual cases, with appropriate burdens and presumptions in favour of individual rights, cannot be a larger justification for any broad change a government chooses to make.

Similarly, it appears that the war-versus-crime binary, often asserted by the US after the 9/11 attacks, is in fact somewhat misleading. The two are not equally available choices, depending entirely on Executive discretion, so that is a first problem with this binary. Beyond that, as argued in this chapter, the US is not really following a war paradigm in its Guantanamo Bay proceedings, but instead appears to be following a hybrid paradigm of its own making, with elements cherry-picked from the existing paradigms to facilitate the government's objectives, and with a significant bias against any person brought up on charges before the Military Commissions. As demonstrated by comparisons the US government has made to Article III proceedings and to courts martial, the US has also constructed a narrative of fairness around its Military Commissions that is at odds with the reality.

Finally, the binary between 'old' and 'new' detention mechanisms after 9/11 is, in some ways, misleading. As explained in this chapter, this was a binary that was more implied than stated, but it is unavoidable when assessing, in particular, US governmental actions and statements regarding terrorism detentions. While many of the wartime detention and interrogation structures employed by the US are indeed new to the US, they are not new in the sense that many have been used in other jurisdictions.

It is obvious that the US drew from practices taken in the past, prior to 9/11, by places like the UK and Israel, both of which have had long-term experience in dealing with different types of terrorist threats. While drawing from these experiences is actually a positive thing, the way in which this was presented to the public was misleading. First, it undermined the point of departure described above in chapter four that the 9/11 attacks were different in a way that required building new detention paradigms, as the structures constructed were obviously not new at all. This point is also important because, in drawing from the experiences of these other jurisdictions, the US appears to have disregarded many of the experiences those jurisdictions have had, which could have been of benefit. It is for this reason that this was presented as a binary because, by presenting these approaches as entirely 'new', versus 'old' (ie, based on systems that have been used elsewhere), the US was able to proceed in a way that suggested a trial-and-error situation, but may really have been just a way of suggesting that it was creating the structures from the beginning, when this was really not true. In so doing, the US created these mechanisms in a way that clearly avoided pre-existing legal constraints, and that might have been more difficult if it had acknowledged and incorporated the trial and error that had already been undertaken by other jurisdictions.

This chapter, like the others in this book, addressed one particular form of argumentation, which was layered with others that are described throughout the book. No one argumentation tool stands in isolation and all were used in conjunction with other argumentation tools, and on multiple levels, even within the same type of tool. Some forms of argumentation have been quite obvious, while others are more subtle. Some forms of argumentation served multiple purposes. In considering the binaries presented in this chapter, it is important to remember that this involves one component seen through the turning of the proverbial kaleidoscope. The objective of this chapter was to demonstrate, via example, some examples of matters that were presented in a binary form that did not represent the true state of affairs. Some political argumentation was certainly valid, but too much was not, and was instead designed to persuade towards particular actions rather than to explain. It was designed for and directed at an audience that was predisposed to be persuaded to a particular form of action. As so many current terrorism detention approaches are variations of those put into place on the foundation of this flawed argumentation after 9/11, a re-examining of these underlying foundations can only improve responses going forward.

Conclusion: Turning the Kaleidoscope

> All stories have a curious and even dangerous power. They are manifestations of truth—yours and mine. And truth is all at once the most wonderful yet terrifying thing in the world, which makes it nearly impossible to handle. It is such a great responsibility that it's best not to tell a story at all unless you know you can do it right. You must be very careful, or without knowing it you can change the world.[1]

I. The Conversation Continues: Can, or Should, the Fracturing in the Post-9/11 Terrorism Detention Narrative be Repaired?

A. Going Back in Time to Change a Narrative

The Introduction to this book made it clear that this work does not claim to solve all of the problems that it identifies. Rather, as Clifford Geertz pointed out in his own work and as discussed in the Introduction, this book acknowledges that it may be closer to the beginning of a conversation than to the end.[2] The book has accomplished what it set out to do, opening a conversation about the way that political discourse can directly create realities, which, in turn, develop into legal norms. In the case of the 9/11 terrorism-detention regimes, problematic political discourse led to fragmented practices, both within and across jurisdictions. Part of this conversation suggests that a past narrative is not set in stone for all time, especially when it continues to impact the future.

Can a long-standing, false narrative, especially one that has a continuing impact on the future, be changed? This book began with an example that demonstrated that it can, with the Mayor of New Orleans giving a remarkable speech, demanding that the narrative of glory that had been built around the US Confederacy be changed. As described in the Introduction of this book, Mayor Landrieu insisted on a backward look, to the point when that false narrative began, and then a new look forward from there, through the lens of a different perspective. Doing so, he argued, would paint a very different picture of the Confederacy from the one

---

[1] Vera Nazarian, *Dreams of the Compass Rose* (Winnetka, CA, Norilana Books, 2010) 174.
[2] See the discussion of the speech in the Introduction, and the entire speech, which is reproduced in the Appendix.

so commonly accepted by particular people. And, in so doing, he insisted that this new narrative, not the long-accepted false one, should be the basis for future action. This action included removing monuments that glorified the Confederacy.

As this book began with that example, it seems fitting to close with another US example of challenges to a long-standing historical narrative. In July 2017, archaeologists at Monticello began unearthing a room that is believed by some to be the place where Sally Hemings lived. The windowless room was adjacent to Thomas Jefferson's room. After the room was found, NBC News set off a firestorm of controversy by describing Hemings, who had six children with Jefferson, as Jefferson's 'mistress'.[3] Other media, including the *Washington Post*, also called her his 'mistress'.[4] The way in which this issue subsequently played out in the media and on social media speaks to how a false narrative can be deconstructed because people in general simply refuse to be bound by it. It also shows that it is possible to go back more than 200 years to undo a narrative that has been accepted over time.

The common, sanitised version of the relationship between Hemings and Jefferson, a long-venerated 'Founding Father' of the US and author of the Declaration of Independence, ignores important, foundational facts. First, Hemings was enslaved by Jefferson, as were the children she had with him. Second, Hemings was approximately 14 years old, while Jefferson was 44, when their 'relationship' began.[5] Accounts of this story often mention that Jefferson's wife had died when he began his 'relationship' with Hemings, as if the story is somehow better if he is not perceived as having been unfaithful to his wife. This further perpetuates the myth that Hemings was Jefferson's 'mistress'.[6]

Although this story was known even in Jefferson's time, it did not stop the creation of a narrative about him as the noble American hero, for his role in the American Revolution, as the author of a foundational document that speaks of values of equality and as the US's third President. To acknowledge the truth about his relationship with Hemings is to change a narrative that seems comforting to some and to demonstrate that he was not so noble at all.

---

[3] NBC News, 'Thomas Jefferson's Mistress Sally Hemings' Secret Living Quarters Finally Discovered' *Twitter* (3 July 2017), @NBCNews, twitter.com/NBCNews/status/881812957822431232 (the word 'Mistress' had been removed from the headline for the story, linked in the tweet); see Britni Danielle, 'Sally Hemings wasn't Thomas Jefferson's Mistress. She was His Property' *Washington Post* (6 July 2017) www.washingtonpost.com/outlook/sally-hemings-wasnt-thomas-jeffersons-mistress-she-was-his-property/2017/07/06/db5844d4-625d-11e7-8adc-fea80e32bf47_story.html?utm_term=.6e3b5c70e8a3.

[4] See Donovan Harrell, '"He Raped Her": Twitter Users Bash NBC for Calling Sally Hemings Jefferson's Mistress' *Kansas City Star* (3 July 2017) www.kansascity.com/latest-news/article159493264.html (containing a screenshot of a *Washington Post* headline, also calling her Jefferson's 'mistress'. The headline was changed after the controversy and no longer appears on the original article site).

[5] Danielle, above, n 3.

[6] See Thomas Jefferson Foundation, 'Thomas Jefferson and Sally Hemings: A Brief Account', *Monticello*, www.monticello.org/site/plantation-and-slavery/thomas-jefferson-and-sally-hemings-brief-account.

While the Hemings story is the most famous, she was one of hundreds of people who Jefferson claimed to own as slaves.[7] These people included his own children with Hemings.[8] Records suggest that Hemings, born in 1773, went to live at Monticello as Jefferson's 'property' in 1774, two years before Jefferson's Declaration of Independence, famously proclaiming values of equality, was signed.[9]

Hemings herself is believed to have been the child of Jefferson's father-in-law and a woman he enslaved, Elizabeth Hemings. This made Hemings a half-sister to Jefferson's wife, Martha, but she lived at Monticello as the Jeffersons' slave.[10] The narrative of what happened to Hemings was reflected back in time in her own family and in the countless untold stories of other women who were similarly enslaved.

After the NBC story, numerous commentators responded with outrage to the description of Hemings as Jefferson's 'mistress', a designation that suggests agency and the ability to consent.[11] Some people pushed back, trying to retain the pre-existing narrative about Jefferson.

As an example of some of the public commentary and attempts to introduce competing narratives, one person wrote a letter to the editor, responding to an editorial by Britni Danielle, saying, among other things:

> Yes, Sally Hemings was Thomas Jefferson's slave. That in itself does not prove that any sexual contact was rape. Ms. Danielle may project all she wishes, but there is no proof that rape was involved. (Okay, in today's laws, sex with someone under 16 is statutory rape. I'm not sure about the laws in Virginia or, for that matter, France, at the time.)

> Hemings may not have been able to say no, but there is no proof that she wished to do so. She appears to have been quite clever in her negotiations with Jefferson and got from him the concessions she wanted. And while he did not acknowledge Hemings's children as his (although, interestingly enough, he kept extensive records on everything, including both parents of all his slaves, he never named the fathers of Hemings's children in his records), he did arrange for their futures.[12]

This disturbing statement suggests that somehow Hemings was cunning and that this was a driving force in the relationship she had with Jefferson. Aside from perpetuating long-standing racist stereotypes about black women, it also shows a determination to cling to the positive idea of Jefferson in the face of

---

[7] See Thomas Jefferson Foundation, 'Thomas Jefferson: Liberty and Slavery', *Monticello*, www.monticello.org/slavery-at-monticello/liberty-slavery.

[8] ibid.

[9] Thomas Jefferson Foundation, 'Sally Hemings', *Monticello*, www.monticello.org/site/plantation-and-slavery/sally-hemings.

[10] ibid.

[11] See, eg, Danielle, above, n 3.

[12] Pen Suritz, Letter to the Editor, 'History Has No Record of What Sally Hemings Thought' *Washington Post* (12 July 2017) www.washingtonpost.com/opinions/history-has-no-record-of-what-sally-hemings-thought/2017/07/12/7b753440-659c-11e7-94ab-5b1f0ff459df_story.html?utm_term=.a7a283e4ab68.

irrefutable facts to the contrary. The writer is willing to concede that maybe—but only maybe—it is a problem that Jefferson had a sexual relationship with a child, but is not willing to recognise the fact that Hemings' status as a slave meant that she had no capacity to consent. Instead, this letter implies that the relationship happened, not because of wrongdoing on Jefferson's part, but because of cunning on the part of a 14-year-old girl being held as Jefferson's slave. It further suggests that Jefferson was a good person for providing for the future of his own children, who he, in truth, claimed to own as slaves and who were the results of a 'relationship' with a woman he also claimed to own.

One can only imagine how, today, a man who enslaved a 14-year-old girl, fathering children with her, would be perceived. Not surprisingly, this letter to the editor drew angry responses. One person wrote:

> There would be outrage if someone speculated that pure blonde white girl Elizabeth [Smart] actually enticed or controlled her abductor, imprisoner, rapist, although she was older than Sally Hemings. Yet it is seemingly acceptable to impute thoughts and actions to someone we know nothing about except that she was legally powerless and she and her children were exploited all of Jefferson's life.[13]

Even after Hemings was wrongly described as Jefferson's 'mistress', people commenting online insisted on clinging to the mythical notion of Jefferson and Hemings having some sort of forbidden, but genuine love. One commenter was quoted as saying that it was possible that Jefferson and Hemings were actually in love, asking if 'she was perhaps not a victim but an agent of change?'[14]

It is actually possible to deconstruct the long-term false narrative about Jefferson and Hemings, based on a few known facts. That she was enslaved by Jefferson suggests no possibility of her giving meaningful consent. This lack of capacity to give consent is also demonstrated by the fact that she was a child at the time their 'relationship' began.

Referring to Hemings as Jefferson's mistress has been aptly described as a 'whitewashing' of the truth. In her op-ed, Danielle sought to change that narrative to one that more accurately reflected the facts when she wrote:

> Language like that elides the true nature of their relationship, which is believed to have begun when Hemings, then 14 years old, accompanied Jefferson's daughter to live with Jefferson, then 44, in Paris. She wasn't Jefferson's mistress; she was his property. And he raped her.[15]

Another writer noted:

> [I]t's insulting to identify the relationship between a slave and a slave-owner using the term 'mistress' when that term denotes a relationship predicated on mutual choice,

---

[13] ibid (comment by tidelandermdva, 13 July 2017) (the original comment referred to 'Elizabeth Smith', but clearly meant Elizabeth Smart).

[14] Danielle, above, n 3.

[15] ibid.

autonomy, and affirmative consent—things slaves do not have. As a slave, Hemings was not afforded the privilege of self-determination, meaning she didn't do what she wanted; she did what she was told. The word to describe that type of interaction is not 'affair'; it's rape.[16]

Leslé Honoré, a Chicago-based poet, has also sought to correct the false narrative that has arisen around Jefferson's relationship to Hemings. Taking the story from the view of Hemings herself, Honoré has shifted the narrative, seeking to give Hemings back her voice in this long-standing story about her. The result is powerful. She writes:

Dear Thomas Jefferson,

I cannot be your mistress
And your slave
I can't be your lover
If you own me
From birth To grave

That wasn't my room
Adjacent to his
It was my cell
For quick access for his pleasure
And my hell

I can't consent
While being owned
I can't say yes
If I'm not allowed a No

I was born from rape
I was born to be raped
And to birth after rape

I was not woman
I was thing
Possession
Chattel
Inventory
Soulless
3/5
A price on a ledger
Breeder
Exploited
Exotic

---

[16] Lincoln Anthony Blades, 'Why You Can't Ever Call an Enslaved Woman a "Mistress"' *Teen Vogue* (27 February 2017) www.teenvogue.com/story/the-washington-post-thomas-jefferson-sally-hemings-slavery-mistress (this publication has become known in the US in 2017 for its political commentary).

Alone
Captive
Dead before death
Not even my breath belonged to me
The slave has no agency

Did it arouse your founding father
When I wept
When I screamed
When from pain I bore beige babies
That would never collect
Their inheritance
But were left denied
Forgotten
Trash from my womb
Reminders of your perversion
The abomination of you wanting me

I cannot be
Your mistress
And your slave
I bear witness

From cradle to grave

And I hold these truths to be self-evident

That all founding fathers were created

Evil

-Sally[17]

Rewriting this historical false narrative is important beyond a mere academic exercise. As Mayor Landrieu explained in his New Orleans speech, a false narrative that is carried forward from the past continues to propel us in the wrong direction going forward and it can perpetuate past wrongs. As Danielle writes:

> Romanticizing Hemings and Jefferson's so-called relationship minimizes the deadly imbalance of power that black people suffered under before the Civil War. It also obscures our collective history as a nation that moved from being built on the blood, bones and backs of enslaved African Americans and indigenous people, to being the imperfect, hopeful and yet still unequal country we are today.[18]

The room at Monticello was excavated as part of an initiative to more truthfully portray the lives of the hundreds of people who were held as slaves there.[19]

---

[17] Leslé Honoré, 'Sally Speaks' in Leslé Honoré, *Fist and Fire: Poems that Inspire Action and Passion* (Chicago, 2017) (reproduced with permission of the author).

[18] Danielle, above, n 3.

[19] Thomas Jefferson Foundation, 'Monticello Archaeology', *Monticello*, https://www.monticello.org/site/research-and-collections/monticello-archaeology.

Time will tell whether the long-standing false narrative about Jefferson and Hemings will shift going forward.

On 11–12 August 2017, white supremacists marched in Charlottesville, Virginia, in a protest that allegedly began after a decision to remove a statue of Robert E Lee, the leader of the Confederacy. Violence resulted in three deaths, including a horrific scene of a car driving into a crowd of counter-protestors. It is clear that the long-standing narratives surrounding the US Civil War and slavery will not be easily changed.[20] However, it is also clear, as evidenced by Mayor Landrieu's speech and by the pushback to the false narrative about Hemings and Jefferson, that these narratives are, at the very least, being publicly challenged. This suggests that other false narratives can also be deconstructed, as suggested throughout this book for post-9/11 detention narratives.

II. Changes to Political Discourse

Various examples throughout this book have demonstrated the power of popular political discourse in the development of legal regimes. Different argumentation tools have been used as examples of the way in which a narrative, favourable to one perspective, can be built, and of how that narrative can be made persuasive. Along the same lines, such narratives can be deconstructed and reconfigured by shifting the various argumentation tools that went into building them to begin with.

As shown from the preceding example about Jefferson, a narrative, once constructed, does not have to stand, unchanged, for all time. By going back and deconstructing problematic arguments, one can change things like the use of labels and euphemisms, points of departure, binary language, fear-based reactions and other factors that went into the original narrative, which may have resulted in a false conclusion. In terms of legal norms, this also means that looking to the argumentation that was used to build those norms might be another way of critiquing the changes that were made.

This book has laid out varying levels of the political discourse that can influence legal actions, including some that appear foundational to changing particular terrorism detention norms after 9/11. One reason why it is described as the beginning of a conversation is because so much more can be said, both about political discourse and about the fragmenting of terrorism detention practices. So many factors go into creating a narrative and only some could be expanded upon here. For example, this book focused on the audience receiving governmental messages, drawing from Perelman and Olbrechts-Tyteca's ideas of the universal audience, as

---

[20] See Jason Hanna, 'Virginia Governor to White Nationalists: "Go Home … Shame on You"' *CNN* (12 August 2017) http://www.cnn.com/2017/08/12/us/charlottesville-white-nationalists-rally/index. html.

opposed to a particular audience.[21] However, this is not the only perspective that might be relevant to how political discourse in this context played out.

Political narratives, by definition, are delivered by a government or by political figures. All of the factors that have been discussed throughout this book went into creating a narrative and persuading a particular audience of the need for detentions for terrorism outside of the criminal justice system. However, particularly in the early days after 9/11, the voices of those affected by these practices were conspicuously absent. This began to change, mostly as some of the people involved were freed or as governmental secrecy became less stringent.

In 2015, Mohamedou Ould Slahi released his book, *Guantanamo Diary*. He was still being detained at Guantanamo Bay when the book was published, so it was heavily redacted by the US government and was actually published with the heavy redaction markings in it.[22] The effect is chilling, as the reader is constantly brought to a halt by the black bars over the next thought, and it serves as an ongoing reminder of the repressive conditions under which it was written. Slahi describes in disturbing detail the circumstances that led to his arrest and transfer to Guantanamo Bay, as well as the extensive torture he suffered there. At one point, he speaks of the futility of trying to prove his innocence in a situation in which his guilt was presumed, and where he faced such a power differential and no meaningful opportunity for a defence. He wrote:

> A Mauritanian folktale tells us about a rooster-phobe who would almost lose his mind whenever he encountered a rooster.
>
> 'Why are you so afraid of the rooster?' the psychiatrist asks him.
>
> 'The rooster thinks I'm corn.'
>
> 'You're not corn. You are a very big man. Nobody can mistake you for a tiny ear of corn', the psychiatrist said.
>
> 'I know that, Doctor. But the rooster doesn't. Your job is to go to him and convince him that I am not corn.'
>
> The man was never healed, since talking with a rooster is impossible. End of story.
>
> For years I've been trying to convince the US government that I am not corn.[23]

Slahi was released from Guantanamo Bay after 14 years, with no charges, even before the Military Commissions there.[24] Although throughout his book, he gives

---

[21] See Chaim Perelman and Lucie Olbrechts-Tyteca, *The New Rhetoric: A Treatise on Argumentation*, translated by John Wilkinson and Purcell Weaver (Notre Dame, IN, University of Notre Dame Press, 1969) 19–26.

[22] Mohamedou Ould Slahi, *Guantanamo Diary* (New York, Little, Brown and Company, 2015).

[23] ibid 317–18.

[24] Rebecca Hersher, 'Author of "Guantanamo Diary" Released from Military Prison' *NPR* (18 October 2016), www.npr.org/sections/thetwo-way/2016/10/18/498420952/author-of-guantanamo-diary-released-from-military-prison.

a detailed account into the many problems with the Guantanamo Bay prison, one point especially relates back to the point made in chapter 6 above that the prison, often described as a wartime prison, is not really quite that. Slahi was not arrested on a battlefield, but in his home country of Mauritania, where he had voluntarily turned himself over for questioning. This is hardly the normal course of proceeding for 'wartime' detentions.[25] Slahi's book became a bestseller in the US.[26] His book is an example of the way in which the post-9/11 terrorism detention narratives continue to evolve.

Considering some of the argumentation factors that went into the creation of these narratives might be a way to steer the narratives in a more positive direction in the future. With Trump currently threatening to expand the prison at Guantanamo Bay, it remains to be seen how much other voices, like Slahi's, who put a human face on the much-debated detentions and torture at Guantanamo Bay, will impact the political discourse and resulting evolutions in terrorism detention practices.

III. Fragmented Practices and Regrets

Overall, the issue of how to address terrorism detentions is a complex matter, influenced by particular facts, constitutional provisions, politics, history and existing approaches to legal regimes, among other things. Such complicated questions cannot be truly addressed through simplified political discourse. Even where fear causes such discourse to dominate, those in positions to create legal norms must go back and deconstruct that argumentation to reconsider changes that resulted from it. A multi-textured issue requires a multi-textured analysis and, while particular discourse may be easy for the public to understand and may have intuitive persuasive appeal, a more nuanced form of discourse is required to address the foundational firmness of detention changes built on this form of discourse.

Across jurisdictions, of course, it is not necessarily unreasonable that different laws and practices might apply. Each jurisdiction has its own legal traditions, legal norms and guiding principles. However, whilst recognising that, it is still a significant difference if one jurisdiction would view the same person as a potentially war-related detainee, while another might view him as an immigration detainee, and a third might view him as a criminal justice detainee—all based on the same conduct and underlying facts. At the very least, given the international nature of terrorism, it seems practical to suggest that there should be some level of harmonisation across jurisdictions in terms of how to handle these

---

[25] ibid.
[26] ibid.

cases, instead of the fragmenting that appears greater than in other traditionally criminal contexts.[27]

Moreover, while much of this book has argued that one jurisdiction has influenced another, there are, at the same time, aspects of the post-9/11 national detention practices that appear to be rather insulated, developed somewhat in silos, more in some places than others, but overall without a significant deference to international law or an expressed will to seek a harmonised transnational law approach to detention practices. Given the international nature of terrorism and even the claim that this is part of why new paradigms were needed, this is surprising.

In the US, the government initially fought even acknowledging the applicability of international law instruments to which it is a party, such as the Geneva Conventions or the Convention against Torture.[28] Given the stark 'us' against 'them' binary that was discussed in chapter five above and the obvious suggestion that terrorism, as an international phenomenon, is not always readily amenable to national criminal justice systems, this failure to actively pursue an international law solution to appropriate detention practices is disturbing. Similarly, it seems strange that, in addressing what has been widely acknowledged, at least in the context of international terrorism, to be a systematic problem involving all 'civilized nations', as Bush expressed it, countries have not pulled together more in developing consistent internal responses to terrorism detentions.[29] On a practical level, this lack of harmonisation across detention practices has arguably created roadblocks across borders.

The second part of this book went into detail about the links between political discourse and fragmented national practices. This fragmenting was obvious within national jurisdictions, with some (or even most) terrorism suspects being processed through the criminal justice system, and others being held outside of that system and subjected to extraordinary practices. The fragmenting of practices occurred across national jurisdictions as well, and it led to some incongruous results when questions arose regarding the transfer of detainees across national borders.

Canada has, for instance, now issued five formal apologies because of its role in working with other jurisdictions in situations resulting in torture of its nationals. It has also paid millions of dollars in reparations, suggesting that, even where such extraordinary practices were used less often, they came at a cost. Maher Arar, who

---

[27] For a different spin on this type of issue, see generally Larissa van den Herik and Nico Schrijver (eds), *Counter-terrorism Strategies in a Fragmented International Legal Order: Meeting the Challenges* (New York, Cambridge University Press, 2015) (containing essays relating to various disciplines in international law and the fight against terrorism).

[28] See *Hamdan v Rumsfeld*, 548 US 557 (2006).

[29] See President George W Bush, 'Address to a Joint Session of Congress and the American People' *The White House* (20 September 2001), georgewbush-whitehouse.archives.gov/news/releases/2001/09/20010920-8.html.

was infamously subjected to the US 'extraordinary rendition' programme, was the first to receive such an apology.[30] He was travelling home to Canada and transferred at John F Kennedy Airport in New York. He was detained and sent to Jordan and then Syria, where he was tortured. He was ultimately returned to Canada and a Commission of Inquiry found wrongdoing on the part of the Canadian government. In 2007, the Government of Canada formally apologised to him and he received a multi-million-dollar sentiment. After he was returned to Canada, the US Congress subpoenaed him to testify before it regarding his ordeal. However, the US government refused to allow him into the country and he had to testify via satellite. The US has never acknowledged wrongdoing or taken Arar off of its no-fly list.[31]

The Canadian government has also formally apologised to Muayyed Nureddin, Abdullah Almalki and Ahmad Elmaati.[32] The three men were separately arrested, detained and tortured in Egypt and Syria, based on information, later discredited, that the Canadian government provided, alleging that they were involved with terrorism. After a public inquiry found wrongdoing by the Canadian government, the government issued an apology and settled a pending lawsuit for an undisclosed amount.[33]

Most recently, information was leaked that the Canadian government was apologising to Omar Khadr, including a settlement reported to be approximately $10 million.[34] Khadr had filed a multi-million-dollar lawsuit against the Canadian government for its role in his detention and torture at Guantanamo Bay. It was reported that this was the settlement of the lawsuit. Although there was no

---

[30] See Commission of Inquiry into the Actions of Canadian Officials in Relation to Maher Arar, *Report of the Events Relating to Maher Arar* (three volumes) (Ottawa, Gilmore Print Group, 2006); 'Harper's Apology "Means the World": Arar' *CBC News* (26 January 2007), http://www.cbc.ca/news/canada/harper-s-apology-means-the-world-arar-1.646481; United States Congress, Committee on Foreign Affairs, *Rendition to Torture: The Case of Maher Arar: Joint Hearing Before the Subcommittee on International Organizations, Human Rights, and Oversight of the Committee on Foreign Affairs and the Subcommittee on the Constitution, Civil Liberties, and Civil Liberties of the Committee on the Judiciary, House of Representatives*, 110th Congress, 1st Session (Washington DC, US Government Printing Office, 2007).

[31] See generally United States Congress, *Reining in the Imperial Presidency: Lessons and Recommendations Relating to the Presidency of George W Bush: Final Report to Chairman John Conyers, Jr* (US, DIANE Publishing, 2009) 143 and generally.

[32] See The Honourable Frank Iacobucci QC, Commissioner, *Internal Inquiry into the Actions of Canadian Officials in Relation to Abdullah Almalki, Ahmad Abou-Elmaati and Muayyed Nureddin* (Ottawa, Gilmore Print Group, 2008).

[33] ibid; see also Nazim Baksh and Terence McKenna, 'Federal Government Reaches Settlement with 3 Canadian Men Tortured in Syria and Egypt' *CBC News* (17 March 2017) www.cbc.ca/news/canada/goodale-freeland-settlement-apology-1.4016572.

[34] This outcome has not been formalised as of the writing of this book, but this information, from media sources, was confirmed by Canada's Prime Minister Justin Trudeau. See 'Khadr Apology, Settlement Based on Violation of Charter Rights, Trudeau Says' *Toronto Star* (8 July 2017) www.thestar.com/news/canada/2017/07/08/khadr-apology-settlement-about-violation-of-charter-rights-trudeau-says.html.

Commission of Inquiry in his case, Khadr has, unusually, been the subject of three Supreme Court of Canada decisions in his favour.[35]

Seventeen British nationals held at Guantanamo Bay were reported to have shared a £20 million compensation fund.[36] The UK did not apologise to the former Guantanamo Bay detainees, which included Moazzam Begg, who has been especially outspoken over allegations of UK complicity in his abuse. Mamdouh Habib was also reported to have reached a confidential settlement with the Australian government over allegations that it was complicit in his abuse at Guantanamo Bay.[37]

Substantial judicial resources have been devoted to certain extraordinary detention cases in the US, Canada and the UK. While more people suspected of terrorism were processed through the criminal justice system, the extraordinary detention cases tended to be higher profile, more challenged in terms of legitimacy and without any clear corollary showing that they deter terrorism. While it appeared at one point that these forms of restraint were being phased out, recent events show that, now normalised, governments are quick to revive them on a claim of necessity.

Keeping these cases out of criminal justice proceedings has done little to enhance a perception of legitimacy to these actions. In some cases, the use of extraordinary measures ensured that the cases could not proceed in criminal justice proceedings. The case of Abdullah Khadr, Omar's brother, provides an example, and it also provides an example of incongruous situations that arose across borders because of fragmented practices.

Khadr was sought for extradition by the US on terrorism charges. If, indeed, the US was seeking Khadr because his detention was necessary for its national security, it did not find a sympathetic audience in the courts of Canada, where Khadr lives, and that lack of sympathy is directly related to US detention and interrogation policies. Although the US government ultimately planned to try Khadr before a criminal court, its prior conduct through its extraordinary detention practices directly stopped it from being able to do so.

Khadr was present in Canada, where he is a citizen, and had been returned after the US had put him through its 'extraordinary rendition' programme. The federal court in Canada denied the US's extradition request for Khadr, a ruling that was upheld on the appellate level and that the Supreme Court of Canada declined to review.[38]

---

[35] See *Canada (Justice) v Khadr*, 2008 SCC 28 (hereinafter *Khadr I*); *Canada (Prime Minister) v Khadr*, 2010 SCC 3 (hereinafter *Khadr II*); *Bowden Institution v Khadr*, 2015 SCC 26 (hereinafter *Khadr III*).

[36] Nick Assinder, 'Gitmo Inmates Settlement: Why Britain Decided to Pay' *Time* (18 November 2010) content.time.com/time/world/article/0,8599,2032004,00.html.

[37] 'Khadr Settlement Far from Unprecedented; U.K., Australia Made Similar Deals' *National Post* (10 July 2017) nationalpost.com/news/canada/khadr-settlement-far-from-unprecedented-u-k-australia-made-similar-deals/wcm/b4779295-1f1e-41fe-8594-82136dd9a2e9.

[38] See *Attorney General of Canada on Behalf of the United States of America v Khadr*, No 34357 (leave to appeal denied) (SCC 2011).

Although extradition to the US is frequently granted, in Khadr's case it was denied because of the way the US treated him when it detained him in Pakistan, in response to a bounty it had offered.[39] The Ontario Court of Appeal put it rather bluntly, saying: 'The United States of America paid the Pakistani intelligence agency, the Inter-Services Intelligence Directorate (the 'ISI'), half a million dollars to abduct Abdullah Khadr in Islamabad, Pakistan in 2004.'[40] The Court then described Khadr's treatment after his arrest:

> Following his abduction, Khadr was secretly held in detention for fourteen months. He was beaten until he cooperated with the ISI, who interrogated him for intelligence purposes. The ISI refused to deal with the Canadian government but did have contact with a CSIS official. The American authorities discouraged the CSIS official's request that Khadr be granted consular access, and the ISI denied access for three months. The ISI refused to bring Khadr before the Pakistani courts. After the ISI had exhausted Khadr as a source of antiterrorism intelligence, it was prepared to release him. The Americans insisted that the ISI hold Khadr for a further six months in secret detention, to permit the United States to conduct a criminal investigation and start the process for Khadr's possible rendition to the United States. When Khadr was finally repatriated to Canada, the United States sought to have him extradited on terrorism charges.[41]

The Ontario Court of Appeal quoted the Superior Court Judge's finding that 'the sum of the human rights violations suffered by Khadr is both shocking and unjustifiable'.[42] Khadr was released after the Superior Court stayed his extradition, and is now living in Canada.[43] His case raises a number of obvious human rights concerns. It also illustrates the fracturing of the anti-terrorism narrative and how fragmented practices have had unintended outcomes. Presumably, the US thought it had evidence to charge Khadr with terrorism, if it was seeking extradition. However, it blocked itself from pursuing any such charges through its previous extraordinary detention and abuse of Khadr. Indeed, if detaining Khadr was critical to the security of the US, it appears that its own actions have sabotaged that detention. Yet this is not to suggest that Khadr is guilty of anything. He has not been charged with any terrorism offences in Canada and was never convicted in any court of law.

Khadr had been criminally charged in Boston, charges that cannot proceed unless he is extradited.[44] It is unclear whether the US pursued the criminal paradigm because it was seeking extradition—a criminal procedure mechanism.

---

[39] See *United States of America v Khadr*, 2011 ONCA 358 (upholding a lower court ruling staying extradition proceedings against Abdullah Khadr, in large part because of human rights violations during Khadr's detention in Pakistan).

[40] ibid para 1.

[41] ibid.

[42] ibid para 2 (quoting *United States of America v Khadr* (2010) 258 CCC (3d) 231, staying extradition proceedings).

[43] See Linda Nguyen, 'Abdullah Khadr Released as Extradition Request Denied' *Global News* (4 August 2010) www.globalnews.ca/abdullah+khadr+released+as+extradition+request+denied/81237/story.html.

[44] See *United States of American v Khadr*, above, n 39, para 16.

Had the US chosen to send Khadr to Guantanamo Bay to try him before a Military Commission, it is unclear whether they would have had any basis for seeking extradition, as the Military Commission is not a criminal proceeding, and it is equally unclear how they could have sought transfer under a wartime detention paradigm that Canada has not adopted. Canada has a history of refusing extradition to the US if there is a risk of human rights abuse, as this has come up regarding the death penalty;[45] however, it is rare. The US's use of abusive extraordinary detention tactics ultimately precluded it from being able to pursue a prosecution in this case.

IV. A Way Forward?

This book has expended considerable space identifying a problem. It thus seems appropriate to suggest a solution, but to do so is not so straightforward. Rather than suggesting a proper paradigm under which to place anti-terrorism detentions, the suggestion is a bit more abstract, relating back to the theoretical approaches enunciated throughout this work.

This book suggested an additional methodology to identify some of the structural cracks in a legal standard, using specific examples of particular political discourse, in general and as connected to fragmented post-9/11 terrorism detention practices. Looking to the argumentation undergirding that change, especially after an event as heavily discussed as 9/11, can reveal rotten structural foundations undergirding those changes. As explained earlier in this book, this is not a definitive or mathematical process and, at best, it can provide one of many indicators as to the strength of the undertakings supported by argumentation. Changes in legal norms that undermine long-standing, foundational principles of the Rule of Law must always be critically assessed, and this is one way to do it, outside of normative assessments of the relevant law.

As René Provost points out in a different context:

> Law is not handed down but rather continuously constructed by all who are involved in its creation and application. Whereas positivism may countenance a responsibility to the law, commanding obedience under certain conditions, legal pluralism speaks to a responsibility for the law, demanding engagement with legal norms over and above compliance.[46]

---

[45] *United States v Burns*, 2001 SCC 7 (upholding a denial of extradition in a case in which there was a risk of the defendant facing the death penalty in the US).

[46] René Provost, 'Asymmetrical Reciprocity and Compliance with the Laws of War' in Benjamin Perrin (ed), *Modern Warfare: Armed Groups, Private Militaries, Humanitarian Organizations, and the Law* (Vancouver, UBC Press, 2012) 31–32.

As terrorism continues to evolve, it would be problematic to say that there could never be a situation that might justify handling a terrorism case outside of the criminal justice system. However, one would assume that the justification to do so would be built on stronger argumentation foundations than much of what publicly emerged on these issues after 9/11. Similarly, one would assume that such a decision would be made on a case-by-case basis, with a government bearing the heavy burden of establishing why it would have to be done in such a case. Simply stating that it is necessary is not enough, and systemic avoidances of the criminal justice system cannot be accepted. Many of the extraordinary detentions undertaken after 9/11 demonstrate the risk of abuse where the sole power over detention rests with the Executive. It is the fear of that abuse that gave rise to foundational principles regarding the criminal justice system to begin with.

In some instances, these practices have expended significant judicial resources, incurred major costs and been plagued with ongoing problems of legitimacy. None of these critiques are new, and they were used in the past in places that used Executive detentions in terrorism cases. When the UK used extraordinary, or Executive, detentions to hold people who were suspected of involvement with terrorism, possibly indefinitely, while dealing with the Irish Republican Army, this approach arguably backfired. One source notes: 'The resulting internment of almost 2,000 predominantly Catholic men was stated to lead to greater civil disturbances and a "diminished respect for the rule of law in Northern Ireland". It was widely reported that the use of internment was among the best recruiting tools the IRA [Irish Republican Army] ever had.'[47] One needs only to be reminded of the horrific images of Daesh members beheading victims in orange prison jumpsuits, resembling those used at Guantanamo Bay, to see the continuing relevance of that critique.

When he spoke after the 9/11 attacks, George W Bush used stark binary language in suggesting that people had only two choices: to side with the US or to side with terrorists. However, it turns out that these were never the only choices. Few would deny that terrorism is a serious issue that has to be addressed and, obviously, this includes detaining those suspected of involvement with terrorism. Nevertheless, it does not follow that the significant deviations from constitutional norms in the detention, interrogation or other extraordinary practices for terrorism suspects that some countries adopted after 9/11 were useful in fighting terrorism.

To move forward, detention paradigms created after 9/11 should not necessarily continue to serve as the basis for changed practices. People may now be more accustomed to extraordinary detention practices, but that is not enough of a reason to continue them. Lord Hope's admonition cannot be forgotten. It was quoted earlier in this book, and it is reiterated here: 'the slow creep of complacency must

---

[47] 'Pre-charge Detention for Terrorist Suspects: United Kingdom' *Library of Congress*, https://www.loc.gov/law/help/uk-pre-charge-detention.php (internal citations omitted).

be resisted. If the rule of law is to mean anything, it is in cases such as these that the court must stand by principle'.[48] Stopping terrorism is obviously a valid and important objective. However, if countries like the US, Canada and the UK do this at the cost of their foundational values, then Lord Hoffmann will have been proven right in predicting that they will be handing terrorists a major victory.[49]

It is difficult to accept, for example, that Canadians are any safer because people like Mohamed Harkat have been subject to a security-certificate regime, with no possibility of a meaningful defence, for 15 years or longer. To accept this is to accept that the foundational principles of the Rule of Law and fair trial proceedings are meaningless. The stated objective of the Canadian government is to deport Harkat. If he were indeed a terrorist risk—something the government has never proven and which he has always denied—one wonders how deporting him to another country would enhance anybody's safety.[50] Moreover, if deportation is not an option, at some point, he should be criminally charged or released, as the security basis for his detention would have become unhinged from the purpose of deportation.

If the government were to expand its security-certificate detentions to citizens, it is assumed that those detentions would not be permitted for long. Canadians would not feel safer, knowing their lives could be destroyed on a mere accusation, and that they would have no rights to defend themselves against accusations used to justify long-term restrictions on their freedoms. Beyond the obvious erosion such practices carry for the Rule of Law, they are simply illogical.

At the end of the day, those who are subject to security certificates also face a major toll on their lives, with no meaningful recourse. When discussing his ordeal, Harkat said last year: 'I thought one day I would have children, a house, a family … everything is destroyed. When I met Sophie, we had a plan to buy a house and have children.'[51] A government seeking to have such an impact on the freedom of people under its control must also be required to prove its allegations in a meaningful judicial proceeding, in which the detainee has a full right to defend himself or herself against the allegations.

In an unusual twist, Alexandre Trudeau, the brother of Canadian Prime Minister Justin Trudeau, wrote a letter to Public Safety Minister Ralph Goodale, asking him to exercise his discretion to allow Harkat to stay in Canada. Trudeau

---

[48] *Secretary of State for the Home Department (Respondent) v AF (Appellant) (FC) and Another (Appellant) and One Other Action* [2009] UKHL 28, para 84 (Lord Hope of Craigshead).

[49] *A (FC) and Others (FC) (Appellants) v Secretary of State for the Home Department (Respondent)* [2004] UKHL 56, para 96.

[50] See Audrey Macklin, *The Canadian Security Certificate Regime, CEPS Special Report* (2009) *Archive of European Integration*, aei.pitt.edu/10757/1/1819.pdf (discussing the regime at length, including discussing the logical flaw in thinking that deportation of somebody suspected of terrorism enhances safety).

[51] Debra Black, 'Mohamed Harkat Girds Himself for Another Fight to Stay' *The Star* (2 August 2016) https://www.thestar.com/news/immigration/2016/08/02/mohamed-harkat-girds-himself-for-another-fight-to-stay.html.

had been a long-time advocate on behalf of Harkat, even offering to act as a surety for him in 2005, and writing, producing and directing a film about abuses of human rights in Canada's post-9/11 security responses, called *Secure Freedom*.[52] In his recent letter, Trudeau wrote: 'I am absolutely convinced that at this moment, he (Harkat) poses no danger whatsoever to the public or to public safety in Canada, but rather offers a positive commitment to the life he has created here.'[53]

Canada's security-certificate system, like so many extraordinary terrorism detention measures, appears to be more problematic than beneficial. However, the narrative continues to develop, as to these and other extraordinary detention measures undertaken in the name of fighting terrorism. Understanding the problematic issues in past narratives can help in avoiding them in the future. Again, the voices of those affected by these practices can be a powerful part of that narrative. In the description of *Secure Freedom*, Trudeau quotes Hassan Almrei, one of the Secret Trial 5, as saying: 'If I'm guilty, charge me, sentence me, and don't shed a tear. But don't deport me to torture without a trial. That's not the Canada I love.'[54]

That quote seems to say it all.[55]

---

[52] ibid; Alexandre Trudeau, Director, *Secure Freedom*, JuJu Films, www.jujufilms.ca/secure_freedom.

[53] 'Justin Trudeau's Brother Urges Canada Not to Deport Alleged al-Qaida Sleeper' *The Guardian* (2 March 2016) www.theguardian.com/world/2016/mar/02/alexandre-trudeau-canada-prime-minister-brother-al-qaida-plea.

[54] *Secure Freedom*, above, n 52.

[55] See *In the Matter of Hassan Almrei et al*, 2009 FC 1263 (ruling that Almrei's security certificate was not reasonable and ordering it to be quashed, which resulted in his release).

APPENDIX: A FULL TRANSCRIPT OF THE REMARKS OF NEW ORLEANS MAYOR MITCH LANDRIEU, IN MAY 2017, ON THE REMOVAL OF CONFEDERATE MONUMENTS IN NEW ORLEANS

Thank you for coming.

The soul of our beloved City is deeply rooted in a history that has evolved over thousands of years; rooted in a diverse people who have been here together every step of the way—for both good and for ill.

It is a history that holds in its heart the stories of Native Americans: the Choctaw, Houma Nation, the Chitimacha. Of Hernando de Soto, Robert Cavelier, Sieur de La Salle, the Acadians, the Islenos, the enslaved people from Senegambia, Free People of Color, the Haitians, the Germans, both the empires of Francexii and Spain. The Italians, the Irish, the Cubans, the south and central Americans, the Vietnamese and so many more.

You see: New Orleans is truly a city of many nations, a melting pot, a bubbling cauldron of many cultures.

There is no other place quite like it in the world that so eloquently exemplifies the uniquely American motto: *e pluribus unum*—out of many we are one.

But there are also other truths about our city that we must confront. New Orleans was America's largest slave market: a port where hundreds of thousands of souls were brought, sold and shipped up the Mississippi River to lives of forced labor of misery of rape, of torture.

America was the place where nearly 4,000 of our fellow citizens were lynched, 540 alone in Louisiana; where the courts enshrined 'separate but equal'; where Freedom riders coming to New Orleans were beaten to a bloody pulp.

So when people say to me that the monuments in question are history, well what I just described is real history as well, and it is the searing truth.

And it immediately begs the questions: why there are no slave ship monuments, no prominent markers on public land to remember the lynchings or the slave blocks; nothing to remember this long chapter of our lives; the pain, the sacrifice, the shame … all of it happening on the soil of New Orleans.

So for those self-appointed defenders of history and the monuments, they are eerily silent on what amounts to this historical malfeasance, a lie by omission.

There is a difference between remembrance of history and reverence of it. For America and New Orleans, it has been a long, winding road, marked by great tragedy and great triumph. But we cannot be afraid of our truth.

As President George W. Bush said at the dedication ceremony for the National Museum of African American History & Culture, "A great nation does not hide its history. It faces its flaws and corrects them."

So today I want to speak about why we chose to remove these four monuments to the Lost Cause of the Confederacy, but also how and why this process can move us towards healing and understanding of each other.

So, let's start with the facts.

The historic record is clear: the Robert E. Lee, Jefferson Davis, and P.G.T. Beauregard statues were not erected just to honor these men, but as part of the movement which became known as The Cult of the Lost Cause. This "cult" had one goal—through monuments and through other means—to rewrite history to hide the truth, which is that the Confederacy was on the wrong side of humanity.

First erected over 166 years after the founding of our city and 19 years after the end of the Civil War, the monuments that we took down were meant to rebrand the history of our city and the ideals of a defeated Confederacy.

It is self-evident that these men did not fight for the United States of America, [*sic*] They fought against it. They may have been warriors, but in this cause they were not patriots.

These statues are not just stone and metal. They are not just innocent remembrances of a benign history. These monuments purposefully celebrate a fictional, sanitized Confederacy; ignoring the death, ignoring the enslavement, and the terror that it actually stood for.

After the Civil War, these statues were a part of that terrorism as much as a burning cross on someone's lawn; they were erected purposefully to send a strong message to all who walked in their shadows about who was still in charge in this city.

Should you have further doubt about the true goals of the Confederacy, in the very weeks before the war broke out, the Vice President of the Confederacy, Alexander Stephens, made it clear that the Confederate cause was about maintaining slavery and white supremacy.

He said in his now famous "Cornerstone speech" that the Confederacy's "cornerstone rests upon the great truth, that the negro is not equal to the white man; that slavery—subordination to the superior race—is his natural and normal condition. This, our new government, is the first, in the history of the world, based upon this great physical, philosophical, and moral truth."

Now, with these shocking words still ringing in your ears, I want to try to gently peel from your hands the grip on a false narrative of our history that I think weakens us and make straight a wrong turn we made many years ago so we can more closely connect with integrity to the founding principles of our nation and forge a clearer and straighter path toward a better city and more perfect union.

Last year, President Barack Obama echoed these sentiments about the need to contextualize and remember all of our history. He recalled a piece of stone, a slave auction block engraved with a marker commemorating a single moment in 1830 when Andrew Jackson and Henry Clay stood and spoke from it.

President Obama said, "Consider what this artifact tells us about history … on a stone where day after day for years, men and women … bound and bought and sold and bid like cattle on a stone worn down by the tragedy of over a thousand bare feet. For a long time the only thing we considered important, the singular thing we once chose to commemorate as history with a plaque were the unmemorable speeches of two powerful men."

A piece of stone—one stone. Both stories were history. One story told. One story forgotten or maybe even purposefully ignored.

As clear as it is for me today … for a long time, even though I grew up in one of New Orleans' most diverse neighborhoods, even with my family's long proud history of fighting for civil rights … I must have passed by those monuments a million times without giving them a second thought.

So I am not judging anybody, I am not judging people. We all take our own journey on race. I just hope people listen like I did when my dear friend Wynton Marsalis helped me see the truth. He asked me to think about all the people who have left New Orleans because of our exclusionary attitudes.

Another friend asked me to consider these four monuments from the perspective of an African American mother or father trying to explain to their fifth grade daughter who Robert E. Lee is and why he stands atop of our beautiful city. Can you do it?

Can you look into that young girl's eyes and convince her that Robert E. Lee is there to encourage her? Do you think she will feel inspired and hopeful by that story? Do these monuments help her see a future with limitless potential? Have you ever thought that if her potential is limited, yours and mine are too?

We all know the answer to these very simple questions.

When you look into this child's eyes is the moment when the searing truth comes into focus for us. This is the moment when we know what is right and what we must do. We can't walk away from this truth.

And I knew that taking down the monuments was going to be tough, but you elected me to do the right thing, not the easy thing and this is what that looks like. So relocating these Confederate monuments is not about taking something away from someone else. This is not about politics, this is not about blame or retaliation. This is not a naïve quest to solve all our problems at once.

This is, however, about showing the whole world that we as a city and as a people are able to acknowledge, understand, reconcile and, most importantly, choose a better future for ourselves, making straight what has been crooked and making right what was wrong.

Otherwise, we will continue to pay a price with discord, with division, and yes, with violence.

To literally put the confederacy on a pedestal in our most prominent places of honor is an inaccurate recitation of our full past, it is an affront to our present, and it is a bad prescription for our future.

History cannot be changed. It cannot be moved like a statue. What is done is done. The Civil War is over, and the Confederacy lost and we are better for it. Surely we are far enough removed from this dark time to acknowledge that the cause of the Confederacy was wrong.

And in the second decade of the 21st century, asking African Americans—or anyone else—to drive by property that they own; occupied by reverential statues of men who fought to destroy the country and deny that person's humanity seems perverse and absurd.

Centuries-old wounds are still raw because they never healed right in the first place.

Here is the essential truth: we are better together than we are apart. Indivisibility is our essence. Isn't this the gift that the people of New Orleans have given to the world?

We radiate beauty and grace in our food, in our music, in our architecture, in our joy of life, in our celebration of death; in everything that we do. We gave the world this funky thing called jazz; the most uniquely American art form that is developed across the ages from different cultures.

Think about second lines, think about Mardi Gras, think about muffaletta, think about the Saints, gumbo, red beans and rice. By God, just think. All we hold dear is created by throwing everything in the pot; creating, producing something better; everything a product of our historic diversity.

We are proof that out of many we are one—and better for it! Out of many we are one—and we really do love it!

And yet, we still seem to find so many excuses for not doing the right thing. Again, remember President Bush's words, "A great nation does not hide its history. It faces its flaws and corrects them."

We forget, we deny how much we really depend on each other, how much we need each other. We justify our silence and inaction by manufacturing noble causes that marinate in historical denial. We still find a way to say "wait, not so fast."

But like Dr. Martin Luther King Jr. said, "wait has almost always meant never."

We can't wait any longer. We need to change. And we need to change now. No more waiting. This is not just about statues, this is about our attitudes and behavior as well. If we take these statues down and don't change to become a more open and inclusive society this would have all been in vain.

While some have driven by these monuments every day and either revered their beauty or failed to see them at all, many of our neighbors and fellow Americans see them very clearly. Many are painfully aware of the long shadows their presence casts, not only literally but figuratively. And they clearly receive the message that the Confederacy and the cult of the lost cause intended to deliver.

Earlier this week, as the cult of the lost cause statue of P.G.T Beauregard came down, world renowned musician Terence Blanchard stood watch, his wife Robin and their two beautiful daughters at their side.

Terence went to a high school on the edge of City Park named after one of America's greatest heroes and patriots, John F. Kennedy. But to get there he had to pass by this monument to a man who fought to deny him his humanity.

He said, "I've never looked at them as a source of pride … it's always made me feel as if they were put there by people who don't respect us. This is something I never thought I'd see in my lifetime. It's a sign that the world is changing."

Yes, Terence, it is, and it is long overdue.

Now is the time to send a new message to the next generation of New Orleanians who can follow in Terence and Robin's remarkable footsteps.

A message about the future, about the next 300 years and beyond; let us not miss this opportunity New Orleans and let us help the rest of the country do the same. Because now is the time for choosing. Now is the time to actually make this the City we always should have been, had we gotten it right in the first place.

We should stop for a moment and ask ourselves—at this point in our history, after Katrina, after Rita, after Ike, after Gustav, after the national recession, after the BP oil catastrophe and after the tornado—if presented with the opportunity to build monuments that told our story or to curate these particular spaces … would these monuments be what we want the world to see? Is this really our story?

We have not erased history; we are becoming part of the city's history by righting the wrong image these monuments represent and crafting a better, more complete future for all our children and for future generations.

And unlike when these Confederate monuments were first erected as symbols of white supremacy, we now have a chance to create not only new symbols, but to do it together, as one people.

In our blessed land we all come to the table of democracy as equals.

We have to reaffirm our commitment to a future where each citizen is guaranteed the uniquely American gifts of life, liberty and the pursuit of happiness.

That is what really makes America great and today it is more important than ever to hold fast to these values and together say a self-evident truth that out of many we are one. That is why today we reclaim these spaces for the United States of America.

Because we are one nation, not two; indivisible with liberty and justice for all, not some. We all are part of one nation, all pledging allegiance to one flag, the flag of the United States of America. And New Orleanians are in, all of the way.

It is in this union and in this truth that real patriotism is rooted and flourishes.

Instead of revering a 4-year brief historical aberration that was called the Confederacy we can celebrate all 300 years of our rich, diverse history as a place named New Orleans and set the tone for the next 300 years.

After decades of public debate, of anger, of anxiety, of anticipation, of humiliation and of frustration. After public hearings and approvals from three separate community led commissions. After two robust public hearings and a 6-1 vote by the duly elected New Orleans City Council. After review by 13 different federal and state judges. The full weight of the legislative, executive, and judicial branches of government has been brought to bear and the monuments in accordance with the law have been removed.

So now is the time to come together and heal and focus on our larger task. Not only building new symbols, but making this city a beautiful manifestation of what is possible and what we as a people can become.

Let us remember what the once exiled, imprisoned and now universally loved Nelson Mandela and what he said after the fall of apartheid. "If the pain has often been unbearable and the revelations shocking to all of us, it is because they indeed bring us the beginnings of a common understanding of what happened and a steady restoration of the nation's humanity."

So before we part let us again state the truth clearly.

The Confederacy was on the wrong side of history and humanity. It sought to tear apart our nation and subjugate our fellow Americans to slavery. This is the history we should never forget and one that we should never again put on a pedestal to be revered.

As a community, we must recognize the significance of removing New Orleans' Confederate monuments. It is our acknowledgment that now is the time to take stock of, and then move past, a painful part of our history. Anything less would render generations of courageous struggle and soul-searching a truly lost cause.

Anything less would fall short of the immortal words of our greatest President Abraham Lincoln, who with an open heart and clarity of purpose calls on us today to unite as one people when he said:

"With malice toward none, with charity for all, with firmness in the right as God gives us to see the right, let us strive on to finish the work we are in, to bind up the nation's wounds, to do all which may achieve and cherish: a just and lasting peace among ourselves and with all nations."

Thank you.[1]

---

[1] Derek Cosson, 'Transcript of New Orleans Mayor Landrieu's Address on Confederate Monuments' *Pulse Gulf Coast* (19 May 2017) pulsegulfcoast.com/2017/05/transcript-of-new-orleans-mayor-landrieus-address-on-confederate-monuments (quoting the Second Inaugural Address of Abraham Lincoln, 4 March 1985, available at http://avalon.law.yale.edu/19th_century/lincoln2.asp).

INDEX